W9-ACC-542

BRECHT: A BIOGRAPHY

WITHDRAWN

Klaus Völker

BRECHT:
A BIOGRAPHY

TRANSLATED BY JOHN NOWELL

A CONTINUUM BOOK
THE SEABURY PRESS • NEW YORK

MILSTEIN
PT
2603
.R397
Z8896713

Bur
PT
2603
.R397

The Seabury Press
815 Second Avenue
New York, NY 10017

English translation copyright © 1978 by The Seabury Press, Inc.

Originally published in 1976 under the title BERTOLT BRECHT,
Eine Biographie by Carl Hanser Verlag München Wien

All rights reserved. No part of this publication may be reproduced, stored in a
retrieval system or transmitted in any form, by any means, electronic,
mechanical, photocopying, recording or otherwise except brief extracts for the
purpose of review, without the prior permission of the publisher.

Printed in the U.S.A.

Library of Congress Cataloging in Publication Data

Völker, Klaus, 1938-   Brecht, a biography.
Translation of Bertolt Brecht, eine Biographie.
Includes bibliographical references and indexes.
1. Brecht, Bertolt 1898-1956 —Biography. 2. Authors, German —20th
century —Biography. I. Title.
Z8116 V58513   [PT2603.R397]   832'.9'12 [B]
ISBN 0-8164-9344-8   78-12610

Contents

PART THREE
Exile

PART FOUR
Before us lie the toils of the plains

Source of Illustrations

We are indebted to Suhrkamp Verlag, Frankfurt, for permission to reproduce the picture of Walter Benjamin on page (iv) . . .; to Andelsbogtrykkeriet, Odense, for pictures on page (ix) . . .; to Roger Melis for the pictures on page (xxvi); all other pictures originate from the archives of the author, most of them, (pages x–xiv) . . . . and pages (xvi–xxiv) . . . . were taken by Ruth Berlau.

ILLUSTRATIVE SECTION follows p. 208.

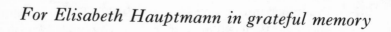

For Elisabeth Hauptmann in grateful memory

The intending biographer pledges himself to tell lies, to hush things up, to be hypocritical, to paint things in glowing colours, and even to conceal his inability to understand, because biographical truth is unattainable, and were one to attain it, one could not make use of it.

Sigmund Freud to Arnold Zweig
(31.5.1936)

PART ONE
Augsburg and Munich

1

Childhood and Youth

'I write plays *(ich bin Stückeschreiber)*. Actually I should have liked to be a cabinet-maker, but obviously one can't earn enough that way,' Brecht once observed, with an assurance that is convincing even if it was ironic. When he returned to Europe from his exile in America and met Max Frisch in Zurich, the latter was reminded of one of Caspar Neher's stylized craftsmen, 'a cabinet-maker perhaps'. Brecht, the 'son of well-to-do people' forsook his class and joined 'the common people'. This repudiation of his class, however, did not extend to his family. Nor was solidarity with the lower orders and the persecuted, his 'downward' path, the reason why he would have liked to be a cabinet-maker. Nor indeed would this occupation have struck his family as unusual, although latterly Brecht's forbears had concentrated more on the technical treatment of wood than on the cabinet-maker's craft. His grandfather, Stefan Bertholt Brecht, owned a small lithographic establishment in the little town of Achern in Baden, one of his sons becoming a printer while in 1893 another, the playwright's father, joined the Haindl paper mill, whose headquarters were in Augsburg. Brecht's brother, Walter, rose to be Professor of Paper Technology at the technical high school in Darmstadt. 'I should have enjoyed working with wood,' Bertholt Brecht declared enthusiastically. 'Really well stained or varnished wood scarcely exists any more, that beautiful wainscotting, those lovely banisters of former days, those light coloured maple-wood table tops, as thick as the width of one's hand, that we found in our grandparents' rooms, yellow with age and polished smooth by the hands of whole generations. And what cupboards I have seen! Looking at furniture like that put better thoughts into one's head.' The Berliner Ensemble's model builder tells us that the 'Chief' actually supervised the construction of the stage models and that even with them he attached great importance to both the treatment and the tinting of the wood.

3

Brecht thus made use of that part of his family heritage that he could apply to his work. He found his way back into his family, as he acknowledged in an early diary entry made in May 1920: 'I have a sense of values inherited from my father. But I am also sensible of the fact that one can leave out of account the concept of value entirely.'

Bertolt Brecht was born in Augsburg on 10 February 1898. The town, situated at the junction of the rivers Wertach and Lech, had lost its status as a Free Imperial City at the Peace of Pressburg and been incorporated into Bavaria in 1806. Its citizens, however, managed to preserve some of their ancient privileges. Thanks to immigrants from western Swabia, who came to the rising industrial town in the nineteenth century, Bavarian influence made little headway in Augsburg. And while it is true that the speech of the Augsburg people took on a Bavarian ring, their syntax and way of thinking remained predominantly Swabian. Brecht never regarded himself as a Bavarian; when asked where he came from, he would say 'My parents come from the Black Forest'.

His father's family lived in Achern; Brecht later recalled it, and above all his grandmother, in the story *The Discreditable Old Lady (Die unwürdige Greisin)*. In 1917, after the death of her husband, Karoline Brecht at the age of seventy-eight permitted herself certain liberties 'quite unheard of among normal people'. While her children exchanged letters in an attempt to solve the problem of what was to be done with her, the old lady took matters into her own hands and enjoyed two more years of independent life, with no obligations, in the company of 'jolly people'. She frequented the house of a well known cobbler in the town, and struck up a friendship with a young woman cook, with whom she went to the cinema and drove over to Kehl for the races. The citizens of Achern were outraged by her behaviour and one of Brecht's uncles complained indignantly at the 'discreditable conduct of our dear mother'. Her grandson, on the other hand, had a fellow-feeling for his grandmother, and, in the words of Robert Minder, acclaimed her 'discreetly as a pioneer' because at the end of her life, 'erect and indomitable', she rebelled against her own class, the class from which at the very outset of his career as a *Stückeschreiber* he too decided to dissociate himself.

His grandparents on his mother's side, Josef Friedrich and Frederike Brezing, lived in the Upper Swabian village of

Rossberg, near Waldsee. They later spent the closing years of their lives in Augsburg, with their children and grandchildren. In 1897 their daughter Sophie married Bertholt Friedrich Brecht in Pfullingen. 'I, Bertholt Brecht, come from the black forests. My mother carried me into the towns as I lay in her body.' The house in which Brecht was born, Auf dem Rain 7, is situated at the foot of the Perlachberg; one of the typical Augsburg dykes runs along the street and at the turn of the century the ground floor of the house was occupied by a file-cutter's workshop. Small craftsmen's establishments and mechanics' workshops, dye-works and spinning mills were to be found in all the houses bordering on the Lech canals.

In 1900 the Brecht family moved into more spacious quarters in one of the Haindl concern's endowed houses in the Klaucke suburb, which had been built a few years previously for employees of the firm. In 1954, when writing the preface to the new edition of his early plays, Brecht still recalled the parkland idyll in front of this house, 2 Bleich Strasse, at the corner of Frühling Strasse, with a view of the Oblatter Rampart: 'An avenue of chestnut trees ran past my father's house, along the old city moat; on the other side was the rampart, with remains of the former city wall. Swans used to swim in the pond-like water. The chestnut trees shed their yellow leaves.'

Little Eugen Berthold grew up in the security and comfort of a middle-class home. His father earned a good salary and was a much liked and devoted member of the Haindl business. He rose very quickly from clerk to *Prokurist,* approximately deputy manager, and in 1914 became managing director of the paper mill. Because he was away a great deal on business the main responsibility for the children's upbringing fell upon the mother, whose whole love was centred on her elder son Eugen, always a rather delicate child and one who, at quite an early age, was to strike people as different from other boys. She took him to the kindergarten every day and, for a time, also to the school run by the barefoot friars. His mother's tender care and attention, though it did him good and he always remembered it with great gratitude, made him the butt of his schoolfellows, a situation he tried to redress by cunning and the use of his wits. He was cheeky in a sly way and in their games and pranks it was always he who set the tone. When they played gypsies or Red Indians he joined in only if he could be the chief. An attraction for the children of the neighbourhood was his puppet-theatre; he got great fun out of acting and reciting his own verses, and satisfaction from the applause of his audience.

Religion played no great part either at school or at home. His father was Roman Catholic only in name, and the children were brought up in their mother's faith. On the whole Brecht was bored by the friars' teaching at the evangelical school, Pastor Paul Detzer's Bible class being the only one he enjoyed and really listened to. And here it was not the message that impressed him, but the vivid descriptions and the magnificent language of Luther's Bible. Even as a schoolboy Brecht had an excellent knowledge of the scriptures and no one was particularly surprised when, at the age of fifteen, he submitted a play called *The Bible*. Thus when, in 1928, he was asked which book had exerted the greatest influence on him, his much quoted answer, 'You will laugh – the Bible', was in fact quite true.

In the autumn of 1908 Brecht entered the Royal Bavarian *Realgymnasium* (roughly a grammar or high school) in Augsburg, where he spent a few more years acquiring a reputation as a 'quiet, well behaved pupil' of average ability; only in German composition did he usually get very high marks. The other boys found it hard to enlist Bert, as they called him, for the usual schoolboy escapades, he preferred to stand on one side, as an observer; he also studied the foibles of the different masters and learned to exploit them for his own ends. While still a very junior boy, a *Tertianer,* he showed that he had learnt to think at school and was able systematically to reverse the pupil-teacher relationship. On one occasion, for instance, he noticed the clumsy attempts of his class-mate, Max Hohenester, to improve a bad Latin exercise he had done: taking his penknife, Max 'scratched out one of the mistakes, stood up, protested and demanded justice. The professor held the page up to the light with his left hand, saw where the paper had been scratched thin, and brought down his right hand with a resounding smack on the side of Max's face.' A few days later Brecht was faced with the problem of improving the marks he had received for a bad essay on Molière's comedies. He went about it much more cleverly than Max: 'Having underlined in red ink a number of perfectly correct passages in his corrected essay, he took it up and asked in a hurt tone of voice what was wrong with them. The master, forced to admit that nothing was wrong, had no option but to rub out the red lines and reduce the total number of mistakes on the page. This naturally resulted in the marks being changed too.'

The pupil was transformed into master and the master had to accept the role of pupil. In this way the pupil avoided being crammed full with 'a whole farrago of utterly useless educational assets': 'In the nine years in which I was bottled up in an Augsburg *Realgymnasium* I did not succeed in materially benefitting my teachers. They were indefatigable in developing my taste for leisure and independence.' The fact was that Brecht wrote astute, original essays that caused his teachers considerable astonishment although, until he reached the *Unterprima* (roughly the lower sixth), he expressed no politically provocative opinions. He published his first literary works in 1913 and 1914, under the pseudonym Bertold Eugen, in the small hectographed issues of the school magazine, *Die Ernte (The Harvest)*: among them were the poem *The Burning Tree (Der brennende Baum)* and his first completed play *The Bible,* a one-act drama in which the action takes place in a Protestant town in the Netherlands under siege by the Roman Catholics. The town succumbs because of the stubbornness of some of the citizens who cling fanatically to their faith, for which they are prepared to fight and die, an attitude regarded by the young people as both questionable and pointless. The Bible quotations, with which their objections are met, strike them as cold and unjust. From a literary point of view the 'drama' is totally unimportant; what is interesting is its underlying tendency, its negative verdict on the spirit of self-sacrifice in a moral cause. To the schoolboy human life seems more important than religious principles. Brecht has little time for martyrs.

The author of *The Bible* felt his vocation to be that of poet and artist. He was already convinced that he was cut out to be a 'genius'. He now wrote regularly, read a great deal, and practised by writing reviews and reflections on the contemporary scene. Surrounded by a few chosen friends, he held himself aloof at school, a gifted solitary who wanted acclaim. At home his family quickly resigned themselves to this; his mother used to say, 'He is altogether different from us'. In his fourth year at school Rudolf Caspar Neher, 'Cas', became his classmate and remained his closest friend. Brecht looked upon him as his 'brother in art' and a searching critic of what he wrote. Neher showed his friend his sketches and drawings.

Wilhelm Brüstle's contention that Brecht was politically left-wing even as a schoolboy is not supported by the facts: Brecht's poems and reviews which Brüstle, as editor of the *Augsburger Neueste Nachrichten*, printed in the paper's literary supplement, *Der Erzähler*, as well as the seven *Augsburg War Letters* written for the *München-Augsburger-Abendzeitung*, are almost all infected by the spirit of the day and imbued with patriotism, enthusiasm for the war and Germanomania. Up till 1915 Brecht praised Kaiser and Empire. Only then did he become thoughtful and critical, and range himself on the side of the victims of the war.

When war broke out he did his duty to his country enthusiastically, like all the teachers and pupils. Men unable to fight in the front line offered their services to the militia, a volunteer defence unit or the territorial reserves. In Augsburg Professor Herrenreiter, whose name turns up later in *Refugees in Conversation (Flüchtlingsgespräche)*, was responsible for finding pupils to work on the land, while a master at the Gymnasium, named Weber, trained the youth squads. No one wanted to be left out. Even now, when orders were issued, not by the gym instructor, but by the Kaiser personally and by the law, Brecht shrank from all physical exertion; on the other hand he was not sparing with words. At the beginning of August he did duty as an 'aeroplane look-out' on the Perlach Tower, a task he took very seriously and enjoyed as a romantic adventure, exhorting other boys of his own age to follow his example: 'It was a beautiful night. Even though we saw no aeroplanes. And, to close, I would like to ask young people and schoolboys who read this: would you not also like to keep watch on the tower for your country? Look-outs are still needed. True, your bed will not march up with you for those two hours, but as compensation you will be performing a small service in the common cause of our dear country and enjoying free of charge the attractions of keeping watch on the tower.'

On 17 August, 1914, only a few days, that is, after the outbreak of the First World War, Bertold Eugen's third contribution to *Der Erzähler* appeared; its title was *Notes on our Times (Notizen über unsere Zeit)*. The scepticism, the accusatory, emotional tone of his play *The Bible*, were forgotten; Brecht wrote apodictically and full of enthusiasm: 'The whole nation stands loyally together. All

8

thought of party has vanished. Among our enemies there is disunity, unpreparedness. We are prepared, morally prepared. The steadfast German character, which has engaged the minds of German poets and thinkers for two centuries, is now proving itself. Our men have gone into battle calm and composed, with iron discipline but ablaze with enthusiasm, not so much exulting in victory as with clenched teeth. And the others, those who remain behind, will show themselves worthy of their brothers and sons. Our women will give the lie to talk about the weaker sex, our youth rebut the suspicion attaching to "modern youth". All of us, all we Germans, fear God and nothing else in the world.'

In the weeks that followed, the sixteen-year-old boy, encouraged by Brüstle to write further contributions for his paper, modified his standpoint and espoused the war and German values in a somewhat more balanced manner. While the war continued to be the great 'storm symphony of our time', Brecht praised Carl Hauptmann for a play that presented war as 'simply large-scale murder'. In November he wrote his *Modern Legend (Moderne Legende)*, an epitaph for 'the dead left on the battlefield', with its picture of mothers weeping 'on this side – and on that'. Enthusiasm for the war was replaced by mourning for the dead, 'among friend and foe alike'. But Bertold Eugen, writing assiduously, continued to have frequent relapses into patriotism until 1915. In *The Subaltern (Der Fähnrich)* the young officer, 'his graceful sword in his hand', leads his company into battle and, 'drunk with rage, in a cloud of blood and mist,' slays five of the enemy: 'then, with a cry, his eyes wild and scared, he collapsed and died'. And finally the young poet took delight in 'Germany's triumphant greatness that ploughs its cemeteries into cornfields'.

Hans Lody, The Subaltern, and *The Soldier from Ching-tao (Der Tsingtausoldat)* fight and die for 'my Germany'. Consequently the teachers of the patriotic Bertold Eugen, who extolled death for one's country so volubly, were somewhat taken aback when, in an essay on Horace's *Dulce est et decorum pro patria mori,* he suddenly adopted a dissenting attitude towards death in battle: 'The saying that it is sweet and honourable to die for one's country can only be classed as propaganda. It is always hard to take one's leave of life, whether in bed or on the battlefield, and it is undoubtedly hardest of all for young men in their prime. Only addle-pates can be so devoid of sense as to speak of an easy step through the dark gateway, and they do so only as long as they imagine themselves to be a long way from their last hour. The moment Death comes near them, they pack up and make off, like the emperor's fat court jester at Philippi, to whom we owe this saying.'

The German master was furious and applied for Brecht to be expelled from the school. But Romuald Sauer, the Benedictine father from St. Stephen's, who taught languages at the *Realgymnasium,* opposed the application at the masters' conference, excusing the boy's aggressive remarks on the grounds that his essay was the work of a 'schoolboy brain unsettled by the war'. Father Sauer, a friend of the Brechts, succeeded in convincing his colleagues, the affair was disposed of by a reprimand and the opponent of the war was allowed to remain at the school. For the rest of his schooldays Brecht was careful to avoid adopting such an unequivocal attitude; he preferred to be cautious and sly.

After July 1916 his contributions to the *Augsburger Neueste Nachrichten* bore the signature Bert Brecht. At this period he followed with the greatest interest all the contemporary literature he could lay his hands on, the most popular penny-dreadfuls and the most trashy little volumes of poems as well as serious literature; his special predilection was for the plays of Gerhart Hauptmann and Frank Wedekind, Bernard Shaw and August Strindberg. He was an enthusiastic adherent of naturalism; he knew, valued and quoted Shakespeare, Büchner, Villon, Kipling, Rimbaud and Verlaine. As a poet and writer he regarded himself as committed to 'reality', claiming that he was dependent on it. 'Reality is the great poet's couch, on which he dreams his dreams', as he had written to Neher when he was sixteen, stating that 'to fuse the laws of nature with idealism is art'. As reading he recommended to his friend the novels of Zola, 'for the post of great (painter=) naturalist is still vacant. The people's soul has not yet been explored'.

Even when he was at school Brecht gave evidence of his great gift for producing work collectively, as well as for recognizing talent and exploiting it. He used to foregather with those of his school friends who had literary tastes in the *Zwinger,* or cage, as he called his hideout in a garret of his parents' house, or by the city moat, or in the meadows along the River Lech. They read each other poems and dramatic scenes. Brecht's position as leader was unchallenged; he criticized the others' works, improved or altered them, and often made use of them for his own verses. The friends were not

10

merely an appreciative audience, Brecht regarded them as 'collaborators' whose criticisms and advice always meant a lot to him. From all of them he demanded a great deal of time, as friends and as working partners. At night the group marched with lanterns along the city moat, through the old town, courting the girls and shocking the citizens. These nocturnal expeditions ended in the open country, where they swam and climbed trees.

Aus verblichenen Jugendbriefen
Geht hervor, dass wir nicht schliefen
Eh das Morgenrot verblich.
Frühe auf den braunen Ästen
Hockten grinsend in durchnässten
Hosen Heigei, Cas und ich.

Orge im Zitronengrase
Rümpfte seine bleiche Nase
Als ein schwarzer Katholik.
Hoffart kommt zu schlimmen Ende
Sprach die Lippe, aber Bände
Sprach der tiefbewegte Blick.

Braunen Sherry in den Bäuchen
Und im Arme noch das Säuchen
Das uns nachts die Eier schliff.
Zwischen Weisen tat ein jeder
In den morgenroten Äther
Einen ungeheuren Schiff.

Ach, das ist zur gleichen Stunde
Wo ihr alle roh und hunde-
häutern den Kaffee ausschlürft
Dass der Wind mit kühlem Wehen
Ein paar weingefüllte Krähen
In die kalten Häuser wirft.

(Youthful letters, faded with age, reveal that we never went to bed before dawn. In the early hours Heigei, Cas and I crouched grinning on the brown branches of the trees, our trousers soaked through—Orge, the righteous Catholic, lay in the citron grass turning up his nose. His lips said pride comes before a fall, but the glow in his eyes spoke volumes. In our stomachs brown sherry, and still in our arms the hussy who in the night had worn us out with her attentions. At intervals we each pissed prodigiously into the dawn air—Ah, that was at the selfsame hour when all of you, callous and unfeeling, now relish your morning coffee. May the cool breeze waft a few crows stuffed with wine into your cold houses.)

The worst 'sinners' and closest friends were Rudolf Caspar Neher, Georg Pfanzelt, known to everyone as Orge, and Otto Müller, known as Heigei but to whom Brecht gave the more dignified name of Müllereisert. Other admirers and followers were Max Hohenester, Ludwig Prestel, Georg Geyer, Rudolf Hartmann and Fritz Schreier. Brecht kept careful track of his friends' artistic output and advised most of them, at every available opportunity, to keep a diary and record in it everything of note. His friends' talents were constantly tested and put to use. One school leaver from St. Anne's was given the task of reading Homer to Brecht in the original and translating the most important passages. Striking phrases and metaphors that might come in useful were written down. He enlisted Orge and Geyer to train his musical gifts – Brecht set his ballads and songs to music himself: the former explained Beethoven's sonatas to him, while the latter had systematically to play him works by Haydn, Mozart and Bach.

'You'd do better to play games like the others', the schoolboy poet, who had himself photographed as the 'modern Schiller' in the poets' corner of the Augsburg *Stadttheater,* was told; but Brecht was not to be won over to physical training. The cardiac defect, with which he was born and which had been medically attested, protected him from excesses in the realm of sport. He refused to expose himself to the possibility that 'sport of any kind' might result in a shock to his heart, which is what he claimed to have suffered during his *Gymnasium* days in Augsburg. His bad heart saved him from being called up for military service until shortly before the end of the war. Most of his classmates had to join up in 1917, although Caspar Neher had volunteered for front line service in June 1915. Just before Easter 1917 Brecht, along with three others who had remained behind, passed a wartime school-leaving examination. With this his education was, in a sense, complete; equipped as he believed 'with a sound knowledge of human nature' he entered life. Political thinking, as he was soon to find out, was something he had not yet learned.

2

Augsburg (1)

'I have never been sparing of boyhood memories in my writing', declared Thomas Mann in a lecture he gave in Lübeck in 1926, when he made a proud acknowledgement to the citizens of his native town, to Lübeck as the 'intellectual pattern of his existence'. Brecht never proclaimed his loyalty to the town where he was brought up in such pompous, vain, complacent terms as Thomas Mann, although Augsburg and its surroundings, the town's character and that of the countryside and speech, form the background to his works as unmistakably as those of Lübeck do in the case of Thomas Mann, and indeed more so. Moreover Brecht never wrote anything deliberately autobiographical, even though many of his plays, prose works and especially poems contain personal experiences and record the attitudes and standpoints of friends and acquaintances. He did not regard his diary entries and biographical notes primarily as literary forms; their main purpose was to provide him with material. With *Refugees in Conversation* he announced his intention to write his memoirs, but confined himself to notes on slips of paper, to reminders of youthful experiences in Augsburg. Here again one cannot speak of an 'intellectual pattern of existence'. Brecht never thought of the people of Augsburg as his 'dear fellow citizens'; and when he returned to his native town, after moving to Berlin in 1924, he did so without attracting attention, in order to work there in peace for a few weeks.

When he had finished school Brecht was in no hurry at first to leave home and Augsburg. His father, it is true, regretted that his elder son made no serious attempt to learn a solid, middle-class profession, but there were no family scenes on that account. Brecht's literary inclinations and the night-time excursions with his friends, which not infrequently caused a stir in the town, were tolerated. When tackled by acquaintances concerning the escapades of his poet and songster son, the father, in addition to

13

uttering general expressions of regret, is said always to have added with a touch of pride: 'that Eugen of mine certainly is a hell of a chap'. The mother suffered a great deal from the neighbours' talk, and from what she saw as the very free life and 'pornographic' expressions indulged in by her son, to whom she still remained deeply attached. Her admonishments did not worry Brecht very much; it was repugnant to him to mince matters, and there were times in his relationship with his sick mother, who meant well by him and in other ways understood him so well, when he felt himself a 'martyr', forbidden to say 'what is': 'My mother says daily: it is dreadful when a grown man does things and says things that would never occur to another man'.

His mother's worried looks and sighs, however, did nothing to curb the schoolboy's erotic independence. When he was seventeen he acquired, from a prostitute in the Hagen Gasse in Augsburg, the 'knowledge necessary' to avail himself of a girl he knew – 'She was fifteen, but very mature'. This, at least, is Brecht's version of his first amorous adventure with a schoolgirl who wanted something more than just to be kissed when out skating. Later, as a sixth-former, he had no success with Therese Ostheimer, a girl brought up on strict Catholic principles, to whom he spoke on her way home from the May devotions and accompanied a few times to the entrance gate of her house where, however, he was always rebuffed. Finally he declared his love in a long letter which the girl's father confiscated and for some time refused to hand over. With Ernestine Müller, a cousin of his school friend Rudolf Hartmann, Brecht's poetic messages and carefully chosen presents of books met with a better response.

At Steinicke's in the Heiligkreuz Gasse, where he regularly bought or borrowed books, the young poet courted the three assistants Käthe Hupfauer, Fräulein Grassold and Franziska, who afterwards married Georg Pfanzelt. What he enjoyed most was to take his girl friends on the swingboats, claiming that it was 'as good as going to bed with them'. In the winter the Brecht clique went skating. When the ice no longer held, Zanotoni's ice-cream parlour was the agreed meeting place. In 1917 'the sweet dream' of cold nights was Sophie Renner, daughter of a dairywoman in the Bitschlin Strasse. The girl was a good swimmer and liked going to the theatre. When she failed to show due appreciation of his proposals, the lover asked his friend Caspar Neher to intercede for him from the trenches: 'Nothing is of the slightest use. You must write to her. That I am desperate. Or better still send her a drawing. But don't make me ridiculous! I count on you for that.' Neher was to draw him 'big, immortal, extraordinary, ironic etc', not 'naked'. Brecht used his friend's drawings, which he thought highly of and praised unswervingly, not only to stimulate his literary work and clarify it visually, but for purely private and directly practical purposes as well. In the same letter he requested 'a little cartoon' for Rosemarie, Rose Maria Aman, the beautiful hairdresser's daughter who, to Brecht's intense annoyance, was having other love affairs as well. When Rose stood her ground he became irritable and restive: 'What are a hundred possibilities against one impossibility?' A few months later, when the girl became more accessible and showed signs of being attached to him, he said sullenly and suspiciously: 'but she sets out to be seduced, like a bitch on heat.' Whereas at first he had assumed that 'her feverish little face betrays consumption', he now interpreted her fascinating expression as a dangerous 'mania to propagate'. This girl, the subject of the celebrated poem 'Souvenir of Marie A.' ('Erinnerung an die Marie A.'), was Brecht's first great love: 'Her eyes are horribly empty, wicked little devouring whirlpools, she has a snub-nose which is too broad, her mouth is too big, red and thick. The lines of her little neck are not pure, she carries herself like a cretin, her walk is slovenly, her stomach protrudes. But I am fond of her.' For a time he tried to hold her, to tie her more closely to him, like many of the women later in his life whom he always gathered round him several at a time. In addition to Rosemarie, Paula Banholzer was also already the object of Brecht's love at this time. He had met her through Müllereisert, when he was seventeen. She was given the name Paul Bittersüss (or Bittersweet), Bi (e) for short, and was accepted into his circle of friends by whom she was respected. In 1917, when his closest friends started to 'migrate' into the armed forces, Bert, suddenly left alone, clung to Paula in particular, inviting her to his garret, and singing and writing poems to her:

Wenn Du gut turnst, bekommst Du einen Gaul.
Dein Vater versprachs. Du willst Dich nicht binden?
Nun: Turnen *ist* schön. Also nur nicht so faul!
Und so manche, Paul, die braucht einen Gaul
Um einen Reiter zu finden.

15

(If you do gymnastics well, you'll get a horse. Your father promised you. You'd rather not be tied? But think: gymnastics *are* good fun. So why this course? And many a girl, Paul, needs a horse to find a man who likes a ride.)

Bi 'tied' herself to the young poet, as he demanded. The love-affair was veering towards marriage, and Brecht wrote to Cas: 'The strongest men are scared of small children'. In spite of the brazen, aggressively direct way in which he addressed women, and indicated what was in his mind, he was a rather shy lover and very tender, always remaining considerate, like a well brought up schoolboy: 'I have given Bittersweet a small ring. She kissed me, trembling. We didn't say a word.'

If a love affair helped him in his work and rendered him productive, Brecht maintained it. If it disturbed him, or consumed too much of his energy, he started to back out: 'Bittersüss is crushing me. Her holidays were a great pleasure and a great strain. Now only being apart can save our love.' His natural inclination to 'polygamy', if one likes to call it that, was a kind of self-protection. He did not wish to lose himself, to seek sanctuary in any form of love. Love served to give him energy, to stimulate his work. In July 1918, when Bi 'missed her period' for the first time, he became very frightened and begged Cas to pray for him quickly, 'because faced with a child I should be beside myself . . . . The scandal would not be worthwhile, if only because it would last too long, and I might be forced to go to India.'

After leaving school, and doing a short spell of part-time work in an Augsburg market-garden, Brecht's main task became clear to him: he had to establish himself as a poet. He was now writing new poems, ballads and songs every day, as well as working at dramatic projects. Apart from his friends no one was interested. For the time being he was unable to earn anything by his work. In September he tried his hand as a private tutor at the Villa Kopp on the Tegernsee: 'For three hours a day I have to be the crammer, after that I am the squire.' It was a holiday task rather than a serious attempt to earn money. Mainly at his father's wish, Bert decided it would be better to continue his studies. On 2 October he enrolled in the Faculty of Philosophy at the Ludwig Maximilian University in Munich.

From the start he had no intention of applying himself to any intensive, systematic study. He registered for lectures on subjects

16

related to philosophy and the natural sciences and for a course in literary criticism, all of which he attended with varying regularity. During his first weeks he tried to absorb as much as he could, without giving any further thought to it all. 'I devour everything I can get hold of and read a prodigious amount. I shall digest it later, in the army.' Apparently Brecht even attended Professor Willstätter's course on 'inorganic experimental chemistry', because in a letter to one of his Augsburg school friends he mentions, in addition to the university and the theatre, the course in a laboratory which he must not miss. The daily to-and-fro between the university, the theatre and the laboratory seems to have forced him to run so hard that he never succeeded in extricating himself 'from a system of late arrivals'. He wanted to find his bearings in all directions. His motto was the saying of Wedekind's Marquis of Keith: 'Life is a switchback'. Brecht found it very difficult to get used to his new surroundings; he went from room to room in search of a better atmosphere to work in, and at weekends he preferred to go to the familiar surroundings of Augsburg in order to write and plan schemes with his friends. In Munich he became submerged 'in the commonplace', and his ideas had to go to waste for lack of anyone to discuss them with. He had no taste for the light-hearted side of undergraduate life or for the social conventions of his fellow students; and those who thought as he did were too refined and too intellectual for him: 'I don't want to make any friends here', he wrote to Neher, 'they are frightful drivellers in spite of their cultured manners'. The young poet longed for his friend's 'grin' and for work that had some meaning for him.

By 'drivellers' Brecht will have meant first and foremost those attending the Kutscher seminar, where style, theatrical criticism and criticism of contemporary literature were studied and discussed. Artur Kutscher knew many of the writers and literary figures of the day personally and introduced them to the members of his seminar. The 'Theatre Professor' was regarded as an expert in modern literature, which he sometimes defended in hymn-like cadences; this distinguished him from his great Germanist colleagues Strich and Muncker. For Brecht, therefore, there was a certain sense in attending Kutscher's seminar. The classes gave him an opportunity to curb his 'contradictory spirit', while at the same time he naturally hoped to make use of Kutscher as a mentor.

17

The most important event of this first term, as far as Brecht was concerned, was the seminar's *Abschiedskneipe,* or close of term party, at the end of January 1918, at which Frank Wedekind was present. Brecht's father had given his son an edition of Wedekind's works as long ago as 1914; the boy had long known and set great store by the plays, and had been in the habit of singing the street-songs and ballads to his friends. Now, in Munich, he admired Wedekind as actor and cabaret artist, and studied his gestures and very individual delivery: 'I have never been so excited and so deeply moved by a singer. It was the man's enormous vitality, his energy, that enabled him, overcome by laughter and scorn, to bring off his indomitable song to humanity, and this also gave him his personal magic'.

When Wedekind unexpectedly died in 1918, his grateful disciple wrote an enthusiastic obituary notice in the *Augsburger Neueste Nachrichten,* in which he paid tribute to his master as a great educative personality. On the day Wedekind died Brecht had gone for a stroll along the River Lech with his friend Ludwig Prestel, who was a trained musician and also composed a little, and on reaching the weir they had sung Wedekind's songs to the guitar. The next morning Brecht read in the paper that the poet he revered had died. He organized a nocturnal memorial celebration in Augsburg and went to the funeral in Munich, where he saw Wedekind in his coffin. In a letter to Neher he wrote: 'One of the greatest surprises I have ever had. He looked like a little boy – just round the mouth for instance. The disdainful, affected set of his lips, the surfeited, cynical expression, had all gone. At first one thought he was smiling, but then saw that he had already given up smiling'. Subsequently a great deal was written about Wedekind's funeral; many of his writer friends are said to have wept distractedly and the engaging, drunken Heinrich Lautensack collapsed at the graveside. Brecht wrote this quatrain:

> Sie standen ratlos in Zylinderhüten
> Wie um ein Geieraas. Verstörte Raben.
> Und ob sie (Tränen schwitzend) sich bemühten:
> Sie konnten diesen Gaukler nicht begraben.

(They stood tophatted, helpless in their plight, as if assembled round some carrion. Distracted crows. And do what—sweating tears—they might, this sorcerer refused a last repose.)

18

In the spring more of his friends had to join up, first Müllereisert and then, in April, Ludwig Prestel and Brecht's brother Walter. Brecht was due to go in May. Hitherto his cardiac trouble had saved him from being called up. Now steps had to be taken against this contingency, because Brecht had no desire to expose himself to unnecessary danger. It was most probably Geyer, who was studying medicine, who gave Brecht the idea of taking an additional course in medicine in his second term, so that if he were called up it would only be for medical service. As a precaution he then asked Neher whether he should go into the artillery or the medical service, at once adding: 'I must say I would rather collect feet and such like things than lose them'. In May, with his eye on the practical advantages to be gained, he diligently attended lectures on medicine, the principal ones being those by Professor Rückert on descriptive anatomy. 'I am studying medicine. The theatres are performing trash. They are waiting . . .', Brecht consoled himself. Although he often spent 'eight hours a day at lectures', and was working extremely hard on *Baal,* he did not fail, even now, to go to Augsburg at intervals to take part in the torchlight processions through the town and 'discuss matters undisturbed in the dark' with Bittersweet. In Kutscher's seminar Brecht read a paper criticizing Hanns Johst's novel *Der Anfang (The Beginning),* this writer being one of the professor's favourite expressionist playwrights. The author of the paper took the opportunity to announce a play of his own, *Baal,* a poetic rejoinder to Johst's play *Der Einsame (A Lonely Man),* which had received its first performance on March 3 at the Munich Kammerspiele.

Brecht took an intense dislike to Johst's play about genius as personified by the poet Grabbe. He castigated it with sarcasm. 'This expressionism is frightful', he declared, and saw his comedy – 'Baal feasts! Baal dances!! Baal is transfigured !!!' – as a counterblast, though it was originally conceived as a play about François Villon. Brecht wrote with an abhorrence of all contemporary art. Strindberg was the height of fashion, his lesser successors played off the 'intellectual' against the 'physical', and in his last works even Wedekind had revised the revolutionary conception of his great plays and prettified their utopian aspect into motherliness and wedded bliss. Brecht wrote to Neher, in the vein of the author of *Frühlings Erwachen (Spring Awakening)* and *Lulu:* 'All feeling for the body's lovely curves and glorious awkwardness fades like the hopes for peace. The intellect is victorious over vitality all along the line. The mystic, clever, sickly, bombastic and ecstatic become inflated and everything stinks of garlic. I shall be thrown out of these people's heaven, these noble, ideal, intellectual people, these Strindhügeln and Wedebabies (Brecht's diminutives of Strindberg and Wedekind), and I shall be forced to write books about your art. And I shall stand on my feet and spit, fed up with the new, and set to work on the old, on what has been tried a thousand times, and do what I want. And I am a materialist and a bad hat and a proletarian and a conservative anarchist and I won't write for the press but for you and myself and the Japanese'. Brecht's *Baal* was his answer to the clever, witty, cultured prattle of Kutscher's seminar, to the tortured stammerings about humanity and the muddled symbolism of the expressionist dramatists.

By the middle of June twenty-four scenes were already finished and typed out by his father's secretaries at the Haindl paper mill, Brecht having successfully explained to his father that he needed a number of fair copies of his play to send to critics and people in the theatre world. The Haindl director was always open to practical business suggestions of this sort. The contents of the manuscript were not discussed. If one of the secretaries expressed a doubt about the literary value of the play she had to copy out, the director assured her that one day Bert would most likely find himself 'in Valhalla'. The father respected his son's work and, even if he did not approve of it either, it was quite clear to him that the question of public recognition of the boy's talent had to be put to the test. Among the prominent people who received copies were Alfred Kerr, doyen of the Berlin critics, and Artur Kutscher. Kerr's reply was unfavourable and he returned the manuscript. Later Brecht was made painfully aware of this mistake on the critic's part, while for his part he never forgave 'Uncle' Kerr. Kutscher, too, could see nothing in *Baal* and appears to have made some rather disparaging remarks about it; his pupil found the 'Leichen-Kutscher's' criticism disgusting and 'enough to make one vomit' (this play on Kutscher's name means literally 'corpse driver').

He was also very keen to have Hanns Johst's opinion; receiving no reply from him, Brecht drew Johst's attention to the fact in these words: 'I shall fully understand if you say that *Baal*, and everything else I write when the spirit moves me, is utter rubbish;

but if you say nothing at all, I can only assume that you want me to take offence'. At the same time Brecht offered to banish the spectre of *Der Einsame* to the periphery of his play. The revised version of *Baal* was then approved by Johst, and subsequently the two dramatists met from time to time to discuss matters connected with drama and the theatre.

Meanwhile the summer term of 1918 came to an end. Back in Augsburg Brecht put his 'worldly affairs in order', because he was expecting his 'sentence of death', his military call-up, any day now. His productivity and entérprise remained unaffected by this. Adequate distraction was provided by outings with Bittersweet into the country round Augsburg and Munich, nocturnal adventures with friends along the banks of the Lech, when songs were written and set to music, parties in his garret and afternoons on the swing-boats. Everything during these summer months was 'marvellous', Neher's absence being all that marred its perfection. In an attempt to persuade his friend to apply for leave and return home at last, Brecht painted Augsburg and all he was missing in the most glowing colours: 'Don't you want to sit on my sofa? I will tune my guitar! The ice-cream parlour! Lanterns! Bittersweet! . . . Come! And art too: My comedy! Songs! Stories!'

Since September 1917 Caspar Neher had received a constant stream of letters at the front; they were intended to keep his spirits up and were larded with exhortations to do all he possibly could to stay alive. Of all his friends at the front in the last year of the war, Neher was the only one who did not manage to wangle any leave. Brecht showed a good deal of concern, because he missed this 'brother in art', with whom he had planned his artistic progress. He regularly asked 'dear childish Cas', the 'Cyclops with a dissolute brain and a virtuous heart', to send him drawings, which he criticized and called works of genius; but all his attempts to place them with periodicals and art dealers were unsuccessful. The plan to get something into *Simplizissimus* also came to nothing, because the editors considered Neher's sketches insufficiently topical. Brecht interpreted their rejection differently: 'But I think their human content is too radical for them. This, of course, is precisely what gives them their value'. All the same he suggested to Cas that it might be quite a good thing to try his hand at something political: 'seen whole of course – symbolic, à la Goya. On the

21

National Association which, along with Wilson, wants to make sure that peace does not arrive like a premature birth!'

Psychological caricatures and visionary faces were much more in Neher's line than illustrations for humorous papers. Brecht was well aware of this and had no intention of advising his friend to turn his drawings into commentaries on the contemporary scene. He himself left it to the expressionists to write plays about contemporary events. What did seem to him important, however, was to collect and record realistic observations, to fix current events in writing. For this reason he lost no opportunity to persuade his friend to keep a diary: 'Remember that Leonardo, whom I adore, also wrote a great deal. He never did anything without good reason'. Neher sent back drawings, pictures, and even the desired diary entries, but he refused to let himself be talked into deserting. He merely bewailed his bitter lot. Bert's most tempting proposals, such as the prospect of spending Whitsun 'alone at home', failed to induce a change of heart.

> Cas ist zornig, denn der Krieg geht weiter.
> Solang Cas zornig ist, ist Krieg der Brauch.
> Cas schmeisst die Waffen weg, doch schmeisst er leider
> Das Bajonett in seiner Feinde Bauch.
> Aber nachts singt Cas wie eine Zofe
> Caspars Lied mit der einen Strophe:
> Wenn nur Krieg aus wäre und ich daheim!

(Cas is mad because the war goes on. So long as Cas is mad war is customary. Cas flings his arms away but flings his bayonet, alas, into the stomach of his adversary. But Cas at night, like any abigail, sings Caspar's song with its repeated wail: Oh if the war were over and I at home.)

When he found that personal arguments had no effect, Brecht reminded him how 'valuable' his life was: 'Art must not suffer from the war', he decided and drew his friend's attention to the fact that 'if you are shot dead, I shall become merely the common or garden singular of people. Please don't be!' The 'great cynic who is just a big baby' submitted patiently to Brecht's reproaches; sometimes, however, the soldier in the trenches felt that the simpleton image was being carried too far, and he became very rude. It was not so much Brecht's admonitions as the detailed descriptions of his love affairs and happiness that tortured and infuriated him. So when Brecht asked his advice as to what unit he should apply for, Neher took it to be sarcasm and quite uncalled-for irony. He didn't 'give a damn' about his military affairs, he replied; Bert should be guided by which uniform his 'little girl' liked best. Brecht apologized. They could each make instant amends for rude or offensive remarks with correspondingly cordial and charming ones, and from Augsburg came yet another imploring ultimatum: 'See that you get here by next week! It can be done! I have asked everywhere. It must be done. A year at the front is too much. Make a shindy! God damn and blast it don't let them kick you around!' At the end of August Brecht sent a last brief protest: 'Are you never coming?' Finally, in September, Neher was given leave and the friends celebrated this reunion bois-terously, in the customary way, with bathing in the Lech, 'shooting the rapids on our backs', climbing the trees in the Wolfszahn meadow and being rocked by the wind as they lay naked in their leafy tops. Now Brecht was far from being a keen swimmer, nor was he an expert tree climber. The fact is that in these exploits he was more of an observer than an active participant, reconstructing on paper the deeds performed by his friends.

Brecht's garret in the Bleich Strasse was the starting-point for everything they did; it was deliberately furnished as the living- and work-room of a genius. 'Twelve suras for my visitors' were nailed to the door, to dissuade fastidious callers from entering. On the wall, and dominating the room, hung a portrait of the Syrian earth-god Baal, painted by Cas; on the table stood one of the skulls which the sixth-former Otto Bezold had brought to Augsburg; in one of the corners a music-stand displayed the opened score of *Tristan* and a baton; on another wall hung Bert Brecht's life-mask, which he had had taken the previous March—in other words all the props the public expected of an artistic genius, assembled by Brecht with mock solemnity but without a moment's doubt that he was destined to be a 'genius'. At night Bert and Orge scoffed 'at God and the anarchists', they themselves being the gods. Brecht announced: 'God cannot exist, because otherwise I could not endure not to be a god myself'.

Personal experiences, the countryside in which he lived and which he enjoyed to the full, his friendship with Cas, Orge and Müllereisert, his numerous love affairs with pretty Augsburg girls,

23

his affectionate relationship with his mother and, finally, his literary impressions, provided the background and stimulus for his writing. What he wrote was always directly connected with experience. This was true of *Baal,* of the wonderful poems and songs later published in *Bertolt Brecht's Homilies for the Home (Bertolt Brechts Hauspostille),* and even of little occasional poems like the 'Song of the Fair' ('Plärrerlied'). For Brecht the Plärrer, the Augsburg fair held twice a year on the parade-ground above the River Wertach, was one of the 'most beautiful things in the world'. Here there were swing-boats to ride in, freak-shows and other sights. Here he had the courage to speak to girls without a lot of preliminary beating about the bush; in one such attempt to start something, in April 1918, 'I messed it up; the girl sent me off with a flea in my ear. I took my revenge by writing a poem. The evening paper paid five marks for it. Five marks precisely'.

> Dort hab ich ein Kind gesehen
> Das hat ein goldenes Haar
> Und ihre Augen stehen
> Ihr einfach wunderbar.

(I saw a child there, she had golden hair, and her eyes become her simply wonderfully.)

At the beginning of October Brecht started his military service. He never reached the front, and after barely three weeks of strict barrack discipline he was posted as medical orderly to a reserve military hospital set up in the courtyard of the Elias-Holl School at Augsburg. Wooden huts served as wards, in which most of the patients were suffering from venereal disease, a petty offence in the army, known as a *Kavaliersdelikt* or gentleman's offence. The young poet immediately wrote a song dedicated to the 'Gentlemen of Ward D', of which only the first verse has survived:

> O wie brannten euch der Liebe Flammen
> Als ihr jung und voller Feuer ward.
> Ach der Mensch haut halt das Mensch zusammen
> Das ist nun einmal so seine Art.

(Oh how love's flame did burn and glow, when you were young and ardour's willing slaves. Ah mankind is mankind's foe, for that's the way mankind behaves.)

24

The song is said to have had three or four verses and a refrain, which Hans Otto Münsterer still remembers:

O diese Weiber, Himmelherrgottsackerment!
Arg schon die Liebe, aber ärger noch der Tripper brennt!

(Oh these women, damn and blast the lot of them! Love's bad enough, but worse the clap that's got of them!)

The war, for Brecht, was something that stood in the way of his development as a person, that conflicted with his idea of vitality. The reports in the newspapers, and the experiences at the front of the men under his care at the hospital, intensified and gave concrete form to his rejection of it. He wrote the *Legend of the Dead Soldier (Legende vom toten Soldaten)* in which the militarists exhume one of their victims killed in the war, declare him fit for military service, bless him, and then send him off to die once more for his country. It was a part-apocalyptic, part-satirical attack on the insane incitements to carry on issued by the military commanders and on the cynicism of doctors and priests who took part in the war. Brecht can never have had an opportunity to sing this ballad to the wounded men and, in any case, he was prudent enough never to risk direct confrontation with the 'enemy'. But his Gentlemen song was received enthusiastically. His superiors, especially the Brecht family friend Dr. Raff, were lenient with the poet. He was not subjected to strict military discipline, being allowed to receive visitors in the hospital and, before long, to go home when not on duty. Early in January he was demobilized. Ten years later he wrote this of his military service: 'At that time I was *Soldatenrat* (Soldiers' councillor) at a military hospital in Augsburg, a job I got only at the urgent request of some friends who claimed to have an interest in my appointment. (As things turned out I was unable to bring about the changes in the state that would have been good for it.) We all suffered from lack of political convictions and I, in particular, also from my old inability to show enthusiasm . . . I scarcely differed from the vast majority of the other soldiers who, as goes without saying, had had enough of the war, but were not capable of thinking politically. So I don't really like to think about it.' No one can swear to the fact that Brecht was ever *Soldatenrat;* it is possible that in the early days of November, when the Bavarian Republic was proclaimed and a Workers',

Soldiers' and Farmers' Council was set up, that his comrades did in fact elect him as their spokesman. But Brecht never got to the point of actually exercising his political mandate. And how would it have been possible for the poet, who was totally inexperienced in political matters, to carry out the policies of a socialist government? A government, moreover, whose members did not even think it necessary to nationalize the means of production and made virtually no attempt to establish an effective system of government by soviets. For Brecht, as for Kurt Eisner the prime minister, revolution at that time was a moral, and not a political, demand.

3

Augsburg (2)

Munich and Augsburg were the centres of the revolutionary events in Bavaria. In January and February 1919 Brecht travelled back and forth between the two towns in order to see for himself and be better able to judge what was happening politically. This was now more important to him than continuing his studies at the University. He applied for leave of absence for the 'Wartime Term of 1919', and this was granted.

Since December 1918 Munich had also had its Spartacist group, which attacked the indecisive policies of the Bavarian government and called for effective revolutionary action. As head of the Government Kurt Eisner, who was a member of the Independent Social Democrats (Unabhängige Sozialdemokratische Partei Deutschlands), occupied a position between all the fronts, contending against not only the Social Democrats but all radical groups that supported the October Revolution and Lenin. He rejected all varieties of traditional parliamentary procedure, as well as the Marxist attitude to class, and coined the phrase '*Räte und Parlament*' or soviets and parliament. He issued alternate threats of resignation and a second revolution. Meanwhile the opponents of revolution moved in to counter-attack. The severe fighting in Berlin ended with the murder of Rosa Luxemburg and Karl Liebknecht, the leaders of the Communist Party. Troops restored 'order'. In Bavaria the controversy continued for a few more months. Following Kurt Eisner's murder a central revolutionary council for the prevention of counter-revolution was formed, and this proclaimed a soviet republic. No communists were included in the newly created Council of People's Representatives. The debates on an effective soviet system came to a head; the discrepancy between the revolutionary programme and any basis for revolutionary action was evident. The soviet government, represented in the public mind mainly by the writers Gustav Landauer, Erich Mühsam and Ernst Toller, proved more or less ineffective in its attempts to establish the new social order from below and protect it adequately. The Communists openly opposed the 'sham soviet republic' and organized a new soviet body with representatives in the factories and among the troops. An action committee of fifteen members, among whom were Axelrod, Max Levien, Eugen Leviné and Ernst Toller, assumed power, their first objectives being nationalization and the establishment of a Red Army. The members of the action committee again could not agree on what part force was to play in carrying through the revolutionary programme. Toller stirred up so much opposition to the Leninists, the 'Russians', that these declared they would resign. Government troops and the Volunteer Corps intervened and, in the first days of May, won back Munich, itself the last bastion of the revolutionaries and defended by the Red Army under Egelhofer, a sailor.

In January Brecht went to some Independent Social Democrat election meetings conducted by Wendelin Thomas and Lilly and Georg Prem. In all probability he was a member of the party for a short period at this time. He had a soft spot for 'Höllenlilli', the brush-maker and spartacist Lilly Krause, whose husband, Georg Prem had been military commander of Augsburg at the time of the soviet. Brecht and Neher had sheltered him for some days when the military and police were hunting down the leading political figures of the revolution. In discussions with his friends Brecht praised the advantages of the soviet system, while dissociating himself from 'Bolshevism'; he admitted that force was necessary because without it the revolution could not succeed.

The clique round the young poet regarded the revolutionary events as an adventure. In most cases their sympathies were with the left, although some actually championed the cause of the employers and the bourgeoisie. Müllereisert, for example, fought in a Volunteer Corps for a time and worked as a spy for General Epp in Munich. He was not intimidated by Brecht's threat not to attend his funeral because of this, but when Brecht announced that he looked forward to Otto's death in battle with equanimity, and had now decided to attend his funeral, he thought better of it and left the Volunteer Corps. Walter Brecht also fought on the side of General Epp's troops.

In spite of the political unrest, Brecht's friends gave a party for him on 19 January at Gabler's tavern. He sang the 'Legend of the

28

Dead Soldier,' some other recent verses and a number of the 'Songs for Guitar' (Lieder zur Klampfe') which he had compiled in 1918 and for which Neher now did some glowing watercolour sketches: 'Baal playing the guitar, Orge with the rope under a tree, gruesome pictures of the dead soldier marching surrounded by flags and commotion under a blue spring sky, and violet shipwrecks'. In the course of the evening Brecht probably performed his 'Song of the Red Army Soldier' ('Gesang des Soldaten der roten Armee') for the first time, a gloomy vision and despairing renunciation of the paradise promised by the revolution to its supporters. It is not a song about the regular army of the Soviet Union; this serves only as a metaphor for the army of the poor and oppressed who parade under the banner of the 'red inhuman flag', trying to escape from hell but never reaching freedom, and are finally left with nothing but 'bloodstained empty hands'. Brecht deplored the cost of the revolution but dissociated himself from the ideals of non-violent prophets like Toller, because he never had any illusions about the real balance of power. Following a protest meeting, at which impassioned speeches and verses in honour of the murdered Rosa Luxemburg were delivered, Brecht wrote a 'Ballad of Red Rosa' ('Ballade von der roten Rosa'), which describes the hopelessness of the fight and in which Rosa, 'the only one set free', drifts down river: 'The red flags of revolution have long since fluttered off the roofs'.

Brecht still lacked sufficient political knowledge, he saw only the suffering, the victims, the deep gulf between dreams and reality. He continued to pour angry scorn on the vapid visions and proclamations of expressionist poets, who wanted to create the new man as the 'singular of humanity'. Unlike the poet J. R. Becher, who had raised his eyes in mystic panic alarm to the divine universe and whose hymnlike strains now extolled Lenin and Rosa Luxemburg, he did not see the October Revolution as deliverance. Brecht's poems reflect the harsh reality, the brutality of the times, man's hopes, doubts and disenchantments.

The November revolution in Germany was betrayed before it began. The majority of the soldiers, an army of millions of beaten and disillusioned little people, could not be won over to the revolutionary cause. In November Rosa Luxemburg had issued a warning, in *Die Rote Fahne (The Red Flag)*, against assessing the situation incorrectly: 'Soldiers who, as gendarmes of reaction, were yesterday murdering the revolutionary proletarians in Finland, Russia, the Ukraine and the Baltic countries, and workers who permitted this to happen, have not become clear-sighted agents of socialism in the space of twenty-four hours'. For the various parties of the left to argue as they did about what form democracy should take, and about the role of force, before the balance of power had been decided proved to be disastrous. The Spartacus League and the Communist Party were formed much too late and as defensive measures; the Social Democrats, on the other hand, supported the reactionary system, and their 'butcher' Noske had the insurgents clubbed down and their leaders liquidated. At the military hospital Brecht had gained an insight into the mentality of the soldiers returning from the war, and left-wing politicians were now hailing these men as heroes of the revolution. He outlined a play round one of these heroes, a love story describing the man's fight to win a bride; 'the revolution in the newspaper district also comes into it'. In January Berlin workers, following a big demonstration, had occupied a number of editorial buildings in the newspaper district. Brecht knew of these events only from the newspapers; in any case he had never yet been to Berlin. He also regarded the external circumstances of his play as relatively unimportant: 'The revolution, which had to serve as a background, was of no more interest to me than Vesuvius is to a man who wants to put his stock-pot on it'.

In this play the soldier, Andreas Kragler, returns to Berlin after spending four years in a prisoner-of-war camp in Africa and finds his fiancée, Anna Balicke, pregnant by Friedrich Murk, a man who has worked his way up in the war. Kragler is a 'corpse'; Murk, on the other hand, is earning money and living 'in the celebrated clover'. Anna's parents, owners of a factory that had made ammunition boxes in the war and was now to switch over to perambulators, are in favour of her marrying Murk. While the engagement is being celebrated in the Piccadilly Bar, the disappointed soldier joins some revolutionary-minded people who want to go into the newspaper district. As Murk and her parents get drunk, Anna falls in love with Andreas again and goes over to join the soldier because he has made up his mind to fight injustice. 'It is this romantic element that comes out when the Balicke girl hankers after the grimy, unworthy Kragler.' Now that he has got his girl, the soldier leaves the revolution to its own devices; he does not want to die and makes his way to safety. 'This then was Kragler, this revolutionary, whom pity turned into an owner again, who wailed and kicked up a row and went home as soon as he had what he had lacked.'

From the Marxist point of view *Spartakus,* later called *Drums in the Night (Trommeln in der Nacht)* is the most 'equivocal' of Brecht's early plays, as he himself was to point out later. It was conceived quite consciously as a topical play and contains political judgements. Moreover there is a discrepancy between what the play sets out to be and what it actually is. *Baal* and *In the Jungle of the Cities (Im Dickicht der Städte)* have a broader basis of reality; because their plots are on a bigger scale they are much more realistic. Nor, in these two plays, was Brecht subsequently forced to change the social attitudes of the characters. But Kragler, the hero of *Drums in the Night,* had to be transformed, and the drama became a comedy.

When he first wrote the play, at the beginning of 1919, Brecht sympathized with his hero, who was conceived as one of the oppressed whom the forces of reaction feared, one of those 'dissolute, work-shy adventurers to whom nothing is sacred any more'. At the same time he was intended to be an anti-hero to the noble proletarian, as formulated by leaders of the left, as well as an answer to the fatuous slogan 'man is good', and all the rest of the revolutionary catchphrases: 'They think up a lot of little sayings of this sort and puff them into the air; then they can sit back, and then the grass grows'. The soldier is not prepared to face death, which he has just escaped by the skin of his teeth, to bring about the victory of an idea. The imperialists also sent him to war for an idea. He sees no difference between the ideas; all he sees are idealistic gestures: 'My flesh is to rot in the gutter so that your idea can join the angels in heaven'.

No doubt this was a realistic end to the play, but its political accents were wrong. The play was not, and was not intended to be, a 'picture of the first German revolution'. The author admitted later that he had acclaimed Kragler as a realist, 'because he refused to be seduced by an ideal that was meaningless to him'. Ignorant of what the revolution was really about, Brecht saw it as a reality but, at the same time, as something that happens to man, like war. He did not want to present the revolution 'as a purely intellectual and moral human upheaval', which is what the expressionists and poet-revolutionaries did. The fact, however, that a man like Kragler will always continue to play the role of soldier, and never under any circumstances wants to be a soldier of the revolution, was left out of account. By his 'ostentatious sympathy for the little realist Kragler' the dramatist did not just fail to show 'respect for the proletarian revolutionaries'. The question why the revolution collapsed was not completely answered by the fact that the revolutionaries failed and the Social Democrats resorted to treachery. Another important reason for its collapse was the different interests of the masses in revolt. The Kraglers were positive and negative characters, proletarians without knowing it, more like petits-bourgeois, underdogs who liked to be top dogs at times, and then were suddenly resurrected as little Nazis. The Kraglers' repudiation of the revolution was also their acquiescence in the existing power structure. *Drums in the Night* could not simply be transformed into a didactic play about 'the Kragler type', as Brecht afterwards claimed to regard it. The soldier Andreas Kragler remained an isolated case, who did not correspond in any way to the typical repatriated prisoner of war; he was an abortive child of Baal, an exotic spectre unhappily cast into the Berlin of the Spartacus era. Both the atmosphere of the play and its language belonged unmistakably to Augsburg; the Berlin setting was simply a concession to the topical nature of the play.

Brecht revised *Drums in the Night,* and in particular its final scenes, repeatedly until its publication in book-form in 1922; this edition then became the basis of a further critical revision in 1953. The action, which originally took place 'between dusk and dawn' on a November night in 1918, was now switched to January 1919 and the part of Kragler's opposite number, the communist bar owner Glubb, was strengthened by the introduction of a nephew who, we learn, was a worker in the Siemens works and fell fighting as a revolutionary in November.

At the beginning of March 1919 Brecht took the play to Lion Feuchtwanger, who at that time was a celebrated novelist and playwright as well as being dramatic adviser to the Kammerspiele in Munich. Brecht, who arrived badly shaved and shabbily dressed and struck the carefully turned out author as 'unkempt', said that he had written *Spartakus* simply 'to make money'. Feuchtwanger's reaction was so enthusiastic that Brecht contradicted him and brought him *Baal,* in his own view a much better play. For the time being *Spartakus* vanished into the cupboard where Feuchtwanger kept his manuscripts, but features and phrases of the play's central character, and of Brecht himself, whom he identified partly with Kragler and partly with Baal, later appeared in his dramatic novel *Thomas Wendt;* Feuchtwanger also announced a stage version of the same material under the title *Thomas Brecht,* but it was never performed. Although Brecht did not object to this sort of 'personality cult', he found the whole affair somewhat embarrassing, and in his view his admirer had made a pretty thorough job of plagiarizing and imitating him. To be on the safe side he now changed Kragler's first name from Thomas to Andreas. It was not until 1920, and then more by chance than anything else, that Feuchtwanger gave the play, which in the meantime, and on his advice, had been renamed *Drums in the Night,* to Rudolf Frank, a dramaturg at the Kammerspiele, whose ability as a director was to be tried out on the work of a young writer. As he always did when one of his plays was to be performed, Brecht started to revise it, but there was a delay in starting the rehearsals and finally Otto Falckenberg, head of the Kammerspiele, took charge of the production himself. The first performance took place in September 1922. Under the Weimar Republic it was given more often than any other play by Brecht, so that his concessions to the prevailing taste paid off, even if a little later than anticipated.

In 1919 the author, who was in such desperate need of money, did not get a penny out of it. Bi, his mistress, was pregnant. Brecht's father advised him to continue his studies, but the son decided he would first make one more attempt to establish himself as a writer and poet: encouraged by Feuchtwanger's interest he revised *Baal.* On 2 May, as the soviet republic was nearing its end in Munich and the 'distant thunder of guns' could be heard in Augsburg, he read parts of the new version to some friends. Münsterer recalls that he read 'large sections of the first part'. The scenes in the newspaper office, 'in which Baal still clings to the idea of an ordered existence', had been cut, as a result of which the play as a whole became less compliant, less bourgeois. Day after day Brecht arrived bringing modifications, alterations, and completely new scenes. 'Furthermore', Münsterer continues, 'this *Baal* exercised a strong influence on our lives, the entire early summer of 1919 was animated by a Baal-like sense of things. But the reverse

33

is also true: much of our life at that time found its way into the play, especially into the second, and best, version. Actual occurrences, of course, are never reproduced, as they are in a *roman-à-clef,* but the flavour of old Augsburg pervades everything. Brecht's garret in the Bleich Strasse, its table piled high with manuscripts, the dense mass of hazel bushes on the verges of the River Lech, the grimy taverns by the moat and in Heddenbach—they are all there. Certain of the characters, too, inherit personal traits from those days, and in some of the dialogue in *Baal* the gap between historical reality and poetic overstatement is not so very wide.'

Georg Pfanzelt, Otto Bezold and Hans Otto Münsterer were the friends mainly consulted by Brecht over the revision, and used by him as go-betweens with his father's secretaries. It was torture to the son to look through and type out his own manuscripts, even to copy out his verses was a burden, so that he was grateful when someone relieved him of this work. Bezold and Münsterer were still boys at the Augsburg *Realgymnasium* when they met the poet in the autumn of 1917. Münsterer's aristocratic appearance and 'gentle' eyes inspired Brecht, who took a delight in dandified men of the Oscar Wilde and Rimbaud type, to compose a small lyric portrait of him, of which these are four of the lines:

> Trug stets einen feinen grauen
> Handschuh verflucht elegant;
> Er gab nur Tieren und Frauen
> Seine nackte Hand.

(Always wore the finest gloves, grey and devilish elegant; to women and animals alone he offered his bare hand.)

One night in May 1919, when Münsterer had just taken his school-leaving examination and intended to go and study medicine in Munich, their friendship was sealed on a bench under some chestnut trees: 'Brecht had just made an awful mess of my clothes, and my person generally, upbraiding me for being such a Philistine—a good thing it was dark, so that no one could see how small and abominable I had become—when suddenly he turned and asked me: 'By the way, don't you want to say Du (the familiar form of you)?' All I know is that I held his hand in mine for a long time, because it meant that I had really been accepted into the outcasts' clique'. During the June nights Brecht sang and wrote in the open air, the friends 'went' to 'India' and 'Tahiti', swam in the

Hahnreibach, lay naked as usual in the grass, and split their sides with laughter in the reeds, while Bert declaimed grotesque funeral orations and May devotions.

At the end of July Bi gave birth to a son in her parents' country house in the Allgäu; he was named Frank in memory of Wedekind. Brecht informed his mistress that, while he had nothing whatever against small children, he was not cut out to be a husband. Marieluise Fleisser remembers it being said of him 'that he had a horror of pregnancies and, if he had been the one to get them into that state, railed against it as if the women had done it to spite him'.

In his Augsburg days Brecht did not regard women as partners, but as objects to be pursued by man as a hunter pursues game. For him, as for Baal, women were only 'wenches', for a man to prove himself on, to 'take'. It is not to a girl that Baal says 'I love you' but to his friend Ekart; and in the case of Hedda Kuhn, Brecht made it clear that it was not her he loved 'but Bi and George'. Bi was no longer a girl, he could be friends with her and permit himself 'weaknesses'. The tie of friendship between Brecht and Bi continued for several years, and when, one day, another suitor appeared Brecht insisted on Bi assuring him, in the other's presence, that it was he whom she really loved. In the poet's eyes Bi, 'sweet Bi', 'that saucy Bi', was 'wise'. He appreciated her intelligence and the practical side of her nature, as well as her sensuality: on the swing-boats she could 'display her knee right royally'. Brecht wrote to her from Berlin, where at first he was rather disappointed in the girls, that he had met only a lot of 'eccentric, played-out geese trying to be clever'; they were 'tarty and sophisticated and so stupid, so stupid!' At the end of 1922 he dedicated to Bittersweet, as a sort of farewell gift, the first edition of *Drums in the Night*. Two years later he asked Helene Weigel to find a job, in an office or as a housekeeper, and a room in Berlin for his former mistress; but Bi could not make up her mind to give up the security of her job in an Augsburg bank. Her marriage, at that time only a few months old, did not seem to be particularly happy; her husband tolerated another man's child only grudgingly, and Helene Weigel arranged for little Frank to be taken care of by relations of hers in Baden outside Vienna. It was not until 1935 that the boy's mother brought him back to Augsburg, where he was trained as a German soldier, only to die later for his country in Russia.

Brecht's resumption of his studies in the summer term of 1919 did not stop him from working at his numerous dramatic projects. The most he did in any case was to attend Professor Kutscher's seminar, and this only to give vent to his anger over the latest plays by his contemporaries. He bestowed on Reinard Goering's *Seeschlacht (Naval Encounter)* the ironic title *Der bekehrte Meuterer (The Converted Mutineer)* and then tore it apart to the delight of most of the students, while Kutscher, glowering, declared 'that the reader of the paper lacked any talent whatsoever'. In Munich the poet found an ally in the dramaturg Jakob Geis, with whom in June he sketched out the comedy *Herr Maier und sein Sohn (Herr Maier and his Son)*. He often spent his evenings at Karl Valentin's, whose twisted logic and involved dialectics impressed Brecht. He even took part as a 'clarinettist' in Valentin's 'Oktoberfestbude' (October Fair Booth). Wedekind's ballad-like delivery and performing technique, Valentin's off-beat thinking and, later on, Chaplin's slapstick comedy became the basis of Brecht's 'epic theatre', at any rate in the form in which we see it in a play like *Man is Man (Mann ist Mann)*.

Autumn saw the completion of as many as five one-act plays, pure Valentin in style, grotesque pictures of everyday life with eccentric dialogue in which logic is stood on its head. The best of them is *A Humble Wedding (Die Kleinbürgerhochzeit)*, in which the total shipwreck of a commonplace family is portrayed in an absurdly comic way. At the end the bridal bed itself collapses with a crash, a sign that even in the erotic sphere nothing more is to be expected of bourgeois society. Reverting to this subject in 1941, when he was reading Diderot's *Jacques Le Fataliste,* Brecht noted: 'Remarkable that here in Germany there is no sign whatever of any of the refinements of sensuality! Love is . . . something divine or something diabolical, a dilemma from which one escaped by making a habit of it! The German aristocracy was incapable of enjoyment, the bourgeoisie was puritanical in its ideals and hence, in reality, bestial. The German university student "did it" after drinking so much beer that, where others would have vomited, he copulated'.

These one-act plays were macabre jokes which, at the same time, were deeply rooted in the German people. As he had already shown in the first two acts of *Drums in the Night,* Brecht was a master at portraying the milieu of the petite bourgeoisie and at ruthlessly exposing these people's sham morality. His habit of working collectively meant that he could write for his store cupboard. All he needed was that his friends should take an interest in what he wrote; to be rejected by publishers and theatres scarcely affected his work. Never in doubt as to his gifts, his doubts were confined entirely to the work in progress and these, far from impeding him, only spurred him on to further work. He never regarded a poem or play as finished; everything he wrote remained 'in a state of flux', it was there only to be altered. Viewpoints he no longer approved of, or considered wrong, he did not wish to see suppressed but corrected. Even in his Augsburg days what he wrote were not works but '*Versuche*', attempts.

In order to make money by literary activity of some sort, Brecht planned and outlined film scripts, as well as material for operas and operettas. Every opportunity that offered was seized upon and tried out. But only Brecht the critic was published. He had written book reviews for the *Augsburger Neueste Nachrichten* while still at school; after he left, this and other provincial papers employed him from time to time as music and ballet critic. His notices were moderate in tone and, in spite of sly criticism, contained a lot of praise and encouragement. It is quite possible that editors played a part in this, anxious to avoid indignant letters from readers. When the young colleague 'committed' himself too forcefully, one way or the other, his notice was turned down, as happened when the dancer Leistikov gave a guest performance in Augsburg in 1918. On that occasion Brecht's enthusiasm made him so 'light-headed' that he saw trees and fountains dancing, the dancer's body sending him into such raptures that he found violent fault with both the clumsy 'extremities' and the graceful legs of the Augsburg 'lasses'. An editor of the *Neueste Nachrichten* regretfully informed the critic that his imagination must 'have played a trick' on him. And even as it was he had prudently refrained from mentioning the dancer's 'divine bottom' in his notice. Thus prevented from singing her praises publicly, Brecht sent her a poem in which he once more drew a host of comparisons and then ended:

> Aus Nachtsturm und aus Morgenlicht
> Schuf dich ein trunkner Gott
> Vielleicht bist du das alles nicht
> Und ich ein Idi=alist

(From night's fierce storm and dawn's first light you were created by a god besot; perhaps, though, what I write's not right and I'm an idi-alist.)

Later, as dramatic critic of the *Volkswille,* he was less gallant. At the end of 1919 the editor, Wendelin Thomas, the first Marxist to exercise a certain political influence over Brecht, got the headstrong university student to assist him on the *Volkswille,* the organ of the Independent Social Democrat party in Swabia and Neuburg. Brecht's notices did not yet contain suggestions for innovations in the theatre, as they did later; he did not yet see the theatre in terms of social problems. He criticized on the basis of the existing system, demanded from those responsible a more progressive repertoire and from the city fathers more money for the theatre; he also demanded the removal of the director, Carl Häusler, who, in his opinion, had no 'intellectual stature' at all. To the actors and actresses Brecht handed out praise and blame in the usual way: as Mrs. Alving, Fräulein Stoff 'gave a distinguished performance, though it lacked feeling'; Hartl's Engstrand 'was a good, respectable achievement'; Aicher's Oswald 'was a surprise'; Frau Aicher acted 'with fine depth of feeling'; Fräulein Wagner as Luise was 'pleasing, instinctive, childlike'. In discussing the plays Brecht struck a completely different note: a silly farce was unequivocally 'execrable', Hebbel's *Judith* 'one of the weakest and silliest plays in our classical repertoire'. Side by side with this were perverse, but intelligent and serious, discussions on Schiller, Hauptmann, Ibsen, Georg Kaiser and Strindberg. His statements of principle, his appeal to the people of Augsburg once in a while to break themselves of their cherished habit of 'having bad theatre', led to a row with the director of the Stadttheater and the actors; the company wrote an open letter to which Brecht replied by defending Augsburg against its theatre: 'When a provincial grumbles about the provinces, he invariably means only one thing, the theatre'. Wendelin Thomas never dissociated himself from his colleague's articles, and he also asked him to write separate notices for performances given for the trade unions, in the selection of which Brecht's opinion was decisive. The *Volkswille,* which in the meantime had become an organ of the United German Communist Party, was forced to cease publication in January 1921. With it went, once again, Brecht's only chance to earn a little money.

It was not worth the poet's while to try to conquer the Augsburg theatre. There could be no question of making his start in the 'provinces'. 'Although I am only twenty-two, grew up in the small town of Augsburg on the Lech, and have seen only a little of the world, apart from meadows only this tree-lined town and a few others, and those not for long, I cherish the desire to have the world completely at my feet. I want everything handed to me, power over animals too, and I base my claim on the fact that I am here only once.' The young Brecht was not exactly modest. He would not hear a word against his egotism; to it he owed his self-assurance and his ability to judge his 'worth': I must have elbow room, be able to spit when I want, sleep alone, be unscrupulous'. But in Munich Lion Feuchtwanger's negotiations remained ineffectual. Hitherto Brecht had done his utmost to avoid getting tied up with any literary groups, establishing contacts, or courting the favour of publishers and people in the literary world. Now he had no option but to do just this. The wild, productive years of his youth had run their course. The man of twenty-two needed new surroundings, he sought means to escape the 'chaos' that threatened to engulf him. For him it was a painful but necessary farewell.

> O, ihr Zeiten meiner Jugend! Immer
> Matter wird Erinnerung jetzt schon.
> Leichte Schatten! Weiss getünchte Zimmer!
> Und darinnen rot Orchestrion.

(Oh days of my youth! The memory already grows dimmer. Faint shadows! Whitewashed rooms! And in them red orchestrion.)

In February 1920 Brecht made a first attempt to gain a foothold in Berlin, to find out exactly what chances he had there. He had talks with the Deutsches Theater about *Baal,* but they came to nothing. He was also fairly assiduous in attending receptions and artists' parties, not omitting the 'Stakugenu', the fancy dress ball at the Kunstgewerbemuseum. At this last he even allowed himself to be inveigled into dancing, the reason being a beautiful creature he had spotted in the throng, dressed as a hula-hula girl, 'authentic African' with a black wig and her skin dyed brown. When the African beauty showed signs of leaving him the poet, who was dressed in the brown habit of a monk, asked 'in a soft rather husky voice' if she would care to dance, adding in the same breath that he was not very good at it: 'His dancing really was more of a make-shift affair. When I had had enough of having my bare feet trampled on, I asked him if it might not be better to sit it out and just talk'. Brecht went on telling 'Fräulein Do', as he called Dora Mannheim, amusing stories until the early hours of the morning and then suggested that he see her home on foot through the Tiergarten: at this hour of the morning 'we shall hear the birds singing there'. A few days later the Kapp-Putsch took place and upset the lover's plans, Berlin being too dangerous for him. Brecht telephoned Fräulein Do to say he had to leave at once because, should anything happen, his place was in Augsburg at his father's side, who was director of a large paper mill there. This reason for his precipitate departure was a pretext. The poet was being cautious, as he always was in situations of this kind: his own safety was what mattered. Back in Munich he immediately wrote an enthusiastic letter telling her he had arrived as merry as a sandboy, trotted off to his pension and spent the evening until eleven o'clock laughing himself almost sick at Valentin's cabaret. He had long since forgotten that he had been going to Augsburg to plead with the workers to be lenient to his father. A few days later, on the other hand, he wants to start a revolution of his own, 'because I am without a job and am worried, and in order to rid myself of thoughts that torment me', for 'there is no sign of green in the trees, the birds hold their beaks trembling, and there are heaps of stories but no amusing ones. I have resumed the great marches in my room, it is dusk the whole day long'. Brecht kissed 'little Do' on paper, 'because you can't do a thing to stop me', and asked her for photographs. The recipient was apparently at a loss, unable to fathom the allusions, and because of this the lover found her answer lamentable: 'It is a miserable piece of paper from every point of view. Such an icy blast comes off the lines that it makes one cough. I feel I am being treated like an orphan'. Later Fräulein Do went to Munich for a few days, and Brecht generally looked her up when he went to Berlin. Dora Mannheim's great merit was that in 1924 she introduced the poet to her colleague Elisabeth Hauptmann.

In Augsburg, after his failure in Berlin, Brecht once more had a feeling of deadlock, disintegration and decay. Many of the poems of this time contain reflections on death and mortality: 'But in the

Cold of the Night' ('Aber in kalter Nacht'), 'Our World is Crumbling' ('Unsere Erde zerfällt'), 'My Brother's Death' ('Meines Bruders Tod'), 'Death Always Soothes' ('Immer beruhigt der Tod').

> Ich beginne zu sprechen vom Tod.
> Viele Irrglauben sind verbreitet
> Aber wenn man den Wunsch von der Furcht
>   abschneidet
> Kommt uns die erste Ahnung von dem, was uns droht.

(I start to speak of death. There are many false beliefs about; but if one detaches the wish from the fear, one has a first inkling of what hangs over us.)

On 1 May 1920 the poet's mother died; in her presence he had felt at home and protected: 'Twenty winters had threatened her, her sufferings were legion, death was ashamed to face her. Then she died and they found the body of a child.' In the meantime Bi had given way, as Brecht's favourite mistress, to the 'dark skinned He', the medical student Hedda Kuhn, although she was not wise like Bi, was continually running around, 'and there was not a thought in her heart'. After she had been his mistress for sixteen months, the poet paid tribute to her in a psalm to celebrate her 'discharge': 'She knew with her brain what a woman is, but not with her knees; she could find the way in the light with her eyes, but in the dark she could not find it'. There was no final separation in 1920, when Marianne Zoff became the poet's favourite, because Brecht was a staunch lover and friend. Those who once became involved with him did not extricate themselves so quickly. 'From time to time I shoot at birds who try to get away and gobble them up again.' Some years later, when looking at a photograph of Hedda Kuhn with the inscription 'Clean. Down to earth. Mischievous.', sentimental tears came into the lover's eyes:

> Sie wusch sich immer mit Mandelseife
> Und von ihr war auch das Frottierhandtuch und das
> Tokaierrezept und die Javapfeife
> Gegen den Liebesgeruch.
>
> Ihr war es ernst. Sie schwamm nicht. Sie dachte.
> Sie verlangte Opfer für die Kunst.
> Sie liebte die Liebe, nicht den Geliebten, ihr machte
> Keiner einen rosa Dunst.

(She always washed with almond soap and hers, too, was the Turkish towel, the Tokay prescription and the Java pipe against love's aroma. She took it seriously. She did not lose her head. She thought. She demanded sacrifices for art. She loved love, not the lover, she was never lost in a rose-tinted haze.)

In 1920 Georg Müller was expected finally to publish *Baal*. The manuscript had already been set up in type, but the publisher did not bring the book out because he was afraid of a law suit, although the author had provided a new, shortened—with a view to what was possible on the stage—and more restrained version. In his diary Brecht noted that he had now probably made a complete mess of *Baal*: 'He is now a thing of paper, turned into an academic, smooth, shaven, wearing bathing-trunks etc. Instead of being more earthy, more un-reflecting, more brazen, more ingenuous!'

Brecht clung to his early plays. He could not detach himself from them until they had been performed. His defiant 'nihilism' and 'anarchism', as well as the 'coldness' one hears so much about, were a necessary contrast to his idyllic youthful romanticism, to the companionable idol of male society, who still continued to receive his fair share of adulation. After an excursion to the Allgäu with Caspar Neher, Brecht noted: 'It is better with another man than with a girl'. In the four pillaging Kipling soldiers—here no longer in the least sympathetic—of the comedy *Man is Man* there is still a lot of the camaraderie of the 'lads' with whom the poet used to wander through the Württemberg countryside in 1920: 'we go bathing every day and don't walk too far. The clergy give us bread or five marks, the farmers their wine. Potatoes we steal'. On these rambles with his friends, difficulties and boredom ceased to exist; the mind could remain 'in exile'. Literature, art and intellectuals were taboo: 'thoughts are impurities'. This, needless to say, was not Brecht's final word on the subject. In addition to out and out swaggering of this sort, his diary entries for 1920 contain astonishing flashes of perception and signs of a mentality more in line with the motto he normally followed: 'In difficult situations note down every possibility and then think it out'.

For more than a year after this Brecht continued to live in Munich as a penniless 'student', most of his time being spent at the theatre watching rehearsals and learning from them; in the evenings he went to Valentin's cabaret. Every now and then he buried himself for a few days in Augsburg; it was there that he sketched out *Galgei,* a first version of *Man is Man,* and, in the autumn, began his play *Garga.* It was a period of indifference and cynicism: 'With unchanging expression, enjoying myself in bed and without responsibility, deceitful perhaps, able to rise above my circumstances, fairly cold, wholly unpolitical'. He became a little uneasy when Marianne missed her period, but announced good-humouredly: 'Let them grow, these little Brechts'. Whereas he himself changed women with as little compunction as he changed his shirt, he became annoyed if another lover entered his preserve. Thus with reference to Marianne Zoff, who wanted to marry Brecht, by whom she was pregnant, but could not shake off her admirer Recht, that 'infatuated swine Malchus' as he is called in one of the ballads in the *Homilies for the Home,* Brecht wrote: 'Timbuctoo is fine, and a child is fine too, one can have both. Whether it's name is Peter or Gise, one can't murder it. Fine. Then I shall do what I can for Gise. And this is best for the woman too; that swine is not the man for her, and a child is better than just anything. So I shall help her, even though I don't marry her, because I am only provisional, I must have room to move in, I am still growing'.

'According to the statutes', Brecht was held not to have attended the summer term of 1921; he had probably forgotten to pay his fees for the lectures, which in any case he rarely, if ever, attended. On 29 November he was informed officially that his name had been removed from the register of students. At this same moment he was negotiating for a second time in Berlin, on this occasion with the publishers Erich Reiss and Gustav Kiepenheuer. In addition he was making unremitting efforts to gain the attention of Max Reinhardt's and Leopold Jessner's dramatic advisers.

4

Baal—An Analysis

His 'Do what you enjoy doing' would yield
rich rewards properly applied.

There was so much of himself in the character of Baal that Brecht remained fascinated by it all his life. The alterations he made to his first play reflect the poet's own changing outlook. Brecht held firmly to Baal's positive modes of behaviour and sentiments, to his enormous appetite for pleasure and his longing for happiness, and he also created other characters in which 'something of Baal' is to be found. First and foremost certainly Galileo, who sublimates his insatiable hunger for the world in the constant acquisition of fresh knowledge, and to whom thinking is sensual pleasure and all sensual pleasures are stimuli to thought. Galileo practices the dialectics of work and pleasure. Baal wants only pleasure and Brecht shows his downfall to be due to the fact that, in the last resort, he is incapable of enjoyment.

Baal came into existence 'for the purpose of demolishing a weak theatrical success by means of a ludicrous conception of genius and amorality'. The first version still bears all the traces of Brecht's quarrel with Johst's play *Der Einsame*. The leading characters and their interrelationships have been appropriated: Baal corresponds to the poet Grabbe, Johannes to the doctor Hans Eckardt, and Brecht's Ekart to the musician Waldmüller. The visionary rapture of the idealistically conceived poetic genius has its counterpart in Baal's healthy materialism and cynicism. Brecht also makes burlesque use of the scenic effects and dramatic construction of the other play in order to polemize against the idealistic contrivances of his model. When Grabbe recites his poetry in a tavern he is 'casting pearls before swine'; the common people don't understand him and cease to listen: genius is predestined to loneliness. Baal, on the other hand, sits down with the lorry drivers and, having gained their attention by announcing that his poems are 'filth', offers them art. The audience is outwitted, Brecht acknowledges the utility value of art.

The underlying idea of *Der Einsame* is the reactionary one that his genius can flourish only if the poet is a solitary figure, outcast by society. To Grabbe literature is life; he suffers, not from bad material conditions, but from the social irrelevance of his genius. Despising the world, he lives solely for his art. When a lorry driver, on hearing one of Baal's poems, remarks 'What it must be to have a brain like that!', the latter replies: 'One has to have a stomach and all that as well!' For him poetry flows only from abundance, it is a by-product of the art of living. It is vitality, not a substitute for a life of misery. His life means more to Baal than his art. His transfiguration is effected through material pleasure. Johst's poet is transfigured through death. Baal ends up whimpering, crawling on his hands and knees into the open: he thought dying would be simpler than that.

The comedy of *Baal* was more than just a rejoinder to Johst's expressionist play. 'The basic assumption of the play is scarcely within my reach any longer today, yet it seems to me that it offers scope for an exceedingly enjoyable approach to the countryside, to human relationships of an erotic, or semi-erotic, nature, to language etc.' The character of Baal accorded with Brecht's view of life and poetry; in creating it the poet proclaimed himself a disciple of materialism and unrestrained vitality. Like the Syrian earth-god, whose name he bears, Baal ravenously devours life in all its forms, sucks his victims dry and spits out what he cannot digest.

The original of Baal was not the Augsburg mechanic Josef K., whom Brecht later invented for the part and who was supposed to have wandered round Southern Germany with a down-and-out medical student, but Paul Verlaine. Brecht related his own experiences and ideas to those he found in literature. Baal's homosexually based relationship with Ekart was a paraphrase of Verlaine's roving, dissolute life with Rimbaud. The wanderings of the two poets through Belgium and England had a substantial influence on the play. Baal was to look like Verlaine: 'His is the uncomfortable skull of Socrates and Verlaine', Brecht wrote in the preface to the 1919 version, and Neher based his portrait of Baal on photographs and drawings of Verlaine. Details in the life of François Villon also played their part in forming the character of Baal, his restless, vagrant existence and the dismal circumstances of his death, his end 'in the undergrowth'. Brecht had already had the idea of writing a *Baal* before Johst's play was performed: 'I want to write a play about François Villon, who was a murderer, highwayman and ballad-writer in Brittany in the fifteenth century'.

Other features of Baal's character show traces of Wedekind and Hamsun. Wedekind loved *coups de théatre,* off the stage as well as on. He always assumed a diabolic personality, as a mask and as an ironic means of self-protection. Baal adopts a distinctive attitude when he sings and recites, as Wedekind did, and like him does so awkwardly and in an untrained voice. Finally Baal's way of speaking reflects the mixture of cynical vitalism and romantic verism typical of Hamsun's prose; later Brecht had strong doubts about this. 'It is always better to crap than do nothing at all' was the pleasure-loving poet's motto in those days. His extreme, materialistically based vitalism, however, exhausted itself with time and gave way to a poetically tinged nihilism, which he also embraced for a while:

> Ich gestehe es: ich
> Habe keine Hoffnung.
> Die Blinden reden von einem Ausweg. Ich
> Sehe.
>
> Wenn die Irrtümer verbraucht sind
> Sitzt als letzter Gesellschafter
> Uns das Nichts gegenüber.

(I admit it, I have no hope. The blind talk of a way out. I see. When we have run the gamut of our mistakes, there, facing us, sits our final companion nothingness.)

When he revised *Baal* for the last time, Brecht wrote: 'The play may well present all manner of difficulties to those who have not learned to think dialectically. They are unlikely to see in it anything but the glorification of barefaced egotism. In fact, however, it opposes an individual to the demands and discouragements of a world that acknowledges a system of production open, not to use, but to abuse. We cannot tell how Baal would react to seeing his talents turned to account: what he resists is having them turned into sausage meat. Baal's art of living shares the fate of all the other arts under capitalism: it is attacked. He is a-social, but in an a-social society'. Whether in 1918, when he drafted the play, Brecht had the detachment from his character that he took for granted in 1954 is unimportant. The question of how far Baal's a-social attitude is to be seen as a reaction against the a-social attitude of society is a secondary consideration compared to the challenge a character like Baal presents to society. During the sociological phase of his Marxist studies, Brecht attempted to revise *Baal* from the standpoint of social criticism, in other words to show the Baal type as the product of social conditions and as a historical person. This 'objectified' *(versachlicht)* 1926 revision subsequently led to plans for the didactic play *Bad Baal the A-social Man (Der böse Baal der asoziale)*. In this Baal appears in several roles, as a progressive clergyman, for example, and as a passport official. In it Baal shows greater awareness. Thus, while he accepts the acclaim of his host, a rich businessman, for himself, he refuses to accept any praise for the instrument he has used to accompany his singing. He enjoys his role as artist and the remarkable 'freedom' accorded him by bourgeois society. All the same he is tempted to see how far he can go in breaking the rules of the game. After the businessman has praised Baal's song and said how much he enjoyed it, Baal says to him: 'I am now going to break a string of your instrument because I enjoy doing that. Tell me again, Sir, do you like the song?' The businessman smiles, sends for a new string and repeats his praise. Baal breaks the new string as well and repeats his question. His host says nothing. The artist expresses his thanks for the businessman's hospitality by smashing his instrument, in order to show his contempt for him. The a-social Baal knows the society he is moving in. He provokes it only because he risks nothing worse than being thrown out. It is a matter of principle for him to be on the alert, to appraise and use his own resources properly. Any meal, even a bad one, is better than sympathy: this is the lesson that life teaches him.

This didactic play was intended to demonstrate that Baal and his output were not to be used for the state. For the 'bad state' as Brecht made a point of stressing. The purpose of this play, which remained a fragment, about the a-social Baal, was to eliminate the anarchistic character of Baal by means of Marxism: 'The great mistake that prevented me from completing the little didactic plays about the "Bad, a-social Baal", lay in my definition of socialism as a great system. Whereas it is much more practical to define it as production on a grand scale, production, of course, being understood in its broadest sense, and the struggle as the liberation of all human beings from all fetters'.

In 1954 Brecht decided once more in favour of his original conception of the character of Baal, remarking only: 'I admit (and give warning): the play lacks wisdom'. It is not enough to see in Baal an anti-bourgeois hunk of flesh, who subscribes to a philosophy no less philistine than the attitude to life of the class he professes to be fighting: Baal as an egotistical being, ruthlessly devouring his fellow men, and as a voluptuary cynically accepting the bestiality of the world. Brecht's thinking had already gone beyond this when he wrote the play: 'For enjoyment's not an easy thing, by heaven!' as he says in the 'Hymn of Baal the Great' *('Choral vom grossen Baal')*. This suggests a criticism of the petit bourgeois concept of materialism along the lines of that formulated by Friedrich Engels: 'By materialism the philistine means eating, drinking, the lust of the eyes, the lust of the flesh and an arrogant nature, avarice, niggardliness, covetousness, profiteering and market-rigging, in short all the sordid vices to which he himself is secretly addicted.' Of greater interest, therefore, than the ordinary Marxist interpretation that sees in Baal merely a petit bourgeois who gets out of materialism only what the philistine, as defined by Engels, understands by it, is the question whether the character of Baal is not a successful artistic projection of a man who dares to try to take the freedom due to him by right of nature and to realize something of the 'happiness' that will eventually accrue to human beings liberated from work that has become alien to them. Baal's mistake, and the questionable nature of his actions, lies only in attempting to put into effect his idea of happiness under existing social conditions. His egotistically motivated attempt is doomed to failure, but what remains is the fact that his claim to happiness is justified.

With the *Life History of the Man Baal (Der Lebenslauf des Mannes Baal)* of 1926 and the didactic play of 1929/30 Brecht wanted to show that the Baal type 'is completely unsusceptible to socialization and his method of production quite impossible to turn to account'; his only regret was that his play had to be performed before an audience that was unsympathetic to socialism. Brecht the poet wanted the proletarian to be Baal's antagonist. But Brecht the dialectician thought it more to the point to awaken in the proletarian a desire to be like Baal. The word 'enjoyment' must not be taken to mean, on the one hand, what specific social groups can permit themselves in the form of luxuries or, on the other hand, what is suggested to the worker as the happiness he should aim for and for which he is expected to toil and drudge under miserable conditions. The human desire for happiness can be fulfilled through work, among other things, but only when the work serves to satisfy a need and is not a means, as Marx puts it, 'of satisfying needs beyond this'. Work is inhuman as long as it serves only to secure the existence of a human being. Under these conditions life itself seems to the person concerned to be 'only a means to existence'. What is desirable, on the other hand, is a social condition which guarantees that 'socially useful work at the same time represents the genuine satisfaction of an individual need' (Marcuse).

Brecht does not regard as excessive the amount of happiness which Baal demands for himself, all he criticizes is the uncompromising rigour with which he procures his right. To seek only enjoyment makes one incapable of all enjoyment. Baal is not transfigured through enjoyment, as at first he hopes to be, but dies like a rat in the woods. People see Baal, as they see Wedekind's Lulu, as an animal, a creature without a soul. He, too, wants to realize his 'nature', to bring the laws of reason into harmony with the interests of the senses. His ambition, therefore, is to wring as much enjoyment out of the world as he can. Unlike Lulu, Baal appears to understand the world, and he accepts the role of animal as Schigolch does, who tells Lulu: 'The animal is the only genuine thing in man . . . What you have experienced as animal, no misfortune can wrest from you again. It remains yours for life'. Baal's aim is to realize, without regard for anyone or anything, 'the image of man as a free subject', in a society which tries to prevent the liberation of all libidinous forces. The enjoyment he obtains does not satisfy him, but he is ready to destroy himself rather than offer himself as a sacrifice to society.

In the preface he wrote to his early plays in 1954, Brecht mentions in connection with *Baal* the plan for an opera, *Travels of the God of Happiness (Die Reisen des Glücksgotts)*, which he sketched at the end of 1941. This opera is also concerned with man's longing for happiness: 'There is a Chinese figure, usually

49

the length of one's finger, carved out of wood and marketed by the thousand, which represents the fat little god of happiness stretched out contentedly. This god, arriving from the east, was to enter the cities ravaged by a great war and persuade the people to fight for their personal happiness and well-being. He gathers round him a varied group of disciples and then finds the authorities on his trail when some of the former start spreading the doctrine that the peasants should be given land, the workers take over the factories, and the children of both of them seize the schools. He is arrested and sentenced to death. And now the executioners try out their skills on the little god of happiness. But when they give him poison he finds it delicious, when they cut off his head it grows again immediately, on the scaffold he performs a dance that infects everyone with his own gaiety, etc., etc. It is impossible wholly to destroy man's desire for happiness'. Brecht planned *Travels of the God of Happiness,* and later *Songs of the God of Happiness,* as 'a wholly materialistic work', intended to show the need to reconcile reason and sensuality, the principles of reality and pleasure. Eating, drinking, living, sleeping, loving, working, thinking are set side by side by the poet as 'the great pleasures'.

If a state of society is achieved in which man's productive powers are really used and no longer exploited, the individual's quest for happiness will no longer be seen as egotism but as an element of universal bliss. But Baal's inflexible determination to reconquer the lost paradise and secure for himself a 'heaven filled with trees and bodies' is powerless to withstand the world's afflictions and proves to be a consuming force which destroys others and in the end kills himself.

5

The Lord Of The South Sea and the Lord Of The North Sea

When Brecht went to Berlin in the autumn of 1921, he thought at first that his chances there were very good. Since the appearance of his buccaneering story *Bargan Lets It Be (Bargan lässt es sein)* in the September number of the Munich *Der neue Merkur* he had been regarded by avant-garde publishers as a dark horse. People showed an interest in the author of the controversial *Baal,* wove legends round him, wanted to meet him and to hear him sing to his guitar. Wherever Brecht appeared he attracted attention; he fascinated his listeners and involved them in heated arguments. Within a few weeks he had made the acquaintance of more people than others did in years. The dramatist Arnolt Bronnen, who became friends with Brecht at this time, has written: 'He still did not have a single contract in his pocket, although he had discussed the casting of his plays with Klöpfer, Krauss, Wegener and George. He knew all the dramaturgs, such as Reinhardt's Felix Holländer and Jessner's Dr. Lipmann; he knew the leading figures in the literary world, such as Ludwig Berger, Heinrich Eduard Jacob; and in at least three publishing houses—the Drei Masken Verlag, the Propyläen Verlag and the Kiepenheuer Verlag—he had an enthusiastic following that extended from the head of the firm to the youngest secretary'. Brecht needless to say was interested only in negotiations at the highest level; he refused to be fobbed off with interviews in ante-rooms and, from the very beginning, planned to present his plays in the leading theatres and only with leading actors and actresses. He never adopted the role of an unrecognized genius, of an author anxious to be published and performed at all costs. He imposed conditions and made equivalent financial demands, because he wanted to live on his earnings as a writer. He had waited long enough and had acquired a realistic attitude to his work: 'I know my throat is better than my song, and the things I sing of are better too. I don't yet 'have' to write, as so many do who can't write at all.'

To the small-town dweller the unaccustomed activity was stimulating only for a time. When it developed into a 'chase', and sapped his physical strength, he no longer enjoyed it. Added to this his negotiations with the publishers had reached deadlock again and the theatres still hesitated. Non-committal arrangements, plans, vague promises and recommendations were all he had. Brecht was on the move from morning till night, spending himself on activities that did not even repay his efforts. Nothing he did could be turned to account. He needed a convivial atmosphere: people, ideas, problems, not cliquishness and business zeal. The big city became an exhausting jungle. 'Cold' uncongenial Berlin struck the poet as like 'Chicago'. 'I am fed up to the teeth with it, truly', he wrote to Bi in Augsburg, and enumerated for her the events of one especially bad day, so that she could visualize the strenuous life he was leading in Berlin. 'In the morning I wrote an act of a film until 10, then I went to the university, then on to the Deutsches Theater for the rehearsals, had a quick bite to eat standing up somewhere at 3, went to the café to meet Klabund, who is manipulating the contract with Reiss, chatted till 6 about this business with the publishers, during which time we made our way in and out of three bars with a young man who had got some cash in advance and paid for the drinks, then I went by underground to the Skala, where Matray and Kata Sterna were dancing, then with Warschauer, Matray and Kata Sterna by car to Warschauer's, where I stayed for two hours while I "supped" and drank wine. Then I went with Matray to Maenz's restaurant where Granach introduced me to a lot of theatrical people, and at 2 sauntered home with a cigar. And all these people manipulate one another, write about one another, envy, despise and deride one another!!!'

Frank Warschauer, a left-wing writer who admired Brecht, used his modest means to act as Maecenas, offering the poet his room and asking him to an occasional meal. For Brecht a supper was a luxury worth mentioning because he had gone to Berlin with scarcely a penny, and lived mostly on thick pea soup at Aschinger's and cheap cigars. He no longer wanted to ask his father for pocket money, although he accepted gratefully occasional gifts of money from him. He had what he called 'a vague relationship' with his father, 'and that is already a great deal between people like us'. As he had to stay longer than he expected in the capital, Brecht asked

52

Marianne Zoff to join him for Christmas; following a two-year engagement in Augsburg, she was now singing at the opera in Wiesbaden. Marianne, a tall, slim, dark-eyed Viennese, with plenty of temperament, generously took over the housekeeping and always managed to find something to eat, if it was only a half-finished tin of sardines, 'out of which the three of them ate half a sardine each, using one fork between them'. The third eater was Arnolt Bronnen, now a bosom companion of Brecht's, to the intense annoyance of the jealous Marianne who saw her influence slipping away. With what he earned as a temporary assistant at Wertheim's department store Bronnen could not contribute much to the housekeeping. Brecht wanted to take the Berlin theatres by storm with him, on the assumption that if the two of them worked together this would be easier and less boring.

The two writers had met at the house of Otto Zarek, a Berlin literary figure, and immediately taken a liking to each other. They were so close and understood each other so well that explanations were never necessary. If, in spite of this, Bronnen did press his friend to explain something or other the latter would refuse categorically to talk about 'feelings' and make some practical suggestion instead: 'We'll go to theatres and rehearsals together, study the directors and learn how it is done'. The all-important thing for Brecht was the working relationship; he saw his friend as a partner and collaborator. Bronnen, on the other hand, looked up to Brecht in admiration, 'fell under his spell' and, like a schoolboy, wanted to serve his idol: 'For Brecht, Bronnen was only one among many friends, for Bronnen, Brecht was the only possible friend'. Bidi, as Brecht was now usually called, serenely accepted the role of father. But he expected Bronnen at least to show a degree of self-assurance and self-confidence. Every opportunity was taken to discuss things in public. For business reasons Brecht joined his first name to that of Bronnen and the firm Arnolt and Bertolt, the two 'Fasolts' of German literature as Karl Kraus scathingly called them, quickly became known and the object of much ridicule in the gossip columns of the cheap press. Brecht did not regard publicity as disreputable; after all he had two plays up his sleeve and was working on a third. Later, after reading Brecht's plays and poems, Karl Kraus revised his earlier adverse opinion; an incorruptible critic, he had been put off by Bert Brecht's methods of pressing his claims as a writer.

Publicity alone brought in no money. The two playwrights suffered from cold and hunger. When, at the end of January, Brecht was admitted to the Charité hospital, suffering from undernourishment, Marianne Zoff came from Wiesbaden once more, having in the meantime terminated her agreement there. She went to the hospital every day, but then, upset by letters from Bi in Augsburg, she too fell ill. Unable to persuade Bidi to return to Munich, because he did not want to leave Berlin until he had won his victory, she finally left him in the care of Bronnen. The two friends enjoyed their 'mental clinch'. What Brecht would really have liked would have been for Bronnen to occupy the bed next to his in the hospital. Nothing, in his opinion, was more instructive for a young dramatist 'than to be in a big hospital ward'. It was not so easy to keep the patient from his work and other habits. He had a constant stream of visitors, of friends and women admirers. Brecht left the hospital prematurely, before he had been pronounced fit, and continued his onslaughts on the theatres. Starting in the mornings he and Bronnen visited the theatres, trying to get the ears of actors and directors; in the evenings they watched the current shows. Finally, in March, they were able to report two successes: Hermann Kasack, Kiepenheuer's chief reader, gave Brecht a contract for the book edition of *Baal;* and Moritz Seeler accepted Bronnen's play *Vatermord (Patricide)* for performance by the newly formed 'Die junge Bühne', with Brecht as director.

'Die junge Bühne' was not a commercial undertaking. It was one of the so-called lunch-time theatres *(Mittagstheater)*, which had no home of their own and usually gave guest performances on Sunday mornings in other theatres. All those taking part worked for nothing. Brecht saw it as a good opportunity to learn. Bronnen's play bore a strong resemblance to *Drums in the Night;* its hero was also a sham revolutionary. Brecht, having recognized the play's main weakness, set out to expand the father–son conflict into a social conflict and make this the central point of his production.

'Die junge Bühne' had to work under wretched conditions. Each rehearsal took place in a different theatre, and Brecht had to make do with actors and actresses whom he did not want to work with. At first his assurance and decisiveness amazed everyone, but it was not long before he told them flatly, in his dry, precise voice, 'that everything they did was lousy'. The cast, whom Brecht did not like, put up with his abuse extremely patiently. Heinrich George, on the other hand, whom Brecht did like and for whom he fought hard, was not prepared to see his part ruined; he shouted Brecht down and stormed out of the rehearsal. The embarrassed director took the opportunity to withdraw and told the author: 'It would never have been any good with that lot anyway'. It was a severe defeat for Brecht, because a young director, who quarrelled with his actors, could not expect to be asked to direct another play in a hurry. As a loyal friend Bronnen had to side with Brecht and could not show any active interest in the production, which was taken over by Berthold Viertel. Viertel and Brecht made friends and got on splendidly; later Brecht gave him the name *Städtebauer*, or builder of cities, because throughout the whole reconstruction period he gave assistance to all and sundry, with the result that all he had to show of his own house was the doorpost, 'a nice one, by the way'.

Cursing Berlin and all its theatres, the unhappy conquerors continued to eat their pea soup at Aschingers. Brecht, having set out to experience life in a big city, had entered the jungle brimming over with energy and ideas, but his feet never touched solid ground. 'Chicago' rebuffed him. Like Garga, in his play of that name, the poet seemed to come to grief there, to lose his humanity in the place. 'Brecht suffered. One could not tell by looking at him whether he was starving or freezing; to such an extent did he live on his own inexhaustible capital that it seemed almost as if he had no needs'. Bronnen thought he recognized Brecht in the character of Garga; the play seemed to him to be built on the latter's closing speech: 'Those were the best days. The chaos is spent, it let me go without a blessing. Perhaps work will console me. It is without question very late. I feel quite alone'.

Garga survives his antagonist Schlink. He wins through, but at what a cost? 'Back alive, anyhow, from that stinking alligators' pit', is Garga's summing up, with its inhuman conclusion: 'One has to grind one's enemy into the dust, one cannot get the better of him'. It is Schlink who issues the challenge and starts the fight, but he never gets to the point of actually fighting and is exterminated. Unlike Garga he preserves his humanity. Who was Schlink? Certainly not Bronnen. Nor was he Feuchtwanger, as Bronnen supposed. Both characters, Garga and Schlink, reflect Brecht's experiences in the big city. It is the clearest of Brecht's early plays. Perhaps it was for this very reason that, consciously or unconsciously, Brecht left unaltered the strange and puzzling nature of the play's action.

The play's theme had already been established in Augsburg; the dialogue about man's loneliness and the inadequacy of speech as a means of communication was written there in the summer of 1921. Berlin merely provided corroborative material. A general theme, the animosity and impenetrability of the modern world, was given concrete form as a result of personal experience. Brecht had come to question Augsburg and his happy boyhood. That sense of safety and security threatened to turn into a mere idyll. There was no longer much difference between Augsburg and Germany:

> Deutschland, du Blondes, Bleiches
> Wildwolkiges mit sanfter Stirn!
> Was ging vor in deinen lautlosen Himmeln?
> Nun bist du das Aasloch Europas.

(Germany, blond pale Germany, with your wild clouds and gentle brow, what happened in those silent skies of yours? Now you are the carrion pit of Europe.)

The poet, in search of a different reality, contrasted Augsburg with the big city, Germany with America:

> O Aasland, Kümmernisloch!
> Scham würgt die Erinnerung
> Und in den Jungen, die du
> Nicht verdorben hast
> Erwacht Amerika!

(Oh carrion land, pit of misery! Shame stifles your memory; and in the young, whom you have not corrupted, America awakes!)

America became the positive counterpart, the pioneer land of technical progress and opportunities for the young. Even there, however, there was no evidence of social reality. The alternatives seemed to be decay or merciless war. Brecht presented the inconsistencies, he had nothing to say about their causes.

He sent the play to Neher in Augsburg, asking him to suggest changes and tell him if it was 'on the right lines'; personally he considered it 'at least as good as *Baal,* and more mature'. At the same time Neher was to get in touch with Fräulein Marie Roecker, the Brechts' housekeeper in Augsburg, who was responsible for having the manuscript copied at the Haindl factory. Brecht distributed the typed copies among the theatre people in Berlin, read them scenes from the play when opportunity arose, and counted on a performance under Reinhardt or Jessner. The actor Paul Wegener was his choice for Schlink, Alexander Granach for Garga. This project also came to nothing.

Meanwhile Brecht 'consoled' himself with work: he began with a *Pope Joan* for Tilla Durieux and had another look at two earlier projects, the Ephesus play *Summer Symphony (Sommersinfonie)* and *Galgei,* on the subject of a man on the swing-boats. There were also film projects; these provided an opportunity to enlist the help of Bronnen, who did not want to write another play. On a visit to the journalist, Stephan Grossmann, at his fisherman's cottage in Geltow at Easter 1922, the two playwrights learned of a competition, organized by the film director and producer Richard Oswald, in which one hundred thousand paper marks were offered for the best plan for a film. In spite of the progressive devaluation of the currency this was still a considerable sum of money. Grossmann, who was on the jury, there and then promised his visitors the first prize. On their way home Brecht sketched out the story of the film, which was to be called *The Second Flood (Die zweite Sintflut)* and show 'the downfall of three admirable characters who are forced to become wild beasts and who do more and more damage to each other's lives the more technically competent they become to earn their livelihoods'. The earth is struck by a catastrophe which leaves only three survivors, who establish themselves on an island where they found a super-civilization; being uninformed, however, they continue to fight and head towards their final destruction. The subject gave the two authors an opportunity to get over their 'Chicago' experience. They worked on the material until far into the night, Bronnen suggesting the rather more romantic title *Robinsonade on Assuncion (Robinsonade auf Assuncion).* The next day Brecht suddenly went back to Augsburg; but a few weeks later he sent the manuscript to Bronnen, who edited it and sent it to Richard Oswald. *Robinsonade on Assuncion* received the first prize as planned, the only trouble being that in the meantime the prize money had become almost worthless. The value of the currency fell every day.

In Augsburg the 'Lord of the South Sea' finished two more films and sent them to the 'Lord of the North Sea' for his opinion and to forward to the dramatist Hans Kyser, who had shown an interest in them in Berlin. Kiepenheuer's forthcoming edition of *Baal* was the only success Brecht had to report on his return home from Berlin. Bronnen, on the other hand, had meanwhile been surprised by three widely discussed first performances of *Vatermord* and had signed a general contract with the publisher Rowohlt. In addition Herbert Ihering, the dramatic critic of the Berlin *Börsen-Courier*, had selected him for the Kleist prize. Apparently Bronnen did not feel justified in accepting this, his sudden success relative to his friend embarrassed him. He therefore introduced Ihering to *Baal* and *Garga* and recommended that Brecht should be awarded the prize. The latter was unprepared for such magnanimity. When he heard of Bronnen's plot he took it for granted that the prize was to be divided. This idea struck him as unwise and bad from a business point of view. He informed his friend that he could not agree to half the prize: 'We must each receive the whole prize in turn'. No one must get the impression that neither had 'won' the whole prize. For Brecht only first prizes were possible; they had 'publicity value'. Later this same viewpoint determined his attitude to the East German national prizes. In 1949, when he was to be awarded a second prize for *Mother Courage,* while Heinrich Mann and Johannes R. Becher were proposed for first prize, he let it be known that he did not wish his name to go forward, he regarded such classifications as prejudicial: 'One must see these things quite impersonally and be keenly alive to their advantages and disadvantages . . .' Herbert Ihering was enthusiastic about the Brecht plays. He was at once convinced of their author's importance, and became Brecht's staunchest and keenest champion in Berlin. The Kleist prize went undivided to Brecht. The presentation, however, did not take place until the autumn.

Lion Feuchtwanger received the unsuccessful conqueror of Berlin with open arms. He had his 'personal poet' on his doorstep again. What he admired in Brecht was his unbourgeois attitude, his posture of an uncouth Don Juan; he must have seen him as a Baal in workman's overalls who had wandered into a big city by mistake: 'It was exactly as if Feuchtwanger had to find someone on whom to vent what was disturbing him. And what was disturbing him was Brecht: so obviously a genius, bold and insolent as a young god, the darling of a machine age'. Feuchtwanger saw in him the wild, unrestrained genius, the adventurer, whereas he was the embodiment of discipline and order. Feuchtwanger's home became the meeting place of Brecht's followers, although the poet himself came only at irregular intervals from Augsburg. He had no room of his own in Munich, nothing but a little *pied à terre* in Starnberg where he sometimes wrote by the side of the lake. Neher was also a frequent visitor at Feuchtwanger's home, while for Brecht's friends Müllereisert and Münsterer, who were studying in Munich, it offered the best opportunity of getting a glimpse of their Bert. 'One ate well, drank well and thought well'. A great many young writers in those days made their pilgrimage to 'Uncle' Feuchtwanger for advice and encouragement; he was a careful and conscientious mentor. Brecht later 'took over' his two most talented pupils, Marieluise Fleisser and Emil Burri.

When the Kammerspiele announced *Vatermord* Bronnen asked his 'herald' if he would be welcome in Munich. Brecht suggested that they both stay in Augsburg, but then had to put him off because of Marianne: 'There is an exasperating atmosphere here, I shan't be able to eat and drink in peace much longer. So at the moment I am still busy studying the problem of how you could feel at ease here between two lines of fire'. Marianne claimed that she saw much too little of her Bidi and reproached him violently when she learned of the proposed meeting.

There was yet another person who kept jealous watch over Brecht's relationship with Bronnen: Cas, the painter, who as a token of sympathy and approval also wore the steel-rimmed glasses which, together with the leather cap, had been part of Brecht's 'get-up' since Berlin. Exercising his particular brand of diplomacy Brecht, the 'dompteur', lodged 'black panther Bronnen' with 'tiger Cas', thus bringing together the rival 'beasts', who were contending for his favour, while at the same time making certain that he would remain the chief topic of conversation between them. One evening at Feuchtwanger's, Neher, when it was already late and he had already drunk a large quantity of alcohol, lost his temper and tried to kill his troublesome rival with a bottle. Their host managed to avert the catastrophe at the last moment and calm down Cas, who was mumbling incoherent threats.

At long last Brecht got his chance in Munich. Following the success of *Vatermord* Falckenberg announced *Drums in the Night* as the first new production of the coming season, while Erich Engel and Jakob Geis succeeded in getting *Garga* accepted by the

Staatstheater. Brecht turned himself into a casting-agency. He had long ago established relations with the actors and actresses he personally favoured and considered suitable. He now talked to them at length about their parts and set in motion a new working procedure for his plays. They usually met at the 'Malkasten', an eating-place near the Kammerspiele fréquented by artists; occasionally, too, they went out to the edge of the woods where Brecht sang ballads and accompanied himself on the guitar. There was one party after another. Among those who took part were Maria Koppenhöfer, Erwin Faber, Kurt Horwitz, Blandine Ebinger, Sybille Binder, the two dramaturgs Geis and Zarek and the director Erich Engel. Bronnen stayed away, he felt out of it because he could not write in this turbulent atmosphere. The attitude to their work of the two friends was too dissimilar. 'Brecht needed to be relaxed when he worked, Bronnen needed to be tense.' Brecht strolled leisurely about the room, puffing at his cigar; the more people there were the better he liked it, as long as they provided material and arguments. It was his way of finding what he wanted, which was often only a single phrase, that was important at that particular juncture to enable him to continue. Bronnen could not adapt himself to this '*Köpfekollektiv*' or brains-pool. Marianne Zoff did not much care for all this activity round Brecht either. She kept a close watch on her lover, and not without reason, because women weakened rapidly when he sang ballads in his shrill voice, and Brecht's interest in an actress was frequently more than merely professional. He was attracted by Blandine Ebinger, one of the candidates for the part of Anna Balicke, and Carola Neher too, then in Munich on a short visit, was a particular favourite of Brecht's; but unable to find permanent work in Munich, she went to Breslau and later married the poet Klabund. When Gerda Müller made a brief stage appearance in Munich, on her way from Frankfurt to Berlin, Brecht nominated Arnolt Bronnen to represent him. Brecht had an insatiable capacity for gathering new people round him: 'He collected acquaintances like mushrooms, knowing that this was the right time for it. On his collecting trips he took Bronnen with him, to act as a shield to ward off the lances, while Brecht stood in his shadow, watching and learning'.

The 'black panther' returned to the capital alone. The 'dompteur' promised to follow him there immediately after the opening performance of *Drums in the Night,* saying as they parted: 'Find a place for us to live.' Not long afterwards Neher was sent north with similar instructions. 'Be nice to Cas,' Brecht wrote to the other friend who was waiting for him, 'show him cold Chicago, rub him with snow when he shivers, and in the evenings, when he discovers he has been hurt, put salt in his wounds . . . in short, initiate him with piss into the mysteries of cold Chicago and wipe his little arse with a rasp and make sure he feels it. But absolve me, because you are a sinner.' Brecht deliberately avoided any clear-cut decisions; he did not want to lose sight of his friends, but at the same time did not want to enter into any firm commitments.

'The twenty-four-year-old poet Bert Brecht has changed the literary face of Germany overnight,' wrote Herbert Ihering after the first performance of *Drums in the Night,* for which he had travelled from Berlin at Brecht's personal invitation. This opening night was attended by all the 'Brechts', by his father, his brother, the housekeeper Marie Roecker, Marianne, as well as by Bi and his closest friends.Even Karl Valentin, who never went to the theatre, did his faithful disciple the honour of going. The rehearsals had not been without serious incidents. The playwright had in-tervened actively and emphatically, constantly supplying new text and trying to influence the director's concept of the play. Only in a few points did the performance conform to Brecht's own ideas, and yet he could feel satisfied with this first success.

On the very next day, 30 September 1922, there was another first performance in which Brecht was involved as an author: *Die rote Zibebe (The Red Raisin).* This was the name of a tavern in *Drums in the Night,* whose landlord, Glubb, now appeared as compère, announcing the individual items and summoning the members of the cast, who stepped out of cabins like puppets. There were poems by Brecht and Klabund, as well as a 'penny-farthing bicycle number' which Brecht had devised for Valentin: 'Liesl Karlstadt, as master of ceremonies, announces the act. First: three circuits of the stage on the penny-farthing. Valentin makes a great business of climbing onto the antediluvian machine and rides three times round the stage. Second: three circuits of the stage on the penny-farthing to the sound of bells. Exactly the same procedure, except that this time Liesl Karlstadt rings a cowbell. And finally third: the horrible death ride through the darkness and mist. After a short but eerie silence, to intensify the effect of this gruesome announcement, Liesl Karlstadt erects two posts between which is stretched a paper band with the inscription 'Darkness and Mist.' Valentin now wobbles nervously past this a few times until finally he takes a run at it and rides between the two posts, breaking the banner as he does so. To tremendous applause Valentin has a laurel wreath hung round his neck, Liesl Karlstadt proudly holds up to the audience the severed scraps of paper, as if she were an executioner exhibiting the victim's head'. The closing number was a performance of Valentin's *Christbaumbrettl (Christmas Tree Cabaret)*. It was an evening of literary cabaret such as Brecht loved; its main purpose was to pay tribute to Valentin who, normally appearing only in inn parlours, in this way conquered the Kammerspiele.

Ihering now mobilized the dramaturgs in Berlin. Felix Holländer wanted to secure Brecht's three available plays on the spot for the Deutsches Theater, in order to forestall his colleagues. Brecht went to Berlin to look carefully into every offer. For him it was a question of gaining acceptance not only as writer but as director. His proposal to do *Baal* with Eugen Klöpfer was turned down, and Holländer did not want Brecht to direct *Drums in the Night*. The *Vatermord* disaster had not been forgotten. Finally they agreed on Otto Falckenberg, a safe choice for the Deutsches Theater and a partner whom Brecht felt he could influence, as he had already done during the rehearsals in Munich.

It was also agreed that Brecht's new project, an adaptation of Grabbe's *Hannibal,* should be produced at the Deutsches Theater. In any event Brecht wanted to stage this play himself, 'for things cannot go on indefinitely with this sort of acting if they are not to become Germanized, civilized!' He had been prompted to make the adaptation by a performance of *Hannibal* in Munich with Albert Steinrück. The first scenes had been drafted in August; in the middle of October, after he had returned to Augsburg from Berlin, he continued working on the play 'with quite a lot of pleasure' until, on hearing from Herbert Ihering that the Deutsches Theater did not intend to do *Hannibal,* he abandoned it.

Grabbe had done no more than provide the incentive for an original play. The few surviving scenes, fragments and notes are very far from being an adaptation; they point rather to an entirely different Hannibal play, based on a highly personal view of history. It is possible that Brecht was still insufficiently versed in Shakespeare to be able to find the formal structure he needed for the dramatic lines and curves he had devised and to which he was already committed. From the standpoint of language, at any rate, *Hannibal* is one of the best things Brecht ever wrote. He conceived Hannibal as a negro and a soldier, endowed 'with some of the wisdom of primitive peoples'; 'he has haunches of course, but he also has a feeling for the comic, a nose for wind and the scent of men'. He wanted to examine the strange circumstances surrounding this hero, because he considered the official portrait of history to be untrustworthy and handed down by the nation that defeated him. But the most important angle for Brecht was the theme of Hannibal's inability to communicate with his soldiers, who did not speak his language: 'Roman historians know of no one who hated Rome as Hannibal did, and it was this same Hannibal who showed himself to be a consummate craftsman, and who somehow had to divide his time between fighting battles, which were tests of his engineering skill, and drafting treaties, in the same way as Rockefeller had to divide his time between his oil concerns. What mastery of his craft was demanded simply by the problem of holding together those polyglot armies without any popular cause to help him (because to fight something for thirty years is never popular, even if that something is Rome)'.

Meanwhile Bronnen and Neher were waiting in Berlin, each hoping soon to set up house with Brecht. But his friend's assurance that 'I am bringing a lantern for the trousseau, as well as the guitar and typewriter', did not satisfy the 'black panther'. He wanted to know for certain now, and went to Augsburg. Bidi, however, had just left for Berlin, to put his theatrical affairs there in order. But the theatres were not prepared to enter into any long-term agreements. To settle there for good at this stage seemed premature to Brecht. Nothing would induce him to risk a second defeat. So he preferred to sign an agreement with the Munich Kammerspiele to work for them as a dramaturg, a post which assured him a steady income, adjusted to the current value of the mark. By the end of 1922 it had become almost impossible for an author to live on his fees alone; by the time the agreed sum had been paid, it had long been so much worthless paper. And finally Munich was not far from Augsburg, where his father's home offered some protection against the worst adjuncts of inflation.

Not least among Brecht's reasons for staying in Munich for the time being was that Marianne was pregnant again. This time, after long hesitation, he agreed to marry her. The wedding took place almost unnoticed; Feuchtwanger and Müllereisert acted as witnesses. The 'deserted brides' in Berlin, who learned of the marriage with some consternation, now set up house together. Brecht made light of his 'treason' and announced new plans for Berlin. He arrived in a bad humour for the rehearsals of *Drums in the Night*. Falckenberg was annoyed; he did not want the author's collaboration. He wanted nothing re-thought, nothing changed, for him it was simply a question of repeating the Munich performance with a different cast. Brecht disliked the routine and the 'varnish', which he wanted to scrape away. The performance was only a partial success, a further reason for Brecht to continue to shun Berlin. What rankled most was the biased, spiteful review by Alfred Kerr: the author's greatest fault in this critic's eyes was to be praised by Herbert Ihering.

In Munich Brecht's interest was focused on the forthcoming première of *Garga*. He once more went through the play, now re-named *In the Jungle (Im Dickicht)*, scene by scene with Feuchtwanger; simultaneously the two of them began working on a joint project for the Kammerspiele, a new version of Marlowe's *Edward II (Leben Eduard des Zweiten von Engeand)*. *In the Jungle* could not be staged without Neher, because his sketches had played a decisive part in shaping its scenic outlines. Unlike Falckenberg, Erich Engel was immediately ready to try out the hitherto unknown stage designer. Cas was urgently summoned from Berlin; apparently, however, he still felt resentful. At any rate he did not appear in Munich on the proposed date. Brecht turned to Bronnen, as he always did, asked him to come to Munich too and complained of Tiger Cas's unreliability: 'Successes affect the ovaries. Isolated successes in big cities last two winters'. Neher came and there was a reconciliation. Bronnen stayed in Berlin, a solitary lover whose grief was only intensified by generous invitations to come to the island in the South: 'Can you really not come, you old rake?' lured Brecht. There would be things to do for their 'big sister' Gerda as well. 'You are wanted. You will be received with honour . . . When (Bidi) and his friend "Caskopf" smoke, they dream of their brother in the asphalt jungle and their eyes grow moist.'

Bronnen's new play *Der Verrat (The Betrayal)* was to be put on in Berlin, again with Brecht as director. The author was invited to read his work to a body of directors and producers from the Staatstheater. Here the question of whether Brecht should direct was no longer under discussion, and Jessner, who was keen to stage the play, was disappointed by the reading and turned the project down flat. 'It all depends on before whom and with what one comes a cropper,' declared Brecht consolingly, though not without a hint of malice. By the time that 'villain Arnolt' finally reached Munich, Brecht's marriage with Marianne was at breaking-point. There was insufficient room in the little apartment in the Akademie Strasse. 'Brecht found the child's screams and the matriarchy unbearable. He couldn't find anywhere to write.' There were frequent quarrels over the numerous visitors who often stayed the night, and Brecht split up and shared out Marianne's precious furniture without a qualm. Now Bronnen was also given temporary lodging there.

In 1923 the fascists held their first meetings in Munich; Nazi followers, wearing uniform and parading patriotic and anti-Jewish slogans, marched through the streets. Hitler spoke in Krone's circus. At first Brecht saw only the bombastic theatrical effects, the gestures that struck him as comic more than anything else. He scented material for his work. Hitler, he said jokingly to Bronnen, 'has the advantage of a man who knows the theatre only from the gallery'; there followed a conversation about a play in Krone's circus that would employ groups of people instead of individuals and 'portray hunger, inflation and liberation'. When people started breaking Feuchtwanger's windows and sending him threatening letters, and when *In the Jungle* had to be taken off after a few performances, Brecht too became more keenly aware of the danger foreshadowed by these 'cavalcades of drab little sots'. He coined the word 'Mahagonny' for the local fascism of Bavaria and the hysterical slogans of the Hitlerites: 'It came to him after seeing the crowds of brown-shirted petite bourgeoisie, wooden figures with their wrongly dyed red flag riddled with holes. The idea grew out of the word, changing as he changed; but during that summer it will have signified more than anything else a petit bourgeois Utopia, that cynically stupid *Stammtischstaat* (beer-hall state) which, out of anarchy and alcohol, concocted for Europe's melting pot the most dangerous brew ever known'. As Brecht saw it in

65

those days, fascism was not a political, but solely a Bavarian, phenomenon. Bronnen was too much a victim of the times and his own problems to emerge untainted from his attempts to grapple with the high-sounding clichés and the nationalistic magic. He became drunk on intoxicating phrases. What his own experiences in the war should have taught him to loathe had a strange attraction for him. Brecht paid no attention to this insecurity on his friend's part, he overlooked his susceptibility to violent gestures.

Brecht wanted to use the summer to write a popular hit that would at least bring in the money he needed so urgently for his family. The most suitable thing he could think of was a dramatization of Selma Lagerlöf's popular novel *Gösta Berling*. Very carelessly he started work on it before reaching an agreement with Ellyn Karin, whose stage version had been authorized by the Norwegian novelist. There was a long and bitter fight over royalties, but he never came to terms with Frau Karin and her publisher. The prologue and two acts were already finished. But there is no cause for regret that Brecht's version never reached the stage. The play is written in good honest doggerel, in the style of Gerhart Hauptmann's *Festspiel in deutschen Reimen,* a Play in German Rhyme to Celebrate the Centenary of the Wars of Liberation; in other words the dialogue rattles along with a great deal of fustian in the manner of an old German woodcut:

> Gösta! Gösta! Was treibst du allhie!?
> Gösta! Du bist gerächt! Beir Jungfrau Marie!

(Gösta! Gösta! Why act so contrary? Gösta! You are avenged! By the Virgin Mary!)

Brecht had abandoned Gösta and to Berlin gone, when an agent named Jo Lhermann, who with the writer Emil Szittya was planning an authors' theatre, asked Bronnen to put on and direct a play. The enterprise was called 'The Theatre' and Brecht did not have much confidence in it. He had more ambitious plans for his own plays. Bronnen proposed *Pastor Ephraim Magnus* by Hans Henny Jahnn, a fiery, wildly extravagant drama about adolescence which appealed to Brecht and which he immediately started to 'prune'. When Bronnen suggested that in such chaotic times, when millions of working people were starving, it might be better to do something else, Brecht retorted angrily: 'What business is it of yours if the people starve? Are you going to satisfy their hunger by writing plays about it?' This sounds cynical and devoid of feeling, but in fact it was only the non-Marxist variant of his materialistic concept of art. One does not have to go to the theatre to learn that one is hungry. One has to know what one lacks, how it is procured and how to acquire it. 'The theatre is nothing where there are no appetites.' Later Brecht, the dialectician, put it this way: 'A good beef broth goes excellently with humanism. Do you know how it feels to wear decent shoes? I am talking of light ones made to measure from fine leather that make you want to dance and well cut trousers made of soft material—which of you knows that? But this is an ignorance that takes its revenge. Ignorance of steaks, shoes and trousers is a twofold ignorance: you don't know how they taste and you don't know how to acquire them; but ignorance is threefold when you don't even know that what you are ignorant of exists'. Brecht condensed Jahnn's play to a bare two hours; only the main features of the plot remained. The author, who came from Hamburg for the final rehearsals, was horrified; he no longer recognized his work, and found himself at cross purposes with the two poet-directors who, in his view, had grasped neither the plot nor the tenor of his play. The performance did not even result in the expected scandal, it went completely unnoticed and a few days later Herr Lherman's enterprise collapsed because of uncovered cheques. So Brecht's and Bronnen's final attempt to work together once more ended in defeat. Any idea of successful collaboration in the future was out of the question. But the bond of friendship between them was to continue. Bernhard Reich later said of this attitude: 'Loyalty to his sympathies and attachments exercised a very great power over the sceptical and practical Brecht'.

Brecht ignored the fact that their views clashed although, with his constant need to develop new ideas and find new collaborators, it no doubt annoyed him that Bronnen chose to go a different way. 'It makes my blood boil,' he once said, 'that Bronnen's theory is different from mine.' He continued to have a fairly high opinion of his friend's plays.

It was through Bronnen that, in the autumn of 1923, Brecht met the actress Helene Weigel, who had been engaged by Leopold Jessner for the Staatstheater. She was a friend of Gerda Müller's and had played a small part in *Vatermord* in Frankfurt. Bronnen had already spoken to Brecht of her marked predilection for

67

realistic presentation. Helene Weigel had taken a studio in the Spichern Strasse. She was known for her hospitality, and her Viennese cooking became famous. In Bronnen's view she was an actress who would inevitably interest Brecht and one evening, when the two friends happened to look up and see Helli's studio window brightly lit, Bert turned in. The poet now started to move back and forth more frequently between Munich and Berlin in order to see his new mistress and shield her from other lovers. Brecht was in raptures over his 'Helletier'; he had still to discover Helene Weigel the actress.

6

Towards an Epic Theatre

When I get my hands on a theatre, I shall engage two clowns. They
will come on in the interval and act the public. They will exchange
views on the play and the audience. And make bets on how it ends.'
Brecht wanted the actor's concept of his part, and the audience's
attitude, to be objective: the theatre not as an experience but as fun
and an intellectual adventure. His aim was to liberate everyone
involved from his restraints. He also wanted theatre audiences to
bet, to behave as if they were at the circus or the races. What took
place on the stage had to be 'real', entertaining, readily
understandable. Brecht invited his audience to participate in the
'human stakes' on the stage; in the preface to *In the Jungle of the
Cities (Im Dickicht der Städte)* he writes: 'Assess impartially the
contestants' form and keep your eyes on the finish'. His proposal to
introduce clowns was to prevent the audience from 'identifying
itself' with the characters. Heroes were to be treated as private
individuals: not ironically, in the manner of Shaw, but as a means
of detaching oneself from them, of portraying and appraising them
realistically. The clowns were to say of David, for instance, 'He
doesn't wash enough', and of Baal, 'He's obsessed with gutter-
snipes'.

Up till now the poet had had no opportunity to try out his ideas
in practice. His two attempts at directing with Bronnen had been
merely preparatory exercises, under the worst possible conditions.
Not until he staged *Edward II* at the Munich Kammerspiele was
he given as many rehearsals as he wanted and allowed to choose his
own cast. Originally he was to do *Macbeth* but, as he still felt shy of
attempting Shakespeare, he decided on Marlowe's *Edward II,* a
colourful and bloody panorama of savage passions. The existing
translation, by Walter Heymel, did not appeal to him much.
Feuchtwanger, who had an excellent knowledge of English,
suggested that they should combine to prepare a new text from the
original. Out of this translation grew a radical adaptation.

69

Feuchtwanger's share consisted for the most part in reviewing technical problems connected with the verse: he criticized passages when they were too 'smooth' and helped to roughen the verse and make it 'uneven', like the Schlegel–Tieck translation of Shakespeare. 'The problem was simple: I needed exalted language, but I found the oily smoothness of the usual iambic pentameter repugnant. I wanted rhythm, but not the usual clatter'. The language had to reflect the uneven development of human destinies and the ups and downs of historical events, the 'fortuitous elements'. It was both a protest against the smoothness and harmony of conventional verse and an attempt 'to show human events as conflicting, struggle-ridden and violent'.

Brecht simplified the plot of the original and reduced the number of characters. The social background, the political action, had to give way to a human one. There was no question of presenting history. The sub-title 'History' refers to the form, which also dictated the narrative arrangement of the material. The precise dates that head the scenes are mostly invented, a means of making the story more concrete—'story', to Brecht, being what people do and what happens to them. This story precedes the play in the form of a street-ballad: 'Herewith is presented to the public the history of the turbulent reign of Edward II, King of England, and his lamentable death, together with the heyday and end of his favourite Gavestone; further, the obscure and tangled fate of Queen Anne, together with the rise and fall of the great Earl Roger Mortimer. All of which took place in England, and for the most part in London, six hundred years ago'.

Themes, images, the dramatic conflicts of *In the Jungle of the Cities* reappear. And in *Edward* the battle between two men in the 'jungle' of time plays an important role. The characters are 'coarsely intertwined', they lack the independence which they have in Marlowe's play, they do not act in the interest of their positions. Marlowe's Edward also wants to keep his paramour Gaveston at all costs, but the king gives way as soon as he sees his position seriously in danger. He agrees to his favourite being banished for a second time, and then political considerations lead Mortimer and the peers to decide that he can return. Brecht omits the second banishment altogether. His Edward acts strictly in accordance with the tenet 'I fall or live with Gaveston'. Against all the dictates of reason he opposes the laws which guarantee his sovereignty. He does not care a jot for his kingship and prepares his own downfall. The very first battle ends disastrously for Edward. He survives only because he succeeds in luring the peers into a trap and murdering them cravenly. He grants Mortimer his life: the king wants to keep him as an opponent with whom he can 'fight.' He spares his enemy for his own 'evil pleasure'. The court, his kingdom, safeguarding his power are of no importance to him, he remains in the field with his companion: 'The rain washes the kidneys and anything is better than London'. Having taken up the fight he cannot turn back, he is caught up in events: 'Enmeshed in camps and campaigns, the man can no longer extricate himself from the war over the fallen Gaveston'. Even Mortimer does not fight the king for political reasons. Brecht presents him as a philosopher who has gained an insight 'into the vanity of human things and actions' and can only with difficulty be persuaded to leave his study, for 'a man who starts by plucking a rooster in order to eat it, or because its crowing has disturbed him, may end up, sated and with a taste for flaying, by acquiring a desire to skin a tiger'. Mortimer, for his part, is attracted like a lover by the idea of fighting the king, for whom he assumes the role of Gaveston: 'And so I wrap myself, shunned as if I had been burned at the stake, in another's skin, in the skin of this butcher's son'. Before he has Edward killed, Mortimer faces him once more and is forced to realize that he, the physical victor, is the human loser. Edward 'knows' himself and 'having no desire to die, he tastes the usefulness of shrivelling annihilation'. As he dies Edward assumes a regal bearing, he regrets nothing and refuses to renounce the throne. 'You fight well,' the defeated man admits. Edward praises 'darkness' as the best, the queen laughs at the emptiness of the world, and Mortimer reminds the young heir to the throne of the wheel of 'Dame Fortune' that turns eternally, that bears one upwards and then downwards, 'for it is round. Who has witnessed this, does he fall, boy, or does he let go? The question is amusing, Savour it!'

Brecht rehearsed for several months. Working with him were Bernhard Reich, artistic director at the Kammerspiele, and his wife Asja Lacis. Caspar Neher built the scenery, which was kept very simple, thus throwing into strong relief the gruesome elements of the play. Erwin Faber played the king, Erich Riewe Gaveston, Oskar Homolka Mortimer, Maria Koppenhöfer Queen

71

Anne, Hans Schweikart the traitor Baldock and Kurt Horwitz Lightborn. Asja Lacis, a Latvian who had studied in Moscow and was able to tell Brecht a lot about the revolutionary events in Soviet Russia, the new Russian theatre and Russian cultural policy, had to take over the part of the young Edward because no suitable actor could be found. Her Latvian accent was not felt to be a disturbing factor, the needed harshness and sharpness which she brought to the part being more important in the director's eyes: 'To speak German with an accent and yet convey the character is better than a wrong interpretation spoken in faultless stage German'. To Brecht the underlying attitude (Gestus) was more important than the spoken word. He never passed careless or badly executed work. To say 'Die then!', and not accompany the words with skilful sword-play, was out of the question. Bernhard Reich tells us how much attention Brecht paid to such things and how hard he worked at them in rehearsal. The soldiers who hanged Gaveston, for instance, had to do it like professionals and with a great deal of imagination: 'Brecht stopped the actors and told them to do it properly, to tie the noose and make it fast to the cross-beam. Shrugging their shoulders the actors did their best to follow the director's unexpected instructions. Brecht stopped them again and, refusing to give way, insisted relentlessly that they repeat the hanging, but to do it like experts. The audience had to get pleasure from seeing them put the noose round the fellow's neck'.

As the rehearsals proceeded the director discovered weaknesses in the dramatist. Brecht made alterations, re-wrote the text. He adapted himself to the needs and abilities of his actors. 'He deprived the actor of the easy-going disposition that insinuates itself so forcefully', as Herbert Ihering put it. 'The actors had to account for what they did. He insisted that they keep their gestures simple. He made them speak clearly, coolly. No emotional faking was tolerated. By these means the objective, epic style was established.' Thus *Edward II* became, as it were, the foundation stone of the Brechtian theatre. Later on the poet used often to tell a story about the rehearsals and the moment when the idea of the 'epic theatre' was born. They could not get the soldiers right in the battle scene. How do soldiers behave in battle? Brecht asked his assistants. No one knew the answer. They asked Karl Valentin who said: 'Soldiers are scared, they're pale'—'*Furcht hams, blass sans.*' This answer gave Brecht his clue. 'The soldiers' faces were given a thick coating of chalk. And that was the day when our style was formed.' The production, though still very imperfect, was received enthusiastically, people spoke of the poet's unusual gifts as a director. It made him attractive to the Berlin theatres. Most of the critics still scoffed at what he was trying to do; they did not understand his concept of theatre. As Bernhard Reich says: 'Scarcely anyone realized that it contained the seeds of a new way of writing plays and of a new technique of acting'.

Since the collapse of the soviet republic, Munich had been the most reactionary town in Germany. For many artists the new threats uttered by *Mahagonny* in November 1923 were a signal to leave. Heinrich Mann left the town on the very day of Hitler's putsch. At the beginning of 1924 Feuchtwanger, Erich Engel, Bernhard Reich and Asja Lacis were preparing to leave for Berlin. Brecht announced that he would go there for good in the autumn. Jessner had taken *Edward II,* and the Deutsches Theater, where *In the Jungle of the Cities* was still awaiting production, offered Brecht a contract as dramaturg.

'Human relationships suffer, and often founder, because the existing contract between the people involved is not observed.' Brecht liked to regularize his personal relationships 'contractually'. He had married Marianne, for example, only on condition that his independence was safeguarded and his friendships with other women tolerated: 'Some things a wife has to accept as irrevocable'. Brecht, on the other hand, expected his women to be unconditionally faithful. If he had reason to feel jealous, he cited the contractual agreement; this, however, was applied so 'elastically' that those concerned actually derived a certain pleasure from it. The obvious pungency of the situation was cleverly ignored. But Marianne suffered under the conditions of the contract, which she was unable to alter in her own favour. She was forced to give up any hope of prevailing on Brecht to lead a normal family life.

Shortly after the opening night of *Edward II* the couple went to Capri. The southern climate had a beneficial effect on Marianne's low state of health; Brecht, on the other hand, was not particularly taken with the blue Mediterranean landscape. Before long Neher followed them and suggested Positano as a permanent place of residence; it was a sombre, more roughly-hewn place which lacked Capri's 'gaudy' beauty. With Cas there it was already less boring.

The friends went off to Naples together. In a town Brecht felt better at once, and in Naples there were bars round the harbour and colourful fairs. The country tended to make him impatient, to irritate him. He had no 'Italian experience'. At that time neither the ancient remains nor the 'Roman tradition' interested him. Passing through Rome, after a short trip to Munich, he walked unseeing through the city and spent the time, until his train left for Naples, in a cinema. He discovered to his satisfaction that one was allowed to smoke in an Italian cinema: a man smoking in the stalls was a favourite idea of the young Brecht. He refused to have anything to do with 'culture'. His passions were sport, the cinema and detective stories. To him this also meant repudiating nature.

As usual Brecht spent the summer in seclusion in Augsburg. He was anxious to go to Berlin with a new play, his comedy *Galgei*. This was an old project, 'the vision of a hunk of flesh who grows and grows and who, just because he has no core, survives every change, as water flows into any form'. The vision of Galgei as a man who is manipulated, a human automaton, immortal because he is incapable of living. This man 'is lived'. The assertion *Man is Man* had not yet been made. Galgei was conceived as a great figure, a colossus of nature like Baal, Shlink and Edward; his animality was stressed and a part of it even retained for the later character Galy Galy, whose individuality was not to be recognizable any more.

In 1924 Brecht was no longer so obsessed with the idea of 'transforming' the harmless stevedore into a human fighting machine. He wanted to write a play about the 'superficial veneer of individualism in our time'. He declared himself an enemy of 'personality', of the 'great individual'. Social processes and mechanisms were beginning to interest him.

7

In the Jungle of the Cities—An Analysis

A battle as ideal as the one to be seen in the
play *In the Jungle of the Cities* can at present
exist only in the theatre; it will be fifty years
before it can exist in real life.

In 1926 Brecht planned a series of plays in which he intended to
deal with the subject of 'Man's entry into big cities'. *In the Jungle of
the Cities,* which he was then in the process of revising once more
for publication in book form by the Propyläen publishing-house,
was to be the first play of this cycle. *The Fall of the Egoist Johann
Fatzer (Der Untergang des Egoisten Johann Fatzer)* and *Joe
Fleischhacker* were to be the second and third. The disintegration
of the Garga family in the jungle of Chicago was meant to typify
the fate of the masses who had left the villages in the wake of
advancing industrialization in order to find work and better living
conditions in the towns. The play described the alienation of men
and women in a society dominated entirely by capital. Continuing
from there, Brecht conceived the egoist Johann Fetzer as typical of
the little man who tries to grow rich by cunningly adapting himself
and to buy promotion into the ranks of the privileged, at the
expense of members of his own class, but who comes to grief in the
process. Joe Fleischhacker was to portray the struggle at the top,
the rise and fall of a dollar baron on the Chicago wheat exchange.

Why did Brecht so often choose Chicago as a setting for his
plays? The city is a concrete example of the close juxtaposition of
industrial progress and human devastation, of social advance and
criminality. It had been described as a 'morass' and a 'jungle' by
Upton Sinclair and Johannes Vilhelm Jensen, whose novels
influenced Brecht. His Chicago, however, is real only up to a point;
it would be truer to call it unreal, a vivid background, an
imaginative archetype, whose purpose is to give concrete form to
the abstract idea of a plot. Instead of Berlin, for instance, Brecht

75

preferred Chicago. He needed to see things from a distance, to 'alienate' them, in order to be able to present them as typical. By this means the characters, which otherwise would merely be romantic freaks in a familiar setting, also become interesting and exemplary. Their patterns of behaviour become remarkable: 'My choice of American settings does not spring, as is often supposed, from any liking for romanticism. I could as well have chosen Berlin, but in that case the audience would not have said 'that person is acting strangely, strikingly, remarkably', but simply 'a Berliner who acts in that way is an exception'. By using a background (namely an American) which conformed naturally to my types, so that it endorsed instead of exposing them, I thought I should be able to direct attention most easily to the strange behaviour of numerically large contemporary human types. In a German setting these types would have been romantic: they would have contrasted only with their surroundings, instead of with a romantic audience'.

In 1921, when Brecht wrote *In the Jungle of the Cities,* he was scarcely aware of the social background and he was not yet interested in social problems. The play was originally called *Garga* and harked back to *Baal.* Only the face of the landscape had changed, and the poet's outlook was now consistently nihilistic. Baal stills feels secure in his landscape, he is a 'chap with spring in his veins and indestructible entrails', full of vitality, in search of happiness and pleasure and with no scruples as to how he gets them. Garga and Shlink are no longer capable of happiness, they suffer from man's terrible isolation and are incapable of feeling a common bond even in a negative sense, in a fight to the death. Physical union itself would not end their isolation. Under capitalism all human relationships are merely relationships between commodities. 'Mankind would give endless happiness to be able to wage war. Its wars are camouflage, make-believe. Nowhere on earth is there the slightest connection between murderer and victim.' Thus even wars are vicarious acts. All fighting is an expression of man's immeasurable alienation, it remains 'pure shadow-boxing'. Baal is permitted to operate on alien soil and to put reality on one side in order to realize something of Utopia. Garga and Shlink live and fight in the capitalistic world.

Brecht declared that with *In the Jungle of the Cities* he wanted to improve on Schiller's *Die Räuber (The Robbers),* a play in which 'a most furious, savage, destructive battle' is fought 'over a bourgeois inheritance with partly unbourgeois means'. He sees in Garga a sort of Karl Moor who has to fight a 'desperate battle for freedom against an ever denser jungle of Shlink's intrigues'. 'It was the savagery of this fight that interested me and because, during these years, I enjoyed sport, and especially the sport of boxing as being one of the "great mythical pleasures of the vast cities on the other side of the Atlantic", I wanted to have in my new play a "fight for its own sake", a fight for no other reason than the pleasure of fighting, with no other aim than to determine the "better man".' Out of this intention there finally came a play 'about the difficulty of bringing about a fight of this sort'. The ideal fight, as envisaged by Brecht, is possible only when the social conditions have been created that allow man to realize his own potential, when man, as Hegel puts it, sees himself 'to be the result of his own work'. Fighting is seen as the motive force of the original modes of behaviour that correspond to man's nature, and these admit of no impure motives for fighting, such as 'the desire to gain possession of women, the means of production, material for exploitation'. For Brecht these are motives that 'can disappear, as they can simply be organized away'.

He took the theme of the play from the novel *The Wheel,* by the Danish writer Johannes V. Jensen, which tells the story of a fight between a young poet, Ralph Winnifred Lee, and an ageing sectarian preacher, Evanston. Lee is a high priest of morality and honesty; in his verse the wheel is enthroned as the symbol of the technical age. Evanston is a degenerate, a cynic, who, as founder of a religion and prophet of happiness, is intent on acquiring power and wealth. He attaches himself to Lee, 'eats his way into him', because he wants to win him over to his own warped view of life. The decisive encounter between the two 'spiritual great powers' takes place on a bridge in the heart of Chicago: 'And now began the fight between two human beings, two different nervous systems, an implacable fight that could end only with the extermination of one of the contestants, because by one it was waged blindly, with the whole force of an elementary appetite, while for the other it was a question of life itself'. Being no match for his opponent's methods, Lee decides to kill him. Evanston sees through this plan and disarms Lee by abasing himself before him. Once again the young poet proves to be the weaker of the two; the only force he is able to mobilize against Evanston is his instinct for survival. Lee then tries to 'digest' his opponent philosophically, and suddenly sees his mission in 'enduring him'. But when Evanston comes too close physically with his declarations of love, he kills him all the same. Lee does not regard his act as murder, but as self-defence against a force which it is one's duty to eliminate from the world. He feels that he has overcome a 'devil'. The winner vows to lead an active life, gives up poetry and becomes a businessman. Americans 'live and work', says Lee; 'intellectual life is simply the talk that pitiable people indulge in about us and on and under and near the subject of what we do . . . . From the standpoint of reality, all aesthetics is only an illness . . . when it is not actually a furtive attack by man on the right of ownership. . . .' In his novel Jensen dilates very long-windedly and emotionally on the Darwinian thesis of a ruthless battle for existence and combines it unquestioningly with social problems.

Whereas Lee, in *The Wheel,* goes into raptures over Walt Whitman and recites his poetry, Garga's hero is Rimbaud. 'George Garga looks like Rimbaud,' Brecht comments. 'Essentially he is a German translation from the French into American.' Garga quotes Rimbaud's and Verlaine's poetry and identifies himself with the poetic self of Rimbaud's *Une Saison en Enfer* and *Les Illuminations*. Like Rimbaud Brecht seeks to give his nihilistic speculations a formal setting, to fix his immediate sensual impression in words: 'I mixed and put together words like strong drinks, whole scenes in words of specific texture and colour such as would appeal to the senses. Cherrystone, revolver, trouser-pocket, papergod— mixtures of that sort. At the same time, of course, I worked at the story, at the characters, at my views on human conduct and its effectiveness; I may have overdone the formal element a little, but I wanted to show what a complex business that sort of writing is, and also how one thing dovetails into another, how the form grows out of the subject-matter and then reacts on the subject-matter again'. The work remains in essence a monologue, it establishes no relationship between the persons involved.

Brecht's conclusion at the time was that a fight with any meaning was impossible owing to human isolation and the inadequacy of speech as a means of communication; later, as a Marxist, he saw the capitalist system as the reason why human relationships were impossible. On looking back, the dialectics of *In the Jungle of the Cities* seemed to him to be of a purely idealistic nature: 'the play, in spite of all its weaknesses, represents an enormous advance in the drama; this had to overtake Hegel's idealistic dialectics before it could make any progress. At the time I (in common with the whole of our drama) did not know a line of Hegel'. Today its idealistic dialectics turns out to be the play's great virtue. The problem of human alienation cannot be solved merely by introducing a socialist order of society. To see man's existence, 'human reality', as dependent only on economic facts is to ignore the philosophic demands of Marxist theory. 'All attempts to thrust aside and shamefacedly conceal the philosophic content of Marxist theory,' as Herbert Marcuse also says, 'show a total failure to recognize the original historic basis of this theory: they assume that philosophy, economics and revolutionary practice are fundamentally separate, and this comes from the very concretization which Marx opposed and which he had already seen through at the beginning of his critical work.'

The dialectical construction of the play necessitated a different title from the one originally planned. Instead of *Garga* Brecht called it first *In the Jungle* and then *In the Jungle of the Cities*. The longer he worked at his material, the more detached he became from the character of Garga; this was especially noticeable when, revising the play for the last time, he eliminated many autobiographical passages. Brecht could still identify himself with Baal, but in the case of Garga no accord was possible any more. Garga's relationship to Rimbaud, unlike that of Baal to Verlaine, was now only the relationship of an actor to his part.

In the opening scene Brecht already indicates the works that prompted him to write *In the Jungle of the Cities*. Garga, an assistant in a lending library, recommends as his favourite books *Une Saison en Enfer* and *The Wheel*. Mention of Tahiti introduces a further literary reminiscence. Garga has also 'assimilated' Gaugan's *Noa Noa:* he dreams of Tahiti, of another would in which he can shut himself off when the monotony of daily life gets too much for him. One day the lumber merchant Shlink comes into the library, not to borrow a book, but to buy Garga's opinion on books. Shlink tries to pin the assistant down, to convert his opinions into a commodity and so into money. The merchant is impressed when Garga refuses to comply and persists in maintaining his freedom. Garga's reaction is untypical, his attitude appears not to have been capitalized: for instance he still has a personal relationship to the books he recommends. The lumber merchant thinks that, in this library assistant, he has found someone who longs, as he does, to 'communicate' and overcome his personal isolation. It looks as if Garga will make a 'partner' for him. Capitalism distorts people, forces them to act contrary to their natures, prevents them from fulfilling themselves. This alienation also affects the businessman, even though materially he is benefited by the capitalist system, because 'ownership does not give him free scope for self-fulfilment and activity; what he possesses is simply capital' (Marcuse). Shlink wants to find out if people can get close to one another by 'fighting'. He wants to switch the daily fight for existence, which admittedly presents itself to him in a different light from Garga and which he also sees differently, on to a 'mental' plane; in other words he wants to leave reality out of his scheme of action.

What Shlink wants is an 'ideal' fight, a fight for the pure pleasure of fighting, in which he has only a human, and no material, interest. Having convinced himself that Garga is a suitable antagonist the lumber merchant opens the fight. His first 'blow' is aimed at his opponent's economic existence. Garga is dismissed. By this means the conditions necessary to his 'freedom', to which he referred so proudly, are removed his 'platform' is shaken to its foundations. Garga is quite unaware of what is going on. A blow at his economic existence is nothing new to him. He refuses battle, beats a retreat and, initially, still thinks he can preserve his freedom. He now finds himself really involved in the fight. Shlink is responsible for all the action; Garga, it is true, parries his opponent's blows, but he reacts only when provoked. Tahiti, the 'essence' of his freedom, the idea that enabled him at least to pretend he was free, is also destroyed by Shlink. The lumber merchant simply takes the dream at its face value and gives Garga his steamship passage. By showing him how to get to Tahiti, thus assuming the active role even in this, he makes it impossible for the dreamer to go there. Once again Garga realizes much too late that the way to Tahiti has been blocked. At first all he is able to grasp is that he has been 'skinned alive'. He removes his clothes, steps symbolically out of his 'skin' and, quoting Rimbaud, takes refuge in the role of an outlaw, ostracized by society: 'I am an animal, a nigger, but it's possible I have been saved . . . I don't understand the rules, I have no morals, I am a brute. You are wrong!' The quotation illustrates the perversion of the natural order brought about by capitalism: 'The result, therefore,' declares Marx, 'is that man (the worker) feels himself to be a free agent only in his animal functions, in eating, drinking, procreating and, possibly, in his choice of dwelling, adornment, etc; while in his human functions he feels himself to be merely animal. The animal becomes human, the human animal'. The worker is commonly accused of thinking only of material things, of lacking all feeling 'for higher things'. Garga, mindful of his social degradation, acknowleges the animal in himself and tries to conform to the picture which the oppressor has of the oppressed. He sees Shlink's eagerness to fight as the whim of a rich man, as a hobby. The reason for the fight which Garga, in his own way, now takes up is a mystery to him, a mystery he has no desire to solve. The only thing he is clear about is that he has been 'harpooned'. Two weeks after the incident in the lending library he goes to see Shlink in his office, intending to kill him. The lumber merchant disarms his opponent by giving in to him. He makes over his lumber business to him, thus providing Garga with a 'similar field of action'. Garga's response is revenge pure and simple. Without his property, his material basis, Shlink, he is convinced, is finished. Garga sells lumber twice over, destroys the firm's books, gives the building to the Salvation Army and says he is off to Tahiti. 'What a defeat for you!' his sister Marie tells him, though the fight is only just beginning.

In order to be free, Garga leaves his family, which has been drawn into the fight. Shlink takes lodgings with the Gargas and earns money as a coal-heaver. Over and over again Garga wants to give up, 'to throw in the towel', but once he has got the 'nut' in his mouth he can neither spit it out nor crack it open. The cords with which Shlink has bound him are fast. Garga cannot rid himself of his opponent: 'That brute Shlink; in my dreams I call him my "Satanic spouse"'. When he becomes aware that the lumber merchant loves him, he marries and tells his sister, who is in love with Shlink, 'Love him! That will sap him!' Shlink is to marry Marie, but the girl prefers to throw herself at another man's head because she realizes she is to be made an objective in the fight. It is Shlink's move again. Garga has to account to a court of law for selling the lumber twice. He refuses Shlink's offer to go to prison

81

for him, partly out of pride and partly in order to degrade his opponent morally. He is prepared to break up his family to prove his moral stamina. The family disperses: the father is incapable of work and takes to drink, the mother goes off to find a job somewhere, Garga's sister and wife go on the streets. As he cannot get the better of Shlink, Garga plans to grind him into the dust. In a letter he hands to the press when he is released from prison he accuses the lumber merchant, who is of Malayan origin, of fornication with his sister. Garga, in fact, has discovered his opponent's weak point: his yellow skin. So he sets the racial fanatics on to him. Garga has long ago ceased to be of any interest to Shlink, who in the meantime has applied himself to his business affairs once more; now, after three years, he is reminded of Garga by the yells of the lynchers. He makes a last attempt to win Garga as a fighting partner, but fails because of the latter's false attitude to fighting. The lumber merchant makes over his business to him for the second time and then poisons himself before the lynchers track him down.

Garga still manages to make use of his lamentable social position: he drags his 'shattered' family into the glare of publicity in order to make capital for himself out of them. Denouncing Shlink as the guilty party, he takes over his role in society. He becomes a profiteer. 'The chaos is spent. Those were the best days.' With this acknowledgement Garga sets out for New York to make his fortune, having first made some money by selling the lumber business. His days as an outlaw are over, his dreams buried. He has learned the capitalist lesson.

What Shlink gains as a man, Garga loses. It is only in the capitalist sense that he is the winner. The fight, as Shlink intended it, never takes place: 'The isolation is so great that there cannot even be a fight'. The opponents are forced to realize that their conduct is influenced by the social conditions under which they live. They don't know what the connection is. They are aware only of the 'jungle' into which man is cast. Their fight is revealed as a 'wild distortion of the desire to compete'. Shlink is the moral victor, although initially his methods of fighting are no less dirty than those of Garga. At the outset he unscrupulously appropriates the library assistant's fiancée in order to bind him to him. Garga, on the other hand, pursues the fight solely on this level: all he wants is to preserve his life; he is interested only in destroying his opponent, not in measuring himself against him. What matters to him is that he is the stronger. That his victory ruins other human beings he regards as a law of nature. Only Shlink offers 'to act humanely'. His degradations are intelligible erotically, they are not weaknesses but are part of his human make-up. His love, naturally, is not the only component of his desire to fight Garga. At the moment when his opponent, rather than the fight, becomes his main interest, Shlink also behaves shabbily and paves the way for his defeat. His jealousy of Garga's fiancée Jane, for instance, is a blunder. His erotic interest explains why he sticks to Garga even after he has realized that there can be no question of reaching an understanding with him. At the end, against all reason, he approaches Garga and stoops to confess his love. Shlink clings to the young man with all his soul and with all his wealth, just as Bargan, the pirate captain in the story *Bargan Lets It Be (Bargan lässt es sein)* clings to the traitor Croze: 'And for the simple reason that he wanted something he could be of use to, he had attached himself to this outcast and left everything for him and was probably happy that the man he loved was not a good man but a vicious, gluttonous child who swallowed him at a single gulp like a raw egg. For I am ready to be quartered if he did not enjoy going to perdition for the little brute on whom he had cast his eye and all he possessed, and on whose account he left everything'.

PART TWO
Marxist Studies

8

I am at home in the asphalt city

Cities

Beneath them there are sewers, within them
there is nothing, and above them there is
smoke. We were within them. We found
nothing to enjoy. We vanished quickly. And
slowly they vanish too.

Berlin was responsive to signs of the times. It was in Berlin that
people were first aware of America and the effects of modern
civilization. The monetary crisis had been overcome, the German
economy was recovering thanks to American capital investment.
Speculators, big and small, gathered in Berlin; there were prize
fights and fights for existence. City and battlefield in one.

Brecht did not look upon himself as a Berliner. But he was now a
city dweller by conviction. He forced himself 'to make sparing use
of nature'. He also resisted the city's scenic backcloth. 'It is
impossible to imagine anyone less susceptible than Brecht to the
city's charms, to its sea of houses, to the breathtaking speed of its
traffic, to its world of show business.' The city in Sunday dress, the
residential suburbs, were anathema to him. He preferred the ugly
parts that reeked of industry. Here, as Marieluise Fleisser recalls,
he came alive. What interested him were people's attitudes and
reactions: 'It was enough for him to catch sight of a corpulent pimp
sending one of his charges out on to the street, observing her from
behind and calling out "Erika, your handbag, more jaunty!",
whereupon she would grow visibly in stature as she swung her
patent-leather bag, exuding optimism—little details like this made
him happy'.

Brecht took a passionate interest in all the non-literary activities,
going to almost every film, to performances at the Sportpalast, and
to bars frequented by whores and pimps. He was quite content to
write for sporting papers and fashion magazines, to compose copy

for the gramophone companies and verses for publicity purposes. Conversely he rifled sports reports and the texts of hit-songs, noting down good lines and usable passages, which he then incorporated in his poems and plays. Despite his enthusiasm for the big city and his violent repudiation of the 'heroic' landscape of his youth, Brecht, in his personal habits, remained bound to Augsburg and his parents' home. As a rule he liked to eat only what people in Augsburg ate. Once anything had become 'a part' of him, he wanted to keep it and have it always by him. He would have been happiest if he could have had all his old friends with him in Berlin; even his servant, Marie Hold, came from Augsburg and had once kept house for his father in the Bleich Strasse. The tailor, who made his self-consciously ordinary and shabby-looking clothes, was also a man he had known in Augsburg. And Marieluise Fleisser, like all Brecht's mistresses, had to wear black coats of marengo wool made by the man who quoted a special price if one came from Brecht; they were close-fitting and reached almost to the ankles: 'And the coat, which was never buttoned, had to be held close to the body with one's elbow over one's stomach—this was the height of fashion in Berlin'.

Brecht and his followers got themselves talked about. They gave interviews and took part in opinion polls. This afforded them an opportunity to declare war on the great names in literature, the officially recognized drama and the established cultural activities; scandals and literary feuds were the order of the day. Old helpers and friends were joined by new ones, whose opinions were as concrete and categorical as Brecht's, and who were able to follow his methods of learning and supply him with the material and ideas he needed. At Dora Mannheim's he met Elisabeth Hauptmann, who made a big impression on him because she listened so attentively and because she made notes. It later transpired that she had remained silent at their first meeting simply because she had a heavy cold. In the early days she was perplexed, rather than convinced, by the poet's radical views. Elisabeth Hauptmann knew English and so was made to collect cuttings from English and American newspapers for Brecht; eventually by means of a trick, she was 'engaged' as his secretary. Brecht got her a job with his publisher by persuading Gustav Kiepenheuer that, without her help, it would be almost impossible for him to prepare for publication the three books for which he was under contract. The publisher behaved very generously and did not even insist on the new assistant coming to the office. From now on she dealt with all Brecht's business with his publishers, acted as his editor and worked with him on his plays. In his little story *Fatty Ham (Der dicke Ham)*, which appeared in the *Frankfurter Zeitung* in July 1925, the poet not only described the appearance and physical characteristics of his faithful assistant but also paid tribute to her indispensable help in difficult times.

The young writer Emil Burri was a man very much after Brecht's heart: he was a boxer and assisted the light-heavyweight Samson-Körner in the ring. Brecht welcomed Burri as a new type of writer, calling his plays *Amerikanische Jugend* and *Das Mangelhafte Mahl* progressive, because of their conscious selection of viewpoints and because of the 'broad lines on which they were planned and the truthfulness of their action'; they were examples of 'objective theatre'. Burri had to tell Brecht about his experiences in the ring and describe the various positions and moves. Anything remarkable or typical was noted down; the following sentences, for example, which were incorporated in the comedy *Man is Man:* 'Oh, we wrestlers have our own code of behaviour. There are specific rules. When a wrestler enters a room full of people, for instance, he raises his shoulders as he stands in the doorway, lifting his arms to shoulder height, then lets his arms swing casually down again, and saunters into the room'.

When, in February 1926, Brecht demanded *'More Good Sport'*, he will not have been thinking of physical training. What interested him was combatant sport between professionals, sport as a passion, its risks and records. 'Great sport begins when it has long ceased to be healthy.' What he wanted was not to found a movement to promote sport but to win those interested in sport as an audience for the theatre. Brecht the dramatist pinned his faith on the sporting public's discernment. A play should be judged like a game of football, an actor like a champion boxer: 'The rotten state of our theatre audiences stems from the fact that neither stage nor audience has any idea of what is supposed to happen. In sports arenas people know, when they buy their tickets, exactly what is going to happen, and it is precisely this that happens when they are sitting in their seats; in other words trained people, with the keenest sense of their responsibility, display their particular skills in the manner best suited to them, but in such a way that one is

89

forced to believe they do it mainly for their own enjoyment'. Brecht wrote a story called *The Uppercut (Der Kinnhaken)*, and wanted to write Paul Samson-Körner's life story, on the basis of what the boxer had told him. Parts of it were published in advance and illustrations appeared in the press; one of the latter, a carefully posed photograph of Samson-Körner cradling Brecht's gently inclined head like a nut, became especially popular. 'Samson-Körner is a great and significant type', Brecht told readers of *Die literarische Welt,* 'I wanted to put him on record for myself. The simplest way was to get him to give me an account of his life. I attach great importance to reality. Realities like Samson-Körner, moreover, can be counted on the fingers of one's hand—strokes of luck. What first struck me about Samson was that he seemed to box according to a sporting principle that was completely un-German. He boxed objectively. This has great plastic charm. The way in which Samson-Körner puts an ordinary railway ticket into his pocket, for instance, is quite simply inimitable. This means that he is also a considerable film actor'. The boxer, for his part, let it be known that he never read the classics but was working on a book with Brecht, who was a 'splendid fellow'. He also went to the theatre, but never to 'anything sad'. He liked operettas, but what he liked best were variety shows. This attitude to literature and the theatre impressed Brecht enormously.

Sport, not as an ideology, but as a technical model for writing and all other forms of artistic activity. Poetry or writing should have a 'utility value', one should be able to regard it as a document. To describe sporting events and do honour to the contestants seemed to Brecht to be both more valuable and more difficult than to create atmospheric effects in poetry. He found reading sports reports more rewarding than reading poetry. He took a series of articles in a boxing paper, on middle-weight champions of the world, as a starting-point for his *Memorial to 12 World Champions (Gedenktafel für 12 Weltmeister)*, and the 'most poetic' lines of the poem, which Fritz Kortner recited at a sports festival in 1927, are taken almost word for word from this boxing-paper:

Stanley Ketchel berühmt durch 4 wahre Schlachten
Gegen Billie Papke
Und als rauhster Kämpfer aller Zeiten
Hinterrucks erschossen mit 23 Jahren

An einem lachenden Herbsttage
Vor seiner Farm sitzend
Unbesiegt.

(Stanley Ketchel, famous for 4 real battles against Billie Papke and as the roughest fighter of all time. Shot from behind at the age of 23, on a smiling autumn day, sitting in front of his farm. Unbeaten.)

The only sport which Brecht himself went in for was driving a car. In 1925 he obtained a driving-licence and a second-hand car which Müllereisert had bought cheaply. Even acquiring a car was a form of sport. When he had had his fill of second-hand cars, and the trouble they caused, Elisabeth Hauptmann devised an original method of getting him a new Steyr—all the firm asked in return was a poem to use in advertising. Brecht wrote a tribute to the 'singing Steyrs', and laughed at poets who turned down such commissions as beneath their dignity. Within a short time he had driven the car to pieces, and the problem of acquiring a new one became acute. The advertising manager of the Steyr company conceived the brilliant idea of an account of Brecht's 'instructive motorcar accident'; this appeared in the magazine *Uhu,* illustrated 'with the kind assistance of the Steyr–A.G.': 'Recently the poet Brecht had a motorcar accident typical of many others. He was driving his Steyr down the Fulda road at 70 kilometres an hour. The road was not especially narrow, but a much more powerful car than his overtook an approaching lorry on the wrong side of the road, without first assuring himself that another car (Brecht's) was approaching. For Brecht the situation was extremely dangerous: he could not veer to his left because of the lorry, which was travelling at a fair speed; on his right there were trees, and beyond them a bank with a drop of about 5 metres. Two possible courses were open to Brecht: he could either drive down the bank and turn several somersaults in the open car, or he could drive into a tree at 70 kilometres an hour and be smashed to pieces. The distance between the oncoming car and his own, with each travelling at 70 kilometres an hour, was very small. Brecht thus had no option but to move out of the way and, by applying the brake sharply several times and releasing it immediately, he was able to drive straight at the nearest tree. He succeeded in hitting it exactly in the middle of the radiator, and thus in halting the car. The radiator broke and the front of the chassis, which took the blow, wrapped itself round the tree; but this also meant that the car was held fast. The accident resulted in only slight injuries'. By this means Brecht was soon the owner of a brand-new Steyr motorcar.

Brecht felt only contempt for people who regarded sport as a sort of physical education and means 'to promote the movement of the bowels'. And he had no use whatever for the theory that physical education is necessary to creative work: 'Whatever the gym-instructors say, it is certainly true that works of the mind in considerable numbers have been produced by ailing people or at least by people whose bodies have been very neglected, by human wrecks distressing to look upon, who by virtue of their fight with a reluctant body have achieved a whole stack of good health in the form of music, philosophy and literature. What is true is that the greater part of the cultural output of the last decades could very easily have been prevented by simple gymnastics and suitable exercise in the open air—this I admit'. When, early in 1927, Brecht became familiar with the work of over four hundred lyric poets, he was so appalled that he could not resist saying, 'these people should first join the army'. *Die Literarische Welt* had asked Brecht to act as judge in a poetry competition. All he could find was evidence of 'sentimentality, insincerity and unreality'. The young poets had modelled themselves on Rilke, George and Werfel, whose work Brecht rejected and therefore could not judge: 'Here they are again these quiet, refined, starry-eyed people, the sentimental element of a worn out bourgeoisie with which I refuse to have anything to do!' Unable to recommend an award to any of the entrants, Brecht decided in favour of a poem by Hannes Küpper, 'He! He! The Iron Man!', which he had found in a bicycling-magazine; it was a song about 'Iron Mac', the six-day champion Reggie MacNamara. One of the entrants, a poet named Hellmut Schlien, protested publicly against Brecht's decision. He felt he had been judged without being understood. For answer Schlien received the advice to subscribe to a bicycling-magazine, from which he would learn, in addition to other things, 'that among uneducated people, far removed from *Die Literarische Welt,* it was considered unfair to refuse to accept the judge's verdict after a race'.

Rainer Maria Rilke, Stefan George and Franz Werfel were targets for attack, to Brecht their art had neither use nor beauty. 'I would draw your attention to the fact that Rilke's form of expression, in dealing with God, is wholly homosexual.' His poetry aside, however, Rilke gave the impression of being 'a truly good man'. Stefan George's poetry was too empty for Brecht, too complacent in its form; the views it expressed were 'trivial and haphazard', merely unusual: 'He has absorbed a mass of books with nice bindings and associated with people who live on their incomes. The result is that he makes the impression of being an idler instead of an observer, which perhaps is the one he wishes to make. The pillar selected by this saint has been selected too artfully, there is too much cloud about, the view from it is too picturesque'. What Brecht disliked about Franz Werfel's poetry was its blend of humorous gesture and deficient knowledge of the world; he could read the eclectic verses of this 'universal friend' only with an 'ugly grin'. Werfel became the object of Brecht's scorn mainly because of a matinée at the Staatliches Schauspielhaus in Dresden that did not go quite according to plan. The episode created a considerable stir at the time and was a heaven-sent gift to the literary editors. In March 1926 the Dresden opera had given the first performance of Verdi's *La Forza del Destino* in Werfel's translated version. The directors of the Sächsisches Staatstheater decided to celebrate the performance as a literary event, and invited the three much publicized authors Brecht, Bronnen and Döblin to a poetry reading in the Schauspielhaus the following day. The 'three gods' came from Berlin; they did not want to let slip this opportunity to appear as guests of honour and representatives of the younger literary generation. But the expected honours were not showered upon them. At the box-office they learned that the directors had only allotted them very inferior seats for *La Forza del Destino,* and Brecht, Bronnen and Döblin were not considered sufficiently important to be invited to the gala reception for Werfel afterwards. Furious, they returned their tickets and threatened to leave. The next morning Leo Franck, of the Sybille publishing house in Dresden, stepped in as mediator and the poetry reading took place after all. Meanwhile Brecht had vented his spleen 'in a little ballad-like allegory', which he then went on to recite but which was understood only by those in the know. In biblical strains he described the disgraceful treatment of three deities in Alibi, on the River Alibé, where celebrations were being held in honour of the 'great Alea', as a result of which there was no one to pay homage to the gods:

Sprach Sibillus, Mann aus der Stadt Alibi:
Lasst uns hingehen zum Tische des Dicken Alea
Welcher ein Weltfreund ist, dass wir aufsammeln
    die Brosamen
Die von seinem reichen Tische fallen.
Und sie gingen und kamen an vor den Tischen.
Es fiel aber da kein Brosamen.

(Said Sibillus, the man from the town of Alibi, let us hence to the table of Fat Alea, who is a universal friend, that we may gather up the crumbs that fall from this rich man's table. And they went and came to the table, but no crumbs fell.)

Bronnen then made certain of a theatrical scandal by telling the audience what had happened the previous day and violently abusing the Dresden directors and Werfel.

Brecht used every public appearance, and even the most idiotic newspaper questionnaires, to parade his status as a member of the literary opposition. He was intolerant in his viewpoints, which he held to be matters of principle. Few among the recognized and representative literary figures were not attacked by Brecht at this time. 'Fine' writing was without exception 'kitsch'; any sort of literature was preferable to that, provided it did not claim to be literature. At least it had 'utility value'. 'When I say that Franz Werfel is kitsch, I have to admit that Edgar Wallace is kitsch too. The most this can do, however, is to stop me from reading Werfel. I refuse to be deprived of the great Wallace.' Detective stories always provided Brecht with an opportunity to insult literature. Throughout his life he permitted himself the pleasure of reading one a day. He was interested in the basic scheme of this literary genre, and compared it to the way in which a physicist works. Altogether he considered it very important to pursue a scheme. It could only be an advantage for the author to be able to assume that the public knew the scheme: 'When you cut the pages of a detective story, you know exactly what you want'. The reader of a detective story is as familiar with the rules as are the onlookers at a sporting event. Brecht also wanted to develop a scheme for his 'epic theatre', which he hoped to see established as an independent art form, like the detective story, the wild west film, the revue, operetta and football. 'The idea of a scheme is sound. What I mean is that on the day when our plays, for instance, acquire significance again, they will resemble one another as one egg resembles another. They will have a scheme. A scheme is the best inner defence for the writer. He cannot get along without it. When one has written some 100,000 plays over a period of 300 years, as we all have, it may be very tempting simply to omit the defences; but if we do so we pay for it. There will be those who need material, or in other words content, as a defence for their formalistic requirements, but the sounder plan will be to maintain a defence for one's material in the form.' Not originality, but form made concrete. The scheme tells us about the attitude from which a book or a play is written. Its variations are the measure of its strength.

Only a few artists of his day were considered by Brecht to practice 'young art'. First and foremost came the faithful followers among his immediate entourage, people like Bronnen, Burri, Marieluise Fleisser, Caspar Neher; in addition there were directors like Erich Engel and Erwin Piscator, stage designers and painters like George Grosz, John Heartfield and Rudolf Schlichter. 'Young' and 'old' had nothing to do with generations. As far as Brecht was concerned Karl Valentin continued to be a 'young' man. So did Feuchtwanger, whose efforts on behalf of the 'dramatic novel', and the presentation of epic material on the stage, influenced Brecht's plan for an 'epic theatre'. Besides Feuchtwanger Brecht had a high regard for Alfred Döblin, of whom he saw a great deal, especially during his Marxist apprenticeship, and in whose novels and theories he saw his own ideas confirmed. 'It is really only a question of finding a form', he wrote to Döblin, 'that will make possible on the stage whatever it is that differentiates your novels from those of Mann!'

In Brecht's eyes Thomas Mann was above all one of the old people, one of those writers who clung to outdated bourgeois ideas and accused the young artists of 'disorder' and 'chaos', who merely confirmed, but never questioned, the existing social order. Brecht poked fun at their democratic 'insipidity, feeble-mindedness and inoffensiveness'; unlike many of his friends, however, he did not attribute these qualities to lack of talent but to the fact that these people were 'inherently venal, lazy and weak-willed'. Referring to Thomas Mann and his novel *Der Zauberberg (The Magic Mountain)* he put it this way: 'These old people employ forms which have become so far removed from their original purpose that the most magnificent material no longer suffices for anything better than successful books'.

As far back as 1920 Brecht already grudged the author of *Der Zauberberg* his large readership when the latter gave readings from his novel in the Börsensaal in Augsburg, a hall whose atmosphere was much better suited to variety and stage performances, in other words to theatre in the Brechtian sense. With sly irony he declared himself to be the advocate for Thomas Mann's art: 'While the hall obligingly fulfilled its main purpose of accommodating as many (future) subscribers as possible, its style and dimensions made it quite impossible for the writer to do justice to the exquisite chamber music of his beautifully chiselled and delicately shaded verbal art'. Towards the novel itself Brecht, in 1920, still adopted what was by and large a sympathetic attitude, while discreetly parodying Mann's style. Later he was particularly scathing about this work and about using pretended irony as a principle of narrative writing. He made no attempt to dispute Thomas Mann's greatness as a narrative writer, expressly drawing attention to his formal skill and the relevance of his 'apparatus'; it was only the ironic attitude behind this, its purely subjective application, that he rejected: 'Here is someone who discovers in the sweat of our face a host of things at which he can smile ironically. This man sees everything ironically before a word goes down on paper. I have an eye for methods. It would give me pleasure, for example, to see one of our people, wanting to produce a death scene, set up a number of small pieces of apparatus round a deathbed—a phonetic one, an optical one, and so on—and then combine the resulting pictures ironically; but I feel a growing sense of anger when a man, in need of something ironic for his apparatus, imagines that the bold step of using a death scene for this purpose will by itself procure him a place in literary history (where, incidentally, all his apparatus most certainly belongs)'. Unlike Thomas Mann, Brecht preferred to give character to an idea rather than 'to invest all his ideas in his characters'.

There were other reasons for the antagonism. Thomas Mann had written *Betrachtungen eines Unpolitischen (Reflections of an Unpolitical Man)*, a book about inward emigration, about withdrawing from society in order to construct the world anew from the mind. The author's adherence to bourgeois ideals, which were always at variance with current bourgeois practice, was the primary source of his irony. Thomas Mann lamented the decline of the bourgeoisie, its ideological decay, Brecht longed for it. He pinned all his hopes on America, which Mann in turn rejected as a 'virtuous democracy'; and the more democratic Mann's bourgeois ideal became until, by way of Weimar, he became an 'American', the further Brecht moved away from America. The very fact that Thomas Mann had once held an opinion was proof 'that he no longer held it', Brecht later remarked disparagingly in *Refugees in Conversation*. Brecht accused Thomas Mann of being an opportunist, saying that he adapted his opinions to circumstances and with an eye to his 'reading public'.

Thomas Mann, as he wrote in one of his *German Letters* for the American monthly review *The Dial,* saw 'much storming and stressing' in the plays of the young Brecht. He praised the first two acts of *Drums in the Night,* while considering *In the Jungle* less good; but after the careful and balanced appraisal typical of him he held both plays to be extreme examples of intellectualistically and Bolshevistically orientated art. He deprecated the protests of reactionary observers as a matter of course. Not because of political acumen but because he had been well brought up. Cat-calls were not seemly: 'Even at Bolshevist art one does not protest by booing'. Subsequently *Edward II* made 'a strongly intellectual impression' on the reviewer, but the author's 'proletarian shabbiness' again disturbed him very much and he dismissed the play once more as an offshoot 'of dramatic "Proletkult"'.

All the same Brecht recognized the essential features of Thomas Mann's prose, even though he rejected them categorically. Thomas Mann's critical objections, on the other hand, were based on a misunderstanding: he saw no difference between Brecht and the expressionists; the former's gesture of realistic speech was merely common, 'proletarian' and unliterary. In spite of his adverse criticism, Thomas Mann sought reconciliation and compromise. He always liked to give fatherly advice: the young would also grow wise with time and then anger would evaporate. He expressed a similar opinion on 'the new children' in an interview he gave to the magazine *Uhu* in July 1926: young people were now showing more understanding for their parents, they were different, they had grown older and showed better judgement. A wave of 'analytic revolution' was crossing Europe, personally he had no use for Bolshevism, collectivism,

97

Americanism and the adulation of sport; he believed in the spiritual and intellectual forces of Germany or France. 'The Bolsheviks', he said with discreetly horrified bourgeois charm, 'hate the soul'. The younger generation, alas, had no aims, succeeding generations were becoming constantly 'more sickly'. Finally he cast a wistful glance at the 'last of the old school', at Bjornson and Tolstoy. In the same issue of *Uhu* Thomas Mann's son Klaus wrote an article on 'the new parents', in which he dissociated himself from the 'revolutionary children'. The days of patricides were over, he and those like him bore the opposing attitudes of parents and children without rancour: 'It is not the shrill outpourings and sensation-seeking compositions of "revolutionary youth" that we chiefly admire, but the great works of those who today are fifty or sixty or who died at the turn of the century'.

This was grist to Brecht's mill. He replied promptly and categorically: 'I saw *Uhu* this morning. Within its pages Herr Thomas Mann (who is Thomas Mann?) looks anxiously at his famous son (who does not know him?) and says (after a pause): when I think of those giants Bjornson and Tolstoy . . .! I won't hear a word said against this successful pair, but no one can blame me if I dislike hearing a whisper of this sort pass through the glades of the press. But I ask you! If statistics really show that rather fewer fathers have been murdered of late (in any case it was only done to keep in practice and can be resumed at any time)—this surely is no cause for comfort! It might happen, for instance, that our eyes should fall covetously on our sons! At this very moment, having given these babies the cannon-balls, with which we were received, to play football with, one of these quiet little ones is slipping off, when our eyes are turned, to play once more in the rectum of his late grandpapa!!' In Brecht's view the children's attitude and their efforts to preserve their fathers' legacy were dangerous. He insisted on the very opposite, and now declared war on the children too, 'whose greatest experiences, on their own admission, are the sixty-year-olds'; he left no one in any doubt that he would worthily uphold his reputation as a champion of the 'strict principle' and a Bolshevist 'nightmare': 'Today when we have barely set our hands to the first purely technical preparations for the excesses we have in mind, today when not even a moderately satisfactory state of disorder is so much as in sight, these boys are

98

already tired of watching. But should they really have the audacity to try to emulate the quiet refinement of their grandfathers (whose little edifices, let it be said once and for all, have vanished irrevocably from sight), we shall add to our controversial fame as patricides the totally incontrovertible one of child murderers. In order to stay young'.

Thomas Mann was offended. He was repelled by the healthy vulgarity. In spite of this, however, he wanted to avoid the break which Brecht had effected long ago. He had no feeling for the boldness of Brecht's dramatic designs and the linguistic power of his poetry. He was unaware of the qualities in Brecht's writings that were prophetic of the future; he regarded the young dramatist as a weaker successor to the naturalists and expressionists. What Nietzsche, naturalism and George had achieved, Mann retorted, had been 'more revivifying, more revolutionary', and had done more to 'break up the ground' 'than the little bit of speed, dynamic energy, cinema technique and bourgeois-baiting with which our rising generation has vainly tried to turn us pale with rage'. The difference between his generation and Brecht's, however, was only trifling, he claimed, and in *Worte an die Jugend (Words to the Young)* he recommended, as a New Year resolution for 1927, that all 'men of intellect' should join forces so that they could hold their own against the 'unintellectuals and anti-intellectuals'. Brecht wanted no alliance. 'It is in our nature that you should fight in a gentlemanly and I in an ungentlemanly way. You, for instance, are not intent on my destruction! I am on yours though.' In a dispute between a cab and a motor car it was quite obvious that only the cab 'finds the difference trifling'.

The polemics were directed in the first instance at Thomas Mann, because Brecht saw in him the most successful type of 'bourgeois producer of artificial, empty and useless books'. 'Intellectual giants' like Mann, in Brecht's view, prevented revolutionary reorganization, they merely jammed the means of production and gave the bourgeoisie an aura of liberality: 'Permit me to inform you, therefore, that the battle between your generation and mine (so far intimated by twenty to thirty little skirmishes between outposts) will not be a battle over opinions but a battle over the means of production. To take an example: in this polemic we shall have to fight for your place, not in the history of German thought, but in a newspaper with 200,000 readers. To take another example: in the theatre it is not Ibsen's opinions and Hebbel's plaster casts we have to fight, but the people who are unwilling to hand over to us the theatres and actors. Your opinions are harmless, your aesthetic forms innocuous, your political attitude (to the bourgeoisie: respectfully ironic) unremarkable (and already disposed of by the bourgeoisie themselves)'. Brecht was not concerned with his objections to Thomas Mann's style, he simply wanted to stop his books, and 'many others', from being published: 'I frankly admit that I would actually make financial sacrifices in order to prevent the publication of certain books'.

In the years that followed Brecht began to realize that the artist's struggle for the means of production could not be carried on in isolation but only within the framework of the class struggle. An appeal to the mind only made him laugh; he pointed out the importance of social theory and practice. He burst into 'peals of laughter' at Thomas Mann's assertion that the difference between his and Brecht's generation was not really big at all.

Brecht's hostility to Thomas Mann lasted until the day he died. It made him furious that he never managed to stem the bourgeois novelists's popularity. Even in the socialist countries Thomas Mann's standing was always higher than Brecht's. Animated by a mixture of envy, impotent fury and his love of sarcasm, he later wrote two 'pornographic' sonnets in which he contrasted Thomas Mann's gentlemanly, grandiose and intellectualized style with Baal's vitality and love of life. The poems, 'Sauna and Sex' ('Sauna und Beischlaf') and 'On Seducing Angels' ('Über die Verführung von Engeln'), were signed by Brecht with Thomas Mann's name. They are linked to the Augsburg Sonnets which he planned to publish in 1927, erotic poems in the style of the *Sonetti lussuriosi* and the *Ragionamenti* by the Italian renaissance poet Pietro Aretino. Brecht called them Augsburg Sonnets because he wrote the greater part of them during the summers he spent in his native town, 'out of sheer boredom' as he said, but also we may suppose in happy recollection of the *Baal* days.[1]

---

[1]Brecht wrote these 'Achilles verses' all his life; most of them remain unpublished. That he liked showing them to people, and gave copies to his friends, is clear from a reference by Gershom Scholem in his book on

'My poetry is more personal in character', Brecht explained in 1926 to Bernard Guillemin, a colleague on *Die Literarische Welt:* 'It is meant to be accompanied by piano and banjo and needs to be performed in mime. In my plays, on the other hand, I do not project my own mood but the mood of the world, as it were. In other words, they are objective in their approach, the very opposite of mood in the ordinary and poetic sense of the word'. Brecht was disturbed by the manifest discrepancy between the more subjective character of his poetry and the more factual and markedly progressive character of his dramatic output; at all events he went to considerable pains to minimize the importance of his poetry, claiming for some time that it was a vice, or more accurately a luxury, which he did not find it easy to give up. Quite early in life he gave a special place to his explicitly sensual poems; they were his 'Achilles verses', poems, that is, on the subjects of his Achilles heels: smoking, aversion to water, women, billiards and cooncannot[2]. Writing poems was directly dependent on personal circumstances and was done for amusement, like other things he did. The prerequisite was an atmosphere of productive idleness, ease and physical wellbeing. But Brecht was aware of the danger inherent in the prodigality of his poetic gifts, of the self-destructive, random nature of his output. In his path to communism he was not searching for an ideological anchor but acquiring a better method of working.

Walter Benjamin, *Geschichte einer Freundschaft:* 'At that time he read me several wonderful and, as he said, still unpublished poems by Brecht. I vividly recall the way he recited Brecht's 'Sonnet on Dante's Poems to Beatrice' ('Sonett Über die Gedichte Dantes auf Beatrice'), in which he spoke the privately circulated obscene version of the second line with an absolutely straight face, as if it were the most natural thing in the world, while looking at me with raised eyebrows. He promised to write it out for me, which he did; but he did not conceal the fact that this copy, as I well recall, differed from the version he had recited. He told me that Brecht had written a lot of obscene poems, several of which he considered to be among his best'. The unofficial second line of the sonnet in question runs: 'in which she lies whom he was not allowed to fuck'.

[2]cooncannot – a Brechtian joke on cooncan, a popular card game in the 1920's.

Publication of Brecht's ballads under the title *Homilies for the Home* had been planned since 1922. The author, who in the meantime was receiving a monthly payment from his publisher, took his time in completing the manuscript. With Elisabeth Hauptmann's assistance the final arrangement of the poems, selected from his output over a decade, was established and prepared for publication. The publisher's request to take out the *Legend of the Dead Soldier* still further delayed the book's appearance. Brecht refused to make cuts and told Elisabeth Hauptmann to negotiate with other publishers for publication of the *Homilies*. In 1926, owing to the stupid demand of his reactionary financial backer, Gustav Kiepenheuer lost his best author for a period of four years to an associate of Ullstein, the Propyläen publishing-house, which assumed all contractual obligations. As a friendly gesture to Brecht, Kiepenheuer had twenty-five copies of the *Pocket Homilies* printed on India paper for the author's personal use. Because the poems were printed in two columns, with titles and numbers in red, and because Brecht had some copies bound in black leather and some in red, the little volume resembled a hymn-book. At the beginning of 1927 the Propyläen publishing house published *Bertolt Brecht's Homilies for the Home, with Instructions, Notes for Singing and a Supplement (Bertolt Brechts Hauspostille mit Anleitungen, Gesangsnoten und einem Anhange)*; the text differed only slightly from that of the *Pocket Homilies*.

The poems were arranged according to their applicability; the book was intended for use. Brecht wanted to demonstrate what he meant by 'utility value' in reference to his poems by means of texts written in a different connection. The poet assumed the role of guide to his breviary. The title was ironical. Brecht adapted the form of the Christian devotional book, but what he had to say was anti-Christian. It was theology turned on its head. Logical atheism. All transcendence is denied. The world is pure immanence:

Über der Welt sind die Wolken, sie gehören der Welt.
Über die Wolken ist nichts.

(Above the world are the clouds, they belong to the world. Above the clouds is nothing.)

Man's true reality is 'coldness, darkness and decay'. In the context of the *Homilies* the statement of most of the poems of the Augsburg period now sounded harsher, more critical. Their target was bourgeois society. The poet was issuing a warning against the teachings it propagated.

The appearance of the *Homilies* was already overshadowed by the first texts for a *Reader for City Dwellers (Lesebuch für Städtebewohner)*, poems in which the poetic subject was put completely into the background by what they set out to demonstrate. The poet now saw his role as an intermediary for objective laws. The new lessons dealt with city dwellers and it was for these that they were intended. The Reader was a poetic undertaking parallel to Brecht's plan to write a cycle of plays on Man's Entry into the Big Cities.

Wenn Sie noch etwas sagen wollen, dann
Sagen Sie es mir, ich vergesse es.
Sie brauchen jetzt keine Haltung mehr zu bewahren:
Es ist niemand mehr da, der Ihnen zusieht.
Wenn Sie durchkommen
Haben Sie mehr getan, als
Wozu ein Mensch verpflichtet ist.

(If you still wish to say anything, then say it to me, I shall forget it. You no longer have to hold yourself in check: there is no longer anyone there to see you. If you pull through you will have done more than a man is obliged to do.)

The laws of the 'jungle' are harsh. It is a free-for-all. If a man wants to hold his own in the fight for money and possessions, if he wants to make his way, he must adjust himself ruthlessly. Pity, goodness, kindness lead only to ruin. Even friends, parents, neighbours, must be regarded as enemies. Everything is permissable, except to act like a human being. This can be fatal. One must never attract attention, the advice to 'cover your tracks' must be followed at all times. Conditions make it advisable to appear as a non-person. Brecht, like Marx, sees man as the 'product of circumstances', but he considers it virtually out of the question 'that circumstances will be changed by man'.

Lasst eure Träume fahren, dass man mit euch
Eine Ausnahme machen wird.

Was eure Mutter euch sagte
Das war unverbindlich.
Lasst euren Kontrakt in der Tasche
Er wird hier nicht eingehalten.

Lasst nur eure Hoffnungen fahren
Dass ihr zu Präsidenten ausersehen seid.
Aber legt euch ordentlich ins Zeug
Ihr müsst euch ganz anders zusammennehmen
Dass man euch in der Küche duldet.

Ihr müsst das Abc noch lernen.
Das Abc heisst:
Man wird mit euch fertig werden.

Denkt nur nicht nach, was ihr zu sagen habt:
Ihr werdet nicht gefragt.
Die Esser sind vollzählig
Was hier gebraucht wird, ist Hackfleisch.
[Aber das soll euch nicht entmutigen!]

(Give up your dreams that you'll be made exceptions. What your mothers
told you had no binding force. Leave your contracts in your pockets, such
things are not adhered to here. Give up your hopes that you are
earmarked for high office. But put your backs into your work. You'll need
to take yourselves in hand quite differently if you're to be accepted in the
kitchen. You've still to learn the ABC. According to this ABC, you'll find
yourselves the underdogs. Never think of what you are going to say, you
won't be asked. There are eaters and enough, what's wanted here is
mincemeat. But this must not discourage you!)

This poem is identical in feeling with the Final Chapter of the
Homilies. Life is a wretched business. One should not cherish false
hopes or let oneself be fobbed off with religion, bourgeois morality
or contracts. The anarchistic perspective, which links the *Reader
for City Dwellers* to the *Homilies*, is reduced by the possibility of
taking full advantage of life in the present. There is no longer any
such thing as enjoyment. The sum total of human effort is already
exhausted in safeguarding one's mere existence, in the fight for
survival. In his interpretation of the *Reader* Walter Benjamin also

refers to the revolutionary perspective of the poems: 'To the discerning communist the last five years of his political work in the Weimar Republic denoted a crypto-emigration. Brecht saw them in this way. This may have been the immediate occasion for the genesis of the cycle. Crypto-emigration was the forerunner of real emigration; it was also the forerunner of the underground movement'. In the light of this, the instruction 'cover your tracks' has to be seen as an injunction to underground workers. Only someone who fights without any illusions, who is clear that the issue does not depend on him, that he is being used simply as 'mincemeat', can also decide not to take himself in hand and to let things take their course. He will become a fighter in the class struggle. 'The man who best serves his cause is the man who starts by letting go of himself.'

Von diesen Städten wird bleiben: der durch sie hindurchging,
    der Wind!
Fröhlich machet das Haus den Esser: er leert es.
Wir wissen, das wir Vorläufige sind
Und nach uns wird kommen: nichts Nennenwertes.

Bei den Erdbeben, die kommen werden, werde ich hoffentlich
Meine Virginia nicht ausgehen lassen durch Bitterkeit
Ich, Bertolt Brecht, in die Asphalt städte verschlagen
Aus den schwarzen Wäldern in meiner Mutter in früher Zeit.

(What will remain of these cities is what went through them: the wind! The house rejoices the eater: he strips it bare. We know that we are forerunners, and after us will come: nothing worth mentioning. In the earthquakes that will come I trust I shall not let my cigar go out, through bitterness. I, Bertolt Brecht, borne within my mother from the black forests to the asphalt cities in days gone by.)

9

Sociological Experiments

> In practice the theatre does not fulfil its social
> function. At a time like this the really practical
> talents are relegated to the field of theory in
> order to remain active.

Jürgen Fehling's production of *Edward II* at the Staatstheater and
Erich Engel's production of *Jungle* at the Deutsches Theater, both
of which took place in October 1924, were successes within the
framework of the normal theatre. The new plays were staged as if
they had been old ones. A wrong, even a terrible performance,
Brecht told himself, was better than no performance at all. He was
not greatly interested in perfection anyway. What was of
paramount importance to him was to try out new methods. The
'almost solid exodus of the better elements to the cinema and of the
best to boxing-matches' gave him confidence. Brecht's reasons for
holding on to the post of assistant dramaturg at the Deutsches
Theater were purely financial. He had no say in the theatre's
repertory. An 'assumption of power', such as he and Carl
Zuckmeyer, another of the theatre's dramaturgs, had envisaged,
was out of the question. It was not long before the two of them
confined their activities to drawing their salaries. At the end of the
year their contracts were not renewed.

In his search for 'epic material' Brecht's only rewarding
experience was Engel's production of *Coriolanus*. Instead of
working up to a dramatic climax, the director told the story of
Coriolanus in such a way 'that each scene stood on its own and use
was made only of what it contributed to the whole'. Totality,
Brecht emphasized, stood 'fast' in every scene. Decades later,
when he was starting to work on his own adaptation of *Coriolanus*
he still recalled in detail his talk with Engel and the latter's
production of the play. His *Hannibal* project, on which he was still
engaged in 1925 and the subject of which he brought up once more,
was turned down by the Deutsches Theater.

But an opportunity occurred to adapt *The Lady of the Camelias* (*La Dame aux Camelias*) by Dumas. Bernhard Reich was preparing the play in Ferdinand Bruckner's version, but was not impressed by it. He suggested to Brecht that he bring Marguerite Gautier's romantic death more into line with reality and give more weight to the social elements of the plot. As Elisabeth Bergner, who was to play the title part, liked the idea, the theatre's dramatic advisers agreed to it. It was thought better not to inform Bruckner of what was being done; when he received his royalties, he would accept the alterations. Brecht agreed that his name should not be mentioned, but asked a good fee. He found the fourth act easy to adapt: the love of pleasure and the extravagance were stressed, and the ailing 'noble' courtesan was counterbalanced by two brazen demi-mondaines, who could not afford to be scrupulous. Esther, one of the demi-mondaines, was played by Asja Lacis. The fifth act was completely re-written. Marguerite Gautier dies in abject misery; it is clear to her that she is no longer loved. Her lover, Duval, only pretends to be in love with her out of pity, and quickly gives up the pretence under the impact of her lamentations. Love has only hastened the courtesan's decline into misery. 'The idea, fostered by Dumas and Verdi, that one day the unhappy but good prostitute would find happiness was regarded by Brecht as an ideological canard that had to be refuted.'

Reich never really mastered the new conception of the play; what was, after all, a clever boulevard play became merely weak Ibsen, and Elisabeth Bergner raised a great many objections because she was afraid the public would disapprove. The notices were all unfavourable. Ihering thought it a mistake to touch the play at all, Kerr spoke of a 'performance, with little to recommend it, of a superfluous arrangement', and Monty Jacobs described the adaptation 'as timid meddling with small secondary themes, without risking any crucial interference, the only effect of which was to wreathe the act of dying in embarrassing monotony'. The performance resulted in a great deal of annoyance to all concerned. Ferdinand Bruckner sued the directors of the theatre and demanded that his version of the work be performed as agreed; he also demanded compensation for loss of royalties from the provincial theatres, which were unwilling to stage his version after its failure in Berlin. Inside the theatre Reich and Brecht were execrated, Elisabeth Bergner saw herself robbed of her success, and Brecht, whose part in the affair was now public knowledge, was doubly furious because the play was a failure and he had not been paid. It was really because of his ruinous financial position that he had decided to collaborate in the first place.

Meanwhile Brecht had to raise money to educate three children, Frank aged six, Hanne aged two, and Steff, his son by Helene Weigel, who had been born in October 1924. The divorce from Marianne Zoff dragged on; she and Hanne lived with relations in Vienna, then for a time in Münster and, at intervals, in Berlin. Brecht lived alone in Helene Weigel's old studio in the Spichern Strasse. During his first months in Berlin his financial situation remained pretty bad. Not until he concluded his five-year contract with Kiepenheuer, later with Ullstein, was he in a position to refuse unrewarding work on the side, such as re-writing *The Lady of the Camelias*. The publisher guaranteed him a monthly advance payment of five hundred marks. This was solely in respect of works he was to write within the next five years, so that *The Threepenny Opera (Die Dreigroschenoper)*, which later was to be the means of swelling Brecht's bank account, was not covered by the terms of the contract. The dramatist, who was always well versed in business matters, once told Fritz Sternberg that this must have been one of the rare cases 'in which Ullstein was exploited by an author'.

Brecht tried over and over again to get *Baal* put on at the Deutsches Theater. He wanted to produce the play himself, no longer as the wild, extravagant work of his youth, but in an objective version designed to bring out Baal's 'abnormality'. His intention was to give Baal's life story the significance of a document. Brecht accepted, though reluctantly, Moritz Seeler's offer to stage *Baal* at the 'Junge Bühne'. Seeler had very little money and the only point of his enterprise, in Brecht's view, was the constraint it was under 'to have to be bold'. It performed plays which the Staatstheater considered risky and the right-wing press objectionable. Its style of performance, too, was traditional and, for the most part, rather more amateurish than at the big theatres. During the rehearsals Brecht quarrelled with Seeler, who criticized many features of the new version and refused to admit that the new elements introduced by the author compensated for the cuts. Oskar Homolka and Paul Bildt, who played Baal and Ekart respectively, sided with Brecht.

108

Brecht also persuaded the 'Junge Bühne' to stage Marieluise Fleisser's play *Die Fusswaschung* under the title *Fegefeuer in Ingolstadt (Purgatory in Ingolstadt)*. Paul Bildt took over the production while Brecht directed in the background, constantly revising the play in rehearsal, and ruthlessly deleting everything that smacked of atmosphere, in order to throw into relief the action and stress the authoress's powers of naive observation. Seeler was even more horrified than he had been in the case of *Baal* and did everything in his power to get Marieluise Fleisser on his side. But she had to stick to Brecht, and patiently allowed him a free hand with her play. 'You must write like a child', had already been his advice to her on a previous occasion; 'the naiveté is what matters, write quite naively. Make mistakes if you like, that is not important.' On the whole the teacher was proved right. The play was well received by the press. After this production Brecht wanted no further dealings with Seeler. The 'Junge Bühne' was not in a position to undertake the principal task of the new drama, which was 'to transform the theatre completely and create a new theatrical style, this latter being also much needed for older plays of real value'. Seeler was a man with literary ambitions, a genuine supporter of the new literature, but he had a bourgeois approach to art and this clashed with Brecht's views.

'We and our plays are no more in place in the old theatres than Jack Dempsey could show to full advantage in a pub brawl, where someone would only have to hit him over the head with a chair to knock him out.' The fact that practical cooperation with bourgeois theatres did him more harm than good turned Brecht's attention to theory. Up till now his main interest had been in developing new methods of production, devising gestures and attitudes, and presenting plays as if they were documents. By drawing up documents he meant: 'Monographs on eminent men, outlines of social structures, precise and immediately utilizable information on human nature and the heroic presentation of human life, everything seen typically and not rendered ineffective in its application by the form'. Epic forms of presentation alone, such as he had tried out in his Munich production of *Edward II,* were incapable of fulfilling this task. In the course of his work on the play *Man is Man* Brecht used the term 'epic theatre' for the first time. Existing dramatic form no longer seemed to him appropriate to the presentation of social processes and the courses of people's lives. 'These things are not dramatic in our sense, and if one "recasts them as poetry" they are no longer true and the drama is no longer drama at all; but when one realizes that our present-day world is no longer related to its drama, it follows that its drama is no longer related to our world.'

For *Joe Fleischhacker* Brecht obtained literature on political economy. He needed the Chicago wheat exchange as a background for the play. He was fascinated by Gustavus Myers's *History of the Great American Fortunes,* and studied the tricks and methods of pioneers of capitalism like Dan Drew and Vanderbilt. Elisabeth Hauptmann interviewed a number of specialists, collected information about the exchanges in Berlin and Breslau, and studied the manoeuvres of the speculators. In Vienna Brecht obtained an introduction, through Egon Erwin Kisch, to the professional economist Dr. J. Singer, whose name had been given to him as an authority on the Chicago exchange. He could find no one able to explain adequately to him the transactions of the exchanges and the banks; the monetary practices remained a mystery: 'I got the impression that these processes simply could not be explained, in other words were not rationally compre-hensible, and this in turn meant that they were simply irrational. From every standpoint, other than that of a handful of speculators, this grain market was one big morass'.

After the Darmstadt production of *Man is Man* Brecht acquired some Marxist literature as well. Only then did he find answers to his questions. Shortly afterwards he wrote to Elisabeth Hauptmann: 'I am eight feet deep in *Das Kapital*. I must get to the bottom of it'. His study of Marx made a general readjustment of his work necessary. For Brecht saw that Marxism was a scientific method that would enable him to analyze the things that interested him as a dramatist and produce them on the stage: 'The total metamorphosis of the theatre obviously cannot be allowed to follow an artistic whim, it must simply be in line with the total intellectual metamorphosis of our time'. The demand for a new theatre was at the same time a demand for a new order of society. It was not Marx who first caused Brecht to speak of the decline of the bourgeois theatre and to put forward the theory of an 'epic theatre'. Marx confirmed him in his views and helped him to understand his own plays: 'Needless to say I did not discover that I had written a whole pile of Marxist plays without knowing it. But this man Marx

110

was the only audience for my plays I had ever come across. For these plays could not help but interest a man with his interests. Not because they were intelligent, but because he was. They provided illustrative material for him'.

At the beginning of 1927, in Schlichter's artists' restaurant which belonged to the brother of Rudolf Schlichter the painter, Brecht met the sociologist Fritz Sternberg, whose book *Der Imperialismus* had just been published by Malik and was much talked of. Sternberg helped the dramatist to dig deeper in his study of Marxism; under his influence Brecht assimilated historical categories into his thinking, although these were still purely sociologically determined. After several discussions on the decline of the drama and the need to liquidate it, the two men set out their points of view in a polemic correspondence which Herbert Ihering published in the *Börsen-Courier*. Sternberg explained that the decline of the drama, far from being a historical accident was a historical necessity, a consequence of the replacement of the individual by collective entities. Shakespeare's plays reflected the meeting-point of two epochs: 'All that we comprehend under the term Middle Ages found expression within them; but medieval man had already broken his bonds as a result of the dynamic vitality of the epoch. The individual as an individual, indivisible and not interchangeable, had been born . . . . Relationships between individuals had become possible, relationships and conflicts between the individual and the state as a whole and society were more and more in evidence. And Shakespearean drama became the drama both of medieval man and of man who began to discover himself increasingly as an individual and, as such, to find himself in dramatic situations relative both to others like him and to higher authority'. With the victory of the bourgeoisie over feudalism, 'which, viewed from the standpoint of this history of the human mind, corresponded to the ever growing prominence of the individual', it became the dramatist's task to present conflicts between individuals, those conflicts 'which were to be characteristic of the age'. The bourgeois drama had then developed an increasing uniformity until now it revolved exclusively round the man-woman relationship. The social outsider as a subject for drama (Strindberg, Wedekind) was also played out. As the capitalistic age drew to an end, the collective would once again become the decisive factor, while the individual

111

as an individual, indivisible and not interchangeable, would progressively disappear. Contemporary drama had to take this into account. The modern collective forces were the classes 'which today not only determine history but are seen more and more clearly to be the decisive factors in what is taking place'. So why did Brecht hesitate to liquidate this drama 'that is nothing but a photograph of yesterday, a historic remnant'?

Brecht agreed with this summary of the situation. Except that he did not speak of drama in general but of the 'old', or 'present day', drama whose right to exist was to be denied because it had no 'sociological place'. The aesthete still regarded an improvement in the drama as a possibility; now, however, the decisive attitude was that of the sociologist, whose criteria were not 'good' and 'bad' but 'right' and 'wrong'. The younger generation had both the duty and the opportunity 'to conquer the theatre for another public'. This was a task that could be carried out by the 'epic theatre', which was 'in harmony with the sociological situation'. Sternberg now came round to the view that the drama 'in the form in which we now have it' should be liquidated, and that no 'modification' could any longer save it; assuming, however, 'that at the same time there is to be a change of form and content', the word drama could continue to be used: 'And I hope I have understood you correctly in assuming that your addition "epic" is intended to indicate this new element'. At first Sternberg had been afraid that Brecht's 'epic theatre' was too personal an affair, because he had used the term as a formal category before he understood it sociologically. This hint was unnecessary, the poet had long been aware of what he owed to Marx. But it had to be made clear to the public that Brecht's 'epic theatre' was not a new type of drama that had come into being by blending the epos with the drama, but a theatre based on social realism, a theatre that sought to acquire scientific standing.

For a short time Brecht attended courses by Sternberg at which 'certain connections between Marxism and the humanities' were discussed. Then the sociologist agreed to hold more intimate discussions where there was an opportunity to see the subject matter applied practically and to test its usefulness. 'You don't think in straight lines, you think round corners', Sternberg told him. 'You think in terms of associations that would never occur to anyone else.' Under the sociologist's influence Brecht's rejection of classical literature hardened, he regarded it as a sort of

112

'superstructure' in the service of the exploiters. Herbert Ihering, in most matters a loyal advocate of the playwright, expressed it more guardedly: 'Classical drama served to confirm a world which it came into existence to oppose'. He distinguished between the objective content of classical literature and its role as cultural asset and 'mental prop' of the bourgeoisie. Although, in his discussion with Sternberg, Brecht had stressed the historical relativity of a work of art, he rejected any attempt to represent the classics as historical. They were 'old' and were to be regarded only as 'junk'. All he was prepared to accept was their value as raw material.

> Dieses oberflächliche Gesindel
> Das seine Stiefel nicht zu Ende trägt
> Seine Bücher nicht ausliest
> Seine Gedanken wieder vergisst
> Das ist die natürliche
> Hoffnung der Welt.
> Und wenn sie es nicht ist
> So ist alles Neue
> Besser als alles Alte.

(This superficial riff-raff that does not wear its boots out, that does not read its books to the end, that forgets what it thought yesterday, this is the natural hope of the world. And even if it is not, everything new is better than everything old.)

Brecht's enthusiasm for 'Americanism' was no longer boundless. He tried to incorporate it in Marxism simply by means of an ideological realignment of its technical skills. He now acclaimed the Soviet Union as the country of the future. In a discussion with Ihering and Sternberg broadcast from Cologne he stated: 'From a technical point of view the Ford factory is a Bolshevist organization: it is not appropriate to the bourgeois individual, it is more appropriate to the Bolshevist society'. There was a certain rightness, he claimed, in the fact that Americanism made apparent the symptoms of decay in the 'old'; it speeded development but was, at the same time, 'morbid'. While rejecting the 'new realism' (neue Sachlichkeit), then being promoted as an art trend, he nevertheless saw it as inevitable: 'Realism will come, and it will be a good thing when it does come—I could wish to see it in Lenin—until it does so one cannot proceed at all; but this inevitable and absolutely essential advance will be a reactionary affair. This is what I want to say: the new realism is reactionary'. Poets like Hannes Küpper, to whom in 1927 he had awarded the poetry prize, he saw barely two years later as opponents, and in the poem '700 Intellectuals Worship an Oil Tank' ('700 Intellektuelle beten einen Öltank an') Brecht scoffed at the idolatry of technology by the advocates of the new realism and criticized their spurious collectivist attitude. The poem was, at the same time, an ironic farewell to his own cult of technology and to his intellectualism with its hostility to art.

> Eilet herbei, alle
> Die ihr absägt den Ast, auf dem ihr sitzet
> Werktätige!
> Gott ist wiedergekommen
> In Gestalt eines Öltanks.
>
> Du Hässlicher
> Du bist der Schönste!
> Tue uns Gewalt an
> Du Sachlicher!
> Lösche aus unser Ich!
> Mache uns kollektiv!
> Denn nicht wie wir wollen
> Sondern wie du willst.

(Come quick, all you who saw off the branch on which you sit. Working men! God is come again in the form of an oil tank. You ugly beast, you are the loveliest of all! Violate us, you realist! Extinguish the 'I'! Make us collective! For not our will but thine be done.)

Through his preoccupation with politics and socialism Brecht became interested in the theatrical work of Erwin Piscator. When the management of the Volksbühne dismissed Piscator in 1926, it meant that Brecht could also strike this undertaking off the list of theatres which might still produce his plays. He also took this opportunity to comment on Piscator's productions. He gave him great credit for the interest in politics which these had occasioned in the theatre. Piscator, he said, had raised the theatre to the technical standards of the day, thus guaranteeing a modern production to both old and modern plays. New plays were not absolutely essential to this kind of staging. He even denied 'that Piscator's staging made possible a new kind of drama'.

In 1927 Piscator opened the Theatre am Nollendorfplatz and established a directors' collective in which Brecht worked for a full year. He used this opportunity to study technical innovations such as the use of films, projections, new forms of stage design and assembly-belt production. It was Piscator, not Brecht, who was really a dramatist as specified by the sociologist Fritz Sternberg. In place of individuals Erwin Piscator peopled the stage with groups as the units of action. Private, personal scenes were raised to a historical level, and this became the starting point for what occurred on the stage. By this, however, was meant only that everything was transferred to the political, economic and social level. A play, for him, was simply a means of bringing contemporary events immediately to the stage. 'What Piscator makes possible', said Brecht, referring to the productions at the Theater am Nollendorfplatz, 'is the inclusion of new material.' This did not satisfy Brecht. For him it was an established fact that technical means must not be made a substitute for form. New material had first to be made 'old', otherwise it remained outside the range of drama. Although outwardly Brecht was at one with Piscator, he was fundamentally at variance with his stage productions, greatly though they often fascinated him in detail. 'There is today a tendency to regard as revolutionary Piscator's attempt at theatrical innovation. It is not so either with respect to production or with respect to politics; it is so only with respect to the theatre.' How widely Brecht's and Piscator's concepts of the theatre differed can be seen from a recorded discussion between the two men in 1928, on the subject of *Drums in the Night,* in which Sternberg also took part. Piscator made some unusual suggestions for altering the play, putting his finger on the weak points of the story but shocking Brecht by the practical solutions he had in mind for revising the play for performance. For Piscator, and Sternberg no less than he, elucidated the play with political facts and supplemented it with his own points of view. He wanted to show Berlin in revolt, Noske's troops in battle array, the deaths of Rosa Luxemburg and Karl Liebknecht, the 'network' of orders and commands, the breath of revolution: 'Throughout your play these were haphazard and accidental'. Brecht turned down all the suggestions, they were too impressionistic and too direct. Piscator,

115

he objected, did not proceed dialectically. He idealized, he was not interested in contradictions. He wanted to dramatize history and the daily struggle. Brecht wanted things translated. He did not regard the theatre as a moral institution but as a place of entertainment that elicited verdicts. With regard to Piscator's theatre Brecht noted: 'To requisition the theatre for the purposes of the class struggle is to endanger the true revolutionizing of the theatre. It is not an accident that this idea of requisitioning comes, not from the side of the producers, but the directors. From the first these fighters in the class war, who usurp artistic means, had to have recourse to new means (jazz and film) and could not go on to revolutionize the theatre itself. Politically laudable transmission of the revolutionary spirit through stage effects, which merely create an active atmosphere, cannot revolutionize the theatre; it is a makeshift that cannot be extended but can only be replaced by a truly revolutionary art of the theatre. This theatre is in reality anti-revolutionary, because it is passive and reproductive. It has to rely on pure reproduction of existing, that is prevailing, types, which as we see it means bourgeois types, and will have to wait for the political revolution to get its own archetypes. It is the ultimate form of the bourgeois naturalistic theatre'.

Brecht employed new principles of construction, and changed the style of acting, for every work, whereas Piscator confined himself to a complete reconstruction of his stage for every work. Subsequently, in *The Purchase of Brass (Der Messingkauf)*, Brecht again assessed Piscator's merits somewhat differently, acclaiming him as the only 'competent' dramatist, apart from himself, and as 'one of the greatest theatrical figures of all time', although what he had attempted had at times had 'very little to do with art' and he had shown little understanding of the art of acting. 'It seemed to him easier to master critically the great subjects at his disposal by means of ingenious and imposing scenic presentation than by means of acting.' Brecht's share in adapting plays for the Theater am Nollendorfplatz was small and had no sequel. Piscator wanted to put on the *Fleischhacker* play at that time; it was announced for the 19275/28 season under the title *Wheat (Weizen)*. Other plays were planned, but never realized. It was not until after Brecht's death that Piscator staged *Mother Courage and her Children (Mutter Courage und ihre Kinder)* and *Refugees in Conversation*. After 1929 the advocates of the epic and the political theatre still

116

considered collaborating from time to time, but it always proved impossible. According to Piscator: 'If the stage is the most fleeting, most transient of the arts, it is precisely this transitory nature that gives it the advantage of being directly open to the currents of the moment. The theatre constantly refuses to acknowledge its own history, and in this refusal lies the essential condition for its vitality. It is the present, pure and simple, or it is nothing'. In contrast to this Brecht, in his work, recognized the difficulty of keeping the drama open to the currents of the moment. He needed distance, he was in search of parables, transcriptions, translations.

At the beginning of 1929 he decided that 'the future of the theatre is a philosophical one'. Piscator, he pointed out, had posed the 'question of subject-matter' and had been successful. But only twice in recent years had the 'question of form' been broached: in *The Threepenny Opera* and in Jessner's production of *Oedipus*. 'The big form is aimed at turning the material to account for "eternity". The "typical" exists also on the temporal plane. A writer who employs the big form tells his story as well, or better, for future generations as for his own time.' Brecht combined his efforts to find the big dramatic form with his fight for a new social order.

10

Man is Man

In fascism socialism sees its own distorted
image. With none of its virtues but all its
vices.

The comedy *Man is Man* summarizes Brecht's general outlook
and theories on the theatre in the mid-nineteen-twenties. The
problem of human alienation, which was the subject of *In the
Jungle of the Cities* and which appeared to be insoluble, is now
relegated to a secondary place and seen cynically as the price of
technical development. Brecht adopts an affirmative attitude
towards man's surrender of his personality, the elimination of
individuality. The individual is exchangeable, he no longer has any
unmistakable characteristics: *Man is Man.*

In the preface to his play, written in 1927, the author
distinguishes between an old and a new class of people, between an
age in decline and an age in the ascendant. The members of the
former, he declares, are no longer capable of expressing life
productively, they no longer develop 'appetites'. They can no
longer create art or assimilate it. Brecht sees huge cities and
technology as the last great achievements of the old class, though
they will be unable to stop its downfall. In these statements one
seems to see the Marxist idea that the social entity alters human
consciousness: 'The great buildings of New York City and the
great electrical inventions alone have not yet given humanity a
greater feeling of triumph. Because now, at this very moment, a
new type of human being, more important than these, is emerging,
and the whole interest of the world is focused on its development'.

Brecht had great hopes of this 'new' human being of the machine
age, and was firmly convinced that, by surrendering his
personality, he could only add to his essential human nature, and
that only in the mass would he acquire significance and strength.

'This new type of human being will not correspond to the picture formed of him by the old type of human being. I believe that he will not permit himself to be changed by the machines but will change them, and that whatever he looks like he will above all look like a human being.' Brecht overlooks the fact that under capitalism mechanization intensifies exploitation, because it increases still further the worker's dependence on the means of production, which do not belong to him, just as he overlooks the 'crippling' of the individual caused by machine work, to which Marx refers: 'The very abatement of his work becomes a means of torture, since the machine does not relieve the worker of his work but the work of its meaning'. By eliminating his personality man is made still harder to recognize as man, weaker and easier to manipulate. Only in a socialist society which encourages man's individual talents, and allows his personality to evolve within the collective, instead of being abolished by it, is the development of this new type of human being conceivable.

Galy Gay, the main character in *Man is Man*, is not a socially positive hero. His 'reassembly', his transformation from a stevedore to a 'human fighting machine', from a character to a collective being, tells us, not that he has become a human being, but that he has been brain-washed. Brecht sees the proceedings mainly as an 'amusement', which everyone is to interpret in his own way. His own view is is that Galy Gay gains as a human being through his transformation, but he can understand someone else taking a different view, 'to which I am the last person to take exception'. In spite of this, however, the play does not admit of two opposing interpretations.

Herr Bertolt Brecht behauptet: Mann is Mann.
Und das is etwas, was jeder behaupten kann.
Aber Herr Bertolt Brecht beweist auch dann
Dass man mit einem Menschen beliebig viel machen kann.
Hier wird heute abend ein Mensch wie ein Auto ummontiert
Ohne dass er irgend etwas dabei verliert.

(Herr Bertolt Brecht maintains that man is man. And that's a thing that all of us can maintain. But then Herr Bertolt Brecht goes on to show that one can make exactly what one wants of anyone. Here tonight a man will be reassembled like a motor car, and he loses nothing whatever in the process.)

119

One morning the stevedore Galy Gay goes to the market to buy some fish, but lands up in the army barracks at Kilkoa because he can't say no. Three soldiers from an English machine-gun detachment persuade him to attend roll-call as the fourth member of their group, who is missing after breaking into a pagoda. At first Galy Gay reacts as ponderously as an 'elephant', but once he gets going he moves 'like a goods train'. He plays his part well and enjoys it: 'In this world it is all a question of taking off from time to time and saying 'Jeraiah Jip', as another man says 'good evening'; and this is how it is when people want you because, after all, it is so simple'. When Jeraiah Jip fails to return the soldiers ask him to continue in the part. When he hesitates they tempt him with a 'deal': they know where they can lay their hands on an elephant, for which they also have a buyer, and they will let him have it. The stevedore agrees and even goes so far as to disown his wife, when Sergeant Fairchild brings her in to identify the man who broke into the pagoda. For all that Galy Gay is a man to be trusted. He has 'tasted blood'. The soldiers completely 'reassemble' him, even before the army sets out for the northern frontier, for they know that one man is the same as another, 'too much fuss is made about people'.

The elephant, which the soldiers lead in, consists merely of two men and a few squares of canvas. But Galy Gay suppresses his doubts because the widow Begbick, who runs the canteen, buys the animal unconditionally. The stevedore is arrested for fraud, sentenced to death in a sham trial and shot. As Jeraiah Jip he is allowed to survive and deliver the funeral oration for the executed man. Galy Gay can no longer distinguish between reality and make-believe and at the end of the proceedings he asks, completely at a loss, 'but who am I?' The soldiers assure him that he has become a man 'who will play his part in the coming battles'. The stevedore still has relapses and expresses doubts about the obliteration of his individuality. The sad fate of Sergeant Fairchild, once famous and feared as the 'bloody fiver' and the 'human typhoon', and now a miserable wreck, a civilian whom no one respects, decides Galy Gay finally to put his trust in the collective and relinquish his personality. The old type of colonial officer, a common sadist subject to fits of humanity, has had his day. Fairchild wants to remain the 'bloody fiver' and castrates himself in order to keep his reputation. Galy Gay gives up his reputation, no longer has any desire to be a character, and consequently becomes a 'man'. Only as a soldier does he acquire vital energy and self-assurance, and turn out to be 'as irresistible as a fighting elephant', a 'human fighting machine'. The insignificant stevedore thrives, at last he is able to realize his potential, he enjoys the game of war as if it were an orgasm. He destroys an entire fort and opens the way to Tibet for the army. The ability to conform, to subordinate oneself to the needs of the collective is here seen by Brecht as a sign of strength. It was as a 'human fighting machine' that he also admired the boxer Paul Samson-Körner at this time. No questions are asked about the sacrifices of war. What matters is the sporting achievement. And when, at the end, Galy Gay captures an entire mountain stronghold, 'it is only because by doing so he apparently carries out the peremptory will of a large mass of people who wish to pass through the narrow defile blocked by this stronghold'.

The transformation theme determines the structure of the play. In all there are four transformations, three peaks in the so-called montage act, the ninth tableau, which is divided into several numbers. The bonze of the pagoda broken into by the soldiers transforms Jip, the soldier left behind, into a 'god' and collects gifts of money and oblations from the faithful who want to see the miracle. The soldiers not only have to 'reassemble' Galy Gay, they also have to convert the widow Begbick's canteen, to make their beer-wagon ready for the march. In return they transform Sergeant Fairchild into a civilian. Gongs, a megaphone and jazz accompany the various transformations, divide one from the other and lead from one into the other. A play as a sporting event and great fun. The technical apparatus provides a framework for grotesque comedy, circus acts and clowning in the spirit of Valentin and Chaplin. Kilkoa, where the play is set, is half Indian and half Chinese. Kipling's 'Barrack-Room Ballads' and Döblin's novel *Die drei Sprünge des Wang-Lun (The Three Leaps of Wang-Lun)* gave Brecht the idea for the play.

In April 1928 the author still saw the behaviour of the main character of *Man is Man* as an affirmation: 'This contemporary, Galy Gay, surprising though it may seem, is very much against his case being turned into a tragedy; he gains something as a result of the mechanical infringement of his spiritual essence, and after the operation reports that he is in radiant health'. A little later, in the didactic plays, Brecht amended his idea of the individual and the crowd. Although he required the individual to take his place in the collective, he did not have in mind 'a mechanical adjustment or the production of average types', but the development of social awareness within a collective intent on fighting for a socialist order of society. The individual was to be established on the basis of the mass. The 'person' was to be demolished, or in other words each individual sector, which under capitalism represented a sort of sanctuary and was an unconscious protection on the part of the individual against the inhuman conditions of life, was to be sacrificed to the demands of the people as a whole. The individual would become the 'smallest unit' and recognize his 'new and true indispensability within the whole': 'Only when he is established in great movements, which are themselves in active and vigorous motion, does the individual acquire a measure of security and become calculable. The Marxists make allowance for a certain latitude, even though they declare the "great" individual to be comprehensible only when he can be associated with great movements of great classes, and even so they are most successful when they concede to him movements of his own that are not completely predetermined. The "average" is in reality only an imaginary line, hence no single person is really an average person. That the type is as dead as a door-nail, shoddy, sham and non-existent, is notorious'.

The 'quality' of a collective, therefore, is important, as is the role it assigns to the individual. The British colonial army, for instance, was an a-social collective, being merely an instrument to enforce political aims and uphold the policy of exploitation. The First World War, as Brecht explains in his notes for a 'dialectical dramatic art', demonstrated the role 'appointed to the individual in future. The individual as such was effective only as the representative of many. But his effective intervention in the great politico-economic processes was confined to exploiting them. The "mass of individuals", however, lost its indivisibility through its assignability. The individual was constantly being assigned to something and what began then was a process which took no account whatever of him, and which could be neither influenced by his intervention nor ended by his end.'

For the second Berlin production, which Brecht directed himself at the Staatstheater in 1931, he tried to revise his comedy to make it conform to these ideas. Galy Gay now became a socially negative hero, the revised version presenting the 'reassembly' of a poor wretch, who has nothing to lose, into a bloodthirsty soldier and anonymous slave to orders. As the dialogue says: 'If we don't keep an eye on him we can turn him into our own butcher overnight'. The Kiplingesque colonial romanticism was eliminated and the jazz band cut out. Brecht ended the play with the transformation scene because, as he said later, 'he saw no possibility of giving a negative character to the hero's growth within the collective'. The main problem was cleverly skirted in order to avoid any discussion about the quality of the collective to which the stevedore was attached. In 1931 *Man is Man* was performed as a grotesque anti-war play. The soldiers were fearful monsters on stilts, partially masked and with enormous hands. At the end Galy Gay, played by Peter Lorre, was transformed into a similar monster.

It was not until after the Second World War that Brecht decided to show his hero's development into a criminal. 'The problem of the play', he now realized, 'is the false, bad collective (the "gang") and its power to corrupt, the collective recruited in those years by Hitler and his financial backers, exploiting the inarticulate demand of the petite bourgeoisie for the real and historically timely social collective of the workers'. Accordingly what had to be brought out was the point at which communism and fascism come very close to one another and yet are worlds apart. Brecht had neither the strength nor the time to undertake a revision of *Man is Man,* in which the problem of the positive and negative collective would be logically treated. He merely proposed that the two last scenes of the 1926 version be given again, and added a few sentences which stressed the imperialistic nature of the war in which the British army was involved.

Brecht also made important changes in the widow Begbick's part in 1931. She no longer roused the soldiers with romantic stories of adventure but approached them with poetry. Instead of the Kiplingesque song, 'Ah, Tom, are you in the army too?' ('Ach, Tom, bist du auch beir Armee, beir Armee?'), she sang 'The Song of the Flow of Things' ('Das Lied vom Fluss der Dinge'), as a commentary on Galy Gay's transformation:

123

Wie oft du auch den Fluss ansiehst, der träge
Dahinzieht, nie siehst du dasselbe Wasser
Nie kehrt es, das hinunterfliesst, kein Tropfen von ihm
Zu seinem Ursprung zurück.

Beharre nicht auf der Welle,
Die sich an deinem Fuss bricht, solange er
Im Wasser steht, werden sich
Neue Wellen an ihm brechen.

(However often you look and see the river pass lazily by, you never see the same water twice. Never does a drop of what flows down return to its source. Do not insist on the wave that breaks over your foot; as long as this stands in the water there will be new waves that break over it.)

It was clearly the author's intention, by means of a poetic commentary, to present an affirmative idea of transformation. In its philosophic content, however, the song is closer to the ideological theorems of the early Brecht than to Marxism. Here the idea of the flow of things is still conceived quite undialectically, everything being subject to constant change; not only personality but things as well are relative and transient. The change, of which the widow Begbick speaks, has neither content nor historical dimension. All that is certain is that everything flows; the question of how it flows and how it can be made to flow is not raised. In Meti Brecht points out the 'dangers inherent in this idea of the flow of things': 'Disciples of evolution often have a low opinion of what exists. The notion that it is transient makes it seem unimportant . . .. The fact that they move makes them forget that they are'.

11

Plays for the Theater am Schiffbauerdamm

> What Germany needs for its future is no
> different from what other countries need: the
> most skilled possible application of Marxist
> viewpoints to society and the economy. Then,
> naturally, it would have the same chance as
> other countries to emerge from its cultural
> morass.

His encounter with Marxist theory, and the 'readjustment' this
necessitated in his work, resulted in Brecht being unable to write a
number of plays. On the one hand these could not be completed
without preliminary theoretical work and, on the other hand,
coming to grips with Marxism introduced too many new elements
into the conception of the plot. These projects still centred round
typical characters like the meat king Joe Fleischhacker and the
railway king Dan Drew. Brecht now had to begin by sketching out
plays for his own use, so that in these drafts he could give
immediate expression to his new-found knowledge and better
document his own learning process. Only with *St. Joan of the
Stockyards (Die heilige Johanna der Schlachthöfe)* did he succeed in
achieving a synthesis of the big form with the scenic demonstration
of Marxist theory.

It was music which led Brecht to the form of the didactic plays.
His own compositions were no longer adequate to his needs. In his
productions of *Edward II* and *Baal* he still used music in the
traditional way: songs and marches motivated by the text and
adding lightness, variety and poetry to the progress of the story.
For his 'epic theatre', which envisaged the 'separation of the
elements', he needed a different sort of music. It had to exist in its
own right and comment on, rather than illustrate, the action.
Brecht called it 'misuc'. Misuc expressed his demand that music
should be rational too, a polemic against the 'emotional confusion'
so often experienced at symphony concerts and the opera.

In the spring of 1927 Kurt Weill, a pupil of Busoni, approached Brecht about a text for a work he wanted to write for Baden-Baden. A meeting between the two men had been arranged by Georg Kaiser, the only expressionist playwright accepted by Brecht, who also counted him among his teachers. As Brecht was busy at the time with other work, he suggested to Weill that he should set to music the old 'Mahagonny' songs from the *Homilies*. The composer, however, managed to interest Brecht in the idea of collaborating, and they had great fun together re-working the songs and assembling them into a 'Songspiel', which they then produced and performed in Baden-Baden as part of the Deutsche Kammermusik festival. The stage revealed a boxing-ring, behind which was a wall onto which pictures by Neher were projected. The fact that Weill, who hitherto had written rather complicated serious music, agreed to compose 'more or less banal words' greatly impressed Brecht. The composer also fell in with the poet's ideas about descriptive music: 'Precisely because it behaved in a purely emotional way and eschewed none of the usual narcotic stimuli, the music played its part in exposing the bourgeois ideologies'.

Brecht and Weill decided to continue their successful collaboration and wanted to write a full-length opera together. A subject would no doubt occur to them and, if it did not, they would turn the Songspiel into an opera as Hans Curjel, the dramaturg of the Kroll Opera house, had suggested. In 1927 Elisabeth Hauptman, always on the look-out for suitable material for Brecht, heard of John Gay's *Beggar's Opera*, which had been resuscitated in 1920 by the Lyric Theatre in London where it had played for over two years. She began to make a German translation of this eighteenth century satire, in which Sir Robert Walpole's government is portrayed as a band of thieves and beggars, and Brecht immediately decided to adapt it. Together with Weill he went through the original music by Pepusch and found it insufficiently aggressive. It was wholly unsuited to the tone of the couplets, songs and ballads he wrote for the adaptation, in which he also used poems by Villon and Kipling. He asked Weill to write a completely new score.

But *Riff-raff (Gesindel)*, as the adaptation was originally called, was regarded by Brecht merely as a secondary work. When, in the spring of 1928, the actor and impresario Ernst Josef Aufricht approached him about a play, with which to open his Theater am Schiffbauerdamm, Brecht told him about *Joe Fleischhacker,* at which he said he was then working; but he could give him no idea when it would be finished, and in any case he had already promised it to Piscator. Only then did Brecht casually mention that he was adapting the *Beggar's Opera,* six scenes of which were already done. Aufricht said he would like to see them. The next day Heinrich Fischer, dramaturg of the Theater am Schiff-bauerdamm, went to the Spichern Strasse to collect the manuscript. Brecht did not mention the fact that Kurt Weill was a party to the adaptation, and was writing a new score for it, until *Riff-raff* had been accepted. Aufricht was appalled: how could such a man as Weill, who composed atonal music, possibly be in a position to write effective music for a play. As a precaution he asked Theo Mackeben, whom he had engaged for the musical side of the production, to have the Pepusch score available as a substitute. The first night was planned for 31 August. The play was still unfinished, most of the songs were not yet written. While Aufrecht and Erich Engel, who was to direct it, were assembling the cast, Brecht and Weill were writing the final scenes at Le Lavendou, in the South of France, and at the Ammersee. Rehearsals started at the beginning of August.

After about ten days Carola Neher, who was to play Polly, left to visit Klabund who was dying in a sanatorium in Davos. Following his death on 14 August she withdrew from the rehearsals. Nothing that Brecht and Engel could do would persuade her to change her mind. Four days before the play opened Roma Bahn took over the part of Polly.

Helene Weigel wanted to play the Madam of the brothel in Turnbridge as a woman with no legs. She had herself brought onto the stage in a wheel-chair and lifted on to a table, from where she could run her business as a lady who did not exist from the waist down. Threatened appendicitis suddenly forced Helene Weigel to withdraw. The part was cut out and the scene re-written. One misfortune followed another. Everyone connected with the theatre thought the play would be a failure. Rosa Valetti, the cabaret star who played Mrs. Peachum, railed against the 'lousy play' and wanted to get out. She signed a contract with the Kabarett der Komiker, because she was certain she would be free to appear there the day after the play opened. When the operetta singer Harald

Paulsen, who was vain anyway, insisted on wearing a sky-blue cravat for the part of Macheath and, in addition, demanded a more effective first entrance, Brecht started to shout. He could not stand this type of actor. Then he had an idea: 'Let's leave him as he is, with his sickly charm. Weill and I will bring him on to a ballad proclaiming his gruesome crimes—his light blue tie will make him all the more sinister'. Thus was born the famous ballad of 'Mack the Knife'. In the end Erich Engel quarrelled with Brecht who wanted to introduce a stage effect to distinguish between the action and the songs: when the songs started the author had the stage darkened, with old-fashioned oil lamps hanging from above, while a dummy organ, in front of which the musicians sat, was visible in the background. Rather than accept this arrangement, Engel wanted to dispense with the music altogether. But he did not get his way. The others found Brecht's obsession with the theatre more convincing than Engel's practical experience.

The dress rehearsal of *The Threepenny Opera (Die Drei-groschenoper)* as the play was now called at Feuchtwanger's suggestion, lasted until the small hours of the morning. At the last minute Brecht cut out the Solomon song and shortened Peachum's part. As a result Erich Ponto, who played the beggar king, nearly walked out. 'The final chorus must go too', demanded Aufricht and Engel, 'it sounds like Bach.' Weill refused and was supported by Caspar Neher, who begged him to stand up for the chorus: 'If you give in and take it out, it will be all over between us'. So the chorus remained. There was another rehearsal in the afternoon. The messenger was supposed to enter on horseback. The machinery for this had only just been completed and it did not work. 'The horse will appear or the play will not be done', announced Brecht, leading the animal onto the stage with a beaming smile. But as Aufricht said he was not going to have the thing turned into a pantomime, the messenger had to enter on foot after all. Before the performance Weill started to rant and rage because his wife Lotte Lenya, who played Jenny, was not mentioned in the programme. Meanwhile the actor playing Filch, an out of work apprentice who wanted to be a bookseller, appeared in Aufricht's office demanding a higher salary, cash in advance and a two-month contract: 'I am not an actor and have no wish to be one. You can't put me on the black list or do anything to me, I am penniless. I want thirty marks an evening or I am off this instant, you won't find me and there will be no first night'. With a broad grin on his face Brecht, who had recommended the apprentice, beat his protegé down to twenty marks. The man had apparently learned a thing or two during rehearsals.

The première of *The Threepenny Opera* has gone down in theatrical history as the greatest success of the nineteen-twenties. The play ran for almost a year in Berlin. The stormy rehearsals, the numerous quarrels and disagreements, were quickly forgotton. Carola Neher was the first to offer her congratulations and asked how long Roma Bahn's contract had to run: 'I must play Polly'. Brecht agreed at once. In his view Carola Neher was the better actress. Under these circumstances moods did not count. After Polly she was given the part of Lilian Holiday in *Happy End,* and finally Brecht wrote *St. Joan of the Stockyards* for her. In a little didactic poem he wrote at this time he gave Carola Neher instructions on how she should wash in the morning, 'like a famous person and so that painters could make pictures from it':

> Erfrische dich, Schwester
> An dem Wasser aus dem Kupferkessel mit den
> Eisstückchen—
> Öffne die Augen unter Wasser, wasch sie—
> Trockne dich ab mit dem rauhen Tuch und wirf
> Einen Blick in ein Buch, das du liebst.
> So beginne
> Einen schönen und nützlichen Tag.

(Revive yourself, sister, with water from the copper jug containing lumps of ice—open your eyes under water, wash them—dry yourself with a rough towel and cast a glance at a favourite book. Thus will begin a pleasant and useful day.)

It came as something of a shock to Carola Neher when Brecht, meeting her at the station one day in April 1929, casually said that he had married Helene Weigel. 'It couldn't be avoided, but it doesn't mean anything', was the gist of his explanation.

But it was Elisabeth Hauptmann to whom Brecht's decision came as the greatest surprise. Dispirited, she tried to commit suicide; fortunately she recovered. Finally she accepted the behaviour of her friend who, in a poem, craved indulgence and appealed for 'special understanding':

129

Auf dich wurden Lasten gelegt, die man
Nur auf die sichersten Schultern legt,
Du wurdest übersehen wie das Nächstliegende.
Von dir wurde erwartet
Die besondere Einsicht.
So essen am letzten die, denen das Werk am nächsten
     steht: die Köche.

(Burdens were heaped on you that one heaps only on most reliable
shoulders, you escaped notice as very familiar things do. In you one
looked for special understanding. Just as those eat last to whom the work
is closest: the cooks.)

Marieluise Fleisser, on the other hand, insisted on separation.
She simply was not prepared to accept the marriage and the
scandal caused shortly afterwards by Brecht's adaptation of her
Pioniere in Ingolstadt (Engineers in Ingolstadt). To show her
defiance she rushed into an engagement with the strange writer
Helmut Draws-Tychsen with whom she then left on a trip across
Europe. She firmly resisted all Brecht's attempts to win her back.
It was above all as a writer that she wanted finally to free herself
from his dominating influence, more especially as she always felt
very out of it with Brecht and his friends. Now Draws-Tychsen,
whom she started to put into a play as 'Deep Sea Fish', wanted to
take possession of her 'whole being'. In 1933, when her two suitors
were forced to emigrate, Marieluise Fleisser went back to
Ingolstadt for good. Forbidden to write under the Nazis, who
burned her books, the only thing left seemed to be to marry a
girlhood friend by whom, out of gratitude, she now allowed herself
to be exploited. Later she used to describe these bitter years as
'quite simply a foretaste of hell': 'I had brought it on myself. The
man obliterated me and no guardian angel came to my aid, only my
hand was still my own and I was forced to drink myself into a
stupor'.

Following the success of *The Threepenny Opera* Aufricht
regarded Brecht as his resident author and Brecht the Theater am
Schiffbauerdamm as his theatre. In the main it was 'his' actors—
Helene Weigel, Carola Neher, Lotte Lenya, Oskar Homolka,
Peter Lorre, Theo Lingen and Ernst Busch—who formed the
nucleus of the company. Only a few plays were given, only a few
actors were schooled. 'His actors', as the dramaturg recalled in *The*

Purchase of Brass, 'were not waiters whose job was to serve food and whose personal, private feelings were regarded as impudent obstrusions. They were servants neither of the poet nor of the public. His actors were not functionaries of a political movement nor were they high priests of art. As political men and women they had to advance their social cause by means of art and by means of every other means.' According to Aufricht *The Threepenny Opera* was a 'literary operetta with flashes of social criticism'. Later Brecht tried to give a keener edge to the political message—man does not live in a moral code but by a moral code—in order to make the play less acceptable to a bourgeois audience. But the 'dubious myth' of *The Threepenny Opera* survived all its author's corrections. Only from the production point of view can the work be called 'epic theatre'; as a play it is at the most a successful attempt 'to counteract the tendency of opera to become totally inane'.

The critics, moreover, were by no means as enthusiastic as the public. The abuse of the right-wing press could give Brecht nothing but satisfaction; praise from this quarter would have been embarrassing to any poet with claims to be taken seriously. What was exasperating were the objections from the left. Brecht was very sensitive to left-wing feuilletonism, to critics who treated art as a question of outlook. Those who wanted political theatre could go to Piscator, not to Brecht who took very little interest in plays about contemporary events. The 'desperate attempts of literary people to echo the views of the proletarians' struck him merely as 'unspeakably funny'. When laymen accused Brecht of being insufficiently concrete in his social attitudes, he would discuss the matter seriously; but politicizing literati, left-wingers and ideological dramatists were angrily snubbed. It amused Brecht to take the opposite line to these critics and impute vain and personal motives to them. In the case of Harry Kahn, for example, who had described *The Threepenny Opera* in *Die Weltbühne* as an 'artists' skylark, much too grandiosely staged', and a 'Swabian studio romp', he was fairly certain that a bad seat in the theatre had been responsible for the bad notice: 'You said at once that, in the interests of objective criticism, I should have seen that you had a seat nearer the front. At the time I considered that your place was not too far back for an objective criticism, but that is where I was mistaken. Now that I read your criticism I see that I was wrong

131

and you were right: your place was too far back for an objective criticism'.

It was a silly controversy but it was pursued with great zest and little humour. From *Die Weltbühne* came the schoolmasterly retort: 'Herr Brecht expects to be praised and imputes base motives because our critic did not hand out the desired quantity of laurels. A foolish attempt at terrorization unworthy of a poet like Brecht'. Kurt Tucholsky, one of the co-editors of *Die Weltbühne,* later repeated Kahn's allegations in an article discussing protests against Brecht in provincial towns: the poet's 'conviction' was hard to fathom, life was not at all as it was portrayed in *The Threepenny Opera* and *Mahagonny;* the connection with Germany in 1930 was 'far fetched', the background was 'stylized Bavaria'. Alfred Kerr then enlivened the discussion about *The Threepenny Opera* by accusing Brecht of quoting several lines by Villon, in K. L. Ammer's version, without mentioning the translator's name. The playwright answered the absurd charge of plagiarism by a brief explanation: 'A Berlin newspaper has noticed late in the day, but has noticed all the same, that in the Kiepenheuer edition of the songs from *The Threepenny Opera* the name of Ammer, the German translator, is not to be found alongside that of Villon, although of my 625 lines 25 are in fact identical with Ammer's excellent translation. An explanation is demanded. I therefore declare, in accordance with the truth, that I unfortunately forgot to mention Ammer's name. This, in turn, I explain by the fact that I am fundamentally lax over the question of literary property'[1].

---

[1] Brecht also defined his attitude to the problem of plagiarism in the *Film-Kurier* of 4 May 1929. As this piece is not included in the *Gesammelte Werke,* it is given here: 'It is already widely known that my thinking where literary property is concerned is pretty lax. It was because of this that I also nearly forgot to mention the name François Villon on the play-bill; but my attention was drawn to this in time and his name was included. I also had Kipling's name put on the play-bill, because I had intended to include a ballad (of his). This plan, however, was not carried out.

'Thus Kipling's name is now to be found on every play-bill in the country, for the simple reason that I forgot to take it out. Just as I forgot to put in the name of Villon's German translator.

132

Brecht regarded Kerr's allegation as philological pettiness, the action of a cultural philistine speculating desperately on his readers' lack of culture. A writer's greatness, he maintained, was demonstrated primarily not by the originality of his mind, but by the suitability of what he wrote for quoting: 'Pretty well every literary heyday, of course, is based on the power and innocence of its plagiarisms'. Kerr's 'disclosure' was reproduced and circulated by all the provincial newspapers. At last someone had seen through the playwright and the cue had been given for his literary despatch. Herwarth Walden had already spoken of plagiarism after the Berlin production of *In the Jungle of the Cities,* pointing out that the author had used lines by Rimbaud and Verlaine. On that occasion Brecht had been able to refer to his manuscript, in which the passages in question were clearly indicated by quotation marks: 'It seems that the stage has no technique for giving expression to quotation marks. Did it have one it might make a lot of other favourite works more palatable to philologists, though fairly intolerable to the public'. Brecht's admission that he was 'lax in matters of literary property' was seen by writers concerned for their royalties as a 'sinister determination to get rich at other people's expense'. *Die Weltbühne* also took the matter up again. Using a play on Brecht's name, Tucholsky punned on what is sauce for the goose is sauce for the gander ('Was dem einen brecht ist, ist dem anderen billig'); and in the following number he printed the 'Song of the Guns' from *The Threepenny Opera* with the remark, 'In spite of his fundamental laxity in matters of literary property the author has waived his fee'. The author of the song was named as Egon Jacobson. The attacks gave a huge boost to Brecht's popularity and to that of *The Threepenny Opera;* even Ammer's translation became famous. Brecht persuaded Kiepenheuer to publish a new edition of Ammer's renderings of Villon, and wrote an introductory sonnet enjoining people to make diligent use of the little volume:

'So there is one name more and one name less—both as a result of forgetfulness. And this forgetfulness is to be explained by my assuredly reprehensible indifference to literary property.

'Literary property is an item that should be classed with allotment-gardens and such like things.'

133

Nehm jeder sich heraus, was er grad braucht!
Ich selber hab mir was herausgenommen . . .

(Let each man help himself to what he needs! I too have helped myself to
this and that . . .)

Brecht slyly offered his apologies: it was only because on the
stage there had to be an emphasis on gesture that he was forced, 'in
places', to make radical alterations to the extracts he had used in
The Threepenny Opera; 'Clarity on the stage is a different thing
from clarity on the printed page'. He described Ammer's work as a
'classic rendering'; and in a postscript the translator in turn paid
homage to Brecht, and compared Macheath to Villon.

Karl Kraus now took over the task of dealing with Kerr: 'There
is more originality in the little finger of Brecht's hand, which took
twenty-five lines from Ammer's translation of Villon, than in Kerr
who found him out . . . . That any literary figure would be relegated
to oblivion who sought to gain lustre by appropriating a single line
from someone else, is as little open to doubt as is the utter stupidity
of trying to make one believe that a writer so constituted, so gifted
and so manifestly out of the ordinary as this one, would have found
it necessary, or imagined it possible, to put on paper, as literary
contraband, lines he considered as much to the purpose of the play
as the scenery and the characters, and the author's rights which
he forgot to acknowledge in sending the work to press. To
insinuate that such a thing, which in this case also involves
copyright, is done deliberately is not the malice of satire but the
malice of idiocy, or even indicates a state of mind that does not
scorn to appear idiotic in order to score a fleeting success with
idiots'.

But Kraus and Brecht did not become allies simply through
their mutual hostility to Kerr. They both hated left-wingery and
the politics of the social democrats. Karl Kraus had no leanings
towards Marxist theory, but for a time felt drawn to the
Communist movement. He was harnessed to the extreme poles of
the aristocracy and the workers. Walter Benjamin saw in Kraus an
'interplay between revolutionary practice and reactionary theory'.
Liberals he despised; in his eyes they represented a dubious, anti-
social, bourgeois morality, and liberalism aided and abetted to an
enormous degree the overthrow of cultural standards. The voice of

the liberal bourgeoisie was the press, the 'free' press, which Kraus blamed for the greatest of all evils, the debasement of language through the use of hollow phrases. Kraus's 'reactionary theory' was the point of departure of his thinking, the denial of any possibility of future happiness; the world, in his view, was irretrievably following the course of his nightmare. His 're-volutionary practice' was the uncompromising destruction of all 'values' carried merely as ballast and which caused nothing but harm, together with the realization that changes were effected, not by reforms, but by revolutionary acts. Brecht noted in admiration: 'In a gigantic work Kraus, the leading writer of the day, describes the degeneration and vileness of civilized man. His criterion is language, the means of communication between human beings'. Kraus had been present at the rehearsals of *The Threepenny Opera* and became convinced of Brecht's theatrical gifts, in which he could detect 'no trace of anything speculative'. In his enthusiasm he had even contributed a few lines to the 'Jealousy Duet', a gift of which Brecht availed himself as naturally as he did of the lines by Villon and Kipling.

Ernst Josef Aufricht did not want to rest on the success of *The Threepenny Opera*. He leased a second theatre, in order to be able to mount new productions at the Theater am Schiffbauerdamm. In choosing Peter Martin Lampel's *Giftgas über Berlin (Poison Gas over Berlin)*, he opted for a topical play of the kind favoured by Piscator. The play's target was the *Reichswehr,* proof enough of the company's left-wing sympathies. Zörgiebel, the social democrat chief of police, demanded that the play be withdrawn and threatened to close the theatre. Brecht, although no supporter of Lampel and his dramatic technique, advised opposing the censorship and gave his support to the association formed by Aufricht and his fellow-workers to oppose reintroduction of censorship. When the dramatic critic Monty Jacobs suggested that they should first investigate the literary value of the play on whose behalf they were proposing to do battle, Brecht snapped at him: 'To form a literary coffee-circle may fit in with your ideas. We are fighting all forms of censorship unconditionally, even if they ban *Lilac Time*'. Aufricht was given permission to stage a single private performance for the press and guests selected by the chief of police. Behind the scenes Brecht, who was not exactly a brave man, organized the actors' resistance and suggested that the officers in the auditorium be invited to leave their swords in the cloakroom before the performance started. It never came to this because some young communists, who had acquired tickets, assumed the task of welcoming Zörgiebel: 'Bloody tyrant! Crook! Slave driver! String him up!' On the grounds that its performance would endanger public safety, *Giftgas über Berlin* was banned permanently.

While Aufricht was still negotiating with police headquarters, Brecht had already started rehearsing Marieluise Fleisser's second play *Pioniere in Ingolstadt:* 'This comedy describes habits and customs in the heart of Bavaria. It provides an excellent opportunity to study certain spheres of atavistic and prehistoric feeling. Primitive love, for instance, occurs in it in an almost pure state of preservation, as certain primitive plants are preserved in limestone formations'. The actual director was Brecht's Munich friend Jakob Geis, but he found it difficult to assert his authority over the actors. Brecht remodelled the play to suit his own purposes. 'Here the procedure was not the same as in other theatres, where a single text is adhered to. Here the text was of no interest . . . Here the method was to study, here things did not just happen, they were tried out . . . . A text was never finished, this was its leading characteristic and, remember, a text was raw material and the author came last, in the theatre every actor counted for more'. Marieluise Fleisser tried to resist, to escape from Brecht's influence, but that was a very difficult thing to do. Most of those who worked with him had the same experience. Throughout her life Brecht remained the 'supreme authority' as far as she was concerned. At that time she had no real idea of the political significance of her play. She had wanted to tell an almost workaday story. Some engineers arrive in Ingolstadt, build a bridge, flirt with the girls, and leave again. 'For a night time rendez-vous she had written, quite naively, "by the cemetery". She wanted a deserted spot. It turned out that on the stage the tombstones were directly behind the lovers. Death immediately behind the deadly sin; the setting was too good an opportunity to miss'. The authoress was not prepared for the scandal caused by the performance. The cemetery scene, the love scene in a crate, and the sergeant's odious behaviour at punishment drill all had to be cut out. Otherwise this performance would have been banned too. The whole country, led by Ingolstadt, set upon the authoress, so that for a time she was frightened and withdrew. Kerr and Ihering praised both the play and the production; for once the two critics, normally at daggers drawn, saw eye to eye. Using the simplest means, Brecht had brought out the play's realism and poetry. 'The play was directed with such a light hand that no one noticed it', wrote Ernst Josef Aufricht, who considered *Pioniere in Ingolstadt* the most successful production under his directorship of the Theater am Schiffbauerdamm.

The didactic plays, on which Brecht was working in the meantime, were not suited to the Theater am Schiffbauerdamm. They were not intended for consumption by a bourgeois audience, but for the instruction of the actors, of those engaged in production. Brecht regarded the huge success of *The Threepenny Opera* with a certain cynicism. He promised Aufricht another play of the same kind, *Happy End,* but lost interest before he finished it. The plot, which was based on a story by Elisabeth Hauptmann, was dramatized in a great hurry: Lilian Holiday, a lieutenant in the Salvation Army, falls in love with the gangster boss Bill Cracker; she kisses him and, because of this kiss, is dismissed from the Salvation Army. In her distress she goes back to Bill, stops him from committing a break-in, and converts him. He joins the Salvation Army. His companions, who want to kill him, also throw themselves into the arms of religion, and the woman leader of the gangs 'The Fly', sums it up: 'What is a picklock compared to an investment, what is breaking into a bank compared to founding a bank'. The Salvation Army operates as a capitalistic cover-organization, maintained by financiers to hide their fraudulent practices. The banal story and the propaganda are not particularly well matched.

Brecht handed over two acts and then went to Baden-Baden to rehearse his didactic plays. He intended to send the remainder from Augsburg. At the beginning of August, when *Happy End* was going into rehearsal, Neher arrived with the news that Brecht expected Aufricht to go to him, he had no intention of sending the third act. In the end Brecht turned up after all and said he would write the closing scenes during rehearsals. Erich Engel refused to direct the play under these conditions and terminated his contract. Brecht, remarking that Engel was 'a tired worn-out man', took over the production himself, with Emil Burri as his assistant. Slatan Dudov, Asja Lacis and Bernhard Reich arrived. They confirmed Brecht's ideological doubts about the play. They found the clear-cut design, the caustic songs and Weill's music unsatisfactory. Dudov was a Bulgarian student of the cinema whom Brecht had brought in for the film scenes in the Baden-Baden didactic play. Asja Lacis was working at the Soviet commercial agency in Berlin, while her husband Bernhard Reich, who lived in Moscow working as a dramaturg, happened to be in Berlin on a visit. The actors were annoyed by these 'strange people', these 'red agitators', who wanted from Brecht something that clearly prevented him from supplying the urgently needed new text in the normal way.

While the play was going into production Brecht was already thinking ahead, interested only in those aspects of the affair that he could make use of. He was fairly certain that *Happy End* would not be a success. So he withdrew his name and suggested a magazine story by Dorothy Lane, dramatized by Elisabeth Hauptmann. Kurt Weill, however, insisted that Brecht accept responsibility at least for the songs. *Happy End* was taken off after a few performances. This new version of *The Threepenny Opera* no longer drew an audience. The press was scathing.

In the opera *Rise and Fall of the Town of Mahagonny (Aufstieg und Fall der Stadt Mahagonny)*, which followed *Happy End*, Brecht and Weill not only parodied the culinary nature of the theatre, but introduced culinary matters themselves as an ingredient of bourgeois society. Logical degeneration of art as diversion and intoxicant, citing Freud who, in *The Malaise in Civilisation (Das Unbehagen in der Kultur)*, blames these functions for the fact that 'large quantities of energy, which could be used to improve human existence, are ineffectually lost'.

Brecht had coined the word 'Mahagonny' as a term for that petit bourgeois dream which he saw as a mixture of anarchy and alcohol. The first songs on this theme expressed the discrepant fascination exercised over him by the male eccentrics he had met in the suburban taverns of Augsburg and Munich. He clearly enjoyed the posturing and lewd familiarity of these lumberjacks, lorry drivers, tramps and card players. He portrayed the 'Men of Mahagonny' as a bunch of failures and showed how, in a collective, they develop energies of which they are not capable on their own. In the *Songspiel* of 1927 the anarchistic character of the milieu had already been displayed in a pleasing, romantically-cynical light. In

138

working with Weill Brecht now became interested in presenting the hitherto sketchily outlined proceedings in the form of a parable; in any case he now realized that the subject presented him with a good opportunity to treat capitalism's proneness to crises in theatrical terms. There was now little similarity left between the Mahagonny of the opera, the 'net-city', and its Bavarian predecessor. The almost cosy, comfortable world of gin shops and gaming tables was given the dimensions appropriate to a big city. The new Mahoganny was organized like a big business in which everyone is allowed to do what he likes if he has money, but in which lack of money, being the worst crime of all, is punished with death. Brecht got the idea for this capitalistic paradise in Berlin's Kurfürstendamm: from the Gedächtniskirche to the Halensee bridge, and a little beyond that into the amusement parks. In this 'glittering, sparkling excrement' of the great 'crazy' city of Berlin cavorted the pleasure seekers, 'the discontented from every continent'; the Salvation Army worked here, beggars and disabled soldiers lounged about. As early as 1926 Brecht was using expressions like 'witches' cauldron' and 'Babel of wickedness' to describe Berlin's amusement centres, where women were Americanized and turned into 'girls', and dreams of the South Seas were sold to the little man.

The Mahagonny world reflected the capitalist world as Brecht saw it at the end of the nineteen-twenties. In the working-copy of the play used in their 1931 production at Aufricht's Theater am Kurfürstendamm, Brecht, Neher and Weill used the expression 'pictures of twentieth century life'. The town of Mahagonny was intended as a 'symbol of contemporary life'. It was not a parabolic morality play. Brecht was realistic in his assessment of what went on in the net-city, in whose laws of happiness man was enmeshed: in Mahagonny the law of money is supreme, and brings with it the total materialization of human relationships. There are the exploiters and the exploited, the group of founders and the group of newcomers. 'The cock-eyed, childish view that feeds on sea stories and books about Indians', writes Adorno, 'becomes the means of breaking the spell of the capitalist system, whose farms are turned into Colorado deserts, whose crises are turned into hurricanes and whose machinery of power is turned into revolvers held at the ready. In Mahagonny the Wild West is shown to be the fairy story inherent in capitalism, as children see it in their games.'

139

In their subsequent work both playwright and composer tried increasingly to stress the didactic elements at the expense of the culinary ones: 'In other words to develop the educational material from the means of enjoyment and to turn certain institutions from places of entertainment into organs for disseminating information'. The appropriate forum for these pedagogic experiments was the Baden-Baden music festival.

Members of the musical avant-garde wanted to change their traditional apparatus for the production of music. They wanted their music to be performed mainly by non-professionals. It was not intended for passive concert audiences. A sort of musical youth movement grew up in connection with the aims of the 'New Music': 'Their music-making was based on the conviction that a musical work communally performed stimulates forces conducive to forming a community'. Music was to be used in the education of the young. The slogans were 'musical appreciation' and the 'cultivation of music'. The pedagogic aims of the 'New Music' did not satisfy Brecht. To him art itself was a pedagogic activity. Instead of education in art he wanted education through art.

In July 1929 Brecht arrived in Baden-Baden with two didactic plays. One, *The Flight of the Lindberghs (Der Flug der Lindberghs)*, was written for broadcasting, although its purpose was to change this medium rather than to serve it: 'The increasing concentration of mechanical means, as well as the increasing specialization in training—processes that should be accelerated—call for a sort of revolt on the part of the listener, his activation and his reinstatement as producer'. In the play the radio and the listener confront each other. The radio stands for the town, the continents, a ship, the forces of nature and the crowd; Lindbergh personifies the listener. It is not the airman, the first to fly the Atlantic, whom we should celebrate, but his deed. He appears in the plural as the Lindberghs:

Sieben Männer haben meinen Apparat gebaut in
    San Diego
Oftmals 24 Stunden ohne Pause
Aus ein paar Metern Stahlrohr.
Was sie gemacht haben, das muss mir reichen
Sie haben gearbeitet, ich
Arbeite weiter, ich bin nicht allein, wir sind
Acht, die hier fliegen.

140

(Seven men built my machine in San Diego, often for twenty-four hours at a stretch, from a few yards of steel tubing. I have to make do with what they have made. They have worked, I continue the work; I am not alone, there are eight of us flying here.)

The director of the Cologne broadcasting station, Ernst Hardt, was interested in *The Flight of the Lindberghs* and took over the Baden-Baden production. Kurt Weill and Paul Hindemith wrote the music. 'On the left of the stage was the radio orchestra with its equipment and singers, on the right was the listener who, with a score in front of him, played the airman's part, the pedagogic part. He sang his music to instrumental accompaniment supplied by the radio. He read the spoken lines without identifying his own feelings with the feelings expressed in the text; at the end of each line he broke off, as if he were practising. Against the backdrop was displayed the theory under demonstration.' Brecht himself arranged a further, concertante, performance of the *Lindbergh Flight* in which the airman's part was sung by a choir, to avoid any chance of the audience identifying itself with the hero. 'Only if the "I" is sung in concert is it possible to preserve something of the pedagogic effect.'

The second didactic play which Brecht put on in Baden-Baden was linked thematically with the first: four ocean fliers, who have come down in the sea, want to be rescued. The play starts by examining the question whether it is usual for 'man to come to the aid of man'. The answer is no. The men who are down in the sea cannot be helped. The collective advises them to acquiesce in their fate, to consent to the loss of their individualities. Only the pilot objects; he dies. The three mechanics give themselves up and escape death.

For his production of the *Baden-Baden Didactic Play on Acquiescence (Badener Lehrstück vom Einverständnis)*, for which Hindemith had written the music, Brecht made use of films and projections, which he subsequently incorporated in the play. In an interlude he introduced three clowns one of whom, played by Theo Lingen, gradually had every limb of his body sawn off by the other two. At this point some members of the audience are said to have fainted. Gerhart Hauptmann, who was present, walked out in disgust. The author and composer remained on the stage during the performance and issued instructions to the actors and

141

musicians in order to provoke the audience and challenge them to comment. When pictures of dead people were shown and the audience became very restive Brecht told the announcer to call out, the moment the projection was finished: 'Repeat showing of the ill-received portrayal of death'. And the pictures were shown a second time.

The form of the didactic play very quickly caught on, and had many imitators. Unlike Brecht, however, who wanted to teach, they used the didactic play for purely experimental purposes. Even Paul Hindemith had misunderstood Brecht, and from the moment when the latter identified himself with the working-class and the Communist Party, further co-operation became impossible. To Hindemith their joint appearance in Baden-Baden meant something entirely different, the sole purpose of the *Baden-Baden Didactic Play* being 'to get everyone present to share in the performance of a work'. He regarded both text and score as suggestions to be altered at will. 'Omissions, additions and modifications are possible. Whole musical numbers can be left out, the dance can go, the scene with the clowns can be shortened or omitted. Other musical pieces, scenes, dances or lectures can be inserted, if this is necessary and the insertions do not affect the style of the work as a whole.' Meanwhile Brecht had further extended his Marxist studies and was in the process of giving concrete form to the teaching at issue for him. The educational purpose advocated by Hindemith, which was purely musical and formal, seemed to the playwright quite immaterial: 'It is obvious that the didactic value of this sort of musical exercise, based on a "thoughtful" text, "which appeals to the imagination of the student", would be much too small. Even if one expected that the individual would "adjust to something in the process" or that the musical basis would produce certain formal intellectual congruences, a shallow, artificial harmony of this sort would never be able to counterbalance even for minutes the widely based collective organizations that exercise a disintegrating effect on the people of our time, by using power of a very different kind'. It was in Hanns Eisler that Brecht now found the composer most congenial to him. Quite logically their first joint work *The Measure Adopted (Die Massnahme)* was rejected by the artistic leaders of the 'New Music'. *The Measure Adopted* was to have been performed in the summer of 1930 in Berlin, as part of the music festival. Some weeks

142

before this Heinrich Burkhard, Paul Hindemith and Georg Schünemann invited their colleagues Brecht and Eisler to show the text of their didactic play to a programme committee 'in order to allay political doubts'. They both refused and proposed that performances given under the auspices of the 'New Music' should be freed from dependence on anyone and anything and be given by those 'for whom they are intended and who alone have any use for them, by workers' choirs, groups of amateur actors, school choirs and school orchestras, that is by those who neither pay for art nor are paid for art but who want to practise art'.

12

Study of Marxism

> Lichtenberg says: 'What convinces a man is
> not important. What is important is what his
> convictions make of him'. In Brecht this
> 'what' is 'attitude'. This is new, and the
> newest thing about it is that it can be learned.
> WALTER BENJAMIN

In the early days of his interest in Marxism Brecht concentrated on
grappling with Marxist theory. His teacher and chief adviser was
Fritz Sternberg. In 1929 his friendship with Karl Korsch and
Hermann Duncker brought him into contact with workers, trade
unionists and representatives of the Communist Party. Thanks to
the success of *The Threepenny Opera* he was financially in a
position to pursue his studies more intensively and more
fundamentally. If one wanted to gain a 'halfway complete
knowledge of Marxism', it involved considerable expense.
Courses and discussions alone were not sufficient. One had to
acquire a large number of books and subscribe to the leading
specialist journals. Brecht, for instance, bought the complete
issues of *Neue Zeit,* which he found indispensable as working
material and which later became a great attraction of his library in
Svendborg.

In those days there were also cheap editions of the most
important writings of Marx and Engels, as well as other
introductory pamphlets to Marxism; Brecht ordered several
copies of these at a time and used them to form a small reference
library. He showed them to every writer who went to him to ask for
an opinion on his plays. If the visitor did not already know the
books, he was given them as a present and told they were essential
reading: 'If, after reading them, you stand by your play, come
back'. His studies not only took up a great deal of his time, they
were also, from the standpoint of bourgeois society, bad for

business; the didactic plays brought him in almost nothing and, as a communist, the author had to expect to be victimized. The group of didactic plays was the result of Brecht's learning process. The constant revisions and alterations tell us a good deal about his method of grappling with the writings of the Marxist classics. The plays were not of a kind to popularize the communist doctrine among outsiders; they were attempts on the part of a student of Marxism to explain the subject to himself, and could only be of benefit to other students grappling with it. Brecht examined several themes simultaneously, and these then contributed to the formal concept of the plays. What seemed important to him was to work out new modes of social behaviour, to demonstrate a communist ethic that incorporated a new historic and humane quality. 'We derive our morality from the interests of the proletarian class struggle.'

The school opera *He Who Says Yes (Der Jasager)* was first performed in the summer of 1930 at the Zentralinstitut für Erziehung und Unterricht in Berlin. When Brecht and Weill returned from the South of France, where they had spent their summer holiday together, they were astonished at the extraordinary success of their didactic play based on the Noh play Taniko, by Seami's son-in-law Zenchiku, which Elisabeth Hauptmann had translated from the English. The little play dealt with the problems of socially right and wrong acquiescence. A boy attaches himself to an expedition led by his teacher in order to get medicine and instructions for his sick mother 'from the great physicians in the city beyond the mountains'. On the way the boy also falls ill. An ancient custom ordains that anyone who falls ill on such a journey must be thrown into the valley below. But the person concerned has to acquiesce in this. The boy, as required 'by custom', does so and is killed; the other members of the expedition continue their journey.

The 'custom' theme of the original had been secularized by Brecht. In consequence of this the idea behind the play had been falsified and made reactionary; its message sounded unpleasantly authoritarian. The 'acquiesence' intended by Brecht was of a different kind. He was rather horrified by the curious interest in the work and the approval given to it, especially by the church. Walter Dirks, for example, hailed the school opera as a 'sermon', and spoke of a 'fundamentally moral law' being taken into account, and of God's voice 'which has to be listened to and freely obeyed'. In view of this Brecht asked his friends at the Karl-Marx-School in Neukölln, both teachers and pupils, to rehearse the work and study the effect of both play and performance on the school audience. The report he received persuaded him to write a new version of *He Who Says Yes*. In this the boy's mother is ill as the result of an epidemic which has struck the whole town. The teacher's expedition to the city beyond the mountains, which the boy joins, is being undertaken in order to fight the epidemic. When the boy falls ill the members of the expedition decide to ask him if he will acquiesce in their killing him, because the whole town is waiting for the medicine. he answers 'yes', not in obedience to 'custom' but in obedience to 'necessity'. In addition Brecht then wrote *He Who says No (Der Neinsager)* to supplement it, and directed that 'if possible the two little plays should not be performed separately'. In *He Who Says No* the boy no longer acquiesces in the custom: 'To say A does not mean one must say B'. His intention to fetch medicine for his sick mother has been invalidated by his own illness. He asks for a new custom to be introduced: that one should think anew in every new situation. There need be no hurry to learn it. The negative answer refers to the situation, and the way the question is put, in the first version of *He Who Says Yes*. The second version and *He Who Says No* are intended to supplement each other; the boy's 'no' does not refute his 'yes' in the other play, it justifies it.

But it was in *The Measure Adopted* that Brecht, assisted by Hanns Eisler and Slatan Dudov, really stated the problem of 'acquiescence' in concrete terms. The play invites discussion of a 'measure' adopted by three Communist Party agitators who had been given the task of preparing the revolution in China. They have killed a young comrade, who joined them, because his behaviour prevented them working successfully for the party and endangered the movement. The young comrade acquiesced in his execution in order to further the advance of the proletarian masses. He responded 'in accordance with reality'. Finally the chorus of controllers also acquiesces in what the agitators did; their measure is approved.

The Communist Party representatives, who attended the first performance at the Berlin Grosses Schauspielhaus on 10 December 1930, did not much like the play. In the main it was seen as a commentary on Bolshevist practice, which only played into the hands of the bourgeois campaign against the terror and the inhumanity of the Bolsheviks. It was also criticized for being insufficiently explicit historically and for posing questions in too abstract a way. Brecht was expected to dramatize revolutionary events and experiences. Because of the way he worked, however, he saw no contradiction between grasping reality poetically and understanding it intellectually. One did not become a party worker, he claimed, through a passionate belief in the working class but by acquiring political knowledge and assimilating the teachings of the Marxist classics. In *The Measure Adopted* Brecht attempted to translate essential points in Lenin's ideas to the stage. He had no instinct whatever for abstract truths. He regarded Lenin's postulate, 'truth is always concrete', as a fundamental dialectical principle.

And those critics who conclude that Brecht's intention was merely to advocate party discipline overlook the play's Marxist statement of the question. Acquiescence cannot simply be equated with party discipline. The young comrade is not punished for his mistakes. He is removed from sight because he has jeopardized the agitators' task and put their lives at risk by underestimating the dangers of unlawful activity and failing to learn by his mistakes. He must not be seen because the police know him. Since his comrades-in-arms cannot spirit him out of the town, they decide to kill him. Force and terror, according to this, are permissable as a consequence of revolutionary work designed to change the capitalist world into a humane one, but not as a justification for doubtful decisions on the part of a central committee. *The Measure Adopted* is not a premature key-play to the Moscow trials.

Criticisms from the left forced Brecht and his collaborators to make the play's theme still clearer. In the second version the reasons for the young comrade's failure are different, his guilt is made more obvious. Whereas, for example, in the first version his task is simply to spread communist propaganda among the men who haul the rice boats, in the second it is to induce these men to demand shoes with wooden skids to facilitate their work. The young comrade's 'mistake' no longer consists only in putting stones under the coolies feet because he is sorry for them; his pity also means that the agitation, which was so successful at first, is ineffective. Instead of encouraging the coolies to refuse to work, he

147

helps them; and when he reminds them to demand more practical shoes, they no longer see the need for them, because the result has been the same. The overseer is once more in command; the downtrodden coolies even obey his order to drive the 'fool' away. The young comrade makes a further mistake when distributing leaflets outside the gates of a textile factory. When a worker is wrongly arrested for distributing the leaflets, the young comrade intervenes, the policeman kills the worker and is then disarmed by the other workers. 'As a result the textile workers went on strike, but the coolies' organization demanded that the policeman be punished, which he was; the strike, however, was interrupted for a long time and the guards in the factories were reinforced.' The spontaneous strike, triggered off by the young comrade's sense of justice, merely diverted attention from the economic and political demands. Alfred Kurella declared that Brecht's line of argument was 'right wing opportunism': the agitators should have continued to provoke the textile-workers' strike by revolutionary means instead of allowing it to be throttled by the reformative attitude of the coolies' organization. In the altered version the strike in the factory is already in progress. The workers involved in the incident with the policeman are strike breakers. The young comrade's task is to effect solidarity among the workers. His sense of justice, however, leads him to call one of the strike-breakers a 'corrupt swine'. His behaviour is a blow to solidarity. While it is true that in the second version Brecht clarified the situation, the question of 'spontaneity' is put in a much more extreme form in the first version.

Although he was so alive to critical comments and constructive suggestions, Brecht adhered to the didactic character of his experimental plays; at the same time he warned people against finding prescriptions for political action in a play like *The Measure Adopted* 'without a knowledge of the A B C of dialectical materialism'.

Fritz Sternberg, who at the end of the nineteen-twenties was much more dogmatically inclined politically than Brecht, later accused his pupil of being uncritical in his championship of the aims of the German Communist Party. But Brecht was never a party man; he was uncompromising in his insistence on political independence and also refused to take any part in the petty feuds of left-wing communist groups. He was just as loyal and just as critical towards the Communist Party as he was towards men of learning and officials who had been expelled from the party for their deviationist views. Brecht appraised each individual's performance in the class struggle and made use of his knowledge. He did not become a communist because, after his somewhat anarchistic past, he 'felt a desire or need to be identified with something', but because he found that Marxist–Leninist theory introduced a new quality into his work as a writer. The social struggles of which Brecht was a sympathetic observer, hastened this process and shaped his social awareness.

Of the experiences that caused the playwright to turn communist, the most enduring were the events of 1 May 1929, which he saw from the window of Fritz Sternberg's apartment in the immediate vicinity of Karl–Liebknecht–Haus, the Berlin headquarters of the German Communist Party. Zörgiebel, the Social Democrat chief of police, had forbidden any public demonstrations on this particular day. It was not the first time the Social Democrats had supported the employers' cause. As the workers had no intention of letting themselves be deprived of their right to demonstrate, there were serious clashes with the police, who finally opened fire on the workers. Brecht saw people mortally wounded. In the afternoon he drove with Sternberg, in his Steyr motorcar, to a number of places where protest actions were expected. Not being 'riff-raff' they were treated politely by the police, who told them of the traffic diversions. Whole streets had been closed to traffic and taken over by the police. Brecht's attitude in the years that followed was deeply affected by the battles waged on that day and by the treatment of the workers as riff-raff. He blamed the Social Democrats' disastrous policy of expediency for what happened on 1 May 1929. Noske had been responsible for the deaths of Rosa Luxemburg and Karl Liebknecht, Zörgiebel for the murder of thirty-five workers. Anti-Communism had been shown to be an integral part of Social Democrat policy, and a contributory cause of the breakdown of democracy. It was very clear to Brecht that, if the worst came to the worst, the Social Democrats would be prepared to join forces with the National Socialists but would never agree to form a united front with the combined labour parties, as the Communists proposed. Further events confirmed this view. The speech made by Otto Wels, leader of the Social Democrats, in the Reichstag on 21 March 1933, when the

government's Enabling Act was debated, was not 'the only worthy
farewell of dying democracy' to which party historians since 1945
have elevated it; it was an indication that his party had decided,
under certain conditions, to conform to the system and cooperate
loyally with it. The Nazis rejected the offer contemptuously,
Hitler retorting: 'Nor do I want you to vote for the Enabling Act.
Germany must be free, but not thanks to you!'

The victory of National Socialism was made easier by the fact
that the Social Democrats and Communists were engaged in such
bitter quarrels among themselves. The result of these disputes was
that the petite bourgeoisie and a large part of the proletarian
masses went over to fascism. Brecht now seized every opportunity
to draw attention to the contemptible role played by the Social
Democrat Party in the rise of fascism. After he had emigrated he
sketched this portrait of Friedrich Ebert, the first president of the
Weimar Republic, in his *War Primer (Kriegsfibel)*:

> Ich bin der Sattler, der dem Junkerpack
> Von neuem in den Sattel half. Ich Sau
> Liess mich von ihnen kaufen, noch im Sack
> Des Armen Groschen. Gabs für mich kein Tau?

(I am the saddler who helped the Junkers into the saddle again. Swine
that I am, I let myself be bought by them, with the pennies of the poor
still in my pocket. Was there no rope for me?)

Out of consideration for Ebert's son, who had become chief
burgomaster of East Berlin and a member of the Socialist Unity
Party, the photograph of the Social Democrat German president
and the above quatrain were deleted from the manuscript; as this
was also politically inopportune for other reasons it could not be
published until 1955. 'It is not enough for the middle classes and
the proletariat to use political means to extract advantages for
themselves, unless production as a whole is reorganized. Socialism
is not a question of distributing, but of producing, goods.' Brecht
the Marxist rejected socialism in the form of a Social Democrat
welfare state. Although he supported the anti-fascist policy of the
United Front, he did not want to relinquish free discussion of the
political antagonisms between the Communists and the Social
Democrats which, of course, still continued to exist. This was his

150

position before 1933 and during his years of exile; even Ullbricht's post-war policy of forming blocks did not make him change his opinion. Brecht had no leanings towards revisionism.

13

Saint Joan of the Stockyards

The didactic plays were written more for a theatre of the future in a Socialist state, where the audience were to be no longer merely spectators but active participators. For the present these texts were of use mainly to the actors, who studied them for their own benefit; their effect on the outside world was revolutionary only in so far as the bourgeois state showed no interest in sponsoring the performance of such exercises. Side by side with the didactic plays Brecht was working at the big dramatic form which he considered essential if the crucial subjects of the day were to be presented in the theatre. This new form of drama had to be adequate to the 'enormity' of present-day subject-matter. In all the dramatic plans he worked out in this connection he sought a way of tracing the supposedly impenetrable laws of capitalism back to simple economic antecedents. As a model he had in mind the battles on the wheat exchange or the exchange operations of the meat kings in Chicago. In the course of his roundabout attempts to clarify Marxist theory and economic processes there finally emerged, out of the material for various projected plays, the play *St. Joan of the Stockyards*. The immediate stimulus was the effect of the world economic crisis, which had been sparked off by the crash on the New York stock exchange in October 1929.

The action of St. Joan is made up of the threads of three stories: the story of the Salvation Army lieutenant Joan Dark, the story of the meat king Mauler, and the story of the workers in the Chicago stockyards. The three stories, actuated by the same contradictions, are related to the classic periodicity of the trade cycle spoken of by Marx in *Das Kapital*. The underlying idea of Marx's work, 'to reveal the economic law of movement of modern society', is the common denominator of what originally were three different, simultaneously developed, projects for plays. The oldest of these is the outline of a play about the squalid life and death of a worker in

152

the jungle of a big city, based on Upton Sinclair's novel *The Jungle*. The path followed by Jurgis Rudkus, 'who is starved to death in the stockyards of Chicago', is already clearly recognizable in the relationship between Garga and his family in the early versions of *In the Jungle of the Cities*.

Sinclair had drawn attention to the appalling state of affairs in the stockyards which made it possible for a worker to have an accident, disappear into one of the boiling vats and be turned into lard. One of the chief consequences of the novel in America was that the laws governing the control of food were made more stringent, and there was a temporary fall in the demand for meat. Because the reader's attention was drawn more to the scandalous conditions under which meat was processed than to the fight against the capitalist exploiters, Lenin called the author 'a sentimental socialist without theoretical training'. While Brecht found many references to the machinations of monopolists, trusts and cartels in Sinclair, he found nothing about the backgrounds and causes of the economic upswings and crises. All that emerged from the novel and from *The Money Changers,* another book by Sinclair, was that in those days the stock exchanges occupied a key position in capitalistic production. The state of the labour market also seemed to be determined by stock market transactions. On this point he learned from his reading of Marx that 'expansion and contraction of capital' controlled the demand and supply of labour.

The second group of dramatic projects dealt with the rise and fall of a hero of the Chicago exchange. Biographies of key figures in the world of American high finance gave Brecht the idea of writing an ideological play on strictly classical lines in which industrialists like Vanderbilt, Pierpont Morgan or Carnegie would appear as the Macbeths or Hamlets of the wheat exchange, who do evil in order that good may come of it. Thus Joe Fleischhacker, a crafty profiteer and passionate philanthropist, was planned as a type of industrialist whose presence serves to stress the fact that the historical process is sustained by effective individuals, as it is in Shakespeare.

One of the favourite targets of industrial philanthropy was the Salvation Army. As this sounded suspiciously like combining business with religion, Elisabeth Hauptmann undertook to collect the necessary material on the origin, financial sources and structure of the Salvation Army. In this way there came into

153

existence a third play-complex containing the character of a woman lieutenant in the Salvation Army called Marie Andersen; her name was later changed to Lilian Holiday. Elisabeth Hauptmann paid repeated visits to Salvation Army homes, soup kitchens and recruiting centres in Berlin in order to study its religious practices and methods. A photograph taken by Carl Koch, which showed her in Salvation Army uniform and was published in *Uhu* to illustrate her story 'Bessie Soundso', led some of her friends to suspect that she herself was a member of that organization; others said maliciously that Brecht had snatched her from the claws of the Salvation Army.

The main outcome of these enquiries into the world-wide organization, which celebrated the centenary of its foundation in 1929, was the observation that its emissaries gave the 'little people' suffering from hunger and cold not only soup, but a sense of security and emotional values, which acted as a deterrent to political awareness and political protests. The powerful army of fanatical soldiers of God was supported by little Rockefellers in every country. It was a case of a firm doing good business with religion. What more obvious than to transfer this species of criminality in high places to the milieu of rogues and crooks. In *Happy End* Brecht and his collaborators had wasted the Salvation Army theme in a merely amusing, superficially aggressive way. And so now, side by side with the resumption of work on current projects like *The Fall of the Egoist Johann Fatzer (Fatzer)* and *Joe Fleischhacker,* the role of the Salvation Army as a supporter of big business in the social struggle was to be presented once more in a new play *The Bread Shop (Der Brotladen);* at its centre was to be the great unemployment crisis of 1929.

In the battle for the bread shops, into which the newspaper-boy Washington Meyer leads the unemployed workers and in which he loses his life, the woman Salvationist Lieutenant Hippler is on the side of the baker who owns them. The religious organization comes to an agreement with the exploiter over the appropriation of wood which rightfully belongs to the widow Queck. The latter, however, submits loyally to the injustice so that, at her death, she may be 'transfigured'. Washington Meyer talks and behaves throughout like a St. John of the Berlin backyards.

Happy End was the immediate forerunner of *The Bread Shop,* and this in turn found its consummation in *St. Joan of the*

Stockyards. Joan Dark, the St. Joan of the title of the play, which was started during this same year of 1929, arose out of a combination of Lilian Holiday and Washington Meyer. In order to give the character more weight Brecht had the idea of modelling her on the peasant St. Joan. It soon became clear that a gangster boss like Bill Cracker in *Happy End* was no longer a suitable character to offset such a champion of the faith. If the historical St. Joan could convince the heir to the French throne, a modern capitalist tycoon might be a suitable target for her missionary zeal. The Chicago stockyards suggested themselves as an admirable field of operation for the Salvation Army. Joan's dauphin was given the name John Pierpont Mauler, whose stock exchange transactions she unwittingly assisted by trying to bring the classes closer together, because she had more faith in God than in revolutionary force.

In a time of great confusion and 'bloody disarray', Joan Dark and her sisters, the 'black boaters', resolve to take up the fight against distress and misery and once again establish God in a world that resembles a slaughter-house. The credulous girl finds herself in trouble because she asks 'thoughtless' questions. The out-of-work men in the stockyards tell her that Mauler is the key figure and the cause of their distress. She therefore goes to see the tycoon and appeals to his humanity. Mauler's heart is softened and he does what the girl asks. But the plight of the starving men does not change. The argument that the poor are 'base' no longer weighs with Joan, who realizes that something must be done about the poverty of the poor. She does not realize that she is being subtly taken in by Mauler. The truth is that her requests are granted because they always correspond exactly to the instructions of his economic advisers. In this way the saint of the stockyards gives Mauler moral backing for his speculations on the stock exchange; she casts a veil over his crimes. In time she sees through the deceit and refuses Mauler's offer of good pay to continue beating the drums for him. She now no longer wants to work for God but for the poor. But she continues to believe that Mauler is approachable as a person; at the critical moment she has more faith in his goodness than in the corporate resistance of the exploited: 'Nothing done by force can be good'. She fails to pass on to every firm in Chicago a letter advising the masses of the forthcoming general strike. Only a section of the workers learns of the strike, and the police are able to disperse this section by the use of force. Joan, who left when 'the snow really began to fall', returns too late to the defeated workers and sinks to the ground exhausted in the driving snow. 'She's not one of us', the workers declare, 'leave her where she is till the soldiers come, they will take her away.'

The police take the homeless girl to the 'black boaters', where the employers are celebrating the return of peace and order. Joan is the very person they want to see: 'We will do her proud, because she has helped us over these difficult weeks by her humane influence in the stockyards, by interceding on behalf of the poor, and even by what she said against us. She shall be our St. Joan of the stockyards'. The dying girl cannot prevent her canonization, her protests are drowned by the acclamations of the butchers and cattle breeders. Finally she realizes that her kindness was fruitless, that where force reigns only force can help, and that 'where human beings are, only human beings can help'. The worst that can be said of a person, she declares, is that he did nothing to change the world: 'make certain, in leaving the world, not merely that you were good, but that you are leaving a good world'.

The structure of the play follows the phases of the recurrent cycle which, according to Marx, runs through modern industry: scenes 1–4 denote the end of prosperity, scenes 5–8 illustrate overproduction, scene 9 presents the crisis, scenes 10 and 11 correspond to stagnation. In the final apotheosis (scene 12) the restoration of the cycle is acclaimed and its conformity with natural law confirmed by the capitalists. Each phase is introduced by a letter, containing economic advice, that Mauler has received from friends in New York. These messages, which spark off the 'movement', contrast with the letter Joan fails to pass on. A successful general strike would have brought about a radical change, the mechanism of the capitalist reproductive process would have been disrupted. The failure of the general strike enables the stockyard bosses to overcome the crisis into which they had been plunged by Mauler's greed for gain. Through wastage of the factors of production—cattle are destroyed to keep prices up— the balance between production capacity and consumption capacity is restored.

If the central points of the story correspond to the phases of the trade cycle, seen in terms of its content it is essentially a counterpart to Schiller's romantic tragedy *Die Jungfrau von*

Orleans (The Maid of Orleans). Starting from his thesis that classical dramatic art and verse forms are incompatible with the complexity of modern subject-matter, Brecht still makes it possible to present the world economic crisis on the stage and to speak of money in iambics. He uses quotations and situations from Schiller 'for the purpose of parodic contrast'. He disposes of classical drama by complying with it. Joan's apotheosis at the hands of the capitalists not only parodies Schiller, it also parodies Faust's deliverance as presented by Goethe at the end of his tragedy. For *St. Joan of the Stockyards* is intended to show 'Faustian man as he is today'. Brecht offers a picture of what the bourgeoisie alone is still prepared to understand by self-realization: successful business management. Mauler is not a 'mere incarnation of capital', he corresponds perfectly to Marx's description of the modernized capitalist, who begins to feel a 'human compassion' for his own Adam and therefore experiences a Faustian conflict 'between the urge to amass and the urge to enjoy'.

Schiller's Joan wants to save France; it does not occur to her that the main result of her victory will be to ensure the king's authority. Her sacrifice finds its fulfilment in transfiguration. Her good will is the decisive factor; the power structure is unimportant. But Joan Dark does not attain her goal. By nature a good person, like the peasant girl from Lorraine, she wants to help the poor. She believes in human goodness. She succeeds in persuading Mauler, the king of the stockyards, to do good deeds, but these, as she finds out too late, benefit only himself. Her goodness does not help the sufferers, on the contrary it weakens still further their position in the fight against their oppressors. Joan Dark's victories fail to change the world. Brecht does not accept Schiller's formula for the good man (which derives from Kant), and so contradicts the classically idealistic view of humanity. Goodness alone is not enough; it is more important to leave behind one a good world:

> Ich zum Beispiel habe nichts getan
> Denn nichts werde gezählt als gut, und sehe
>   es aus wie immer, als was
> Wirklich hilft, und nichts gelte als ehrenhaft
>   mehr, als was
> Diese Welt engültig ändert: sie braucht es.

157

(I, for instance, have done nothing. For nothing will be counted good, good though it may seem, unless it truly helps, and nothing any longer honourable unless it changes this world conclusively—for that's what this world needs.)

Work on the play, in which in addition to Elisabeth Hauptmann and Emil Burri the main collaborator was the teacher Hans Borchardt, was completed in the autumn of 1931. During the months that followed the publisher Felix Bloch-Erben tried in vain to find a theatre that would take *St. Joan of the Stockyards*. Gustaf Gründgens considered putting it on at the Komödienhaus Rotter in Berlin; Piscator had a plan to produce Brecht's play and a dramatized version of Theodore Dreiser's *An American Tragedy* one after the other 'at the same theatre and with the same company'. At the end of 1932 Berthold Viertel had talks in Vienna about a production with Carola Neher and Peter Lorre, that was later to tour Germany; in January 1933 Heinz Hilpert announced a performance at the Deutsches Theater in Berlin, with Eugen Klöpfer as Mauler. Finally it was reported that the Hessisches Landestheater in Darmstadt planned to give the play its first performance, on the advice of the 'typical Jew' Kurt Hirschfeld, as the press put it. A few days later permission for it was refused by the municipal council. German theatre managers, under threat of constant reductions in their subsidies, feared for their jobs; by this time the charge of encouraging 'Kulturbolschewismus' could have serious consequences. Thus the hour-long wireless version, which Brecht had compiled for Alfred Braun's 'hour' on the Berlin wireless, remained the only public presentation of *St. Joan of the Stockyards*. The performance was introduced by Herbert Ihering in these words: 'The day will come when it will be counted one of the most memorable, but most inglorious, features of the cultural history of our time that the theatre was forced to abandon to the wireless the communication of one of the greatest and most important plays of this era'.

Gustaf Gründgens, who in 1959 eventually staged the play for the first time, was also the first German director to whom Brecht offered *St. Joan* after his return from exile: 'In 1932 you asked permission to stage *St. Joan of the Stockyards*. My answer is Yes'. Gründgens wired back: 'Scared to death by letter, but delighted you still remember. Please let me have book by return'. In the spring of 1949 Kurt Hirschfeld, who was in Zurich, endeavoured to realize Brecht's plan for Gründgens, who found the play 'as magnificent as ever' and wanted to cast Fritz Kortner for the part of Mauler, as he had in 1932. Shortly afterwards he asked Kortner to see the project through with him 'despite all past beastliness': 'I have a certain desire to see the symbolic side of the play, and would be happy if we could make good our failure of those days. It would be in the nature of a triumph of the spirit over the times'. Kortner, however, was not prepared to make this gesture of reconciliation out of hand, and probably also discouraged Brecht, who was not over-scrupulous in such matters, from persuading Gründgens to cast someone else as Mauler.

14

In Praise of Dialectics

In the struggle for power the proletariat has
no other weapon than organization.   LENIN.

Communism, for Brecht, was not a confession of faith. He had
made the proletariat's cause his own, but he continued to regard
himself as a bourgeois poet. At first he made no attempt whatever
to merge with the proletariat: 'If intellectuals want to take part in
the class struggle, they must grasp intellectually that their
sociological constitution is homogeneous and determined by
material conditions'. The dominant idea of his literary work was to
show the method of dialectical materialism in action and to present
the world as susceptible to change. He saw himself as a 'Leninist of
the footlights', the name given to him later by Ernst Bloch. The
bourgeois literary world offered Brecht no platform for his literary
interests, and even an association like the 'Bund proletarisch-
revolutionärer Schriftsteller' (Federation of Revolutionary Proletarian Writers) seemed to him no more than a sorry left-wing
species of outworn organization. Conversely the spokesman of the
Federation accused Brecht of seeking to eliminate all 'emotional
factors' with his theory of the 'epic theatre': 'Our concept of the
world is not the result of knowledge alone but of experience as
well'. But Brecht had no intention of waging war against the
emotions; all he, unlike the traditional theatre, wanted was to
subject them to critical examination.

   Before he could even think of writing a 'eulogy' of the
Communist Party, Brecht needed to acquire the information and
technical knowledge necessary to enable him to understand and
analyze social processes. He refused to treat revolution or the
Soviet Union as if they were set subjects for a literary exercise. His
own interest in the 'experiment' of the Soviet Union began at a
time when the first 'sentimental' communists were withdrawing

again in disgust. It was the writer Sergei Tretyakov who, after Asja Lacis, did more than anyone to awaken Brecht's interest in the new social and literary problems facing the land of the October Revolution.

He first came into contact with Tretyakov when the latter's play *Scream, China!* was performed during Meyerhold's guest appearance in Berlin in the spring of 1930. The two men discovered that they held very similar ideas on the social function of the theatre. Whereas the German dramatic critics, together with most devotees of proletarian art, found that this play, too, failed as an 'experience', Brecht hailed Meyerhold's production as an attempt at 'a great and more rational theatre', which was to be seen as the outcome of many discussions. Early in 1931 Tretjakov visited Berlin again in order to talk with German intellectuals about his 'factographic' method of writing and his experiences in a socialist village. It was at this time, too, that his report on the struggle for a collective economy was published by Malik under the title *Field Captains*. Tretyakov's materials were documents, facts and interviews, whose tendentious literary treatment was intended not only to provide information about reality but also to contribute towards changing this reality. Walter Benjamin, who like Brecht was interested in the experimental approach, took part in the Berlin talks with Tretyakov and later referred to him, in his essay 'Der Autor als Produzent', as an example of a writer who had subjected to revision the breach between reader and author because he knew that the political intent, 'no matter how revolutionary it may seem, will act in a counter-revolutionary way so long as the writer's solidarity with the proletariat is simply a matter of conviction and has not been experienced by him as producer'. Characteristically Georg Lukács, the orthodox Marxist literary scholar, was violently opposed to Tretyakov and, in a review of Ernst Ottwalt's journalistic novels, questioned whether artistic totality could be attained if the relationship between fact and intention was treated in this way. The poet Gottfried Benn was still more emphatic in his hostility to the 'inner emptiness of this Tretyakov presentation', to a new collective literature that sought to organize life and not art. To Benn to be an artist meant 'to exclude life, to constrict it, and actually to fight it, in order to give it form'. Akin to Lukács in many ways, Benn wanted to adhere to the traditional definition of art because he saw its purpose as simply to describe the world and to reflect on it; in other words he was prepared to see it only with the eyes of the consumer. Tretyakov, on the other hand, insisted that people and things should be seen with the eyes of the producer. As an 'operational' writer his mission, as Benjamin explained, was 'not to report but to fight; not to play the onlooker but actively to intervene'.

Brecht was also determined to intervene in his capacity as artist. He did this in various ways and made use of any opportunity that came his way to play an effective part, without regard to quarrels over political policy or stubborn theoretical squabbles. Discussions over matters of principle counted for nothing with Brecht; he had friends and dependable comrades-in-arms in all the left-wing groups. The production of *The Measure Adopted* led to the film project *Kuhle Wampe*. The experience gained from the didactic plays was transferred to the medium of the cinema. In order to ensure that their script was treated in accordance with their intentions Brecht, Slatan Dudov, Hanns Eisler and Ernst Ottwalt decided not to make the film on a purely commercial basis. They obtained a contract that made them authors in the legal sense: 'This cost us our title to the usual fixed payment, but it gave us otherwise unobtainable freedom in our work. . . . Obviously the organization of the work gave us much more trouble than the (artistic) work itself, which meant that we came more and more to see the organization as an integral part of the artistic work'. The film was also, and not least, intended to provide an answer to a practice from which Brecht had suffered during the filming of his *Threepenny Opera* script and against which he had unsuccessfully tried to take legal action. This time the production manager was the lawyer Georg Höllering; his task was to allay the doubts of the firms which were extending credit, and to pilot the politically explosive undertaking through the censorship jungle. *Kuhle Wampe* was to remain the only film in which Brecht succeeded in carrying out his ideas in every phase of the work. It was also the only communist film to be made in Germany. It took almost a year to make, owing to the enormous difficulties involved in obtaining the necessary funds in a country in which fascism was constantly gaining ground and unemployment was on the increase. When the film was completed, in the spring of 1932, it was immediately banned by the censor. Protests and outcries in the press, in so far as this was still democratic in outlook, finally obtained its release.

The communist critics again had reservations about this film, although they described the work of the artists' collective as basically 'valuable' and 'capable of development'. The cause of the shortcomings was 'a certain ignorance of the proletariat, which will never be overcome by theoretical study, however assiduous, on its own, but only if this is accompanied by revolutionary practice'. While this criticism was again aimed chiefly at the 'coldness' of the method used by the artists, the objections to the film on the grounds that its radical approach was too idealized touched on its essential weakness: the harsh contrast between older workers, persisting in their petit bourgeois way of life, and young proletarian sports enthusiasts was politically unsound, even though the authors intended it simply as a means of delineating social democrat and communist behaviour. The argument underlying this contrast was really aimed at the languid acceptance of the 'jungle' by certain classes of worker, at the strange effect ownership has on the poor, who give up all thought of revolution the moment they come into possession of an allotment garden or a small pension.

During the shooting of the film the team of Brecht, Dudov and Eisler became involved in another project, which permitted a more distinctive treatment of the questions of class consciousness and joint action. The dramaturg Günther Stark and the writer Günther Weisenborn had been commissioned by the Volksbühne to adapt Gorki's novel *The Mother* for the stage. Weisenborn submitted their adaptation to Brecht, with the result that a completely fresh start was made. This meant that the project was finished as far as the Volksbühne was concerned, because a play by Brecht was no longer politically acceptable there. Another plan for this theatrical venture, an adaptation of *Measure for Measure* which Ludwig Berger wanted to produce in conjunction with Brecht, had just been turned down because Brecht had started to construct an entirely new plot. Only the 'young' Volksbühne, which at that time arranged numerous evenings of recitations and songs, with Brecht, Eisler, Ernst Busch and Helene Weigel, still showed any real interest in getting these works performed. A collective, consisting of a 'group of young actors' who had taken part in *Kuhle Wampe,* was particularly interested in *The Mother.* The 'young' Volksbühne and Ernst Josef Aufricht, who was staging the Berlin production of the opera *Rise and Fall of the Town of Mahagonny*, shared the production costs.

Stark and Weisenborn had reduced all the political details of Gorki's novel to a purely human plane. Brecht was attracted mainly by the character of a worker's mother and her part in the class struggle. Initially he was not in the least interested in presenting the specifically Russian aspects; what he planned was much more in the nature of a 'domestic drama', which would make the political patterns of behaviour practicable for the audience. He took the story up to the victory of the working-class in the October Revolution of 1917. Once again he used reformism and the threat of war to point the differences between the policies of the Communists and the Social Democrats. He presented Pelagea Vlassova as doubly exploited, because she is both a worker and a wife and mother. The theme of the enquiry enacted on the stage was the question whether the social function of the mother, which determines the continuance of the family to the extent that she produces the offspring, can become a revolutionary one, and how. Brecht regarded the adaptation, to quote Walter Benjamin's words after the performance, as 'a sociological experiment in revolutionizing the mother'.

Communist criticisms of the performance, which was the most important theatrical event of the winter 1931/32, were similar to those levelled at the didactic plays: the social content was given abstract emphasis, no experience was communicated to the audience. In Gorki, they said, Marxist theory was not didactically independent as it was in Brecht; the political aspect was inherent in Gorki's characters, whereas Brecht offered scholarly and political digressions; the struggle of the proletariat could only be presented from personal experience. The aesthetic debate had revealed curious vestiges of the spontaneity theory, long since proscribed in the realm of politics. To the advocate of spontaneity socialistic awareness was the necessary and direct consequence of the proletarian class struggle; Kautsky, on the other hand, claimed that socialistic awareness could only be introduced into the labour movement from outside: 'Modern socialistic awareness can only come into existence as the result of profound study and insight . . . . Socialistic awareness, therefore, is something introduced into the class struggle of the proletariat from without, it is not generated from within'. Lenin took up these reflections of Kautsky's in *What is to be Done?:* 'Without revolutionary theory there is no revolutionary movement'. For him the spontaneous element had value and quality only when it represented 'nothing but the embryonic form of awareness'. Finally he gave a reminder that socialism could only become a material force capable of seizing hold of the masses if it were pursued like a science, in other words if it were studied. In *The Mother* Brecht set out to comment in particular on the views of Lenin expressed in *What is to be Done?* and *One Step Forwards, Two Steps Backwards.* Such exercises, he admitted, 'benefit the individual only in so far as they benefit the state, and they only benefit a state that sets out to benefit everyone alike'.

Lenin's demand that one adopt a scholarly, scientific attitude towards Marxism caused Brecht to introduce the evolution of Marxist theory as a permanent stimulus in his development as a writer. Within the Communist Party, however, theory was no longer discussed in relation to practice; there were only expulsion proceedings and polemical statements against theorists who deviated from the views of Party Headquarters in Moscow. The exemplary introductory courses in Marxism by Hermann Duncker, the accepted authority, initiator and most celebrated teacher of the Marxist Workers' Training College, no longer satisfied Brecht. In discussions with some of the trainees at the college his attention was drawn to works by Karl Korsch devoted to reactivating Marxist theory. He was particularly impressed by Korsch's dispute with Kautsky on the subject of the materialistic view of history. With Alfred Döblin he went to lectures by Korsch who also from time to time invited the two writers to talks at his Tempelhof apartment. Brecht supported the specific political interests of the group round Korsch, and the newspaper *Kommunistische Politik,* only in so far as these were aimed at constantly giving a new form to Marxism both as a scientific method and as an expression of the proletarian movement. The didactic play *The Mother,* which for the most part was no longer played to bourgeois audiences but in local halls to audiences of workers, ended with 'In Praise of Dialectics': 'Once a man knows where he stands, what can stop him?' In his talks with Korsch and his friends, Brecht pressed for a new and tractable revolutionary dialectical formula, and suggested for this purpose a 'Dialectical Society'. And so, alongside Korsch's series of lectures on

'Marxism, Living and Dead', a study-group was formed, with Brecht's apartment as meeting-place; those who took part were Elisabeth Hauptmann, Slatan Dudov, the painter and film pioneer Hans Richter and, on Korsch's side, Hanna Kosterlitz, Paul Partos and Heinz Langerhans. Korsch's help was invaluable to Brecht. Nevertheless he reproached his teacher, who had been expelled from the German Communist Party, with having too much faith in the proletariat: 'Sometimes it seems to me that the less he believed in a thing the more he felt bound to do for it'. Brecht criticized the academic perfectionist in Korsch, the absolute side that, in his opinion, prevented him from playing 'an active part' himself. To define dialectics as 'classifying, arranging and seeing the world in such a way that the revolutionary contradictions inherent in it are revealed and intervention becomes possible', did not satisfy Korsch as a working hypothesis, because he also wanted to cut 'the umbilical cord of Leninist ideology', on which Brecht insisted. In his view it was essential to bear in mind that mentally one was 'perpetually in the fight'. Brecht's approach was much more pragmatic; he did not want to cut himself off from the masses for purely ideological reasons. 'And where has one ever heard that the eye simply leaves should its owner make a mistake? Where will it live?' While he agreed with Korsch that, in its dealings with Moscow, the German Communist Party had become utterly spineless, and was, if anything, inhibiting the revolution, it was still, as far as he was concerned, the greatest labour party; he could exert an influence on it and use its organizational platform as an effective outlet for the opportunities at his command.

Brecht was fond of using the word 'teacher'. In doing so nothing was further from his thought than those school teachers who, on the strength of their position and prescience, exercise authority over their pupils, and award or punish them on prescribed lines. Nor did he regard as his teachers specific writers and philosophers whom he admired or especially liked to read, but authors, scholars and friends with whom he collaborated and from whom he not only acquired knowledge but who practised thinking and working as a way of life, and who, like Brecht himself, remained both teachers and pupils, because knowledge is not a fixed quantity, is in constant need of modification, and must always remain 'in a state of flux'. In this sense he counted Lion Feuchtwanger, Karl Valentin, Frank Wedekind, Alfred Döblin, Karl Kraus and Sergei

Tretyakov among his teachers. Helped by Fritz Sternberg, Brecht learned to see in Karl Marx his best possible audience. Karl Korsch then became his 'Marxist teacher'.

The teaching was Marxism, its content dialectics, its practice the class struggle. Brecht was never a registered member of the Communist Party, but as a writer he was its best imaginable teacher and its apt pupil. He served his apprenticeship with the party and, on his side, canvassed for the party as a teacher. 'I came to you as teacher, and as teacher I might have left you. But because I learned I stayed.' He accepted the criticism his plays received at the hands of the party, as long as it was useful to him. What he found hardest to endure were the objections raised by critics sent by the party; but the arguments of an Alfred Kurella or Alfred Durus, as the later versions of *The Method Adopted* show, were scrutinized to see if they were valid. Of much greater value to Brecht were the talks and discussions he had with people with whom he was associated, such as the pupils of the Karl Marx School at Neukölln, and the members of the audience at *The Mother*.

To be both teacher and pupil was the underlying idea of Brecht's work, especially of his theory of the stage. A play was good only when changes improved it. A play, too, had to be a teacher in the Brechtian sense, it had to adapt itself to new ideas. When the Nazis assumed power in February 1933, Brecht was forced to discontinue his attempts to perfect the form of the didactic plays. Now the theatre was once again, though for a shorter period, assigned its duties: it had to enlighten its audiences and stir them emotionally. Brecht had to retreat on two fronts, not only from his position relative to form, but politically as well. The opportunity for an audience to participate in a performance as pupils and teachers no longer existed.

'The development of the German theatre and German drama was brought to a halt by fascism—it had already been obstructed by the last democratic and semi-democratic governments. . . . By then reaction had already gone too far for attempts at camouflage. A stop had already been put to everything that smacked even of artistic advance. We replied with intensified political propaganda. A dramatization of Gorki's novel *The Mother* instructed people to fight illegally, to produce and distribute leaflets, to conspire in prison, to carry on an undercover fight against the ideology of war.

The bourgeois press accorded Helene Weigel, who played the Mother, a place among the greatest German actors for her performance, but the theatre was visited by the police in ever greater numbers until finally she was dragged from the stage and arrested . . . Then fascism came out into the open'.

Brecht was well aware of what he had sacrificed and what he had gained by deciding in favour of Marxism: 'To ally oneself to poverty means impoverishment'. This price was too high for most of his bourgeois colleagues; they wanted to remain poets, not be propagandists. But even left-wing writers and friends, who were not shocked by his partisanship, did not understand his intellectual 'radicality'. The 'jump' from works like *The Threepenny Opera* and *Rise and Fall of the Town of Mahagonny*, whose culinary opulence they repudiated, to the sparse didactic plays was something they could not understand. Only in 1931, when the bourgeois public's enthusiasm for leftist art and political theatre was clearly on the wane, did the unpolitical left notice that the much vaunted freedom of the Weimar Republic was a delusion and that the forces of reaction had not been idle. German nationalist circles now demanded government action against the 'Bolshevist' derision and destruction of the people's most precious possessions. Many artists resigned. Piscator gave up and went to Moscow. Erich Engel switched his attention entirely to harmless film comedies. But the number of those who, like Arnolt Bronnen, deserted to the side of the coming victors was by no means negligible. During his exile Brecht noted: 'I could not tell anyone what to do and others could not either; after an epoch in which everything had moved to the left, but too little, the people were dissatisfied and everything moved to the right, and very far to the right. Then I noticed how my friends now welcomed this epoch and became its friends, because they took it to be the new epoch'.

Brecht did not go the 'usual way'. He was one of those who, to the end, tried to fight the movement to the right. Although in the autumn of 1931 the Berlin police still had no record of any proceedings against him 'in our archives here', as they told Munich in answer to a question, they had known for a long time that Brecht was 'a confirmed communist and as such is also active as a writer on behalf of the German Communist Party'. Once Hitler had been elected *Reichskanzler*, Brecht had every reason to be careful. At the end of February 1933 he had undergone an

168

operation and, luckily for him, was in hospital. On the morning after the *Reichstag* fire, without returning to his apartment, he left Berlin with Helene Weigel and headed for Prague.

PART THREE

Exile

Flight

Brecht knew very well what exile would mean for him: a complete readjustment of his working methods, being cut off from the theatres, his most important means of production, and, in addition, renewed uncertainty as to his financial position which latterly, for the first time, had improved to such an extent that he and his family could live comfortably on the income from his work. His bank accounts were blocked from the day he left, and even the royalties accruing from performances of his plays abroad passed, under the terms of his existing contracts, to his German publishers. Although Brecht had expected the worst, a Nazi dictatorship, the political developments found him unprepared. It was immediately clear to him that he had to go into exile. While his own origins made him an 'Aryan', his wife was Jewish, and this alone would have been sufficient reason for Brecht to leave Germany. Over and above this, however, everything he had written so far had been anti-Nazi. The Nazis hated him, but would certainly have accepted him if, like a good many of his colleagues, he had 'about turned' and declared himself to be in sympathy with the 'new Germany'. Brecht did not leave Germany of his own free will, but because of his political convictions. He was not an emigrant, he was a refugee: 'We are exiles, outlaws. We live uneasily as near the border as we may, awaiting the day of our return'.

That Brecht and his family were able to leave so quickly was due to the many friends who came to their aid, placing money at their disposal and taking care of his manuscripts and working materials. If it could be managed, Brecht wanted to remain in a country bordering on Germany where, being no great linguist, he could easily make himself understood, and where he would have a chance to publish his works. From Berlin the obvious destination was Prague, because the Czechs required no special entry visa and, moreover, the young republic allowed left-wing political and cultural organizations the greatest freedom to pursue their ends. The right of asylum was interpreted generously. But, as was the case in most European countries that offered asylum, the exiles found the economic situation in Czechoslovakia too serious to permit the authorities to issue foreigners with working-permits on any considerable scale. Immigrants had to rely on assistance from Czech friends or the refugee committees.

The Czech writer Franz Carl Weiskopf, who wrote in German and in recent years had lived in Berlin, gave Brecht advice and addresses, and would also have seen that he got the necessary assistance in official quarters. But Prague did not strike Brecht, whose primary concern was to find theatres to stage his works, as a suitable field of operations. The few German language theatres in the city cultivated a non-committal, conservative style of performance, and were also keen to avoid political confrontation. Moreover such German writers and artists as were beginning to gather in Prague did not particularly welcome Brecht. The best thing to do, therefore, seemed to be to go on to Vienna, where Helene Weigel's family lived and big hotel bills could be avoided. In Vienna Brecht found Hanns Eisler, who had just arranged for *The Measure Adopted* to go into rehearsal there, Fritz Sternberg, and Peter Suhrkamp, who was able to give him advice and valuable help in regard to publishers. People no longer cherished any illusions that Nazi rule was a passing affair; nevertheless they hoped to be able to return to Germany again in a matter of months, or in a year or two at the most. At any rate they did not want to give up their apartments there or have their furniture and clothes sent on to them. But although Vienna was an international meeting-place, it was no place to work in; nor could it provide Brecht with the audience he needed. Even Karl Kraus lived there withdrawn and isolated, and when the exiled poet called on him he did not encourage him to prolong his stay. Brecht, as we know from a personal record, regarded Kraus as his main source of help in Austria, and the latter's financial assistance at this time was rewarded by Brecht with a firm attachment such as, owing to his unfortunate political views, many of his followers could no longer give him.

Brecht was not among the inner circle of Kraus's followers, but he was grateful to him and felt bound to him by ties of friendship.

He had a high regard for the authority of this incorruptible critic, who fought as no one else did against stupidity and transgression, against misuse of the language and the decay of the bourgeois culture in every sphere. By his method of reproducing the spoken and printed word unaltered, Kraus subjected everything to question in a highly effective way. Brecht, for his part, saw 'progress' differently: what he wanted to do was not merely to expose 'the degeneration and depravity of civilized man', but also to examine the reasons 'why, given the structure of modern production, man must of necessity arrive at a state in which every new step forward, almost every single invention, must inevitably make human beings more and more inhuman'.

When the Nazis seized power the critic, who for decades had taken a stand against almost indescribable abominations, remained silent; this his admirers found hard to stomach. He could not bring himself to publish *Die dritte Walpurgisnacht,* which he wrote at this time. It was not until 1933 that an issue of his periodical *Die Fackel* appeared, containing a funeral oration for Adolf Loos, and a ten-line poem in which Kraus spoke of experiences that were incommensurable, of the impossibility of giving satiric form to what was happening politically.

> Man frage nicht, was all die Zeit ich machte.
> Ich bleibe stumm;
> und sage nicht, warum.
> Und Stille gibt es, da die Erde krachte.
> Kein Wort, das traf;
> man spricht nur aus dem Schlaf.
> Und träumt von einer Sonne, welche lachte.
> Es geht vorbei;
> nachher war's einerlei.
> Das Wort entschlief, als jene Welt erwachte.

(Do not ask what I was doing all that time. I remained mute; and did not tell you why. And there was silence too, because the earth roared. No word appropriate; one spoke but in one's sleep. And dreamed of a sun that laughed. It passed; and afterwards one did not care. Words took to sleep when that world awoke.)

The emigrant press greeted this poem with bitterness and disgust, opponents with derision. Brecht was one of the few who understood the reason for Kraus's silence; he knew he was the victim of an unease far greater than was 'to be found at all the paper barricades put together'. In a volume of 'voices in celebration of the sixtieth birthday' of the satirist, issued in April 1934, the poet, who meanwhile had fled beneath 'the Danish thatch', published his lines 'On the significance of the ten-line poem in the 888th issue of *Die Fackel*'; in these he exonerated the normally eloquent writer from any blame for his silence: 'When horrors reach a certain pitch, precedents run out. Atrocities proliferate and lamentations are no longer heard. Crime boldly walks the streets and noisily defies description'. The loquacity of left-wing feuilletonists and their indifference to language and grammar persuaded Kraus to take up his pen again. Because his poem had been derided, misunderstood and repeatedly published with a misplaced comma that distorted the meaning, he compiled an issue of *Die Fackel* containing defamatory articles and fictitious obituary notices, together with his appropriate corrections. At the end of July 1934 there appeared a bulky issue, 'Why *Die Fackel* does not appear', in which he inveighed against the 'intellectual riff-raff', against 'all political dabblers starved of anything to write', who went on being convinced of the immortality of the mind and the power of the word over barbarism'. To Kraus, the idea that words could become guns seemed merely an incongruous claim to effectiveness, and the assurance 'you can't kill the mind' to be nothing more than the solace of a phraseology that had 'surrendered power to others'.

From his own standpoint Kraus was right, but he completely misread the political situation. He placed responsibility for the Nazi victory in Germany on the half-hearted, shilly-shallying, opportunist policies of the Social Democrats. Meanwhile he regarded social democracy in Austria as something absurd and on the verge of collapse 'alongside the larger structure of Communism'. Because he had spoken out so strongly against National Socialism the Chancellor, Engelbert Dollfuss, in Kraus's eyes, was the one leading figure who showed courage and seemed determined to resist. But his hope that Dollfuss, like David facing Goliath, could save Austria from Hitler and the *Anschluss* with Germany was based on a false assessment of the policies of the forces of conservatism who, at the time, simply thought they could use the tension between Hitler and Mussolini for their own ends but, in reality, were firmly on the road to fascism. Kraus was incapable of satirizing Dollfuss. The notion that any pact between the Dollfuss Government and the Social Democrats would inevitably break down if Mussolini objected to it he regarded as quite untenable. All the greater, therefore, his indignation at the stubborn attitude of the Social Democrats who, as he saw it, had led the workers in a revolt that was doomed to failure from the start, instead of urging them to resist Nazi Germany at the side of the government.

But the tragedy of what happened in Austria in February 1934 lay precisely in the fact that the party leaders adopted a luke-warm attitude, antagonistic to the interests of the workers, and only decided at the last moment on a general strike and armed resistance. The revolt, in other words, was not instigated by Hitler but was an expression of political intent on the part of the workers to which party officialdom was reluctantly forced to pay attention. Misjudging the true balance of power in Austria, Kraus went so far as to justify the brutal measures taken by the extreme right-wing *Heimwehr* against the proletariat and the republican defensive alliance. Against his better judgement, he had broken his silence. Because he so hated the barbarism of the Nazis, he decided to accept the Austrian form of fascism as the lesser evil. He was soon painfully aware that he had miscalculated.

Kraus's justification of the white terror in Austria was a severe blow to Brecht. To his poem in praise of Kraus he added a second, 'On the Rapid Fall of a Good but Ignorant Man' ('Über den schnellen Fall des guten Unwissenden'), which he sent to Kraus by Karl Jaray. Brecht was still prepared to hear the socialist fighting-literature written off as an 'insult to the intelligence', especially as he had been unreservedly excluded by Kraus in this connection, but he could not pass over in silence Kraus's decision to align himself with the oppressors. Brecht, however, did not withdraw his friendship. The second poem remained unpublished and he still continued to react angrily to unduly biting left-wing criticism of Kraus. When Helene Weigel went to Vienna in the late autumn of 1934 Brecht, who at the time was spending a few weeks in London, asked her not to avoid Kraus but to be nice to him and say that he had just been worried himself at adopting a hostile attitude towards workers who resisted. Brecht's opinion of the offending July issue of *Die Fackel* will have been similar to that of

177

Walter Benjamin, who wrote to Gershom Scholem from Svendborg: 'Here in truth a new Timon has arisen who, with a sneering laugh, distributes his life's earnings among false friends'.

Having heard in Vienna that writer friends like Döblin and Feuchtwanger were toying with the idea of going to live in Switzerland, Brecht made up his mind as early as March 1933 to go to Zurich to see what things were like there. Helene Weigel continued to stay with her relatives for the time being, and it was there that she received an invitation from the Danish writer Karin Michaelis to bring Brecht and the children to visit her at her home in Thurö. Karin Michaelis had once met the actress Helene Weigel in Vienna and had kept in touch with her through their mutual friend Maria Lazar, who lived near Thurö.

The first colleague from Berlin whom Brecht ran into in Zurich was Kurt Kläber, editor of the *Linkskurve* and a member of the Communist Party, as well as of the Association of Revolutionary Proletarian Writers. According to the film pioneer Hans Richter this cultural official, who wrote under the name Kurt Held and had made his name with an American travel-book *Die Passagiere der Dritten Klasse,* was 'a Saxon with a heart of gold who to the end of his life steadfastly defended his ideals, although these differed fundamentally from Stalinist principles'. While Brecht did not contribute to the *Linkskurve* and, generally speaking, was in bad odour with those who did, he had established a very good personal relationship with Kläber and had a very high opinion of him as a man with whom to discuss things. They had met through Bernard von Brentano who, during his last two years in Berlin, had become a radical and been accepted into the Communist Party, albeit with strong reservations, as the reviews of his work *Kapitalismus und schöne Literatur* in the *Linkskurve* make plain; at the end of 1933 he was expelled from the party because of his failure to obey party discipline.

Kläber happened to recognize Brecht's voice in the next room of the hotel when the latter was making an appointment by telephone with Alfred Döblin. As it turned out Anna Seghers was also in Zurich, and they all decided to try to find somewhere to live on Lake Lugano. Kläber and his wife had had a holiday house in the Ticino for some years and promised to take the matter in hand. Brecht accepted the Kläber's invitation to Carona but first spent a few days in a hotel at Lugano where he had arranged to meet

Feuchtwanger. It seems that it had finally become clear to Brecht that he would have to remain outside Germany for longer than he had expected, for he now advised his wife to have 'everything' sent on from Berlin; not least because the prices of new things were prohibitive. The search for somewhere to live in the Ticino, which he soon abandoned and delegated to his wife, was the first and last occasion on which Brecht took the initiative in house-hunting; from then on it was once more Helene Weigel who travelled ahead and saw to this and other necessary arrangements. On this occasion Brecht made a note of all the food prices, worked out the best ways of getting to school and enquired about travel facilities. He liked the Kläber's house very much, but it was too far from a town, too 'lonely', for him. If they were going to remain in Carona for any length of time he thought a motor car would be essential. He would have preferred Zurich, 'a German town', but Lugano was cheaper. This was also confirmed in a letter from Brentano, who described Basle as 'wickedly expensive'. Brecht could envisage living in the Ticino only if Brentano, Fritz Sternberg and Karl Korsch also came. At the very least he wanted to have Anna Seghers and her husband Johann Lorenz Schmidt, the economist, in addition to the Kläbers, to discuss things with: 'If they at least would come! Schmidt is no Marx, but still . . .' In those days of hectic political developments, when some measure of agreement among the widely scattered emigrants was so necessary, Brecht was more than ever in need of clarifying conversations and discussions with friends sympathetic to communism. He and Helene Weigel spent several weeks in idyllic Carona with Kläber and his wife Lisa Tetzner, the well-known author of fairy tales; paralyzed since childhood, she could only hobble about with the aid of a stick. In subsequent letters to his hosts Brecht recalled especially the mornings spent out of doors reading the newspapers: 'One day I would like to read the newspapers with you again. One digests things better together'.

It soon became clear to everyone who had given any thought to the Ticino plans that an extended stay in Switzerland was out of the question. At the most Brecht thought he might remain there for the summer. But then he received Kurt Weill's invitation to come to Paris. Edward James, the husband of Tilly Losch the dancer, who was a friend of Lotte Lenya's, had just formed an international ballet company there under the artistic direction of

179

Boris Kochno. They called themselves 'Les Ballets 1933' and Weill was to write a ballet for them. He hoped that Brecht would provide him with a suitable libretto; Caspar Neher was coming from Berlin to do the sets. The work was completed within a few days, and the first performance of *The Seven Deadly Sins (Die Sieben Todsünden)* took place at the Théâtre des Champs Elysées on 7 June 1933. For Brecht it was more in the nature of a *pièce d'occasion* which brought him in a little money—quite nice, 'but not of much importance'.

The ballet, for a woman dancer, a woman singer, and a male voice quartet representing the family, tells the story of the girl Anna's path to the big cities, where she hopes to earn enough money by her dancing to keep the family and build a house. Her beauty and talent are merchandise which she has to sell. Her alter ego, in the shape of her sister, warns her at every step not to give way to her natural desire for happiness and thus commit one of the seven deadly sins. Anna sacrifices both youth and happiness. At the end of seven years she has achieved her goal, the family home is built. And it has been done by eschewing the seven deadly sins. The Christian moral code classes as deadly sins those sins which result in the loss of the state of grace and in damnation. According to the scholastic Peter Lombard, whom Brecht takes as his starting point, the deadly sins are pride, wrath, envy, lust, gluttony, avarice and sloth. Brecht declares these offences to be virtues. They are sins only to the petit bourgeois because, under capitalist conditions, he cannot afford to live a natural, human life. Pride in personal dignity is bad for business: one must do what is asked of one provided one is paid for it. Wrath over the brutal tricks played in the fight for one's daily bread is not permissible. To eat one's fill can spell ruin: a dancer's market value is determined by her figure. Pursuit of the fleshpots is called gluttony, as a precaution. The lower classes are advised by their rulers not to abandon themselves to 'base material pleasures'. To love for pleasure is penalized and called immoral. Only those who have money and pay money may be loved; but avarice is not to be commended either, if crime is seen to be the result. Similarly the petit bourgeois must not permit himself to be envious of the fortunate ones who disregard the social conventions. As a 'free born' human being he is only free to bow to the norm of the bourgeois order of things. 'Think what will happen if you do what you like', Anna is warned. To do what one likes is to rebel against the existing order and risk being ruined. For Anna her 'sister's' advice and the admonitions of her family prove to be sound. After seven years she starts to climb the social ladder, 'she walks with more and more of a swagger until finally she walks in triumph, while the other Annas are brought low and must humbly make way for her'.

The ballet is in the nature of a parable. It is a commentary on the conclusion that, in a society in which exploitation prevails, it is impossible 'to be good and still live'. Asceticism as a constituent of morality is shown to be a corollary of inhuman conditions. Anna, like Shen Te later, in *The Good Woman of Setzuan (Der gute Mensch von Sezuan)*, is two people in one: the 'practical', 'sensible' manageress and retailer of the commodity love; and the artist, debased to a commodity, who is always on the point of lowering her market value by behaving in a humanly natural way. *The Commodity Love (Die Ware Liebe)*, incidentally, is the title of a play which Brecht was planning to write about 1930, and which he recalled when working on *The Good Woman of Setzuan*. The principal character is a young prostitute who realizes 'that she cannot be both commodity and retailer at the same time. She opens a tobacconist's shop 'where she plays the cigar merchant, dressed in men's clothes, while continuing her career as a prostitute'. The girl leads a double life: as commodity and retailer of this commodity. As her own tout, 'she has, so to speak, a first class commodity at her disposal which she uses all the tricks of the trade to exploit'. Brecht's goal is not a 'good person' but a 'good world'. He does not see 'good' and 'evil' in terms of morality. What is decisive is whether a person's conduct has good or evil results; if it has, the society in which this occurs is worthless. Moral assumptions, Brecht insists, must be socially motivated. As he sees it, the deadly sins have materialistic qualities, they contribute to the realization of human nature. But they are depicted to the petite bourgeoisie by those in power as offences.

For Brecht, as we have seen, this ballet was a *pièce d'occasion,* a simple exercise, which amused him but contained nothing specifically new as regards either form or content. A work on established lines was all that was any longer possible with Weill. The music of *The Seven Deadly Sins* bore to the melodies favoured by the bourgeois world a relation analogous to the method used by Brecht, the intention of which was to cast doubt on the prevailing view of morality and transform it. With as much virtuosity as in *The Threepenny Opera* and *Rise and Fall of the Town of Mahagonny* Weill again denounced the musical forms he repudiated by paraphrasing them ironically. The unforced way in which, by means of an ingenious montage technique, sounds and rhythms from the débris of played-out music were introduced, gave tautness to the work and increased point to Brecht's message. The work did not have the accustomed success, and because of this Weill never again risked a collaboration with Brecht. The playwright, he said, was going through a stage in which all music was anathema to him. He then did what Brecht also tried to do later but without success, he conquered Broadway. But it was a pyrrhic victory on Weill's part, because Broadway took him to itself and robbed his music of all its edge.

Brecht was so impressed by Paris, the big city, and by the number of its cinemas and theatres that for a time he entertained the idea of taking an apartment there. But when Ernst Josef Aufricht's projects came to nothing—he wanted to start another theatrical venture and produce Brecht's *Round Heads and Pointed Heads (Die Rundköpfe und die Spitzköpfe)*—he returned gratefully to Karin Michaelis's offer. Helene Weigel left Carona and took Steff with her to Thurö, where the housekeeper Mari Hold was staying with little Barbara, who had been smuggled out of Germany by an English woman, after spending the hectic days of the hurried departure from Berlin with her grandfather in Augsburg. Brecht arrived in Thurö at the end of June 1933, where in the meantime Ernst Ottwalt and his wife had also found refuge. Between Brecht and Hans Henny Jahnn, who had been staying with Karin Michaelis since Whitsun, no real contact was established: 'We scarcely saw each other', Jahnn regretted later; 'I was preparing to go to Switzerland, and Brecht had other irons in the fire, trying to secure his future'.

In his *Refugees in Conversation* Brecht described the Danes as hospitable and genial people, and lavished special praise on their proverbial sense of humour; but he had some unkind things to say about their sly ways in political matters. Democracy to them, or so it seemed to Brecht as a refugee, was primarily a vested right to make a joke. 'They were all convinced that fascism would make no headway with them, because of their sense of humour: they more or less live from the sale of pigs, so they had to be on good terms with the Germans because they needed pigs. But they made some good jokes about themselves, such as that one has to tread carefully when selling pigs, otherwise it harms the pig.' The picture of Denmark painted by political emigrants like Ziffel or Kalle was inevitably sardonic: one was tolerated but not welcome. For Brecht himself the years spent in exile in Denmark were relatively pleasant. What plagued him was the obvious discrepancy between trying to exert an influence on a Germany dominated by fascism and the obligation to remain politically unnoticed in a country where he was a guest.

Denmark also had not escaped the effects of the world economic crisis; there was large-scale unemployment in the country, which was still to a great extent agricultural in structure. At first the Danes paid little attention to the political conditions in Germany; the Social Democrat coalition government had its hands full with its own extreme communists. On 15 February 1933 Aksel Larsen, the leader of the Danish Communists, had been taken into custody in Stockholm as a precautionary measure, following the call to overthrow the capitalist order of society. The majority of Danish newspapers regarded the dawn of the Third Reich either as a drastic but necessary cure for Germany's protracted sickness, or as a fleeting outbreak of madness. The people made jokes and maintained a cautious wait-and-see attitude. When the first streams of refugees poured into Denmark, the population gradually took a more realistic view of the crime of fascism. They offered what help they could and most of the refugees were generously given shelter. The German authorities tried in vain to persuade Denmark to adopt a more emphatically 'neutral' attitude. In the tangle of economic interests, of the dangers arising from informers infiltrated by Germany and from fascist groups at home, and of diplomatic pressures, the Danish Government acted with its native skill to assist the victims of persecution. From time to time, however, political figures like the communist leader Funcke were handed over to the Nazis.

Thurö, a small island whose southern extremity bordered on Fünen, was a fairly remote part of Denmark not far from the German border. Not very thickly populated, it made a good place of refuge. At the beginning of August Brecht signed the contract for a house they had found, with Karin Michaelis's help, in a village on Fünen near Svendborg. Brecht's chances, as a German writer, of settling and establishing himself reasonably successfully in Denmark were not bad. His name, naturally, was known mainly in connection with *The Threepenny Opera,* although *Drums in the Night* had been performed in Copenhagen. Moreover, shortly before he arrived *The Man Who Says Yes* had been published, while *Rise and Fall of the Town of Mahagonny* was announced for the end of the year. Left-wing theatrical circles seemed also to take a special interest in the didactic plays, and the critic and dramatist Svend Borberg, who on Fritz Kortner's advice had approached Brecht in 1932, undertook the task of introducing Brecht to the Danish public through articles in the newspapers. He also translated *St. Joan of the Stockyards* in the hope of getting the play put on at the Theatre Royal in Copenhagen; in this he was unsuccessful, although a contract had already been agreed and the popular actress Bodil Ipsen wanted to play the title role. When the news spread in the Copenhagen theatre world that Brecht was staying with Karin Michaelis, the actress Ruth Berlau set off for Thurö to ask Brecht for a copy of his play *The Mother,* which she wanted to rehearse with a communist group of amateurs. 'Red Ruth', as her friends had called this former member of the Theatre Royal since the publication of her enthusiastic account of a bicycle trip through the Soviet Union, had already been loud in her praise of the author of this play, in which she had played the part of Anna Balicke in 1930. Her profession of communism and her support of Per Knutzon's Revolutionary Theatre caused something of a stir because her husband was the distinguished doctor Professor Robert Lund and she was a familiar figure in Copenhagen drawing-rooms. When Brecht could not grant her request immediately, because he had with him only his own working-copy of the play, she waited for a suitable opportunity and simply took it. She was convinced she would take it back, because Brecht had made her an unambiguous proposal which so stunned her that she was unable to accede to it on the spot. She had arrived in the company of the young architect Mogens Voltenen, whom Helene Weigel had succeeded in enlisting to help her with the problems of furnishing and equipping the newly acquired country house in Skovbostrand. In this way the first links were forged in the Svenborg-Copenhagen axis, which was to be of such value to Brecht in the years that followed.

The money to buy the house, which cost seven thousand krone, came from sums contributed by Brecht's and Helene Weigel's fathers and from fees. Now that they had decided on Skovbostrand as their permanent residence for the immediate future, they sent to Germany for the crates of books and essential furniture. In corresponding with the friends who arranged for the transport, Brecht used the cover name of Berta; Otto Müllereisert organized things in Berlin, all the Augsburg mail went through Georg Pfanzelt, and the postal address in Svendborg was that of Maria Lazar. Because the house had first to be made ready, and the stable on the west side enlarged to make a study, Brecht decided to spend the next few months in Paris, where in any case he had matters to attend to with publishers and where he wanted to participate in anti-fascist literary activities.

Moreover Margarete Steffin had stayed behind in Paris; she was a young communist whom Brecht had met in Berlin during rehearsals for *The Mother,* in which she played the part of the serving girl in the scene showing metal being collected for the war effort. She and Brecht formed an unusually warm attachment. In the summer of 1933 Brecht wrote to her frequently from Denmark and sent her erotic sonnets. In contrast to his numerous love affairs with other women, this one had about it a tender intimacy, as well as something conspiratorial. At first the two lovers made a pact not to tell anyone else of their feelings for one another. To seal this they agreed on an unobtrusive code word; 'this was to be: I'm touching you . . .. And when we were among strangers we used to say this, and knew at once we cared'.

In the sonnets Brecht restated the unusual conditions surrounding this love, which they had had so little time and opportunity to foster but which was enduring and deep just because it had to be unobtrusive. It was generally Brecht who urged their brief meetings which, in this case, he usually regretted. He arrived in a hurry and had to leave in a hurry, because it was almost impossible for Margarete Steffin to receive him in the lodgings in Zehlendorf where she was living in 1932: 'And this apart one was not glad for him, given short shrift he seemed unwelcome, to have him there seemed far from pleasing! And thus he lost the heart to come. All his wishes now seemed crude to him, and his haste no longer decent'.

Margarete Steffin was a working-class girl from Berlin and joined the communist youth organization while still at school. She was slight in build and suffered from chronic tuberculosis. Brecht not only loved her, he felt responsible for her; she was a comrade whose welfare the party had placed in his hands, so to speak. This 'soldier of the revolution' was tireless in furthering his works. Even after she had become very weak she constantly left her sickbed 'to explain the value of the didactic plays' to workers. To Brecht she was the party's representative: 'So that she might verify everything I said, so that henceforth she might improve my every line, trained in the school of those who fight oppression. Since then she has been my support, weak in health but gay in spirit, not to be corrupted even by me'. On the one hand he paid tribute to the courage, soldierly intelligence and skill of his fellow worker, while on the other he praised her skills in bed, her fire and sensuality. His favourite name for her was 'Jib', because if he put his hand up her skirt when they were working she jibbed and rebuked the 'classic author': 'An angry stranger, you sit facing me. "How dare he, I don't even know the man!" And my astonishment is not yet past, when in you I see signs of joy emerge. And, still severe, you write the new text down, and suddenly you draw my hand to you'. Margarete Steffin was the 'good comrade', the recipient of long political didactic poems and revolutionary messages; but she was also the muse of his 'Achillesverse', for whom he wrote poems as Dante did for Beatrice, except that Brecht did not 'sing at the mere sight of her'. He was most solicitous in seeing that his mistress did not wear herself out with too much work and was always warmly clothed. When she was sent to the Soviet Union for a rest cure in 1934, Brecht bought her woollen things and thick underpants: 'So now I dressed you with as loving care as when I undressed you (those times so few! I could have wished occasions much less rare!) This time must be as if I'd undressed you! Thus well protected and immune from chill, I argued, she'll survive, my loved one still'. Herr Keuner's favourite animal was the elephant: 'His skin is thick and knives break off in it, but he has a gentle nature'. Margarete Steffin liked to wear elephants as charms; she found them sympathetic and badly needed them to take care of her.

Brecht arrived in Paris at the beginning of September 1933, but as most of the people he hoped to see again had left the city during the hot summer months and were not yet back, he went straight on to Lion Feuchtwanger in Sanary, taking Margarete Steffin with him. His mentor and friend, an international celebrity whose novels always sold in large numbers, had bought a villa in this small coastal town in the south of France, where less well-to-do writers were hospitably received and entertained. While Feuchtwanger was a successful writer, his earnings were not of the same order as those of people like Stefan Zweig, Franz Werfel, Emil Ludwig, Vicky Baum or Erich Maria Remarque, some of whom lived like film stars and because of this found themselves exposed to malicious attacks, although in individual cases they undoubtedly helped their poorer colleagues. Thomas Mann in particular, who, as winner of the Nobel Prize, was the most celebrated German writer in the world, gave great offence by a way of life that outwardly was so ostentatiously concerned with his own importance; not least among the reasons for this, however, was his refusal to accept exile as an economic reality. Mann personally never considered himself wealthy compared to other authors. To Feuchtwanger a decent standard of living meant a secretary, a married couple to look after the house and garden, and a car; and in the eyes of most of his colleagues this was the normal standard for a well-established writer. What distinguished Stefan Zweig, Emil Ludwig, Franz Werfel and Thomas Mann at this time from Arnold Zweig, Lion Feuchtwanger, Alfred Döblin and Heinrich Mann was not so much their financial circumstances as the way in which they presented themselves to the world as writers. The first group were 'great writers', the second group 'lesser masters'. All were widely read novelists. But whereas the first group held court and took part in social life, the second were interested in social questions and constantly put the security of their bourgeois existence at risk. In comparison to all these authors Brecht, who owned a farmhouse in Denmark, where things were cheap, and stayed at third-class pensions when he travelled, was almost penniless. 'Extras' were possible only under exceptionally favourable circumstances. The second-hand Ford he later acquired in Svendborg was found for him by Ruth Berlau when he received an advance payment for the Danish edition of *The Threepenny Opera;* and in 1936 the fee for his share in the script of a Richard Tauber film enabled him to buy a small hand printing-press.

Feuchtwanger owed his modest fortune chiefly to the favourable terms he had obtained for his new novel *Die Geschwister Oppenheimer*. Brecht's decision also to try his hand at a novel, which, now that he was an exile, would have a readier market than a play, is traceable to Feuchtwanger's advice and example. He also felt a strong desire to re-tell in greater detail the Marxist version of *The Threepenny Opera,* which he had not been permitted to film, in order to make known his new attitude to the work. Using the technique of the detective story as a basis for the construction of his novel, he approached the narrative mainly in the satiric manner of Swift.

Feuchtwanger's novel was published in Amsterdam by the German language house of Querido, whose literary agent and financial partner was Fritz Landshoff, formerly joint owner of Gustav Kiepenheuer, who had published Brecht's *Versuche.* Two other Kiepenheuer men were also in Amsterdam, in charge of the German language branch of the publisher Allert de Lange: one, Hermann Kesten, as its literary head; the other, Walter Landauer, as its business manager. All three paid regular business visits to Paris because most writers turned up there. They stayed at the same hotel and kept each other informed of their transactions; they also helped writers from time to time by switching them between the publishers when one of these had misgivings about continuing to pay the monthly advances. Brecht came to terms with Landauer. De Lange paid higher royalties, unusually high ones in Brecht's case, but unlike Querido retained the 'normal publisher's' share in the case of translations. To what extent Kesten acted as reader of *The Threepenny Novel (Der Dreigroschenroman)* we no longer know for certain; but after reading a criticism of *Terror and Misery of the Third Reich (Furcht und Elend des Dritten Reichs)* in 1942 Brecht made a note that, 'because of his hostile attitude', he had refused to tell him about his plans for *The Threepenny Novel.* On the other hand in the late autumn of 1933 Brecht and Kesten had several talks at which, in addition to literary plans, business matters were at least discussed. The main feature of a conversation on 14 December was Brecht's proposal that, in spite of their differing outlooks, they should conclude a pact of literary friendship. The two authors, Brecht said, should give a verbal undertaking to treat each other's works with respect for the next five years. But even Brecht's assurance that he had concluded similar pacts with Döblin and Feuchtwanger could not persuade Kesten to abandon his intransigent attitude. He then indignantly repeated his refusal in writing: 'By way of elucidating this

188

comprehensive proposal, you explained that you were not in the first instance a writer and poet but a "teacher of behaviour"; that, as a Marxist, you were antagonistic to the whole bourgeois world, and were compelled and willing to proceed against your opponents with the most drastic weapons of the capitalist world, to which normally you object; that you felt compelled to destroy with every means at your disposal the economic or literary existence of your opponents or non-friends; that you were both willing and able to do this; that you had already often done it; but that, on the other hand, you were prepared to offer your friends the greatest kindness and assistance; that Caspar Neher, for example, owed his livelihood to you'. On receiving this, Brecht asked Kesten and Landauer to meet him in a café, where he expressed his regret at what had happened, said it was a misunderstanding and asked the incorruptible Kesten to retract what he had written. Needless to say Brecht had not made the proposal merely as a joke; in fact he enjoyed concluding pacts of this sort. It was probably only when Kesten took his proposal seriously that Brecht offered the above explanations, in order to goad his companion who was clearly sensitive about things of this sort. In general he attached great importance to such agreements. A notebook for 1933 contains a remark by the politician Ramsay MacDonald to the effect that all contracts are sacred but no contract is binding for ever. Brecht was well known for his 'contracts' with women; he drew up detailed agreements intended to govern the relationship between himself and the woman, and preclude from the start false claims and expectations.

In addition to his contract with Allert de Lange, Brecht also came to an agreement with Willi Münzenberg's Editions du Carrefour for the publication of a volume of poems, *Lieder Gedichte Chöre* which he had compiled with Hanns Eisler and Margarete Steffin, and in the final editing of which Elisabeth Hauptmann also had a hand. At this time, too, Brecht was already engaged in trying to get the most advantageous contract he could for his projected Tui-novel; to this end he played off the two interested parties, Allert de Lange and Editions du Carrefour, against one another in order to negotiate as large an advance payment as possible. Brecht also hoped to find some means of gaining a foothold in the film world. But even those better versed in this world than he was, people of consequence, found scarcely any doors open to them in France, and only rarely backers and producers when they wanted to make anti-fascist films. Max Ophuls and Ludwig Berger succeeded in following up their German film successes, there being a certain demand for their style of work; but after making Molnar's *Liliom,* Fritz Lang received no more commissions. The only political feature film to be made in France during the first years of the German exile was Slatan Dudov's *Seifenblasen,* or *Soap Bubbles;* a large part of the preparatory work for this had already been done illegally in Germany and the French version was made with the assistance of Jacques Prévert. Dudov could offer Brecht nothing, and the latter was forced to restrict himself to theatrical productions; he staged the first performance of *Senora Carrar's Rifles (Die Gewehre der Frau Carrar)* in Paris, as well as scenes from *Terror and Misery of the Third Reich* under the title *99%*. Brecht developed a friendly relationship with Jean Renoir, to whom he was introduced by Carl Koch, and this was later renewed in America. Although no opportunity materialized for them to work together, Brecht profited from Renoir's story-telling and cooking. In the little story *How to Eat (Esskultur),* which he wrote in Finland, Brecht gave a sketch of a dinner with Renoir in Meudon: Brecht asked Renoir to sing some old French songs, which Margarete Steffin accompanied on an old concertina.

In 1933 Paris was the leading trans-shipment centre for emigrant artists, scholars and politicians. It was here that most of the conferences took place, and here that further joint action, and the problems of safeguarding the material existence of the refugees, were discussed. Opposition to Hitler was the one bond that united the emigrants; in other matters their interests and opinions often clashed violently. Even their reasons for being in a foreign country were reflected in the individual political attitudes: some had left because of their convictions, others had been turned out or had escaped arrest. For some the Jewish question was uppermost, for others the problem of fascism. In line with this some considered pro-Jewish, others anti-fascist, solidarity to be the more important. Hermann Kesten, for instance, thought of publishing an anthology of Jewish stories, an idea which Brecht, who on the Jewish question thought as Benjamin, Bloch and Karl Kraus did, declared to be absurd. Anna Seghers, a Jewess and a communist, who had also fled to Paris, replied to Kesten, 'It is precisely at this moment that a book consisting exclusively of Jewish authors seems to me wrong'.

In this medley of differing interests, intrigues and high-minded programmes Brecht remained extraordinarily clear-headed, realistic and disinterested. That Brecht's first concern, like that of everyone else, was to 'keep the home fires burning' in Svendborg goes without saying. He set personal enmities, animosities and political prejudices aside whenever it was a question of pursuing anti-fascist activities on as broad and united a front as possible; at the same time, however, he considered it vital to maintain the contrasting views and differences of opinion, as well as to establish an enlightened political attitude in general. During their discussions in cafés he liked to probe open wounds and provoke the others into adopting standpoints. What he sought was not a popular front policy at any price but an effective front of anti-fascist solidarity. although he had never been a member of the association of revolutionary proletarian writers, he considered an alliance so important politically that he suggested to the association's secretary, J. R. Becher, that a conference be called 'at which the aim and methods of our future work shall be finally determined'. Becher, who was well aware of the lack of theoretical knowledge among working-class writers, was at this time trying to bring together widely scattered authors to form an effective united front. In order to do this he established bases in all the emigration centres. In Moscow he started a German language edition of the magazine *Internationale Literatur;* in Prague he helped Wieland Herzfelde to reorganize the editorial staff of the *Neue Deutsche Blätter;* and in Paris he succeeded in reforming the Federation for the Protection of German Writers of which, in October, Heinrich Mann was invited to become honorary president. Having ensured the continuance of the *Arbeiter Illustrierte Zeitung* in Prague, Willi Münzenberg, with the help of the Comintern and Soviet money, set up large mass-communication systems and publishing houses, mostly in Paris. His aim, too, was to put an end to the disastrous fragmentation of the left and the inter-party struggles for power. Münzenberg, left-wing press lord in the Weimar Republic whose views were diametrically opposed to the Hugenberg concern, was not only an able manager and official, he also published the First Brown Book on the *Reichstag* Fire and the Hitler terror, and founded an institute for the purpose of investigating fascism,

191

which was the envy of Kurt Kläber, who wanted to organize a similar project in Switzerland but could find no one to back him.

In exile the rivalries, the multiplicity of opinions and the obscure sectarianism not only continued, but increased. When a small periodical was started it was generally followed by a rival, and when a writer managed to find a bigger or a committed publisher, another writer was always on the spot to discover the fly in the ointment. The very large number of refugee intellectuals of different origins naturally made a broad spectrum of publications desirable, but when one considers their possible sales and politicial effectiveness there were still too many insignificant little local papers constantly and exclusively endorsing their own opinions. Tucholsky's criticism that 'instead of starting one good newspaper everybody was starting one of his own' was by no means wholly unjustified. In a number of cases publishing firms came into existence not for political reasons but for business considerations. As 'the first confidence trickster on the emigrant fringe', to quote Maximilian Scheer, emerged the figure of Joe Lherman, publisher of *Das Blaue Heft* and a series of cheap books, whom Brecht still remembered well as the man who put on his production of Hans Henny Jahnn's *Pastor Ephraim Magnus* in Berlin 1923, and who was now once more operating his trick of the uncovered promissory note, with the result that whatever he undertook once more promptly failed. Most projects, however, failed because of the political disruption. Instead of a united fighting front, all that emerged were new dissensions. Instead of divergent standpoints combining to form a common policy, an idea, originally put forward as a prescription for integration, gradually engendered a proliferation of unruly offshoots. A multitude of opinions never became integrated into a common standpoint, but a single opinion on the other hand gave rise, in the course of time, to many. At the decisive moment a multiplicity of communist cells did not unite to form the Communist Party, but the once strong Communist Party, which had developed out of the Social Democrat Party when it turned bourgeois, fathered twenty-five splinter groups. And between the two big workers' parties existed a confusion of independent left-wing associations like the Socialist Workers' Party, the International Socialist Fighting Alliance, financed through vegetarian restaurants in Paris and London, the Revolutionary Socialists, and the 'Neue Beginnen' and 'Neuer

Weg' groups. Brecht belonged to none of these, but in almost all of them he had friends or close acquaintances with whom he maintained contact, in order to keep himself informed and exchange viewpoints. He was to be seen at all the important meeting-places of the Paris emigrants; he tried to mediate in all their quarrels by throwing light on the situation, and to play his part in important political projects. He wrote a series of texts for immediate propaganda purposes and wrote revolutionary songs, manifestos, speeches and open letters. He was also working on a second Brown Book. In spite of being so active, however, Brecht remained very detached. He disliked the vain, egocentric attitudes of the intellectuals. People like Jean Renoir, in whom he was interested personally, saw too little of him. The only ones on really cordial terms in those autumn days in Paris were Brecht, Margarete Steffin, Elisabeth Hauptmann, Hanns Eisler and Walter Benjamin. Among them the situation was discussed freely and openly, without recourse either to astrology or to forecasts about the future. Brecht's hotel in the rue du Four was only two houses away from Walter Benjamin's apartment. When, shortly before Christmas, Brecht left for Denmark he wanted to transfer this group to Svendborg. But Elisabeth Hauptmann was on her way to America and Hanns Eisler still had numerous concerts to attend to as well as music for films, although he promised to go in the spring. Finally Walter Benjamin agreed and asked Brecht for a detailed report on the economic situation in Denmark; much though he disliked the milieu of the Paris emigrants, he wanted first to enquire into the chances of earning a living so that he would not be financially dependent on Brecht. Immediately after arriving in Skovbostrand, the latter wrote: 'It is pleasant here. Not at all cold, much warmer than in Paris. Helli says you could manage on 100 krone (60 Reichsmarks, 360 francs) a month. In addition the Svendborg library gets any book one wants. We have the wireless, newspapers, playing-cards, soon your books too, fires, small cafés, an exceptionally easy language, and the world moves to its end more peacefully here'.

16

Under the Danish Thatch

Ah, we are not misled by the peace of The
Sound. The cries can be heard all the way
from their camps.

Although Brecht spent six years in Denmark, he steadfastly
refused to learn the 'exceptionally easy' language. To the people of
the neighbourhood he remained the strange foreigner who, with
his cap pulled down over his face, passed them with a silent
greeting. This behaviour did not imply any unfriendliness on his
part, it stemmed from the impatience which the idyllic landscape
aroused in a man waiting to return home. To furnish his house
comfortably, to do anything which seemed to indicate that he was
coming to terms with his situation, was like treason to him.
Moreover in these first years of his exile Brecht was afraid that, if
he learned a foreign language, it might affect his ability to express
himself in his own. 'Why turn the pages of a foreign grammar?
When the call comes to return home it will come in the language
that I know.'

His refusal to learn Danish was all that remained of the harsh
discipline he prescribed for himself as a token of protest. An
integrated household was a prerequisite for his work. The house
had to be well equipped and maintained if he wished to entertain
invited guests even on a modest scale. And because of the children
too, who had to go to school, he needed to be installed on a more
lasting basis. His Danish retreat was comfortable and safe: 'An oar
is placed across the roof. A moderate wind won't carry off the
thatch'. All the same, 'The house has four doors through which to
flee'.

After the many months of feverish activity devoted to survival
and the political struggle against fascism, Brecht began once more
to work at long-term literary projects. In addition to Benjamin he
tried to lure Karl Korsch to the 'Danish Siberia'. He also praised

the well-stocked local library to him, saying how excellent it was for purposes of research; his chests of books from Berlin including the volumes of *Neue Zeit*, were at Korsch's disposal and so too would be Benjamin's library, which was expected soon. Brecht was anxious to continue with Korsch the Marxist studies to which he had devoted his last winter in Berlin: 'Admittedly the human material is widely scattered; on the other hand, for this very reason one will have to clarify one's methods, otherwise there will be no chance of accumulating under its several headings the work that has to be done'. 'In an agony of uncertainty' up until the last moment, Korsch finally decided in March 1934 to remain in London for the time being, because he hoped that the decisive battle between fascism and socialism in Europe was about to take place: the February clashes in Austria, the anti-fascist general strike in France, and the pre-revolutionary events in Spain seemed to him indicative of this.

It was not until the beginning of 1935, after Brecht's visit to London, that Korsch spent some weeks under the 'Danish thatch' in order to collect material to clear Heinz Langerhans, who had been charged by the Nazis with betraying his country and faced imprisonment with hard labour for at least fifteen years. The case of their mutual friend Langerhans, who had led a resistance group which collapsed in December 1933, encouraged Brecht to recall the many anonymous opponents and fighters of Hitler in the concentration camps and not to lose his faith in a different Germany. Langerhans had distributed leaflets about armaments and preparations for war in Germany, and then told the examining magistrate that he had obtained his information from a Danish newspaper. It was now Korsch's task to draft out a specimen copy of the non-existent publication, which an anarchist group in Copenhagen undertook to print. On the strength of this Langerhans could only be sentenced for high treason. He was sentenced to two and a half years in prison; following this he was sent to a concentration camp, from which he escaped in 1939.

Through intermediaries Brecht was in touch with many underground workers; from time to time he came into possession of their leaflets, and friends from Germany, who visited him or Margarete Steffin during the first years of their exile in Skovbostrand, brought him news of what was happening—this later provided basic material for poems and for scenes in *Terror*

195

and Misery of the Third Reich. When he considered the slight chances his works had of being published or of being effective, Brecht became envious of the young, 'carefree' anti-fascists who were able to fight in Germany. Artists and communists who had fled from Germany and who, like the sculptor Fritz Cremer, were unable to find any sphere of activity, artistic or political, in London that was even moderately satisfying, he advised to return to Germany and engage in unobtrusive trickery and cunning. At any rate he had more respect for the resistance of fighters in the concentration camps, for their courage and unwavering conviction, than he had for the voluble drawing-room communists, who for a time acclaimed Stalin and the Soviet Union, only to turn from them disillusioned. People like Langerhans he always found sympathetic, and his attitude to them was frank and open-minded. With renegades like Sidney Hook or Ruth Fischer Brecht always adopted an inflexibly Stalinist attitude; in 1943 he called K. A. Wittfogel, formerly a radical Marxist Sinologist, a man as 'heated and traumatic as a disenchanted troubadour'. For Brecht, to be anti-Stalinist was not a full-time occupation.

Brecht was no orator, nor was he given to noisy, demonstrative gestures. Slyness and cunning, the methods of the underground fighter, were more in his line than rousing phrases and sabre-rattling appeals. In contrast to writers with a rigidly anti-fascist code of morals, like Klaus Mann or Ferdinand Bruckner, who ruthlessly severed all relations with Germany and felt nothing but scorn and contempt for friends who wanted to avoid the 'worst' and keep their minds and spirits intact during the reign of the brown shirts, Brecht showed a great deal of understanding for the attitude of Emil Burri, Casper Neher, Herbert Ihering and Peter Suhrkamp, who went about their work relatively unobtrusively and as decently as they could, in spite of the fact that they had aligned themselves with the extreme left-wing views of the communist poet. Exile seemed to him to be too high a price to pay merely to preserve one's reputation intact. 'But in relation to the individual a materialist is merely someone who regards, or rather is able to regard, the individual as the material of which he is the concrete evidence and as which he acts.'

When, in the summer of 1935, Karl Korsch's permit to reside in England was withdrawn, because the suicide of a German woman communist friend of his made the other emigrants suspect him of being a Hitler informer, he was obliged to leave the 'ultrareformist Eldorado' of London for good and seek refuge in Skovsbostrand where, until he left for America in the late autumn of 1936, he lived with his family and wrote his book on Marx. 'We don't know when he will go, his suitcases are always packed', said Brecht of his Marxist teacher, whose observations and advice were once again welcome to him as a writer: 'He discovers all one's weaknesses. And immediately makes suggestions. He knows a lot. Listening to him is difficult. He speaks in very long sentences. And this forces me to be patient'. Brecht had more confidence in him as an interpreter of the Marxist method than as a judge of the current political situation. Korsch struck him as an 'all or nothing' man.

Brecht's first major undertaking in Denmark was the completion of *The Threepenny Novel*, which turned out to be much longer than he expected. When Hanns Eisler eventually arrived in Svendborg in March 1934, the first of Brecht's eagerly awaited friends to do so, the long planned revision of the play *Pointed Heads and Round Heads* was taken up; the young Danish director Per Knutzon was very interested in it. The comedy, which had grown out of a projected adaptation of Shakespeare's *Measure for Measure* in 1932, was completely reworked, the fascist racial policy being gone into more deeply and the remains of Shakespeare's plot removed. In addition to this the epic elements were given still more emphasis and a large number of songs incorporated. The title of the play now became *Round Heads and Pointed Heads*. But before Eisler could start on the music he had to leave again, and a new project, the little didactic play *The Horatians and the Curiatians (Die Horatier und die Kuriatier)*, had to be written without the composer's assistance. The Party had unexpectedly sent a telegram to Eisler ordering him to Prague to attend an international music congress, at which the amalgamation of the Social Democrat and Communist working-people's choral societies was to be discussed. It was some time before Brecht, who felt he had been left in the lurch, forgave his friend for his Party loyalty.

Along with Margarete Steffin, who at once learned Danish and acquired a knowledge of the other Scandinavian languages, Ruth Berlau now also became Brecht's collaborator and mistress. She undertook the task of introducing the emigrant German playwright to the progressive theatre people in Copenhagen, to the

197

director Per Knutzon, who had produced *Drums in the Night*, to her colleague Lulu Ziegler, and to the writers Otto Gelsted and Johannes Weltzer, who immediately became prominent as Brecht translators. Most of Ruth Berlau's friends belonged to the left-wing of the Danish liberals. They raved over Brecht the poet. Thanks in the main to them, many newspapers carried interviews and articles about him, although these did not have the desired effect of obtaining performances of the plays, which Brecht himself considered important. The negative results caused Brecht to entrust the same mission to an increasing number of people; in the event of duplications he could always select the alternative that offered the best possibilities. These tactics, which most of his friends found hard to understand, were also used later by Brecht as a precautionary measure. For instance he asked Eric Bentley, apt disciple and first champion of his ideas in America, to translate his plays; at the same time, however, he let Thornton Wilder know that he could imagine no one better able to translate his plays than himself. He gave many of his poems to both Eisler and Weill, and later to both Eisler and Dessau, to set to music; and had Igor Stravinsky, in addition to Paul Dessau, shown an interest in composing his *Lucullus* libretto, he would have been quite happy.

Journalists, writers, and artists generally interested Brecht only if he could learn from them and make them his collaborators. The only one at that time to establish any closer contact with Brecht and his family was the young social democrat journalist Frederik Martner, whom Karlin Michaelis had sent to the normally very tight-lipped author in Skovbostrand with the advice, 'Tell Brecht I want him to do it'. The interviews which Martner published were intended not only to acquaint Danish readers with Brecht's works and theories, but above all to allay interest on the part of the authorities. The object was to safeguard Skovbostrand as a place to work in. Brecht stated that he was living 'quietly and peacefully' and was 'not writing in Danish newspapers'. He also paid a tribute to Denmark as a free country with a social democrat government, which allowed him to work in peace and quiet: 'It is beautiful here, where I am living, and reminds me of the country round my home in Augsburg in Bavaria. From my window the view is exactly the same as it was there. I find it difficult to work in big foreign cities, not in German ones you understand, but in London, Paris and such like places'. Brecht's visits to Copenhagen during these years were infrequent, although the Danish capital was only five hours away. He went there from time to time only to meet Ruth Berlau and accompany her to Vallensbaek, where she had a weekend house. During the first year, as long as he was still working on *The Threepenny Novel*, Brecht found Skovbostrand agreeable, especially as a large number of visitors turned up there. The moment 'boredom' set in, or in other words the uncomfortable feeling that he was cut off from political events and a traitor to those who were fighting, he went to Paris, to London and to Moscow. His visits to these emigrant-centres sapped his strength and embroiled him in unproductive sham battles; they did, however, provide him with material for a satire on intellectuals. Brecht's enormous output during the years 1938—1941 was due not least to his conviction that people were no longer much interested in his concept of art and his political opinions.

As is evident from the plans for his *Tui* novel, which he first discussed in a wider context during Walter Benjamin's visit in the summer of 1934, Brecht saw in the satirical tenor of this work an opportunity to get away from his own position as an emigrant. He still refused to admit emigration as a possible basis for literary plans and undertakings; he wanted to look beyond emigration and continue his previous studies and experiments within the framework of the epic theatre. On the other hand his partiality for satire and irony posed immense difficulties for him, because it was based on an imaginative and fanciful view of art which, as Benjamin noted in his diary, might now clash with his efforts 'to make art consistent with reason'. At the time the play *The Horatians and the Curiatians* seemed to Brecht the only possible way out of the dilemma. He saw it as a didactic poem on a strictly formal basis. When Walter Benjamin read it in 1935 he thought it the 'most accomplished' of the didactic plays.

In Brecht's opinion the audience could no longer learn anything from the plays of Ibsen, Strindberg or Schnitzler, which he considered threadbare in form; they were simply psychological characterizations. The plays had no utility value as historic documents. Only those precedents which had a clearly defined basic scheme were compatible with his concept of theatre. What chiefly interested him at that time were elements of the Chinese and Japanese style of acting, transplanted and rendered less severe by the introduction of various slapstick effects in the manner of

199

Charlie Chaplin. Brecht wanted to teach his audience by the use of effects and jokes. Didactic plays like *The Mother, Round Heads and Pointed Heads*, as well as *The Horatians and Curiatians*, he expressly wished to be performed as comedies; they were to be done with a light, playful, elegant touch. When referring to Eisler's beautiful vocal settings for *The Mother*, or to Joris Ivens's music for the film *Heldenlied*, on the construction of the steel works at Magnitogorsk, Brecht liked to use the expression 'theory in song'. He regarded himself as a strictly pedagogic dramatist, concerned with doctrine and theory, not with commitment. He hated every kind of so-called propagandist art. He was intent, not to generate violent emotions or feelings of anger, but to speak to people's intelligence, to elicit a practical way of thinking. Hatred of Hitler he regarded as politically worthless, unless it stemmed from a knowledge of the causes of barbarism and fascism. He raised no objection if the word 'pedagogy' was applied to his work in the theatre: 'The main content of the play must be the relation of man to man, as it is today; to investigate this and give it expression is my chief interest'. To his Danish friends Brecht was a teacher, and it was a role he enjoyed. It gradually became the custom to address him as 'master' when speaking or working with him. But if his pupils lost their sense of humour and took the word 'master' too literally, Brecht discreetly questioned this and resolutely set about erasing the pedagogic image: 'Remember, I am not a Pestalozzi'.

17

Moscow 1935

The transformation of the old world into the
new does not take place outside the world, as
some critics expect it to.

Brecht returned from his first visit to Moscow, in 1932, greatly
impressed; unlike many of his colleagues however, who later
turned their backs on the Soviet Union in disillusion, he did not
proclaim his views in enthusiastic political manifestos. For him the
decisive gain from the revolution was the benefit to production
that resulted from abolishing profits. But in spite of the fairer
social conditions, the living standard of Soviet workers was still
below that of most workers in western Europe. Brecht considered
the most pressing task of the socialist state to be to increase
production and thereby even out the differences in status of the
various social strata engaged in the production process. To
demand social equality, and above all to demand the abolition of
wage hierarchies, he regarded as idealistic. He warned against
apologetic admirers of the socialist structure, 'who credit the
worker in the Soviet Union with such things as "the inspiring
awareness of dedicating himself to a great cause", and hold out no
prospect of any reward in this world for his privations and
exertions'. By and large he thought Stalin's policies were necessary
and right, but he saw no reason to glorify the form of oppression
still associated with his rule. To those intellectuals who were
worried about personal liberty, Brecht replied that without the use
of oppression and force it would never be possible to end
oppression and force. Brecht did not share the illusion of many
writers who, coming from countries where there was such a lack of
freedom, went to the Soviet Union in order to see freedom. As he
saw it, the revolution had not brought freedom as such; but
freedom to produce had been achieved: 'The state now serves

production. It functions well in so far as it makes production possible, and it is necessary so long as production needs it'.

That Brecht in 1933 did not at once move to the land of the working-classes, which according to his political opponents would have been the right thing for a dedicated communist author to do, was in the first place a corollary of his declared intentions not to go far from Germany, and not to go to any country with completely different cultural traditions, where his dramatic experiments would be unlikely to be understood. But now that one could no longer count on a quick end to Nazi rule, the need arose for a thorough reappraisal of the question whether the Soviet Union was not in fact the country best suited for a Marxist orientated writer to live and work in. It was for this reason that, early in 1935, Brecht gladly accepted an invitation to Moscow, so that he could study the situation there and the opportunities for work. The occasion for the journey was a Brecht evening given at the suggestion of Erwin Piscator by emigrant German artists at the Moscow club for foreign workers, where the 'Deutsches Theater Kolonne Links,' consisting of former members of the Berlin 'agitprop' theatre 'Kolonne Links' and the 'Truppe 1931', was now also installed.

Erwin Piscator had gone to the Soviet Union in 1931 to make his film *The Fishermen's Revolt in Santa Barbara*, based on a story by Anna Seghers, which took much longer than expected to complete. In 1934 he had been elected president of MORT (International Association of Revolutionaries of the Theatre), which he wanted to enlarge into an international communication centre for anti-fascist artists. His idea was that MORT should also publish its own newspaper, produce films and promote plays. But Piscator's most ambitious plan was to establish an anti-fascist cultural centre in the Soviet Union. Once his plans were realized, he wanted Brecht to play a leading role. This was not the least of his reasons for arranging to have an invitation sent to him.

Brecht would probably have been given permission to pay an extended visit to the Soviet Union whenever he wanted, but for less eminent refugees an entry visa was very hard to get. Compared to the countries of western Europe, the first workers' and farmers' state granted exile only on a very modest scale. Entry visas were refused to the majority of emigrants with communist sympathies. Moscow was not an emigrant-centre like Prague or Paris; but all refugees who were eventually accepted, were given adequate assistance and employment. Moreover a great deal of Soviet money flowed into solidarity funds and aid committees in western Europe.

The main concern of writers like J. R. Becher, Erich Weinert, Friedrich Wolf, Willi Bredel, Fritz Erpenbeck, Ernst Ottwalt, Julius Hay and Maria Osten, who were living in Moscow in 1935, was to form a German language theatre. The idea was that it should be mobile and give performances in all the districts where German was still sufficiently understood. The Soviet republic of the Volga Germans, in particular, was an obvious choice for an operation of this sort. But first there was the problem of establishing a position in Moscow, the difficulty being that Piscator's ambitious plans, whose aim was essentially that of artistic experiment, were in direct conflict with the aspirations of artists round Gustav von Wangenheim, whose plans were centred, to a large extent, on the new catch phrases of 'proletarian humanism'.

Brecht's first talks in Moscow made it clear to him that the prospects for a German theatre were in any case very slight, but were non-existent for a theatre such as he and Piscator had in mind. On 1 May 1935 a German regional theatre, which most of the members of the 'Deutsches Theater Kolonne Links' immediately joined, was finally established at Dnjepropetrovsk. In charge of it was Maxim Vallentin. The company drove by lorry to the villages of the Ukraine, where they performed and held discussions in the market places and community houses. In the early days their performances were still very much in the style of the 'agitprop' theatre, but before long they too had to change their ways and cultivate the classical heritage. Finally, after abandoning experimental ventures of every kind, those members of the company loyal to the party took over the Akademisches Deutsches Theater in Engels, with the result that Piscator was unable to exert any further influence. In the spring of 1935 Curt Trepte, who was one of Vallentin's associates at the German regional theatre in the Ukraine, and who in 1937 returned to his Swedish exile, tried independently of Brecht to enlist Helene Weigel's services as an actress. Brecht advised his wife to agree to a tour of at the most two months, in order to take a closer look at things before committing herself further: 'One has no idea what this sort of thing is like down

203

there; it certainly won't be first class and I doubt if it is even third class'.

Meanwhile Moscow provided no opportunity to stage his plays nor could he obtain a definite promise of a part for Helene Weigel either in the theatre or in films. At that time Brecht's epic theatre stood no chance of recognition or success in the Soviet Union. Politically, too, there was little call for it, because in Russia communism was not blindly acclaimed as the finest and greatest thing in the world, but was presented as 'the least that was required', as something created by man for man. The preference was for academic, naturalistic theatre, for appropriately tendentious social drama. If the acting of a Carola Neher, who lived in Moscow, was not appreciated, the possibility of an engagement for Helene Weigel did not even arise. Brecht had only a few friends on whom he could count, and they themselves were now caught in the crossfire of arguments over the correct interpretation of socialist realism. By 1935 the playwright Sergei Tretjakov, whose Russian translation of Brecht's plays had been published shortly before the latter's visit to Moscow, was already out of favour, and Meyerhold, whom Brecht considered the greatest Soviet director, was being increasingly obstructed in his work. Only Piscator's plan to create a model anti-fascist theatre in Engels envisaged a sphere of activity for Brecht commensurate with his status. But the negotiations with government representatives of the German-speaking Volga republic went on for months, and it was not until the summer of 1936 that Margarete Steffin brought Brecht a firm offer from Piscator. Brecht, who in the meantime had been to New York for the rehearsals of *The Mother* and while there had had the same sort of discouraging experiences he had had in Moscow, immediately replied to Piscator: 'Grete has told me of the Engels plan. The idea of creating a big experimental theatre in which we can resume and extend our theatrical research strikes me as splendid. I saw in New York how greedily a great many people absorb everything to do with the new technique. It is becoming clearer and clearer to them that they cannot solve the new problems with the old means and the miserable equipment they have at their disposal'.

A few weeks later, when Piscator was in Paris with Arthur Pieck on a commission for the Comintern, MORT was closed down as an international organization. At the same time Piscator heard from Wilhelm Pieck in Moscow that the proposed Engels contract was in abeyance for the time being: 'With the approval of the authorities concerned I am writing to inform you that there is no need for you to come back and that, for the present, there is no talk of putting the Engels contract into effect'. Piscator knew only too well what this meant and in consequence never returned to the Soviet Union. In so far as they were able to do so, many emigrants moved to the West during the months that followed. Brecht's friends Tretjakov, Ernst Ottwalt and Carola Neher were arrested and died in forced labour camps. As late as the beginning of 1937, however, Lion Feuchtwanger was still able to get the actor Alexander Granach, who had already been arrested, out of the country.

The shilly-shallying, suspicious attitude of the Soviet authorities towards German emgirant communists, and especially towards artists like Brecht, was due not least to the differing assessments of the political situation in Germany. Since 1933 the Soviet people had never been correctly informed about the defeat of the German labour movement, which meant that audiences were perplexed even by the anti-fascist plays of someone like Friedrich Wolf. A play about the 'struggle in the West' by Vsevolod Vishnevsky, author of the *The Optimistic Tragedy*, actually had to be banned, because it called for an alliance between the German Communist and Social Democrat parties, and thus indirectly accused the Comintern policy of being disastrous. In 1935 party headquarters in Moscow was still fostering hopes of a German proletariat, which had long ceased to exist. The years 1935 to 1937, when the policies of the Popular Front were being most actively promoted—policies which aroused very mixed feelings in Brecht because of their purely tactical nature—brought a noticeable relaxation in the attitude of the Soviet party organs to the German emigrants in Russia; understandably, however, this attitude hardened again during the Moscow trials and after the Hitler-Stalin pact. The emigrants genuinely wanted to have no truck with any friendship between the German (Nazi infected) and the Russian people, of which Walter Ulbricht had the temerity to speak in 1940. For two years, until the Nazis' Russian campaign, there was a strict official ban on anti-fascist propaganda. To remain an advocate of socialism in the Soviet Union, and of its socialist achievements, although this was the cause to which in spite of everything Stalin was devoting himself, was excessively difficult in those days; it needed the sort of 'cold' knowledge which a Marxist like Brecht had acquired. Speaking of events which were sometimes incomprehensible on any rational basis, he wrote: 'Inside Su all wisdom was directed towards construction and away from politics. Outside Su everyone rendered himself liable to a charge of corruption if he praised Ni-en's (Stalin's) merits, even when these were undeniable; inside Su everyone rendered himself liable to a charge of treason if he revealed his mistakes, even though they were ones under which he himself suffered'.

In 1935, when Brecht was in Moscow, the brief phase of intensified propaganda for the Popular Front was just beginning. He was able to recite his poem 'To Those who Conform' ('An die Gleichgeschalteten') over the Moscow radio, and he had talks with the relevant cultural authorities which later led to establishing the periodical *Das Wort,* on whose editorial board Heinrich Mann and Lion Feuchtwanger were to serve, as well as Brecht himself. When it became known at the Paris writers' congress in June that the periodicals *Neue Deutsche Blätter* and *Die Sammlung* were shortly going to have to cease publication, Michail Kolsov, head of the Soviet publishing house of Jourgaz, promised once more to do his best to find ways and means of establishing a representative German language magazine for exile literature, which all the delegates were so anxious to have. A magazine of the type planned by Kolsov, Brecht and Feuchtwanger was possible only because of the Popular Front policy. To do what Brecht would have liked and turn the project into a magazine for original writing and Marxist criticism proved impossible, but it would still be better than Becher's *Internationale Literatur.*

In those days the Comintern sent their agents into any country in which the social structure showed signs of instability. The social democrats, hiterto regarded as universal enemies, suddenly became allies; agreements were reached even with bourgeois democratic parties in order to enlist their help in fighting left-wing sectarian groups. In the cultural sector the policy of the Popular Front was to form alliances with the great figures of bourgeois literature like Thomas Mann and Stefan Zweig, but to fight tooth and nail intellectual sectarians like Joyce and Tretjakov. In its early stages this policy meant a cautious departure from incapsulation. A large number of Soviet party men and writers were able to travel abroad to make propaganda for the Popular

Front. Only two years later this entry into the field of agitation cost most of these emissaries their lives, unless they had avoided contact with independent thinkers.

Brecht's first links with Kolsov and his wife Maria Osten, who did all the preliminary secretarial work for *Das Wort*, were formed in Moscow in 1935. Brecht had no close contacts among the emigrant politicians of the German Communist Party; Wilhelm Pieck was the only one with whom he struck up a mild friendship, while he found Béla Kun, the Hungarian party leader, interesting to talk to. The idea of meeting Stalin never occurred to him; only the high priests of humanism and novelists with an international reputation were received at that exalted level. As the most important events in Moscow during 1935 Brecht noted the guest appearance of the Chinese actor Mei-lan-Fan, and the inauguration of the metro on 27 April, the takeover of which by the Moscow workers he celebrated in a chronicle: 'And all this had been built in a single year and by more builders than any other railway in the world. And no other railway in the world had so many owners'.

Those who had worked on it now received the fruit of their labours. Brecht praised these worker heroes and enjoyed being carried away by their enthusiasm. For the first time in human history owners and builders were one and the same thing. For Brecht this was what mattered; he could forget the embellishment of the stations with marble and precious woods, the love of display and the fact that they looked like ballrooms, which offended his sober aesthetic sensibilities and his clear-cut views on art. At the time the 'wonderful' building feat was symbolic of the triumph of socialism. The sacrifices and privations had been given a meaning, the social usefulness of what had been done was apparent, and the pride of the masses in 'their' metro made all criticism trivial.

Meanwhile the social upsurge, the Soviet Union's huge leap from an agricultural country to a powerful industrial state, gradually came to represent the essence and sole aspect of the path to communism. Even Brecht often made the mistake of seeing the 'rapidity' of the socialist build-up as a quality, and as a guarantee that socialistically aware men and women would succeed in their goal. In spite of all the work, all the achievements, all the

207

mechanization and industrialization at any price, this last all too often remained a pious hope. According to Brecht, however, communism should be 'the mean' not 'the extreme':

Der Kommunismus ist nicht das Äusserste
Was nur zu einem kleinen Teil verwirklicht werden kann, sondern
Wo er nicht ganz and gar verwirklicht ist
Gibt es keinen Zustand, der
Selbst von einem Unempfindlichen ertragbar wäre.

(Communism is not the extreme, of which only a small part can be realized; but until it is realized in its entirety, there can be no state of things that would be tolerable even were one insensitive.)

Brecht in his apartment on the
Charlottenburger Knie in Berlin.

Brecht wrote of this photograph: 'To obtain a picture showing how one works is not easy. Tomorrow one will probably have a method of working that can be photographed. But hitherto it has often proved difficult to reconcile working with being photographed. I myself almost always work in conjunction with others; for this reason I got the photographer to come at a time when I had the room full of people, even if not with the specific intention of working. I must also state, by way of excuse, that our unnatural attitudes are due to our decision to behave for once as though we knew we were being photographed.' – The picture was taken in 1927, in Brecht's work-room in the Spichern Strasse and shows, from left to right, Paul Samson-Körner, Brecht, Samson-Körner's manager Seelenfreund, Hans Borchardt, Hannes Küpper and Elisabeth Hauptmann.

Top left: Brecht and the boxer
Paul Samson-Körner taken in
Brecht's work-room in the
Spichern Strasse.
Top right: Elisabeth Hauptmann
in her Berlin apartment, about
1929.
Bottom: Emil Burri and Brecht
in Le Lavandou, 1930.

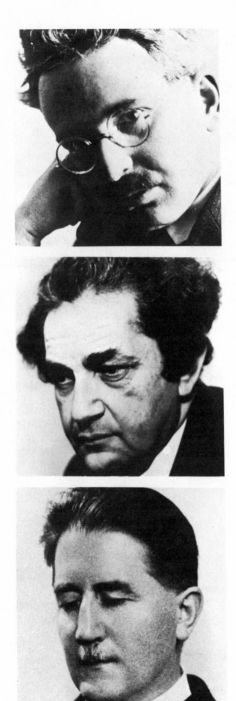

Top: Walter Benjamin
Centre: Fritz Sternberg
Bottom: Karl Korsch

Carola Neher trying on costumes
for her role as Polly in *The
Threepenny Opera*. Taken in
Elisabeth Hauptmann's Berlin
apartment, 1928.

Top: Brecht playing skat with his Augsburg friends Rudolf Hartmann and Georg Pfanzelt in 1934, when they visited him in Skovbostrand.
Bottom: Margarete Steffin, the 'little soldier of the revolution'.

Karin Michaelis at Brecht's,
Skovbostrand 1934.

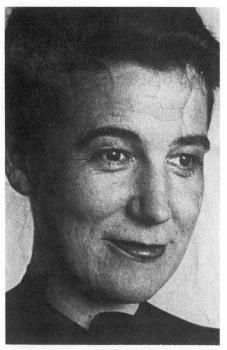

'He whom I love has told me that he needs me.' Ruth Berlau, 'red Ruth', called by Brecht his sister Lai-tu or Ute.

Special performance of Brecht's
Senora Carrar's Rifles in
Copenhagen, 2 February 1934.
Top: Ruth Berlau, the actress
Bodil Ipsen, Brecht and Helene
Weigel.
Bottom: Martin Andersen Nexö
with Margarete Steffin.

Brecht with his son Stefan in Lidingö, August 1939.

1. The one-act play, *What is the price of iron ?*, produced by Brecht and Ruth Berlau in Stockholm, August 1939.

2. 'Care for a smoke? Genuine Austrillos!'

3. Svendson stands and does Swedish drill with his iron bars.

4. A 'customer' enters the iron merchant's shop.

5. 'Your face seems so familiar to me.'

6. 'Then it must be blood. Do you want the money or not?'

7. 'It's only my stomach, it rumbles.'

8. 'Has he also bought from you, then?'

9. A woman shoe dealer.

10. 'Genuine Czech. Eleven krone each.'

11. 'Still your lowest price?'

12. 'But as we are cousins I'll let you have them for eight krone, in other words for the iron.'

13. 'And then a higher power called him to himself.'

14. He wipes a tear from his eyes, and as he does so a revolver falls from his sleeve.

15. Enter a lady and gentleman.

16. 'Frau Gall and I would like a word with you, if you can spare the time.'

17. 'What, Frau Tschek killed?'

18. 'I can assure you I abhor violence of every kind.'

19. 'Ah, quite a gathering.'

20. 'But I see that the atmosphere is hostile to me.'

21. 'I have brought you some shoes.'

22. 'And you are doing well out of it, Svendson.'

23. The customer leaves, heavily laden.

24. 'What is the price of iron?'

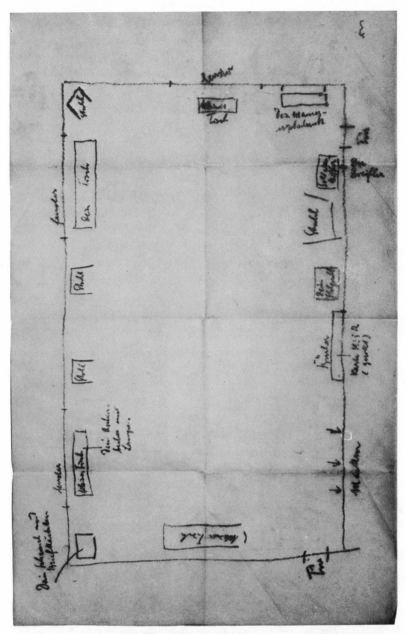

In the middle of August 1942 Brecht moved to a larger house in Santa Monica, with its own garden. Here, for the first time since he arrived in America, he felt 'fairly well'. He wrote to Ruth Berlau, whom he expected back from New York, sending her sketches of the lay-out and pointing out how well his work-room was situated, 'without any need to pass through rooms occupied by others'. In this plan of his work-room he indicated, among other things, the following: your manuscript cupboard, The Doubter, soldier's chest, your standing desk, masks, your stool with compartments for letters, your ash tray and lamp, your table.

Brecht and Lion Feuchtwanger in Santa Monica, 1945.

'How will my home town receive me? Before me come the bombers. Deadly swarms announce to you my return. Conflagrations herald the son.

Brecht in October 1947, shortly before his return to Europe.

Brecht at the entrance of his house in 26th Street, Santa Monica.

Peter Lorre reading the Svendborg poems in the garden of Brecht's house in Santa Monica.

'When I returned my hair was not yet grey. I was happy. – The toils of the mountains lie behind us, before us lie the toils of the plains'. Brecht in the Letzigraben in Zurich, 1949.

Brecht in Zurich, 1949.

Brecht with Fritz Kortner at the stage door of the Zurich Schauspielhaus, 1949.

Max Frisch explains to Brecht the construction of the diving-tower during a visit to the site of the new swimming-bath in the Letzigraben in the spring of 1949: 'Ruth Berlau was there but being a woman soon got bored, while Brecht, in duty bound though nervously, climbed tier after tier of scaffolding and finally even the ten metre diving-tower from where one got the best view of the whole area. Up there, however, he had no ears for explanations, only for respect. . . not until he was down again was he prepared to listen to a lecture on statics.'

Brecht and Caspar Neher in Zurich, 1947.

On 3 September 1949
Brecht went to his native
town of Augsburg, where
he visited Georg Pfanzelt.

Brecht in Zurich, 1949.

Brecht at the Bâle
carnival, beginning
of March 1949.

Right:

Brecht and Helene Weigel at the
book bazaar in the Stalin-Allee,
Berlin, 1 May 1953. In the
background the writer Erwin
Strittmatter.

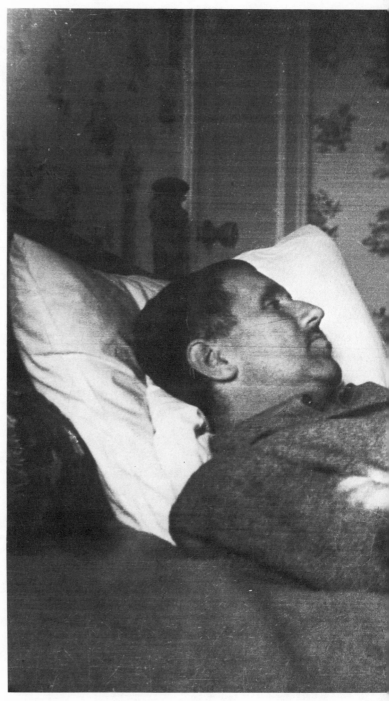

'Friends, what I want is that you should know the truth and speak it!'
Brecht reading the newspapers in his apartment in the Chaussee Strasse in Berlin.

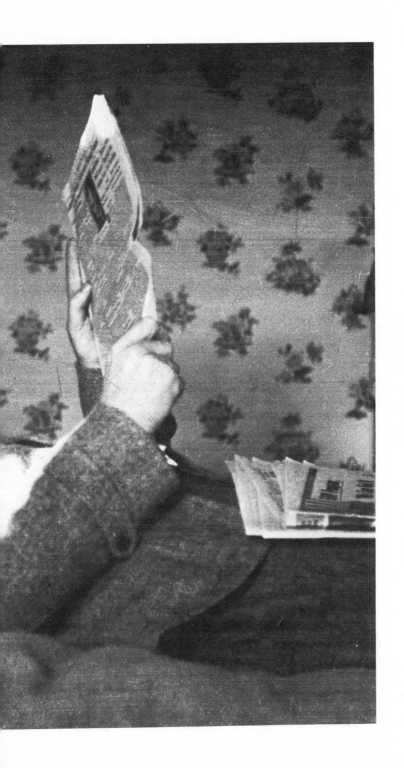

Helene Weigel, 1900–1971

Elisabeth Hauptmann, 1897–1973

Ruth Berlau, 1906–1974

18

London

Brecht spent the autumn of 1934, and a few weeks in the spring of 1936, in London. Karl Korsch had chosen the English capital to live in because it had no specific exile atmosphere and no mutually hostile groups of German emigrants, but contained people from every country in the world with similar convictions and with whom one could talk. If one mastered the English language one could take part in its cultural and political life. The fact that in his case residence there ended as a bad political comedy only confirmed Brecht's view that Korsch was a theorist who found it very hard to reach decisions 'in matters concerning his personal life'. Writers and scholars who emigrated to England wrote largely for the English public, and actors who were able to acclimatize themselves to London acted for English audiences. Among those who were successful on the London stage, or in films, were Elisabeth Bergner, Lucie Mannheim, Grete Mosheim, Oskar Homolka, Conrad Veidt, Adolf Wohlbrück (Anton Walbrook) and Ernst Deutsch. Most of the emigrants found England a liberal and sympathetic country to live in.

Until 1938, it is true, refugees from Nazi Germany had to comply with the usual entry regulations. A resident permit was issued only if the applicant held a valid passport and visa, was in possession of adequate financial means, and knew a British citizen of good standing who would vouch for him. In this way people from Germany seeking asylum were restricted to a small number of privileged refugees who were generally able to adapt themselves unobtrusively to conditions in the host country. They established excellent relations with their British colleagues, and when some official regulation or other had to be complied with they received skilful assistance in circumventing it. Many artists, for instance, acquired British nationality by marriage; many marriages of expediency were concluded merely for the sake of the documents.

The poet Auden married Erika Mann, and a politically broad-minded relative of the British royal family found a suitable husband for the actress Therese Giehse. Auden's young friend, the writer Christopher Isherwood, worked as an assistant to Berthold Viertel, who had been making films in England since 1933. People knew each other, helped each other, put contracts in each other's way, without having to enter into any commitment that underlined their emigrant status.

Brecht hoped to do business in London. The theatre, which he described as 'antediluvian', showed no interest in his plays and even the English publishers offered him no more than a translation of *The Threepenny Opera*. But he had initial talks with Wieland Herzfelde, whose Prague publishing-house was now a London firm owing to conditions in Czechoslovakia, about a collected edition of his works; the first two volumes of this finally appeared in 1938, just before Czechoslovakia was annexed by Nazi Germany. The most Brecht could hope for in England was work on a film project. In conjunction with Leo Lania, who had formerly worked with Piscator and for the new version of whose play *Das Ölfeld* he wrote two poems, he drafted a story about the Viennese doctor Semmelweis, a specialist in puerperal fever. Lania tried to sell the script to the film producer and director Alexander Korda, but he was unable to use it.

Hanns Eisler, whom in London Brecht inveigled into committing further 'vulgar' excesses, in other words into composing workers' marching songs, also put him in touch with Berthold Viertel; but he had no contracts to offer for film scripts. Brecht's inability to express himself adequately in a foreign language was a major obstacle in his attempt to gain a foothold in the film industry. He was at the mercy of experienced script writers, who turned his suggestions into the usual saleable merchandize before he had even formulated them properly. Brecht was an outcast, a man robbed of his place of work, unable to find his niche on foreign soil. Viertel, who had produced films in Hollywood prior to 1933 and was not wholly dependent on the German language, wrote of the 'expatriate' playwright who did not want to be an emigrant: 'Dressed in your leather jacket you wander round in foreign towns, whose idiom you will never learn, because both tongue and soul revolt against the foreign gibberish'. With no great success to his credit, Brecht returned to Svendborg at Christmas 1934; things were tough, but not altogether without prospects, was his verdict.

Brecht's hope that he might still get a slice of the 'international drug traffic' cake came true in the spring of 1936. Fritz Kortner had managed to convince Karl Grune, who was to direct a film of Pagliacci starring Richard Tauber, that Brecht should have a hand in the script. The London company making the film, confident that the inclusion of well known names would help, sent a telegram to Brecht in Denmark offering him a contract for five hundred pounds. A jubilant Brecht reported to Eisler, who was to act as musical adviser and conductor for the film and was surprised at the speed with which Kortner's 'intrigue' had succeeded. While Eisler looked upon his high fee as a means of financing his work on the *Deutsche Sinfonie* and took advantage of every free weekend to go to Paris at the film company's expense, Brecht was grimly determined to take his part seriously. Intent on doing something for his money, he actually made suggestions, which caused the producers considerable alarm and merely upset the script writers Drinkwater and Burford, as well as Tauber himself, in their routine. No one was interested in Brecht's work, and when he persisted stubbornly in his ideas he was simply paid off and shown the door. Brecht was so furious at being treated in this manner by the 'film mob' that, expecting Kortner and Eisler to support him, he asked them not to take any further part in the film. But as both of them had regarded the project from the beginning merely as a source of cash, they had no intention of protesting until they had received their money. It was an occasion when Brecht found conspiratorial laughter very hard to stomach, he had suffered a deeply wounding defeat.

What was right for the film industry was apparently also right for one of the great men in the literature industry. At Eisler's Brecht met Stefan Zweig, whose work he despised and could not read. It was not his wealth that the two Marxist artists held against him, but his attitude of mind which, rooted in his wealth, was glaringly reflected in his work. Eisler called it 'stock exchange humanism'. Brecht took the opportunity of the usual question, 'What are you working on?', to ask his friend to play the famous author the 'song of the stimulating effect of money'. Eisler croaked his way tellingly through this attractive battle song of the 'base materialists', written for the new version of *Pointed Heads and Round Heads,* followed it with the 'Ballad of the Water Wheel' and finished up with the 'Saarlied', an occasional poem. Stefan Zweig listened to the songs poker faced, his only comment being a tentative 'interesting'; but when Brecht apologetically called the little election song a trifle written 'to help the cause a bit' Zweig replied caustically: 'Don't call it a trifle, Herr Brecht, it is, perhaps, the best thing you have written'.

> Hinter uns lassend die Hölle der Enttäuschten
> Gelangten wir in die Hölle der Enttäuscher.
> In einer grauen Stadt, erfüllt von Marktgeschrei
> Trafen wir, die ihr Gesicht verloren hatten.

(Leaving behind the hell of the deceived, we came to the hell of the deceivers. In a grey city, filled with the cries of the market place, we met those who had become faceless.)

In 1934 Brecht had gone to London alone. As he walked through the foggy city, or strolled past the market stalls in the early morning, he missed Margarete Steffin, his little 'soldier of the revolution', who was convalescing in the Soviet Union: 'Write and tell me what you lack. Is it my arm?' When he saw a fruit barrow he automatically put his hand in his pocket for money to buy an orange, as he used to do in Paris, but was forced to the bitter realization, 'there is no you in this city'. On his second visit he was accompanied by Ruth Berlau, whom he called Lai-tu, his sister and pupil: 'It is the essence of love, as it is of other great productions, that lovers take seriously many things that others treat lightly: a mere touch, an imperceptible nuance. The best succeed in bringing their love into perfect harmony with other productions; then their kindliness becomes universal, their resourcefulness a benefit to many, and they assist everything that is productive'.

It was Ruth Berlau, the defender and staunch advocate of his didactic plays, who encouraged him to write a stage hit in the style of *The Threepenny Opera,* so that they would have money to finance a proletarian theatre. In June 1935 Brecht had already intimated, for publicity purposes, that he was working on an operetta, with a woman pirate as the central character. Hanns Eisler was to write the music and he intended to negotiate with Mae West to create the part. In 1936, when they were sitting around in London doing nothing because they wanted to attend a

212

coming anti-fascist writers' congress, Brecht and Ruth Berlau, recalling the prematurely announced plan, began to draft a play with the title *Joys and Sufferings of the Lesser Pirates (Freuden und Lieden der kleineren Seeräuber)*, in which an amorous widow sings:

> Ich bezweifle, ob er meiner wert ist
> Ob es wirklich Liebe bei ihm is?
> Wenn all mein Gespartes aufgezehrt ist
> Wirft er dann die Schale auf den Mist?
> Ach, ich weiss warum ich mich so wehrte:
> Wenn ich ihn nur nicht so sehr begehrte.

(I doubt if he is good enough for me, if what he feels is really love for me. When all my savings have been gobbled up, will he then cast aside what's left of me? Ah, I know why I resisted so—if only I'd not craved him so.)

In all the literary projects initiated by Ruth Berlau the terms demanded for love in a male-dominated society played a central role. At this time Ruther Berlau was working on a volume of short stories, *Jedes Tier kann es,* in the closing stages of which Brecht gave advice and helped with corrections. It concerned seven women, laid out side by side in their coffin in the mortuary, who render an account of their lives. None of them derived any pleasure from the sexual act; they experienced only pain, because each embrace was an 'embrace of wrestlers': 'The women raised their arms in defence as they were enveloped by their possessors'. In a fragment written for the 'Didactic Poem on the Nature of Man' ('Lehrgedicht von der Natur des Menschen'), 'Love's Downfall' was reduced to the following formula: 'Life moves between "let me go" and "I shall hold on", and the hands of each, of the one who holds on and of the one who struggles free, curl into claws. Who can learn to give when to none is given?'

Ruth Berlau herself was unhappily married, a fact of which Brecht reminded her at this time, and slept with her husband only because she was married to him. Her husband, on the other hand, was devoted to her, permitted her every liberty and encouraged the 'third party' so that he could be near her. Brecht reproached her: 'What is the good of finding a third party with whom you are united, and of retaining another third party who reconciles you. It is like taking a piece of bread and washing it down with poison'. Robert Lund respected his wife's feelings and tolerated her whims

213

with great patience. He treated the consumptive Margarete Steffin, and was always at the service of Brecht and his family when they needed a doctor. Ruth Berlau suffered from her insincerity towards her husband, but did not take Brecht's sermonizing too seriously because she knew that he did not follow his own maxims altogether strictly. Essentially he was right, but what really upset him was the fact that she did not sleep exclusively with him. Political events soon forced Brecht to a decision. When the Nazis occupied Denmark and he left Sweden for Finland, he insisted that his 'sister' follow him; and when she received these lines from him, she no longer had any choice: 'I love you. And nothing will change that. However long we are apart. Even in ten, even in twenty years. As for Lai-tu, she is charged with taking care of herself and of seeing herself safely through the dangers until *our* turn comes, the true one for which we have to save ourselves, Ruth dear. Near or far'. Brecht loved Ruth Berlau, but through her association with him she lost her power to organize and control her life. She exhausted herself in her love for Brecht, it possessed and consumed her. She always looked upon the little poem 'Frailties' ('Schwächen'), found among Brecht's things after his death, as her poem:

> Du hattest keine
> Ich hatte eine:
> Ich liebte.

(You had none I had one: I loved.)

19

But why be afraid of what is new?

In a period when it is involved in serious
fighting, and is facing still more serious
fighting, the proletariat must demand of its
theatre the most exceptional efforts, an
altogether exceptional speed of adaptation,
the most rapid achievement of an altogether
exceptional level of political knowledge.

Having found in Moscow, the metropolis of a new, all-
transforming type of society, scarcely a trace any longer of a
progressive proletarian theatre, Brecht renewed and intensified his
efforts to find opportunities in the west for his theatrical schemes.
Since truly epoch-making and revolutionary experiments could
not be conducted without state subsidies, for the time being only
some sort of compromise was possible. Brecht was not prepared to
allow that the only difference between the proletarian and
bourgeois theatres might be the political message. He still believed
that only a different artistic attitude could make the young
proletarian theatre politically effective. Because of this he
concentrated all his hopes on the New York production of *The
Mother,* which the Theatre Union, the most important workers'
theatre in America, was planning for 1935. He was altogether too
hasty in concluding that the choice of his play *The Mother* was a
positive sign that his ideas had the power to convince. To Brecht it
was self-evident that the courage to put on a play like *The Mother*
implied the courage to make changes in the style of production,
without which the necessary political effects could not be
achieved. Meanwhile in New York it had been decided to
concentrate mainly on the dramatization of Gorki's novel, to
present a play, that is, with a revolutionary Russian story, but
without ahdering to Brecht's epic style of performance. When, at
the end of August, Paul Peter's adaptation arrived in

215

Skovsbostrand, Brecht immediately vetoed the proposed naturalistic production of his play: 'For my part I had taken great pains to
avoid naturalistic features, because it seemed to me that the labour
movement needs big, simple forms. I am always afraid of letting
the environment become too predominant, because then the
audience will always explain the characters in terms of their
environment, and the subjective element, right or wrong political
conduct, goes by the board'. As the Theatre Union was a workers'
theatre and promoted by the American Communist Party, Brecht
was prepared to co-operate. With the help of V. J. Jerome, the
cultural representative of the agitprop division of the Communist
Party, to whom he turned in this matter of the production of *The
Mother,* Brecht hoped to be able to convince those collaborating
with him in the theatre that his view was right. He also wrote a
letter in verse to the workers' theatre in which he denounced the
naturalistic elements of the Peters version and contrasted them
with the light, amusing, simple informative style of a performance
imbued with the spirit of the socialist classics: 'Comrades, the form
of the new plays is new. But why be afraid of what is new? Is it hard
to achieve? But why fear what is new and hard to achieve? For a
man who is exploited and constantly deceived life itself is one long
experiment, to earn a few pennies a precarious undertaking not
taught anywhere. Why should he fear the new rather than the old?
But even if your audience, the worker, hesitates you should not
follow him but go ahead of him, go ahead of him swiftly, with long
strides and absolute faith in his ultimate strength'.

Brecht offered to direct the play and said he was prepared to go
to New York 'provided only that my travelling expenses are met. I
am also prepared to pay them back later out of the royalties I
expect'. Brecht's mistake was to regard the Theatre Union as a
workers' theatre, in the sense of the company with which Ruth
Berlau had successfully rehearsed *The Mother.* The actors and
others concerned in the American enterprise were not all
communists; they were a mixture of communists, social democrats
and liberals of every hue. Although the performances were
intended for working people, the greater part of the audience was
middle-class. The company's continued existence depended on
the financial success of each production. This was the main reason
why left-wing American writers and directors, who worked for the

Theatre Union in the nineteen-thirties, were reluctant to embark on experiments.

Jerome, whose attention had been drawn to *The Mother* by Hanns Eisler and who had recommended the play, intervened as mediator between the theatre and Brecht. Initially he was successful. At his suggestion a representative of the theatre, Manuel Gomez, was sent to Denmark to remove the insuperable difficulties. Gomez signed a contract with the author, guaranteed him full control over the integrity of his text and handed him a passage to New York. Each of the signatories was convinced that, on the spot, a feasible solution would be found. Once on American soil, the Theatre Union argued, Brecht would realize that their practice of producing plays in a naturalistic way was the right one. Brecht, on the other hand, had made up his mind that, at the rehearsals, he would insist on directing the play in his own way. On 7 October the 'classic' author left his Danish retreat full of confidence. In a poem, which he gave to Ruth Berlau on leaving, he did not hesitate to compare his journey with that of Christopher Columbus:

Sieh seinen Ruhm wie einen Staub verwehen.
Seit lang ist's nur das Ei, von dem man spricht.
Gern steht das Allerneueste dort im Licht.
Ob sie jedoch ein Lehrstück schon verstehen?
Traust Du denn diesen, dass sie Dich erkennen
Trotz Deiner Grösse einen Grossen nennen?

(See how his fame, like dust has blown away. For long the egg alone's been spared this plight. The last in line now steps into the light. But will they understand didactic plays? Do you trust them to discriminate and, despite your greatness, call you great?)

The talks in America got off to a good start: the two sides liked each other and it seemed as if Brecht's and Eisler's wishes were receiving full consideration. The theatre management agreed at once when their guests advised casting someone else for the part of the mother and furthermore said they were also prepared to do the third act in Brecht's original version. At the beginning of November Brecht reported to Svendborg that he was deep in rehearsals and that the old version had been completely reinstated. 'A nice little bit of dictatorship' had been necessary to bring this about. At first the Americans were prepared to swallow the fact that he thought the cast pretty weak and frequently indulged in blunt criticism, but they found it impossible to countenance the ruthlessly direct political message which Brecht and Eisler brought to bear. In their view it was completely out of place in the theatre. Finally Paul Peters, the translator, and Victor Wolfson, the director, intervened, countermanded Brecht's instructions and ordered cuts to be made. In Germany Brecht had always rejected any intervention by the party, but now in New York an authoritative word from the party leadership seemed to him the only way to convince the artists of the Theatre Union politically. He vehemently upbraided the half-hearted comrades, gave them political tuition and provoked them with extremist slogans. Encouraged by their horror at this, he proceeded to admonish them in a manner unpleasantly reminiscent of a political commissar. He told the Marxist intellectual Sidney Hook that the American communists were 'lousy' and ought to model themselves on the Russian ones. When Hook reminded him of the murder of Kirov, and spoke of other arrests in Russia, Brecht is said to have retorted: 'The more innocent they are, the more they deserve to die'. When those he was talking to annoyed him by their lack of insight into political situations Brecht was often goaded into making much more shocking remarks than that. Stupidity and obtuseness made him passionately unjust.

A bare two weeks before the opening night came the inevitable explosion in the theatre. When Brecht called the work of the musical director, Jerome Moross, 'muck' he was threatened with physical assault unless he left the theatre immediately. The situation was so tense that Brecht and Eisler decided to go. Of all those involved in the production only the stage designer, Mordecai Gorelik, sided with the authors. He had long since got over his anger at Brecht's derogatory remarks about his 'picturesque' sets. In the meantime he had actually come to welcome the suggestions of this man who called himself the 'Einstein of the new theatrical form'. In an initial statement to the theatre management Brecht threatened to withdraw his play, because it had been made impossible for him to enter the theatre to give those in charge of the production 'the directions which I stipulated in my contract'. In a further letter addressed to his 'dear comrades' he said he was still willing to cooperate, although he was not prepared to drop a single one of his demands: 'The fact that a theatre is poor need be no obstacle to good performances, provided that sufficient understanding, hard work and discipline are put into them. Should you really see no possibility of guaranteeing me some final, undisturbed rehearsals, I shall feel obliged to protest against my play being given. You will force me to take the same step if you cannot give Eisler the assurance he asks in order that his music may make its proper effect'. In spite of this the authors were excluded from further rehearsals. Jerome, to whom they again turned for help, demanded from the theatre management that Brecht's requirements be met and that no cuts be made unless authorized by him. At the same time he asked Brecht and Eisler not to take any steps to prevent the performance and not to approach the press. Following this, talks took place with Gomez in Brecht's apartment, Elisabeth Hauptmann acting as contact and messenger with both the party leaders and the Theatre Union. Promises were made and assurances given; the two sides agreed and then promptly disagreed again. Instructions stated to have been carried out proved impossible to carry out.

The result was a total failure for both play and performance; the press, almost without exception, tore the whole thing to pieces, which meant financial ruin for the Theatre Union. Even after the first night Brecht and Eisler did not give up all hope of being able to influence New York's hordes of workers politically with *The Mother*. The verdict of the press did not worry them unduly, it was the people who were still to see the play in whom they were interested. Thinking that further work on the performance would help, they requested permission to put their play 'into a political and artistic form worthy of it'. But rehearsals after the first night were not provided for in the theatre's rules, and apart from this the political and artistic level achieved was regarded as perfectly satisfactory. In a memorandum, in which they once more recapitulated in great detail the events leading up to the dispute, Brecht and Eisler concluded that, to their disappointment, 'The theatre's behaviour is no different from that of any theatre on Broadway, which treats a play simply as a piece of merchandize, or as raw material for an easily saleable piece of merchandize'. A few days later Brecht wrote to Piscator, who was involved in similar disputes in Moscow: '*The Mother* has been ruined here (stupid

219

mutiltations, political ignorance, backwardness of every sort, etc) .
. . . All in all an experience, but never have anything to do with so-
called theatres of the left. They are run by little cliques, which are
dominated by playwrights, and have the worst Broadway
producers' manners without their specialized knowledge which, if
not very great, is at least something'.

When he wrote 'dominated by playwrights' Brecht was thinking
primarily of Clifford Odets, whose play *Waiting for Lefty* had
struck him as quite interesting, but whose *Paradise Lost* provoked
him to a polemical outburst on fundamentals. He accused Odets of
portraying in his play exploiters who 'themselves are ruined'.
Because they fail, he asked, are industrialists any less exploiters, or
'are you trying to tell us that our oppressors have already been
sapped of their strength? Are we to sit back and do nothing?' After
he got back to Svendborg he wrote to Jerome asking him without
fail to initiate discussions on plays like *Paradise Lost,* so that young
people entering the communist movement would not be left in the
dark as to the cause of the evil in the world. Looking back he
regretted that there had not been more opportunities in New York
to discuss literary questions. It was not people like Jerome who
were to blame for the failure of *The Mother* in America, but artists
with insufficient political knowledge. Brecht's didactic play
merely repelled them, disturbed their accustomed modes of
thought and patterns of work. His experiences in New York were a
repetition of those he had had a few months earlier in Moscow: he
was rejected and not understood by party men and left-wing
artists. In Moscow he had struck up a friendship with Béla Kun, in
New York with V. J. Jerome. If Brecht originally saw such
connections in terms of their 'usefulness', in the end they did him
more harm than good: Béla Kun was liquidated, while in America
it was better not to associate with communists. In February 1939,
when their son Fred was born, Brecht sent the Jeromes this little
poem, from the Chinese of Su Tung-p'o, recalling those days in
New York:

> Familien, wenn ihnen ein Kind geboren ist
> Wünschen es sich intelligent.
> Ich, der ich durch Intelligenz
> Mein ganzes Leben ruiniert habe
> Kann nur hoffen, mein Sohn
> Möge sich erweisen als

Unwissend und denkfaul.
Dann wird er ein ruhiges Leben haben
Als Minister im Kabinett.

(Families, when they have a child, want it to be intelligent. I, who have ruined my whole life by being intelligent, can only hope my son will turn out to be ignorant and too lazy to think. Then he will lead a quiet life as a cabinet minister.)

After the failure in New York, after the collapse of Piscator's plans for a German language theatre in the Soviet Union, and after reverses like that in London at the hands of the film company, Brecht's only remaining hope was that in Denmark, at least, people would take him seriously as an artist who wrote political plays. Having to wait so long for the promised production of *Round Heads and Pointed Heads* made him impatient and bitter. Moreover his inflexible determination to have nothing to do with any form of 'naturalistic' theatre was alienating more and more Danish artists hitherto friendly to him. There were fewer people prepared at least to misunderstand him. He welcomed the performance of *The Mother,* which Ruth Berlau had prepared under his and Helene Weigel's supervision with the small amateur Revolutionary Theatre company, as a good piece of work, nicely done. A great deal of patience and endless care had gone into it. Those taking part not only acted a play but, in studying it, adopted its teachings and learned to perform it as actors and teachers combined. Pressed to do so by Ruth Berlau, Brecht wrote for the company the didactic poem 'Address to Danish Worker-actors on the Art of Observation ('Rede an die dänischen Arbeiterschauspieler über die Kunst der Beobachtung'): Actors! Your task is to be investigators and teachers in the art of handling people' It was important for actors, who were also workers, to make use of their knowledge of human nature, to portray the world as made by man and subject to change:

> Du, der Schauspieler
> Musst vor allen anderen Künsten
> Die Kunst der Beobachtung beherrschen.
> Nicht wie du aussiehst nämlich is wichtig, sondern
> Was du gesehen hast und zeigst. Wissenswert
> Ist, was du weisst.

Man wird dich beobachten, um zu sehen
Wie gut du beobachtet hast.

(You, as actors, have to master the art of observation above all other arts.
For what matters is not what you look like but what you have seen and
manifest. What we want to know is what you know. People will observe
you, to see how well you have observed.)

The company met in the evenings for discussions and rehearsals
under the red flag in a cellar in the old town of Copenhagen. Red
Ruth prepared coffee and sandwiches. Helene Weigel sang Eisler's
songs, Brecht played, checked attitudes and gestures. The Danish
poet, Otto Gelsted, who had translated the songs, gave language
lessons. In these surroundings Ruth Berlau was very much the
'one hundred and twenty per cent party communist', constantly
demanding explanations and written commentaries from Brecht:
'There were few communists present when we started rehearsals, a
great many by the time our work was over'.

The Revolutionary Theatre's influence was restricted to a
numerically small audience, and because Brecht was anxious to
make a good start in Copenhagen's big theatres, the bourgeois
press was not mobilized to the extent that perhaps it should have
been. This production of *The Mother* would in any case only have
elicited prejudices against political theatre in general. It was with
his parable play *Round Heads and Pointed Heads* that Brecht hoped
to achieve the success he wanted. The production had been
delayed because Per Knutzon and Lulu Ziegler, who had become
co-directors of an experimental theatre, had opened their new
venture with a piece of social criticism in the form of a musical that
unexpectedly ran for over a year; it was only in the autumn of 1936,
when the run of this *Lost Melody* came to an end, that Brecht's play
finally went into rehearsal. Per Knutzon had reached an excellent
understanding with the author on the dramaturgical problems and
stylistic principles of the production. He was ready to commit
himself wholeheartedly to a completely epic and non-Aristotelian
manner of performance, but then quarrelled with Brecht when it
came to checking each phrase for its social 'Gestus', or attitude.
Brecht retired in disgust to Skovbostrand, where Mordecai
Gorelik found him in the state he knew so well from New York:
railing against the theatre's vicious habit of being interested in a

222

play's climaxes and tensions. Meanwhile Helene Weigel acted as mediator in the Riddersalen Theatre and succeeded in arranging for Brecht to participate again in the final rehearsals. Unlike the New York production of *The Mother,* the Riddersalen performance conformed in the essential points to Brecht's own ideas, and he saw no reason to disassociate himself fundamentally from the final result. Reactions in the Danish press to the play and its performance were to demonstrate to him once and for all that he could not carry on doggedly with his experiments at the point where the Nazis had interrupted him. He was asking too much. The attitudes and conflicts of his characters were communicated only in abstract terms. All he provided was illustrative material. The audience expected actual examples.

The greatest care and diplomatic skill were devoted to publicizing the first night on 4 November 1936. In interviews the political nature of the performance was played down and emphasis laid on the good relations with the censor, who had raised no objections. Nothing was said about it being a world première; instead, reports were circulated of the play's success in New York and Moscow, and of an impending production in Prague.

The reception on the opening night was warm, but this was probably due in the main to Danish friends who were sympathetic to Brecht; among these were Karin Michaelis and Frederik Martner. The bourgeois press claimed that these prominent 'drawing-room radicals' were incompetent to judge. For its part it scarcely touched on the play's political propaganda, being much more concerned to draw attention to what, in its view, was the play's bad construction. The author had laid himself open to this treatment by stating in the programme that he disputed the claim of plays dealing with contemporary events to be called 'dramatic art'. One critic wrote: 'In the programme Brecht commends himself as the inventor of the epic drama; we would be happier if he would invent dramatic dramas for us'. It was unfortunate that Frederik Schyberg, the 'Danish Kerr', who had written in support of Brecht after the performances of *The Threepenny Opera* and *Mahagonny,* now launched a massive attack. He had heard of Brecht's differences with Knutzon, so he praised the production and took the author severely to task, calling him a 'pallid sectarian with a meagre talent'. He not only called *Round Heads and Pointed Heads* undramatic but condemned the play for the scepticism and

223

contempt for humanity it expressed. He wrote of a crude masked comedy without people, in which he could discover only intelligence but no poetry. Almost all the critics, even those further to the left, found the form of the play unsuited to its content; in their view satiric means were not appropriate to treatment of the racial question, they missed any positive human beings. A social democrat newspaper wrote: 'He should have given us some hint—to underline his ideas—that deep down most of us after all are good and are only led astray by a morally destructive form of society'. That the play was not entirely untopical, and that there was fruitful soil for Hitler's nationalist programme in Denmark too, was demonstrated by the conservative and undisguisedly national socialist newspapers, which called for a witch hunt.

Roman Catholics and Nazis united in their efforts to get proceedings taken against the 'Jewish communist', who in addition was instantly given the status of pornographer. One statement, fully worthy of *Der Stürmer,* ran: 'If Brecht's play opens the eyes of Danish Catholics to the true character of the Jews, it will not have been written in vain'. Brecht had become a political issue over night. He was now famous, but in a way that he could not turn to his own advantage. Demands were made that the question of his residence permit be looked into. On the other hand the performance at Copenhagen's Riddersalen Theatre now attracted the audiences which hitherto had been kept away by the bad notices. Thanks to the violently anti-semitic articles, *Round Heads and Pointed Heads* ran for twenty-one performances. When the truth came out that Brecht was not a Jew, the attacks became still more malicious. To be just a communist was even worse. The affair was further aggravated by the fact that, in view of the coming great Brecht première at the Riddersalen theatre, the Theatre Royal, where the repetory was always chosen with great care, also wanted to stage a work by this obviously important writer. Although their courage had long since dwindled from *St Joan of the Stockyards* to *The Seven Deadly Sins,* they did not intend to break their contract entirely. The production was carefully prepared in conjunction with the authors. The director of the ballet, Harald Lander, and the cast retired for several days with Brecht, Kurt Weill and the translator Otto Gelsted to Thurö, where Karin Michaelis had put her house at their disposal. Unfortunately the first night of the ballet coincided with the scandal over the performance of *Round Heads and Pointed Heads*. The fact that in the case of *The Seven Deadly Sins* Schyberg was once more full of enthusiasm, because he could bestow all his praise on Kurt Weill, did not help much. It was simply further grist to the fascists' mill to have this communist author now honoured by the Theatre Royal, where he was permitted to sneer at the Catholic religion and drag the 'faith of thousands through the mire'. The fanatical campaign against Brecht, and a hint from the government following an official complaint by the Nazis to the Danish ambassador in Berlin, forced the management of the theatre to take the ballet off after two performances.

The threatened official action against the author did not materialize, but apart from the communists no one at that time stood up for him in public, because it was clear that a Nazi victory in Denmark could no longer be ruled out. Disillusioned, the writer Hans Kirk expostulated with his colleagues in the progressive liberal party over their silence: 'The bourgeois intelligentsia are so afraid of being mistaken for communists that they simply draw in their heads'. Largely as a result of this campaign it was now clear to Brecht that, as far as the immediate future was concerned, he could no longer think of carrying out experimental theatrical work in public that would have worthwhile results. He had learnt the lesson that if you were a refugee the important thing was to stay out of the limelight. He was a guest in a country that was forced to take notice of Nazi Germany. His reputation as a communist did him nothing but harm. For the bourgeois critics he had to become a poet again, a 'true dramatist', if he wanted to have any political say at all. It had been a mistake to say in an interview in 1934: 'We must get away from naturalistic acting, from the emotionally charged dramatic acting of people like Emil Jannings, Poul Reumert and, indeed, the great majority'. Later Brecht greatly regretted this attack on Reumert in particular, because he was the only actor who might have helped to get *Galileo* staged, and successfully staged, in Denmark. Brecht, who wanted results now, found himself compelled to change his attitude, and consented to make compromises in his way of writing. From now on he wrote plays in which 'emotions' were allowed to play a part. *Senora Carrar's Rifles* and *Galileo (Leben des Galileo)* were proof that he had retracted his postulate of a pedagogic theatre. In a letter to Karl Korsch, who was then emigrating to America, Brecht wrote: 'I could not help being very pleased, after *Round Heads,* that my residence permit was renewed. And, moreover, I have friends enough who tell me that I must choose either a reactionary content or a reactionary form; both together would be too much of a good thing. And a prominent communist said, "if that is communism, I am not a communist". Perhaps he is right'.

20

Short Digression on the Play *Round Heads and Pointed Heads*

Round Heads and Pointed Heads is the only great play by Brecht that has still not found a response commensurate with its importance. The reason why it is so rarely performed is probably because, instead of regarding it as a stage parable on the theme 'the Reich and the rich are birds of a feather', people see it merely as a satirical crypto-play about the racial ideology of the Third Reich and Hitler's role in relation to the big capitalists. Today, however, sufficient time has passed for the play to be set in the imaginary Swiftian country of Yahoo, and to be dissociated in performance from Ausschwitz and the specifically German 'final solution' to the Jewish question. Anyone reading the play today would do well to study the extent to which the alterations made by Brecht in the later revisions of the play, referring as they do to the growth of fascism in Germany, are still appropriate to the play's philosophico-political pretensions. Indeed even in 1936, in spite of the pains to which he went to point out contemporary parallels, Brecht was not concerned with any external resemblance to Hitler: 'The mere fact that in certain respects it is a very idealized portrait of a racial prophet (which is all that is needed for the parable) would have prevented this, even had the police not done so'.

Brecht considered the comedy *Measure for Measure* to be the 'most advanced' of all Shakespeare's plays: 'He requires of those in high positions that they do not judge others by standards they do not wish applied to themselves. And it transpires that they may not demand from their subjects a moral attitude which they themselves do not adopt'. He was not satisfied with attempting to put into an up-to-date, actable form the Elizabethan play whose plot Shakespeare had taken from a play by George Whetstone. The old plot, however, provided an excellent basis on which to construct an entirely new story. Shakespeare's story of Angelo, in which a Duke of Vienna appoints a deputy, whom he allows to become unpopular in order to avoid blackening his own good name, gave Brecht the opportunity to demonstrate how little the principle of justice, so prized by the class dominated society, is worth. His Angeler of the first drafts is a comedy character whose rigorous moral code cannot find expression because the capitalist order of society involves conformity with certain economic laws, which a man cannot simply ignore if he wants to get on. This Angeler was intended to expose reformism of every kind: Brecht wanted above all to demonstrate that all reforms, however well intentioned, turn out to be adroit diversionary measures which only reduce the chances of revolutionary disputes, of the inevitable class war.

The growing importance accorded in 1932 to a man like Hitler led Brecht to turn the character of Angeler, whom he now called Angelas and was finally to call Angelo Iberin, into more of a capitalist puppet, and to show, as the central point of the play, that the purpose of racial ideology is to divert attention from the class war. In the first version of the play, completed in 1932, those in power see the introduction of a salt tax as the only way out of the country's economic crisis, but they lack the courage to enforce this unpopular measure because to do so would risk revolt by the oppressed tenant farmers. As a way out of the difficulty power is transferred to the racial ideologist Angelas who, instead of dividing the population into poor and rich, divides them into round heads and pointed heads. But he has to give an assurance that, after the defeat of the revolutionary tenants, who unite under the banner of the 'sickle' and form an army, he will levy the tax on salt. Side by side with the story of Angelas Brecht introduces another, the story of Callas, that bears a dialectical relationship to Kleist's novella *Michael Kohlhaas;* in this a man becomes a traitor to his class because he considers the new racial theory to be a legitimate means of acquiring two horses he needs to cultivate his land.

Following Hitler's accession to power in Germany, and the mounting persecution of the Jews there, Brecht incorporated a series of further topical allusions in the play which he had conceived as a political parable: he intensified its symbolic character and 'atrocity story' elements, while stressing the emptiness of racial ideology that parades under the banner of anti-capitalism. The salt tax theme was eliminated and the landlords were presented as warmongers who, for the moment, were still able to hide their real intentions. The character of Angelo, stripped of all trace of personal integrity, emerged as an unscrupulous demagogue who, at the end, unhesitatingly follows the line demanded by the big capitalists. The original point of departure of the comedy, the attack on reformism, was completely scrapped in favour of the political symbolism of the successful attempt by the ruling capitalists to unite the people as a community with the help of a racial ideology in order to prevent them uniting under a revolutionary banner.

If one disregards the political development of fascism in Germany and applies the parable more to countries in which revolutionary situations have existed but were unable to develop owing to the military strength of those in power and the lack of unity among the working classes, there is no reason why the parabolic simplification of this 'atrocity story' should not prove convincing and effective.

21

Let us not speak only for culture

At times like these humanity has to become bellicose to avoid being exterminated.

The plays *St. Joan of the Stockyards, The Mother,* and *Round Heads and Pointed Heads,* in their ways all large-scale didactic plays, were an expression of Brecht's markedly revolutionary attitude and they advocate a united front of the working classes. They did not really fit in with the ideological premises of the Popular Front policies as pursued at that time. When he attended the International Writers' Congress in defence of culture, held in Paris in 1935, Brecht again found himself out of sympathy with the strategy pursued by the Communist Party. His conclusions as to the causes of fascism, the essentially barbaric character of bourgeois conditions of ownership, and the need for revolutionary change, accentuated not what this assembly of anti-fascist writers had in common but what separated them. While he considered unity of action among the persecuted writers to be important, he found a congress marked by sheer self-consideration and vanity extremely depressing and was led into making some sarcastic comments.

Thus, as far as he was concerned, the Paris congress, to which he had gone with Karin Michaelis, provided to only a very small extent a forum for political activities and he was forced to confine himself largely to collecting material for his satirical novel about the 'Tuis', the Tellect–Uell–Ins, the intellectuals. For Walter Benjamin the meeting with Brecht, and the latter's speech, provided 'the most enjoyable—almost the only enjoyable—element in the proceedings'. Neither found much of value in the individual contributions of the various speakers, whose political attitudes annoyed them considerably. On the other hand they studied with great interest the facial expressions and demeanour of writers like André Gide, Aldous Huxley and Henri Barbusse. The literary fellow—travellers and mere Communist Party officials elicited little sympathy from them. They were united in rejecting 'people like this Alfred Kantorowicz'. To talk to they preferred scholars with a Marxist background: Brecht, for example, found discussions with the socialist theologian Fritz Lieb from Bâle more interesting than debates on aesthetics with Alfred Kurella.

Preliminary work on the magazine *Das Wort,* the financial means for which, Kolsov had stated in Paris, would soon be available, remained for the time being Brecht's only activity within the immediate orbit of the Communist Party. In the meantime it had been agreed to appoint Willi Bredel as resident editor in Moscow. Of all the 'non-Moscow people' Brecht, at first, had the fewest misgivings that the magazine would turn out to be too one-sided, while Lion Feuchtwanger clung steadfastly to the idea of a literary magazine for all German speaking writers in exile. Efforts to persuade Heinrich Mann to accept the editorship continued until the appearance of the first number in the summer of 1936. He too, pleaded for the magazine to be an 'organ of free German literature' and, with reference to Feuchtwanger, declared: 'Personally I approve of communist democracy as practised in the Soviet Union. For Germany what we need is simply to fight for freedom—without any doctrine; that will come later and will naturally be socialist'. Brecht's view was that, to be effective, the fight against fascist barbarism had also to be a fight against the capitalist conditions of ownership. The idea of first winning the fight for freedom and then propagating socialism did not greatly appeal to him.

On the one hand Brecht was against reformism and in favour of the revolutionary struggle, on the other hand he did not support the allegation of left-wing opposition circles that the Communist Party of the Soviet Union was pursuing a nationalistic form of socialism: 'People who adopt this attitude have so far given no proof whatever that they are prepared to follow an international-istic proletarian policy . . .. By accusing the Soviet Union of pursuing this common policy, in other words of regarding and pursuing the proletarian interests of all countries as common interests, and by holding it against the Communist Party of the Soviet Union that it regards, and wants others to regard, its own affairs as those of all other proletariats, these people themselves are abandoning an international proletarian policy'.

There is no doubt that Brecht overestimated the interest still taken in Moscow in a progressive international movement, and his attempt to interpret as a plausible economic and political necessity the claim of the Russian communists to control all fraternal parties and prescribe the extent of their revolutionary activities, was to gloss over existing practices. On the other hand Brecht was justified in mistrusting revolutionaries who thought they could act without adequate material power and discipline. The Popular Front policy was a necessary defensive measure against Hitler's fascism. In France, in 1935, the Socialist parties joined with the Communists to form a government. The Nazis reacted sensitively to this and when civil war broke out in Spain, in 1936, they immediately hurried to the aid of Franco's generals in order to prevent Spain from turning socialist. In the field of foreign policy the Popular Front government in France was beneficial, but its home policy tended to inhibit the revolutionary will of the workers. When the country was hit by a great wave of strikes, and the resistance of the Spanish people seemed likely to encourage the French workers to take revolutionary action, none of the parties in the government any longer thought of going beyond the liberal and social reformist programme of the Popular Front. Maurice Thorez, the leader of the Communist Party, told the revolutionary socialist Marceau Pivert in July 1936 that it was far from true to say that everything was possible, and that all that mattered at the moment was to settle the strike whose aims, in any case, had already been achieved by the formation of the Popular Front. There was no means by which a Popular Front government so intent on peace and order could counter the hidden forces of fascism. Brecht was well aware of the reactionary nature of such a policy and of the uncritical enthusiasm of left-wing newspapers; in this respect he thought exactly as his friend Walter Benjamin did, who in July 1937 wrote to Fritz Lieb: 'But if you want still further support for your view of the policy of the Popular Front, take a look at the French left-wing press: they all cling simply to the fetish of the "left-wing" majority, and are not disturbed by the fact that it is this that formulates the policy which the right-wing would use to provoke uprisings'.

The threat to the Spanish republic, and the resulting political outlook, temporarily united the emigrants, and in France a big campaign for solidarity was under way which, for the first time

232

since 1933, also made political theatre possible. Brecht sat down to write a provocative play calling for solidarity with the Spanish people and armed intervention. The material for this, which he collected from newspapers, related mainly to events round Bilbao. *Generäle über Bilbao* was the name he gave to the first version of this play, which he completed at the end of March 1937 and for the plot of which the Irish poet J. M. Synge's one-act play, *Riders to the Sea,* was the immediate source. In Synge's little play a mother tries in vain to stop the last of her sons from going to sea, but he too drowns in the raging waters. The mother's grief ends in resignation: 'No man at all can be living for ever, and we must be satisfied'.

Brecht took over the dramatic construction of the play, but replaced the concluding fatalistic lament of his model by the accusatory, revolutionary force of the mother Carrar's affirmative decision. Formally the dramatist became more conventional, politically he remained true to the programme of his Paris speech of 1935. Later, for a performance in Sweden after the cause of freedom in Spain had been lost, Brecht strengthened still further his plea for armed intervention against barbarism and exploitation by introducing an additional piece of action. A sentry in the French internment camp, where fighters from Spain are being held, asks what was the point of the fighting, and Teresa Carrar's brother replies, pointing to his sister: 'She also asked "why fight". She did not ask this question right to the end, but for a very long time, almost to the end. And there were many like her who asked this question "why fight" for a very long time, almost to the end. And the fact that they asked this question for so long was one of the reasons we were beaten. And if, one day, you ask this question as they did, you too will be beaten'. It had to be made clear to the audience that a mother like Senora Carrar was not on the side of the generals, but she had hoped to be able to keep herself and her family out of the war and, for this reason, had refrained from rising against the generals. As things turn out she is forced to see that she cannot remain neutral. Brecht hoped that his play would also be used as a means of attacking the non-interventionist policies of the Western democracies.

Delighted though he was with the play's propaganda effect, he found it hard to accept the disadvantages inherent in the conventional technique in which it was written. Brecht would have

233

much preferred to write a play in which he could have set out the causes of the Spanish civil war and the complicated social contradictions prevailing in the country. He missed the freedom to comment which his use of the chorus had given him in his didactic plays. Because of this he recommended that directors staging *Senora Carrar's Rifles* should use documentary films in the performance to provide the necessary political information. The use of Synge's play enabled him to translate the subject matter into theatrical terms, but at the same time it ruled out the possibility of making explanatory statements about the Spanish civil war. In the course of his work on *Senora Carrar's Rifles* Brecht repeatedly tried out more topical versions of a Spanish play. He sketched out a film for Piscator, the story of a man named Michael Kohlhaas in the Bay of Biscay, the idea for which came from newspaper reports about captains of British ships who tried to avoid obeying their government's instructions to respect the blockade of Bilbao ordered by the generals. A great hit was made at the time by the facetious answers given by one of these captains who, having loaded his ship with potatoes for the starving Spanish people, was detained in the French port of St Jean de Luz. On 19 April 1937 a colleague of this 'Potato Jones' successfully broke the blockade and proved by his action that the only way to help the Spanish people was by positive action, whereas non-intervention only helped the reactionary insurgent generals. This endorsed Brecht's conjecture that the British Admiralty knew quite well that there was not a single Spanish ship at large in the Bay of Biscay. His film about 'Potato Jones' was to centre round talks 'which British officials hold with him aboard his ship on the subjects of peace, the policy of non-intervention and neutrality; they have to hold their noses the whole time because of the fearful stench from the rotten potatoes in the hold'. According to Brecht the whole thing could have been done with five actors, an old barge and a few hundred yards of Spanish news-reel.

As a natural consequence of declaring his solidarity with the Spanish republic, Brecht once again gave up the secluded life in Svendborg which he had imposed on himself following the discussions in the Danish press on the subject of his residence permit. During the winter he had confined himself to working on his plan for a Diderot society: this entailed systematically collecting and recording the technical problems encountered in their work by artists to whom the correct presentation of the world and the conditions necessary for human coexistence were matters of prime importance. Brecht was interested in an exchange of views between artists engaged in experimental work, the idea being that they would supply the society with descriptions of their methods and findings in the form of reports. In this way the members would coordinate their technical vocabulary and help to create a common terminology. The reason why Brecht embarked on this course of self-help was that the aesthetic debates within the confines of the communist parties were insincere and only hampered artistic work. The project originated in discussions with the stage designer Gorelik. The name was Brecht's, who had a high opinion of the French encyclopaedist because of the materialistic philosophy that pervaded his articles on the theatre: 'I simply wanted a name, because every descriptive title sounds either banal or affected'. To Jean Renoir, whom he wanted as a member of the society, Brecht wrote: 'As we are approaching only productive people, it will take a little time, but this will also mean that what finally emerges will be a picture of a modern anti-metaphysical and social art'. Had the list of members been drawn up in the cultural affairs department of the Communist Party, the society would inevitably have been composed of people ranging from J. R. Becher, Alfred Kurella, Georg Lukács and Maxim Vallentin to Sholokhov and Thomas Mann. Whereas what Brecht had in mind was an association of artists like Eisenstein, Ochlopkov, Dudov, Piscator, Renoir, Tretjakov, Hanns Eisler, Fritz Kortner, Auden, Isherwood and Rupert Doone.

In the summer of 1937 Brecht went with Ruth Berlau and Karin Michaelis to a writers' congress in Paris, the main theme of which was the attitude of intellectuals to the Spanish civil war. The tensions which existed between independent communists and the 'Moscow people' were a very large factor in the discussions and basically the organizers were more interested in condemning the opinions of an André Gide than in demonstrating solidarity with the Spanish republic. Very soon Malraux and Kolsov proposed that the congress be continued in Madrid, a suggestion which was received enthusiastically by most of the delegates because it offered them a chance of seeing the theatre of war at first hand. Many writers already belonged to one of the international fighting brigades. André Malraux had been one of the first intellectuals to decide spontaneously in favour of armed intervention on the side of the harassed republicans; he had arrived in Spain in the autumn of 1936 with an air squadron. His example was followed by the writers Ludwig Renn, Willi Bredel, Stephen Spender, Gustav Regler and Ernest Hemingway. Even a brief visit to the starving, beleaguered city of Madrid was far too dangerous for Brecht. He could only fight with words and ideas. Simply to call him a coward is to ignore the fact that a Hemingway's delight in adventure was foreign to his nature as a writer. If he scented danger he had to get to safety; any thought of literary activity under such conditions was out of the question. To live in a Madrid hotel receiving some thirty direct hits a day and write a play on the side, as it were, was something he simply could not imagine. Kolsov, a 'fanatical reporter' like Egon Erwin Kisch and convinced that it was a writer's job to be present at the centre of historical events, was considerably disillusioned when Brecht declined the invitation to Madrid; instead he confined himself to composing a speech, which was then read out to the congress and in which he supported a war, provided it was a real war: 'Culture, for long, for much too long, defended only by intellectual weapons, though attacked by material weapons, and itself not only an intellectual but also, and indeed especially, a material matter, must be defended with material weapons'.

When Ruth Berlau decided to fly to Spain with Kolsov, and fight there, Brecht was horrified and deeply hurt. Having failed to restrain his mistress, he lacked the courage to follow her. He refused to admit that what she did was revolutionary; the art of war, as taught her by him, applied only to a war in which there was no shooting. It also rankled that Kolsov's arguments had been more effective than his advice. Back in Svendborg he feared for the life of his 'sister' in the civil war. A note in verse, which he sent to her in Madrid, was intended to teach her to be careful; she was to read his instructions constantly, morning and evening, and think of his love: 'He whom I loved has told me that he needs me. Therefore I take care of myself, watch my footsteps and live in fear that each raindrop may kill me'. He sent further poems to her in Madrid and asked her to come back and cut short his fears. When Ruth Berlau finally announced that she was returning on a certain ship, Brecht drove 'over the islands' in his Ford to meet her; but he did not find her. Gerhart and Hilde Eisler, who had arrived by the same ship, recollected a woman who answered Brecht's description, but had no idea where she might be. Ruth's failure to arrive was regarded by Brecht as precisely that, a failure; the worst thing, he said at the time, was that in future he would have to judge her by ordinary standards. He wrote in a poem, 'When your mistress writes that she is coming, don't believe her. The natural forces are in abeyance here'. The poet had gone to meet her and take her to Skovbostrand, to the house with the thatched roof. But she turned out to be unpredictable and unreliable. When she told him she was coming, she clearly had still not made up her mind to do so; and, because he thought he was in the right, he said 'I feel ashamed':

> Also fuhr der gekommen war
> Wieder zurück über die Inseln und den Meeresarm
> Und durch alle Stunden der Fahrt
> Schämte er sich.

(And so he who had come drove back over the islands and the inlet of the sea, and throughout the hours of his drive felt ashamed.)

In this case Brecht really had cause to feel let down: Ruth Berlau had travelled on the ship in question, but during the voyage had struck up a friendship with a Swede who had fought in Spain; finding it hard to imagine Brecht waiting for her, she simply continued with the ship to Copenhagen and took the man home with her to Vallensbaek. From time to time Brecht's beloved Lai-tu broke the agreement not to have relations with other men; after all he slept with other women all the time. To Brecht it was as if something 'precious' had been suddenly shattered, the private dialogue interrupted. He was used to treating her as his lover; now, however, she wrote to him that she was right and he, of course, knew that he was wrong.

While Brecht was in Paris again, assisting at the rehearsals for Ernst Josef Aufricht's production of *The Threepenny Opera* and Slatan Dudov's of *Senora Carrar's Rifles*, Ruth Berlau was in Copenhagen engaged on the preliminary work for the first performance in Denmark of the latter play with Dagmar Andreasen, who had already played the part of Pelagea Wlassowa. Brought together by work in this way, his mistress's lack of obedience was soon forgotten; Brecht knew: 'Lai-tu loves me. She comes to me when she is happy and when she is sad . . . .. She laughs with me over her foolishness and is proud with me over her cleverness. And we do the same when I am foolish and I am wise'. Moreover Ruth's Swedish lover, who had appeared so unexpectedly, was later to prove extremely useful to Brecht. He was Georg Branting, a social democrat member of parliament, who in 1939 obtained the visa for him to stay in Sweden.

The Paris production of *Senora Carrar's Rifles,* which was dedicated to the 'Spanish people's heroic fight for freedom', gave fresh impetus to Brecht and encouraged him to finish 'the little plays about Germany'. It was a sound idea politically and at the same time provided the best available opportunity to 'develop the epic style of performance'. Brecht told Korsch that his wife's acting in the play was 'the best and purest form of epic theatre that has been seen anywhere up till now'. The playwright was proud of this 'classic piece of work' by Helene Weigel, and he felt 'very fond' of her again, a feeling he had not had for a long time. Up till the end of 1937 she played the part alternately in Paris and Prague, while Brecht had to take charge of the childrens' birthday celebrations in Skovbostrand; in the intervals he went to Copenhagen for the final *Carrar* rehearsals there. At the end of the year the 'dear comrade' actress was bidden, following a resolution by the Svendborg Council of Husbands and Sons, 'to return without delay and resume your activities here, once your obligations have been fulfilled'.

Apart from another visit to Paris in May 1938, to rehearse some scenes from *Terror and Misery of the Third Reich,* and trips to Copenhagen, Brecht did not leave his retreat on the Danish Sound again. The growing power of fascism, and the depressing way things were going in the Soviet Union, persuaded him to give more attention to the progress of his own work as an artist, in order to preserve as much sanity as possible and avoid sinking into unproductive despair. The guiding spirit behind his work, in which Margarete Steffin and Ruth Berlau usually participated, was the 'Doubter', the wise man on the old Chinese scroll which Brecht had hung in his study:

Nachdenklich betrachteten wir mit Neugier den
zweifelnden
Blauen Mann auf der Leinwand, sahen uns an und
Begannen von vorne.

(Pondering, we looked anxiously at the doubting blue man on the canvas, regarded one another, and started again.)

22

The Realism Debate

Where the slogan 'for humanism' has
not yet been supplemented by the slogan
'against the bourgeois conditions of ownership', literature has not yet turned to the
people.

As the entries for July 1938 in Walter Benjamin's diary show,
Brecht did his utmost to give an accurate account of the political
developments in the Soviet Union. He advocated a sceptical
approach to what was going on in Russia, and finally compared his
attitude to the first workers' and farmers' state with that of Marx to
German social democracy: it was one of 'positive criticism'.
Against the background of the Moscow trials and their consequences for many of Brecht's friends, the publications of the
Marxist Tuis Georg Lukács, Alfred Kurella and Andor Gabor
caused him great anxiety. For him these critics were not only
enemies of artistic productivity, latterly they had also become
political opponents. In his eyes they were ideological opportunists,
members of criminal cliques. The false champions of realism and
the people's entity, whose criticisms he saw as threats, were only
too familiar to him from Berlin, where in the name of the
Communist Party they had pursued a critical policy on the
legislative level which art was then forced to carry out on the
executive level.

The Marxist playwright Bertolt Brecht and the Marxist literary
historian Georg Lukács were never great admirers of one another.
It is true that in 1941 there was a brief meeting in Moscow when
each adopted a conciliatory attitude. Brecht, at the time, wanted a
literary non-aggression pact, similar to the one he had suggested to
Hermann Kesten in 1933, and proposed to Lukács that they
should stop quarrelling in public: 'Look, a lot of people are
continually inciting me against you. There are sure to be a lot of

239

people inciting you against me. It would be better if neither of us paid any attention to them'. Later, in East Germany, the old antagonisms proved to be of no consequence when J. R. Becher and Georg Lukács suddenly became important allies of Brecht's in opposing the dogmatic party officials. In contrast to Becher who, as his sympathy for Benn's poetry shows—a sympathy which he never denied—had retained, along with his party bias, a fair measure of artistic illogicality, Lukács held unswervingly to his out and out bourgeois views on art. In 1947, when reading Lukács's introduction to the correspondence between Goethe and Schiller, where the writer analysed the way in which the German classics treated the French Revolution, Brecht reflected on how German writers, 'again not having (a revolution) of their own', would set about 'treating' the Russian revolution under the guidance of Lukács. The latter had recommended Tolstoy and Sholokhov as suitable models. The ardent plea for Solzhenitsyn, which Brecht did not live to see, came later in the form of a satiric play. For Lukács, Babel, Mayakovsky and even Tretjakov entered the picture only as peripheral figures, and then with the strongest reservations, whereas Brecht was inclined to regard Kafka as the 'one truly Bolshevist writer'.

In the argument between Brecht and Lukács the latter was always more influential while Brecht was alive: the official artistic doctrine of socialist realism in communist countries was built on the slogans of Shdanov and the theoretical writings of the Hungarian scholar Lukács. Since he espoused the rebel cause in Hungary in 1956, the most dogmatic disciples of Lukács have regarded their teacher as a 'revisionist', while in the meantime they, who are much worse revisionists, have canonized Brecht. But it was Lukács who gave the cue for this canonization. Having always regarded Brecht as a secret champion of 'decadence', assiduously working for the liquidation of the classical heritage, he surprisingly delivered a commemorative address at the memorial celebration for Brecht in the Berliner Ensemble's Schiffbauerdamm theatre. On this occasion Lukács declared Brecht to be a 'true dramatist' and conceded that he had sought to transform the masses who saw and heard his works. With Brecht, he said, the aesthetic effect also produced a moral effect: 'But this was the meaning of the Aristotelian catharsis in its profoundest sense. As Lessing rightly understood it, its purpose was to elevate an

240

emotional shock into an aptitude for morality. Because Brecht sought to do this, and in his best works succeeded, he was a true dramatist'.

Thus Brecht was posthumously turned by Lukács into a descendent of Aristotle and Lessing, and admitted to the ranks of his favourite dramatists Ibsen, Chekhov and Shaw. Finally in his preface to the West German edition of *Skizze einer Geschichte der neueren deutschen Literatur,* Lukács made a curious apology for never having given a detailed analysis of Brecht's work: 'In the early thirties I adopted a negative atitude to both his output and his theories. That is reflected in this book. It was only after my return, when I came to know plays like *The Good Woman of Setzuan, Mother Courage and her Children*, etc. that my attitude changed fundamentally.' The fact remains, however, that Lukács found neither time nor opportunity before he died to give detailed theoretical expression to his change of opinion.

His few affirmative, or guardedly favourable, statements about Brecht show no basic change; they do, however, give grounds for suspecting that all he wanted was to prove that he had always been right in his attitude to Brecht and that in his late plays the latter had moved nearer to his own aesthetic standpoint: 'And with his maturity this excessively direct approach progressively diminished and there came into existence powerful plays which, in spite of the "alienation effect", raised the underlying thought to poetic greatness'. In spite of 'formalistic' or 'avant-garde' aberrations, Lukács then admitted that Brecht's late works were informed with 'the correct transformation of reality': 'The reality which avant-gardism denies and sets out to destroy aesthetically is the starting-point and aim of the "alienation effect"'. Lukács continued emphatically to reject Brecht's theory of alienation. He held firmly to his old aesthetic concepts and his theory of realism, which derived from Goethe and the nineteenth century bourgeois novel. Lukács had only to discover the desired style and 'enduring characters' in a writer to call him a realist on the spot. Looking back he maintained that Brecht had created genuine human characters only after abandoning his 'abstract opposition' during his exile. It was then that he had recognized 'with increasing clarity, in his fight against Hitlerism, that the central problem of dramatic creation was to save man's essential nature from whatever threatened it, whether from within or without'. Lukács

241

admitted that the latter plays also contained elements of the abstraction that characterized the output of his middle period; this was because Brecht failed to see sufficiently clearly that the 'poetic rationale' of his programme could also have been realized without the alienation effect.

This schoolmasterly appreciation of Brecht is in line with Lukács laboured first tribute of 1938; the latter, which referred to a scene from *Terror and Misery of the Third Reich*, produced a somewhat astonished comment in Brecht's diary: 'Lukács has already hailed *The Informer (Der Spitzel)* as if I were a sinner who had been received into the bosom of the Salvation Army. But the thing is taken from life! What he fails to see is that 27 scenes have been pieced together to form what is really only a catalogue of attitudes, the attitudes of not opening one's mouth, of looking over one's shoulder, of being frightened etc. The attitudes adopted under a dictatorship. By this means the epic theatre is able to show that not only 'interiors', but almost naturalistic elements too, are within its scope and do not constitute the difference. In any case the actor will do well to study the "street scene" before he plays one of the small scenes. The attitudes to which I have referred are not to be executed in such a way that the onlooker wants to hold up the progress of the scene; empathy must be carefully controlled, otherwise the whole thing goes by the board'.

Lukács attributed the origin of the alienation effect to 'Brecht's violently one-sided polemic, concealing historical facts and relationships', against the theory of empathy. Now it is certainly true that in the nineteen-twenties and early nineteen-thirties Brecht adopted an attitude of extreme hostility to the classical heritage, which he later abandoned. At the same time it would be wrong to attach too great importance to his later pronouncements on the classics, because they have to be seen in the context of cultural and political viewpoints. Frequently it was only a question of saying something pleasing in order to secure from attack a production designed to break new formal ground. On the other hand Lukács's praise of *The Informer* was not given at random either. The series of scenes constituting *Terror and Misery of the Third Reich* really did show greater conventionality of form. It was clearly a more or less conscious withdrawal on Brecht's part, undertaken in the hope of getting his plays performed. When he had finished work on *Galileo* he again regretted having recourse to

242

this sort of tactics: 'Technically *Galileo* is a big step backward, like *Senora Carrar's Rifles* motivated much too much by opportunism. The play would have to be completely re-written in order to catch "this breeze that comes from new shores", this roseate dawn of knowledge. The whole thing more direct, without the interiors, the "atmosphere", the empathy. And everything with a view to planetary demonstrations. The arrangement of the play could remain, as could Galileo's characterization. The work, work I should enjoy, could only be done under practical conditions, in immediate contact with the stage'.

With his work on the *Setzuan* play Brecht wanted 'finally to come up to scratch again', so far as the epic technique was concerned. 'When writing for one's store cupboard there is no need to make concessions'. This remark shows that Brecht's 'opportunism', which Lukács later called 'true dramatic creation', was simply an attempt to write plays which could be performed under the less favourable conditions of exile and which, he hoped, would gradually lead those taking part in the direction of a better epic theatre. In his *Aesthetics*, of 1963, Lukács saw Brecht's 'opportunism' in a positive light: the 'true dramatic creation' to be found in *Galileo* and other late plays was theoretically still illogical, 'but for this very reason its appearance at the centre of things was all the more effective dramatically and poetically'. Lukács continued to regard the epic theatre as a dramatic mistake on Brecht's part. In support of his thesis that the 'poetic rationale' can be realized without the alienation effect he cited Chekhov, who built his plays on the contrast between the subjective intentions of the characters and the objective tendencies and significance. In Chekhov therefore, the play itself constituted the 'alienation effect'. Brecht, however, did not intend the audience to swallow a programme in the guise of poetry. According to Lukács Brecht had invented the alienation effect as a piece of sleight of hand. But he used alienation as a means to clarify his intentions, not to obscure them. He wanted his theatre to teach people in an entertaining way to enjoy socially engaged thought and action. Plays like *Galileo* only appeared to be a concession on Brecht's part to Lukács criteria of realism. Ernst Schumacher points out in his work on *Galileo* that, in spite of his considerable objections to the form of the play, Brecht altered nothing, even later, and that he never realized the 'planetary demonstrations' he considered desirable. In

243

fact *Galileo* is the only play of Brecht's in which he made use of history to 'historicize', alienate, current events. Brecht did not abandon alienation, he arrived at in a different way. 'The answer', writes Schumacher, 'it is only to be found in the fact that he was using a real, not an invented, story with which to throw light on contemporary history'. In order to prevent misunderstandings Brecht tried in this play to find solutions that would make it clear to the audience that here, too, it was epic theatre they were watching. On 23 November, 1938 he noted, alluding to the 'strategem' at the end of the play: 'Here at least even the person who automatically projects himself into a part must be aware of the alienation effect as he projects himself into that of *Galileo*. In a strictly epic performance empathy of a permissable sort takes place'.

Brecht was not satisfied with this compromise. In 1945, when he revised the play in America, he again criticized the traditional nature of its dramatic style: 'In *Galileo*, with its interiors and moods, the scenic structure, taken as it is from the epic theatre, makes a curiously theatrical effect'. Brecht was not 'theoretically illogical', as Lukács said, but simply failed to arrive at a satisfactory result when he gave practical shape to the formal problem. In remarking that the alienation effect is intended not to preclude feeling but above all to ensure that the 'right feelings' are awakened, the playwright is making concessions, from his point of view, to the empathy theory, but he does not abandon it even in *Galileo*. What Lukács says of this play in particular makes it abundantly clear that he is not capable of understanding Brecht's 'theatre of alienation' dialectically. According to Lukács's interpretation Mother Courage is still a tragic figure who goes to meet her doom subjectively, because her actions show her to be in direct contrast to the objective tendencies and significance of the play's general social trend. Brecht, on the other hand, is not in the least interested in Mother Courage as a tragic figure; what matters to him is that the audience realizes why she goes to her doom. To understand her feelings seems to him to be permissable empathy. The consequence of this new quality of empathy on the part of the audience is that, from the standpoint of the socialist society, Chekhov's characters, for instance, are no longer to be regarded as tragic. In an essay in dialogue form on the subject of 'the tragic element', Brecht says that while the epic style of acting is not concerned to produce a tragic mood, this is not to say that a tragic

244

mood cannot be produced by this style of acting: 'It would permit a tragic mood whenever a performance, which respects the historicity and practicability of the social basis, would evoke such a mood'.

To critics, whose legitimate demand, 'to present reality in such a way that it can be grasped', he supported, Brecht replied by arguing that reality cannot be presented 'without recognizing its dialectical nature'. He found it essential, therefore, 'to indicate the conflicting, courtroom-like nature of the situations, events and characters'. The task of the alienation effect was to make it possible to present 'this dialectical nature'; 'the former is explained by the latter'. The tragic element had to become of secondary importance. Alienation meant 'to announce a contradiction'. It had to be possible to give dialectics concrete expression: 'The enigmas of the world are not solved but demonstrated'. Brecht wanted to use the alienation effects to excite conflicting emotions and make dialecticians of the audience. Lukács, on the other hand, was not interested in influencing reality, what he sought was the 'artistic experience'. Brecht's epic theatre was an attempt to wrench this 'artistic experience' away from metaphysics and 'bring it down to earth'. For Brecht it was at this point that the question of form arose, because 'to explain the political uses of non-Aristotelian dramatists is child's-play; the difficulties start in the aesthetic sphere'.

In 1937/38 *Das Wort*, the magazine edited by Brecht, Bredel and Feuchtwanger, inaugurated the so-called 'expressionism debate'. On one side in this debate were Lukács and his followers, on the other were those sinners who were suspected of decadence, modernism and avant-gardism. In retrospect Lukács subdivided the opposition 'front', those 'who defended expressionism through thick and thin', into radical innovators like Benn, whose criticism helped to stabilize what it criticized, and 'honest seekers' like Anna Seghers and Hanns Eisler, 'who were enthralled and shaken to the core by the new phenomena of social life and, at the same time, set out to find a humanistic and revolutionary answer to the specific horrors of that period'. Later Lukács rightly presumed that Brecht, while taking no immediate part in the discussion like Bloch, Eisler and Anna Seghers, was the centre of the socially involved avant-garde. Brecht, for his part, regarded Lukács at that time as the leader of the 'Moscow clique'.

245

The discussions on socialist realism had reached their first climax at the end of the nineteen-thirties. The Stalinist policy for art, originating in Moscow, was to operate internationally. Brecht joined in the discussions, but his views did not get a hearing. Even the programmatic work *Range and Variety of the Realistic Style (Weite und Vielfalt der realistischen Schreibweise)*, in which Lukács is not mentioned by name, was not published at that time. It contains Brecht's demand that the concept of realism be interpreted 'more broadly, more generously and, in a word, more realistically'. In a note to his essay, probably intended for the editors of *Das Wort*, Brecht declared himself in favour of ending the debate, because it had exacerbated the antagonisms intolerably. He wanted to avoid a quarrel in order to prevent any outward disruption of the broad anti-Hitler front: 'I have therefore chosen a positive form for my remarks and written in such a way that the affair can now be allowed to rest'— in the last number of *Internationale Literatur* this affair had taken a very nasty turn because in it Lukács, without further argument, had denounced 'certain plays by Brecht' as formalistic. Brecht's position in the 'aesthetic sphere' was diametrically opposite to that of Lukács. Brecht utterly rejected the theory of art decreed by Moscow, which proclaimed 'the' realistic style; he attacked many of the 'socialist classics', who were accorded exaggerated importance at the time, and exposed the petit-bourgeois background of their concept of realism. Even the most important prose work of the early years of the Stalinist era, Sholokhov's *And Quiet Flows the Don*, was for Brecht more in the nature of an impressionistic novel which, although it made moral demands on its characters, had almost nothing to say about their place in society—hence it was not a realistic novel. For Brecht realistic art was 'an art which leads reality against the ideologies and enables people to feel, think and act realistically'.

Apropos of the disputes of the Soviet literary historians he noted: 'Genuine investigations are not undertaken, or else they assume the character of legal proceedings. They are frighteningly unproductive, venomous, personal, authoritarian and servile at the same time. It is clearly not an atmosphere in which a vital, militant, exuberant literature could thrive. Not only is there no important novel, but even trashy novels like those of Alexei Tolstoy are considered good. And there is not a single play, not one dramatic character, either comic or tragic, not one linguistic achievement, not one philosophic quality in any play, and this with a theatre capable of so much'.

Brecht did not use the disastrously bad artistic policies as an excuse to polemize in general against the land of the October Revolution, a fact that distinguished him from other critics outside the Soviet Union who thought as he did. His criticism of individual aspects was not intended to 'expose deep-seated rifts' or to show that something was necessarily rotten there: 'Probably all that can be said initially is that the Bolsheviks do not understand how to develop a literature. One should not even conclude that their methods have failed in this field; perhaps it is enough to say that the methods they applied in this field have failed. The situation was certainly unfortunate. Literature was taken by surprise when the proletariat seized power.' Later Brecht took these reflections a stage further theoretically when he considered in detail the disastrous consequences of the party's demands to writers: 'By immediately turning the bourgeois revolution into a proletarian one, the Soviet Union has forced existing progressive writers into taking a leap that in several cases has broken their necks, or at any rate their legs. In a Russia led by Kerensky an Ehrenburg would have become a literary figure of world importance. For a great many writers a situation that meant freedom to Mayakovsky meant severe constraint. They revenged themselves on Mayakovsky'. For Mayakovsky, as for Brecht, revolutionary theory and practice in Lenin's sense were one and the same thing. They could write 'in the name of the party'; for other writers, who were only fellow-travellers, or romantics of the revolution, and who sincerely tried to espouse the cause of the people, the party's orders and demands spelt artistic ruin. The party found the obedient writers easier to deal with than the socialist ones. This led to the curious situation in which Brecht and Mayakovsky were criticized by the party for pointing out mistakes and discussing contradictions while, at the same time, they were accused by their bourgeois colleagues of submitting weakly to the wishes of the Communist Party.

In the preface to the West German edition of his book *Der russische Realismus und die Weltliteratur,* published in 1964, Lukács described his championship of the old school in the expressionism, or realism, debate as a *'reculer pour mieux sauter'* in the Leninist sense. He had wanted, he said, to fight 'the state-standardized literature' of the Stalin era indirectly by analysing the great realists of the past. His adherence to tradition had only been an expression of his 'longing for an appropriate artistic reflection of contemporary reality'. This statement, however, was merely a rather strange attempt to gloss over the pernicious role he had played during his Moscow exile. Because he did not only argue in the name of realism against the formalism and decadence of Proust, Joyce, Kafka, Dos Passos and Brecht: the tendencies he strove to 'liquidate' were not to be found among the representatives of the 'highly state controlled, standardized, naturalistic norm of socialist realism', but among socialist writers like Ehrenburg, Olescha and Tretjakov.

Two of his articles entitled *Grösse und Verfall des Expressionismus* and *Erzählen oder Beschreiben?,* and published in the magazine *Internationale Literatur,* preceded the debate in *Das Wort.* It was the second of these in particular—the article *Narrative or Descriptive Writing*—which annoyed Brecht. In it Lukács contrasted the narrative approach of Tolstoy, Balzac and Scott with Flaubert and Zola. In the three former, he asserted, events were portrayed 'which are significant in themselves by reason of the fate of those taking part in them, because these people are significant for the life of society through the rich unfolding of their human lives'. But the people in Flaubert and Zola were observers of events. The decisive factor for a writer was his 'attitude to life'. Narrative and descriptive writing were the two basic methods of presentation characteristic of two periods of capitalism, and these resulted in two different attitudes of the writer to reality. Descriptive writing encouraged a tendency to reduce things to a common level, hence this method was a danger to realism in literature. What Lukács required of a novel was that it should 'present and display life in its entirety, throughout its whole range'. In the moderns a deliberately scientific approach led to 'complete subjectivism'. Because of this there was no place for a 'poetry of things' independent of human destinies: 'Things have a poetic life only through their relations with human destiny. Therefore the true epic writer does not describe them. He tells of the function of things in the chain of human destinies'. People had to be proved 'in real situations', and the 'human destinies of those portrayed' had to be able to move us poetically. Only 'true epic

248

writing' created 'enduring characters'. Modern realists toned down the capitalist reality. Outward descriptions of things were no longer permitted by Lukács; socialist writers in particular had to overcome 'what was left of capitalism'. Flaubert could be forgiven because he did not live to see the October Revolution. But in the Soviet Union a 'reporter's attitude to the problems of epic writing' was no longer permissable.

Lukács's criticism was aimed in particular at the novels of Tretyakov, for whom, he said, people were no longer anything but illustrative material: he wrote 'documentary novels' and advocated the theory of a 'biography of things'. If a novel lacked a 'personal' story, Lukács saw in it purely social and sociological tendencies: 'The infinite richness of life must inevitably be lost when no expression is given to the complex interweaving of the ways and byways by which individual men and women consciously or unconsciously, intentionally or unintentionally, realize the universal'. The descriptive method robbed novels of all tension. Lukács cited Sholokov as a positive example of the opposite: 'It will suffice to call attention to art and the life of Sholokov'. His mode of life was also decisive for the realistic writer, because 'residues in consciousness always indicate similar residues in the person himself'.

Brecht's comment on this article in his diary was, 'this stupidity is gigantic'. He poked fun at the revealing terminology and pointed out to the 'Herr Professor' that the social changes had in fact called the traditional narrative form into question: 'We find a wide range of the "richness of life" in Lukács's early bourgeois novel *(Goethe)*, and this novel does indeed give "the illusion of creating and displaying life in its entirety, throughout its whole range". Imitate it! Except that today nothing unfolds any more and life's range is never wide! The best advice one could give would be to run it to death! Capitalism, by the way, runs things to death in this way, the famous iron heel. We have in truth a great many devious ways, wrong ways, obstacles, braking devices, braking failures, etc to describe. But increasing quantity has brought with it an about-turn. Lukács, who is inclined to take everything out of the world and transfer it to consciousness, sees this about turn (indignantly) only in the sphere of consciousness. In Zola a factual complex occupies the centre of his novels: money, mining etc. Organic diversity of composition leads to mechanical combinations and montage. The novel becoming less and less human! This the wretched man now uses to trip up those wretched writers who have sunk from 'narrative' to 'descriptive' writing. They capitulate. They align themselves with capitalism, they dehumanize life. He refuses to accept their protests. They are too late, they have been drawn into the affair, their radicalism is specious. But what the Professor overlooks is the fact that the dehumanized proletariat puts all its humanity into its protest and enters the fight against the dehumanization of production on this basis. The devious nature of the new ways must not be allowed to refashion the novel. Here he really has a notion of richness (in phrases like that about "this richness of the fabric") that was quickly superseded. Much has become more, and there is no more trace of richness left. To calculate has become to theorize. It does not occupy the same position, it no longer ranks among the 'reflections of the hero'. The writer sees something new when he catches the proletarian generalizing, one has to realize that. The "soulless" factual complexes—mining, money, etc—have brought about the down-fall of the narrative form of Balzac, Tolstoy, etc. All the admonishments of the professors cannot put it together again. All the king's horses and all the king's men couldn't put Humpty Dumpty together again. Gide wrote his principal novel *(Les Faux Monnayeurs)* on the difficulty of writing a novel. Joyce wrote a catalogue of types of description and the one great folk-tale of the day; Hašek's *Schweyk* abandoned the dream-orientated form of the early bourgeois novel'.

Brecht disclaimed Lukács's praise for *The Informer* scene, pointing out that it was precisely here that he had made use of the incriminating montage technique. In fact he also employed it in other works and constantly referred to his experimental use of it in films as well as to its use by other writers. Brecht made use of montage whenever it seemed appropriate; at all events he defended it against the arguments of a Lukács: 'I have no reason to advocate the Dos Passos montage technique through thick and thin. . . . All the same I should not like to see this technique condemned merely to permit the creation of enduring characters. In the first place Dos Passos himself has given us excellent descriptions of "combative and intricate human inter-relationships", even if his battles were not those engaged in by Tolstoy's characters and his intricacies not those of Balzac's stories. In the second place the novel by no means

250

stands or falls by its "characters", and certainly not by the sort of characters that existed in the last century. One should not encourage the idea of a sort of Valhalla of literature's enduring characters, a sort of Madame Tussaud's waxworks of enduring characters from Antigone to Nana and from Aeneas to Nechljudov'.

Brecht also accused Lukács of making the question of realism a question of form, when he meant technique: 'one should cherish no great expectations of people who are over fond of using the word form to mean something different from content or in connection with content or in some other way, and who have an exaggerated abhorrence of the word technique, as something "mechanical" for instance. One should ignore the fact that they quote the classics (of Marxism) and that in these the word form occurs: they have not learned the technique of writing novels. And there is no need for anyone to be alarmed by the word mechanical, as long as it refers to technique; there is a mechanics that has rendered, and still renders, great service to mankind, and it is the mechanics of technique. The "orthodox" among us, whom in another field Stalin distinguishes from the creative, habitually conjure up spirits by employing certain words in the most arbitrary way'. Questions of form were treated by Lukács and his followers formalistically. Their Marxism, Brecht said, was more like 'Murxism' (*Murks* in German means drivel). This is how he described their reasoning: 'The realism of the bourgeois realists was incomplete, they still had idols; leave them out of it and all is well. Their facts are accepted and rearranged. Marx is Ricardo with the right conclusions. Nothing more. Sholokhov is Balzac relieved of a few blinkers. In fact the Sholokhovs have not a trace of Balzac's materialism (a strange brew of romanticism, a craving for facts, a craze for collecting, speculation and so forth) and vastly more blinkers'.

Brecht considered it impossible to treat contemporary problems and subjects without inventing new forms. He rejected as unmarxist Lukács's attempt to make realism a question of form. For Brecht it was a question neither of the old form nor of the new, what he demanded was the appropriate form: 'Everything to do with form that prevents us from getting to the root of social causality must go; everything to do with form that helps us to get to the root of social causality is to be welcomed.' Lukács wanted to

251

retain old forms simply as form. Brecht regarded his essays not as analyses but as rules for constructing up-to-date novels. What use was 'richness of life', when the conditions one had to describe stank to high heaven? With his demands for 'rounded', 'harmonious' and 'spiritually rich' characters Lukács made writers, and not social conditions, responsible for literature's decadence. Brecht described Lukács's concern at the disruption of bourgeois narrative forms as a 'curious fondness for the idyllic': 'Balzac's technique does not turn Henry Ford into someone like Vautrin but, which is worse, it does not permit the creation of characters having the new humanity of the class-conscious proletarian of our age. For such tasks Upton Sinclair's technique is not too new but too old. This signifies not too little Balzac but too much Balzac'.

Prompted by Lukács's violent criticism Brecht turned his attention to some of the avant-garde works. He studied the catalogue of sins such as montage, alienation, change of style and inner monologue, and in this context discovered that James Joyce's *Ulysses* was a 'great satiric novel'. He questioned whether Thomas Mann's *Josef* novel was 'really so much more deeply rooted in the people' than *Ulysses*. In an article *Practical Contribution to the Expressionism Debate (Praktisches zur Expressionismusdebatte)* Brecht wrote: 'I have heard Joyce's book praised for its realism by quite intelligent readers. Not that they would have praised the style as such (some spoke of it as mannered). But it struck them as having a realistic content. I shall probably be told I am a compromiser when I say that *Ulysses* made me laugh almost as much as *Schweyk,* and normally people like myself laugh only over realistic satires'. In fact Brecht found more realism in Joyce than in Thomas Mann or Sholokov, two of the few twentieth century writers whom Lukács accepted, along with Gorki, without serious reservations. Although Brecht was basically right, he was not sufficiently detached, when it came to details, to be able to make valid for a Thomas Mann arguments which he had applied to himself in the case of *Terror and Misery in the Third Reich.* Apart from his judgements on Sholokhov and Thomas Mann, however, Brecht's views on the problems of a realist aesthetic provided a serviceable starting-point for a Marxist theory of realism. Lukács, on the other hand, offered only criteria of a dubious nature in his essays. He formulated guidelines that were derived from the aesthetics of the bourgeois novel. To this day his rules of construction still form the basis of official Marxist statements on the problem of realism. Brecht suggested to the Marxist critics of the day that they study the subject-matter of a play 'as Marxist, historian, politician, economist and dialectician and then, if you wish to pronounce a judgement on formal elements of an aesthetic nature that is to be of assistance in the construction of plays, consider how far these elements are appropriate to the subject-matter'.

The dispute between Brecht and Lukács, which in the days of the Popular Front could not be thrashed out adequately in public, reached its climax with Lukács's work *Marx und das Problem des ideologischen Verfalls (Marx and the Problem of Ideological Decline)*. This was both a summary of his theses up till that time and a general attack on all writers who had failed 'truly to break through to the sources of life'. In his reply Brecht now pointed out that the fascist concept of art and the socialist concept à la Lukács were dangerously similar:

'Read Lukács's *Marx und das Problem des ideologischen Verfalls*. How the man installs himself in every position the proletariat vacate! Once again the talk is about realism, which they have now degraded as successfully as the Nazis have degraded socialism. The realist writer of the "decadent age" (our age, that is; to start with always a few murmurs about "bourgeois decadence", after which simply the "decadent age"—collapse of the whole, not of the bourgeoisie) is absolved from being a dialectical materialist. All he has to do is "give preference as a creator to reality correctly observed and experienced over an acquired philosophy of life and acquired prejudices". Because this is what Balzac and Tolstoy did, they mirror reality!' This vindicates the Sholokhovs and the Thomas Manns, they mirror reality! There is no antithesis between the realists of the bourgeoisie and those of the proletariat. (A glance at the Sholokhovs certainly seems to prove this.) And presumably not between the bourgeoisie and the proletariat either? In the days of the Popular Front too? Long live Pastor Niemöller! A realist of the first water! Again, no knowledge is necessary to "create" (for presumably Thomas Mann creates and he knows nothing). As creators these half-wits (sic) give reality preference over prejudices without knowing it. It is a direct record of experience: you receive a kick, you say Ow! He receives a kick, so let him say Ow! What it is to be simple! This Lukács is attracted to the problem of ideological decadence as if by magic. It is *sua res*. The Marxian categories are here carried *ad absurdum* by a Kantian, not by being refuted but by being applied. Here is the class struggle, a concept rendered meaningless, prostituted and bled white, gutted until it is no longer recognizable; but here it is, making its appearance. "Also to be seen . . .", "among other things . . .": no more facts, nothing concrete. The essay referred to contains a short quotation from Marx. Marx praises the way in which Sue creates the girl from the gutter. He endows Fleur de Marie with splendid qualities and so gives "a slap in the face to the prejudices of the bourgeoisie". Here at last is something concrete, a slap in the face and still more than that; reality is discussed in the shape of the inhuman situation in which Fleur de Marie finds herself. With Lukács all that is left of the class struggle is a demon, an empty principle that confuses people's ideas; it is no longer anything that exists. The writer exists in reality, all he has to do, therefore, is to portray reality and there he is in the midst of its portrayals! And since these people start their formalistic criticism by declaring war on formalism, how closely it all resembles the manoeuvres of national "socialism"!'

A similar line was taken by Ernst Bloch who, as early as 1937, had pointed out in an essay on the expressionism debate how identical in outlook certain schematically inclined Moscow intellectuals were with Hitler. He criticized the 'red fanfares against expressionism' that were sounded by Marxists like Lukács and that derived from a classicism they owned in common with Hitler. To Lukács's charge that the expressionists had shown a contempt for their cultural heritage by profaning it, Bloch replied: 'The possessors of "our fathers' works" of the last century were not heirs but epigones; they were burdened by Goethe's saying, "Woe unto thee that thou art a descendant". Youth, on the other hand, which in the course of this century has been renewed and renewed again, possesses the great past not as a curse but as a witness'. In his contribution to the discussion, which appeared as an article in *Das Wort*, Bloch returned to his criticism of the mechanical, undialectical rebuke levelled by Lukács at all the more recent experiments in art: 'Perennial neo-classicism, or the belief that nothing produced since Homer and Goethe is respectable unless modelled on them, or rather on an abstract from them, is certainly no vantage point from which to judge the art of the last but one avant-garde movement and make sure if all is well with it'. Lukács, said Bloch, had a 'concept of reality closed to objectivity', and this misled him into opposing any artist who attempted 'to demolish a universal image (even if the universal image is that of capitalism)'. Lukács equated the experiment of demolition with a state of decadence: 'The expressionists were "pioneers" of demolition; would it have been better if they had wanted to be physicians at the sick-bed of capitalism?' Bloch used Brecht's works to answer the literary historian who, at that time, employed the word 'liquidate' with striking frequency: 'Brecht wants a "sparse language with a clear-cut use of words", but with it he wants a precise imagination that calls things by name and cannot be debased. This means that Brecht's simplicity has nothing in common with abstract "liquidation"; on the other hand it impresses us with its political tartness and richness . . . The promise contained in an announcement of *Mahagonny* applies to these works: "Yesterday people started asking about you there". And the unenlightened answer: those sympathetic to capitalism, who were not asked, angrily; the left-wing schematists, who do not understand it, stupidly'.

In association with Hanns Eisler, Bloch finally published, in *Die neue Weltbühne,* a polemical contribution to the problem of cultural heritage which gave Lukács the opportunity to take Brecht's composer and collaborator severely to task as well. Eisler regarded Lukács's schematism not only as an artistic, but also as a political, disaster: 'What artists need is not to be told that everything produced today is necessarily, and must necessarily continue to be, rotten, what they need is understanding and knowledge of their specific problems of production . . . Formalism will not be overcome by academicism but only by means of the new subject-matter which is in urgent need of a form suited to it and determined by the content'. Eisler, therefore, suggested a productive takeover of the heritage and said he was against academic cultivation of the classics as practised by the Nazis. The historical heritage, he claimed, should be 'subjected to a thorough critical examination to offset its abuse by the Nazis'. Lukács saw in these remarks an alien, arrogant and negative attitude 'to the glorious literary past of the German people'. He regarded the position adopted by Eisler as avant-gardism of the worst kind. The

255

composer did not leave this unanswered; 'Induced to do so by Lukács's criticism, there are many who, from fear of behaving in an "alien, arrogant" way, might even call anti-fascist practice in Germany barbaric and fall back on an antiquated, schoolmasterly aesthetics conducive to a more introspective experience of the classics. Lukács has made no other suggestion about what should be done in Germany. And a glib phrase like "the glorious literary past of the German people" is a slim morsel to offer for such a very real need. (In Germany, by the way, the word "glorious" was more frequently used to praise the Prussian Army than to honour Goethe and Beethoven.)' Brecht drafted a 'small correction' which again was not published. In it he wrote: 'Lukács has, so to say, wiped the floor with my friend Eisler, whom few will regard as a pallid aesthete, because he is supposed not to have shown the prescribed feelings of respect when the will relating to the inheritance was executed. He rummaged about in it, as it were, and refused to take possession of everything. Perhaps, being an exile, he is not in a position to carry so much around with him'.

One must not forget that these disputes, which left nothing to be desired in the way of outspokeness, took place against a background of the growing menace of fascism and in the face of the Moscow trials. Dissenting opinions on the part of those who shared the same convictions were attacked more violently than fascist ideas. Brecht was horrified by the onslaught. The discussions interfered with his work as a writer. The contributions, above all those by Lukács, were the theoretical justification for the final condemnatation of all progressive tendencies in literature. His trite schematic theory of art, stamped as it was by idealism, ignored the achievements of every modern artist, of Picasso, Stravinsky, Schoenberg, Eisler, Joyce, as well as Brecht. Few of these artists had sufficient knowledge of Marxism to be able to distinguish between the teachings of Lenin and the current Marxism of the Moscow critics. Avowedly bourgeois writers like Romain Rolland, Sinclair Lewis or Thomas Mann, whose support for communism may have found expression in their speeches but not in their works, were rated more highly than socialist writers like Brecht, Mayakovsky or Tretjakov, who presented reality more comprehensively and in a more partisan way. In Moscow the bourgeois writers were put on pedestals as apostles of realism and recommended as models.

256

Although the outlook of the old writers, with whose view of realism Lukács was in agreement, might be permeated with reactionary features, in their case this did not prevent them from 'presenting social reality comprehensively, correctly and objectively'. In the case of a writer like Tolstoy, Lukács divorced the form of presentation from the artist's outlook because the form appealed to him. The moderns, however, were censured by the literary historian for their lack of correct awareness, their allegedly unrealistic writing being put down to this. In the case of Tolstoy Lukács got rid of this contradiction by declaring that his reactionary prejudices had been inextricably allied to a 'healthy popular movement with aspirations and a great future'; 'Tolstoy's case is not the only one in world literature in which an artist has created imperishable masterpieces on the basis of a fundamentally false outlook. But however subtly intertwined the repirocal influences may be, and however great and realistic the creation, it is obvious that not any and every false outlook can be used in support of a great realism. The illusions and mistakes of great realistic writers only become artistically productive when the mistakes and illusions are historically necessary and allied to a great progressive social movement'. Lukács did not offer this way out to contemporary writers. To him expressionism, for example, was 'the literary form of expression of the Independent Socialist Party ideology among the intelligentsia'. All who were not 'true sons of ancient Homer' were in for a rough time.

Brecht's aesthetic theory owed more to realism and political practice than did that of Lukács, whose adherence to old forms was merely an invitation to reside in loftier aesthetic spheres. It was a misunderstanding to imagine that in all this the theoretician took as his authorities Marx, Engels and Lenin, whose literary taste had probably made too deep an impression on Lukács. His method had virtually nothing in common with Marxism. Lukács adopted a distant and dogmatic attitude to the political realities of 1938; decadence, not fascism, was the enemy he called on people to fight. He was guided solely by literature and a few exemplary forms. 'But for literary forms', Brecht argued, 'one must turn to reality, not aesthetics, not even to the aesthetics of realism. There are many ways of concealing the truth and many ways of telling it. We derive our aesthetics, like our morality, from the needs of our struggle.'

257

23

On a little island where the people are friendly

> Does not everything point to the approach of
> night and nothing to the start of a new era?
> Should one not, therefore, adopt an attitude
> appropriate to people who are heading for
> night?

Because political circumstances demanded it and because he wanted his plays to be performed, Brecht felt compelled to make compromises in the construction of his plays. He separated theory from practice. Whereas hitherto practical work divorced from theory had been inconceivable, he now wrote his plays in a matter of a few weeks and, alongside this, worked out the theory of an epic theatre. Side by side with *Senora Carrar's Rifles, Terror and Misery of the Third Reich,* and *Galileo,* he wrote *The Purchase of Brass,* a dramaturgical breviary in dialogue form, in which he demonstrated how a new theatrical form could be obtained from criticising the existing theatre. His work on *The Purchase of Brass* was an antidote to his concessions to practice.

Because, since 1937, his financial situation had been anything but rosy, he decided to follow his friend Feuchtwanger's example and treat political questions of the day with reference to a historical theme. When his plan to write a play on Julius Caesar, which Erwin Piscator wanted to stage in Paris, fell through again, Brecht set about turning the material into a novel, his idea being to apply his plebian way of looking at history to current political events. Almost all his fellow-writers' historical novels were based on a bourgeois view of history, according to which history was made by great men. Moreover Brecht, as dialectician, was more interested in the differences between Caesar and Hitler than in drawing any moralizing comparison between their evil deeds. The important thing was historical appreciation, not moral indignation. But, attracted though he was by the idea of attacking fascist dictatorship through the indirect means of a historical model, the more he worked on it the greater became his scruples at undertaking his intended proof by analogy before he had a proper grasp of the social conditions that had played into Caesar's hands and given him power. In his Paris speech of 1935 Brecht had criticized Feuchtwanger's approach on the grounds that brutality does not stem from brutality, 'but from the business transactions which can no longer be undertaken without it'. Accordingly his Caesar, the prototype of so many dictators, was to be presented as a businessman.

Strangely enough it was Walter Benjamin and Fritz Sternberg who, from what they then knew of it, wanted to see more 'human interest, more of the old type of novel' in the Caesar novel, whereas Brecht was chiefly concerned to display the business talents of his character. As he worked on it his interest in history became overshadowed by his absorption in satirical polemics. And by limiting his hero to one principal quality, he failed to satisfy the requirements of the large-scale historical biography, and alternative to the traditional historical novel, he had planned. The novel remained a fragment; when he was forced by external circumstances to interrupt his work on it in 1939, Brecht was not particularly sorry.

While Per Knutzon succeeded in reconciling to Brecht, with a performance of *The Threepenny Opera* in the Riddersalen Theatre, the bourgeois critics who had been outraged by *Round Heads and Pointed Heads,* Brecht himself won back the goodwill of the progressive liberal and communist artists in Copenhagen with his play *Senora Carrar's Rifles* and its performance. Moreover events in Spain had finally persuaded all artists, who were 'left wing' in the wider sense, to make common cause against all fascist tendencies. On 14 February 1938 a special performance of Ruth Berlau's production of *Senora Carrar's Rifles,* with a cast of German emigrants and Helene Weigel, instead of Dagmar Andreasen, in the name part, was given at the Borup High School in Copenhagen in aid of republican Spain. The celebrated actress Bodil Ipsen read Spanish poems by various authors and, at the end of the proceedings, paid homage to her German colleague by reciting Brecht's poem, 'The Actress in Exile ('Die Schauspielerin im Exil'), in Otto Gelsted's translation. The presence of Martin Andersen Nexö, who held a position in the literary life of Denmark comparable to that of Gorki in Russia, was a clear indication of the support now felt for a writer persecuted by the Nazis as Brecht was. In 1939 the refugee who had been thus honoured repaid the homage with a poem, 'How future ages will judge our writers' ('Wie künftige Zeiten unsere Schriftsteller beurteilen werden'), dedicated to Martin Andersen Nexö on his seventieth birthday:

> Aber in jener Zeit werden gepriesen werden
> Die auf dem nackten Boden sassen, zu schreiben
> Die unter den Niedrigen sassen
> Die bei den Kämpfern sassen.

(But in that day they shall receive their due, who sat on the bare ground to write, who sat among the lowly, who sat with the fighters.)

Although Brecht disliked Nexö's addiction, in his memoirs, to 'dissecting souls and moralizing', he showed a great interest in the contents of these books and praised their 'respectable proletarianism'. He also readily helped in the translation of the first three volumes of the memoirs, which Margarete Steffin was making for a German-language publishing house in Moscow. He was less enthusiastic, however, about a play, *The Defeat,* which Margarete Steffin had translated from the Norwegian; its author, Nordahl Grieg, had spent a short time in Skovbostrand, where he was forced to listen to a brilliantly constructed lecture on dramatic techniques. Brecht subsequently wrote *The Days of the Commune (Die Tage der Kommune)* as an answer to Grieg's avowedly propagandist play. In Brecht's eyes Grieg, who went down in a British bomber over Berlin in the Second World War, was another example of the 'hard-boiled man' (sic) who only produced 'hot stuff' (sic) and worked up people's emotions. He classed him among the romantics, whom he described as 'members of the great emotion racket'.

In the autumn of 1938 Brecht started working on a plan to write a play about the physicist Galileo. This play also was intended to be put to immediate use: he wanted to make a version for workers that would encourage them to resist. Brecht's intention was to portray Galileo as a popular teacher, a sly partisan and fighter for the ideas of progress. He wrote the first version in November and gave it the title *Und sie bewegt sich doch.* At first he still believed that a performance in Denmark would be opportune, but political developments in Europe soon forced him to consider other possibilities. The thought of moving to the United States first occurred to him after the defeat of the Spanish republic and the conclusion of the Munich agreement, which made it clear that the bourgeois democracies had capitulated to fascism. As soon as he had finished the play Brecht sent a copy of it to America to be translated. In an interview published in Copenhagen at the beginning of January 1939 he was careful, in view of the renewed sensitivity in official circles to the political activities of emigrants, to say that he had written a play 'for New York', which dealt with 'Galileo's heroic fight for his modern scientific convictions'. And he went on to assure the interviewer that the play contained no topical allusions to Germany and Italy. Brecht had given up the idea of writing a militant play. While working on it he began to let his own views on the advancing eclipse seep into the play. His fear of the spread of fascism and his horror at the news from Russia led him to put this confession into the mouth of Galileo: 'I adhere to my belief that this is a new age. If it looks like a blood-bespattered old hag, than that is how a new age looks'. Brecht had confidence in the eventual victory of reason and in the fundamentally progressive nature of scientific knowledge. His physicist, a champion of enlightenment, was an implacable enemy of stupidity and barbarity. The announcement in December 1938 that the scientists Hahn and Strassmann had succeeded in splitting the uranium nucleus only confirmed Brecht in his intention to give more importance to the responsibility of the intellectual and to let his Galileo assume an attitude 'appropriate to those who are heading for night'. In the Danish version of *Galileo,* however, the physicist's scientific contribution outweighed his failure as a member of society. His retraction was permissable opportunism committed in the name of science. Galileo's decision to continue his studies in secret and smuggle his knowledge out of the land of oppression was regarded as nobler than heroic martyrdom. For Galileo the rules of behaviour laid down by Brecht in a Keuner story written in 1930 still held: 'A man in possession of knowledge may not fight, may not tell the truth, may not render a service, may not eat, may not decline honours, may not be identifiable. A man in possession of knowledge has only one of all the virtues: he is in possession of knowledge'.

Unnoticed by the Danish aliens department, Brecht left Skovbostrand at Easter 1939 in the company of Ruth Berlau. A week later Helene Weigel and Margarete Steffin followed with the children. An invitation from the National Association of Amateur Theatres to lecture in Stockholm, obtained through Georg Branting and the writer Henry Peter Matthis, enabled Brecht to enter Sweden. Margarete Steffin had to become a Danish citizen before she could safely cross the Swedish border: a Danish comrade offered to go through the formality of marriage with her. In a letter to Matthis, Brecht explained his hurried departure in this way: 'You will, I am sure, have some idea of how embarrassing it is to sit tight on one of these little islands when it looks as if the slaughter is about to begin. This year every week without a world war is simply an incomprehensible stroke of luck for mankind'.

While Ruth Berlau remained in Copenhagen, continuing to supervise the printing of the Svendborg Poems, Brecht and his family found accommodation on the small island of Lidingö, near Stockholm, in a house which the sculptress Ninan Santesson placed at their disposal. As the former inhabitant of Fünen wrote to his Danish friends: 'Once again I have ended up on a little island, where the people are friendly'. The house was ideal: situated in the middle of a small fir wood, it was admirably suited to undisturbed work, while at the same time it was an easily accessible meeting place for emigrants living in the Swedish capital. Through Branting and others who had heard his paper 'On the experimental theatre' at the students' theatre in Stockholm, Brecht was induced to take part in meetings called for the purpose of establishing an amateur theatrical group sponsored by the social democrat trade unions. He agreed to write a short play for the company, who wanted to convince their fellow countrymen of the need for the peoples of Europe to present a united anti-fascist front against Nazi Germany. He had just finished the one-act play *Dansen,* which was intended for Danish audiences and which he was going to send, through Ruth Berlau, to the workers' theatre in Copenhagen. Now he sketched out another play on similar lines, *Kleine Geschäfte mit Eisen* which, under the title *What is the Price of Iron? (Was kostet das Eisen?)*, was first performed in August 1939 by the Amatörteater Riksförbund in a Stockholm school for adult education. Because officially he was not allowed to engage in political activities Brecht wrote this play under the name of John Kent; on another occasion he used the pseudonym Sherwood Paw.

Dansen and *What is the Price of Iron?* are plays in 'knockabout' style, intended to enlighten their audiences politically and incite them to action. Unlike *Terror and Misery of the Third Reich,* which is a series of realistic scenes, each scene being precisely defined in time and place, the one-act plays are short, roughly sketched parable plays, easy to understand and meant to be staged as unrealistically as possible, like robust puppet shows with macabre effects: 'The iron merchant must wear a wig whose hairs can stand on end; the shoes must be very large, the cigars too'. Brecht aimed at poster-like, exaggeratedly clear effects.

The central character of the first play is the pig dealer Dansen, who also has charge of the key to his friend Svendson's iron warehouses. Dansen watches a 'stranger' raid neighbouring businesses. The thief turns Österreicher's tobacconist's shop into the firm Ostmärker & Co, and Frau Tschek's shoe shop into Bemm & Mährer GmbH. The stranger also shows great interest in Dansen's business, and still more in the iron warehouses, to which the pig dealer has the entry. But against his better judgement Dansen very soon finds himself with the stranger as a customer. Brecht comments: 'He no longer asks: what have you done with my neighbour? but only: what are you going to do with my pig? Thus one sees the difficulty of selling pigs and having morals at the same time'. Since the new customer buys a lot of pigs from him, Dansen makes a contract with him. He tries to set his friend Svendson's mind at rest: 'Your warehouse is now absolutely safe'. Dansen considers a joint line of defence unnecessary. Finally the stranger arrives and demands the key to the warehouse. Dansen confronts him with his contract rolled up like a rifle but the customer, who is armed to the teeth, tears the contract to shreds, seizes the key and demands to be supplied with pigs free from then on.

What is the Price of Iron? is set in Svendson's iron merchant's shop. Throughout 1938 and 1939 a sinister customer turns up regularly to whom Svendson sells iron at a good price, although the man has successfully raided Svendson's business friends, the tobacconist Österreicher and the owner of the shoe shop Frau Tschek. Svendson prefers to hold himself aloof from all the 'beastly quarrelling', saying he is neutral. He regards himself as a businessman, not a politician. For business reasons, therefore,

Svendson refuses to join the alliance against the criminal which Frau Gall and Herr Britt want to form. But then war breaks out and the sinister customer turns up with sub-machine guns and helps himself to all the iron. Shortly before this Svendson had made a hurried attempt to raise his prices.

By means of these simple parables, Brecht wanted to explain his views on the political situation to audiences in the countries whose guest he was, and to make it clear to them that the policies of neutrality and non-intervention pursued by their governments would end in disaster. By the time the play for Denmark was finished, there was no longer any question of getting it performed; and when Brecht, with the assistance of Ruth Berlau, who in the meantime had also arrived in Sweden, put on *What is the Price of Iron?*, Sweden was sending large quantities of iron to Nazi Germany. The Second World War was imminent.

During this time of the outbreak of war, Brecht wrote one play after another. When he found it impossible to continue work on the *Setzuan* play, which he had begun in Skovbostrand by taking as his starting-point the fragment *Die Ware Liebe (The Commodity Love)* written in his Berlin days before 1933, he wrote *Mother Courage and her Children* in barely five weeks—that dramatic chronicle of a woman who, refusing to let war get the better of her, becomes a camp follower, determined to make her pile. Even after she has lost her three sons in it, she still continues in the war. In a discussion which he had in 1950 about the proposal to film *Mother Courage* Brecht further underlined this aspect of his play: 'Women who have lost a son are always the most rabid warmongers, because if the war were to end its meaning would remain unfulfilled and the whole thing, in their eyes, would have been in vain'. It was not the mother but the audience who had to draw conclusions from what occurred. Brecht was moved to write the play by the story of the Scandinavian sutler Lotte Svärd in Johan Ludvig Runeberg's *Tales of a Subaltern,* which the Swedish actress Naima Wifstrand had read to him. Naima Wifstrand had translated *Senora Carrar's Rifles* into Swedish and played the title role in Hermann Greid's production of the play in March 1938. She ran a school of acting, where Helene Weigel was now also able to teach. Brecht contributed little exercises for actors, and wrote the part of Mother Courage for Naima Wifstrand, while he turned the part of the daughter Kattrin into a non-speaking part so that Helene Weigel could play it in a Swedish production. Although an immediate start was made with the translation, the play was not given in Sweden. The wireless play *The Trial of Lucullus (Das Verhör des Lukullus)*, which was written in the space of a few days after the completion of *Mother Courage,* was also not broadcast by Stockholm radio, in spite of having been accepted at first; all that took place was a rendering of the text, in the form of a shadow-play, by a small workers' acting company. With the exception of *The Mother* and *Round Heads and Pointed Heads* not a single play since *St. Joan of the Stockyards* had been tried out on the stage.

Brecht took refuge in work, although he followed the progress of the war in every detail and analysed the political situation both with German artists, scholars and politicians, who regularly visited Lidingö, and with the Swedish writers Arnold Ljungdal, Johannes Edfelt and Henry Peter Matthis. With the actor and director Hermann Greid, who had written a book on dialectics, Brecht discussed questions of Marxist ethics. Greid's concept of socialism as a future order of society, in which man would transform brutish relationships into human ones, struck Brecht as idealistic. 'Socialism is nothing but a collection of projects on the part of the proletariat', he declared. In these talks in Lidingö Brecht's chief concern was to remain productive and not let himself become confused by political events which, like the conclusion of the Hitler–Stalin pact, were sometimes hard to fathom. He judged it expedient to attach himself neither to those emigrants who condemned the Soviet Union lock, stock and barrel, nor to those who swore unreservedly by Moscow: 'I do not think one can say more than that the Union is saving itself at the cost of leaving the world proletariat without watchwords, hope or assistance'. In order to make it possible to unite in useful political work with the others taking part in the conversations, who were all at sixes and sevens and consisted of Socialist Workers Party people round August Enderle, former fighters in Spain and trade unionists, Brecht put forward the idea of a 'dictionary of fascist slogans'. Well though he appreciated the requirements of a flexible, pragmatic policy geared to the continued existence of the Soviet Union, Brecht found it very difficult to adjust himself to the stark reality, to 'the disintegration of all ideological cover'. There was no longer any place in political practice for Marxist theory and frank debates on matters of principle.

265

One of the numerous gatherings in Lidingö, at which the defeat in the Spanish civil war was discussed, was recorded by the painter and former miner Hans Tombrock, whom Brecht encouraged to produce an 'oeuvre' and whom he prevailed upon to translate the accidental and romantic aspects of his artistic intentions into the ability to employ 'the principle of the social group as a category of pictorial composition'. In the same way that he regularly gave Eisler, and later Dessau, poems and songs to set to music, in order to add a further quality to their 'utility value', he now got Tombrock to illustrate his plays and poems with drawings. The most notable results of this collaboration were large panels for community houses in Sweden, 'of which one panel always contained a picture and one a text'. The two panels 'Questions of a worker reading', for example, were done for the community house in Gävle. To illustrate his poem Brecht wanted Tombrock to do a worker of 'stature'; he was to look over life-size, ill at ease and menacing: 'One must have the impression that he may still lack the book; otherwise he lacks nothing but the power to rule. One must think: there sits the man who really built Thebes with its seven gates, the conqueror of Asia, grimly studying the lies about his conquests and building feats. It is most important, for these community houses, that the people should be reminded of their strength'. The worker was to be approached as fighter, designer, engineer and politician. Brecht's strength, in his dealings with other artists, was his ability to set aside their weaknesses and scruples, to help them to find a method of work and to keep them productive. It was especially important for the socialist artist to hold his ground in face of the steadily deteriorating situation, and not to let his energies be sapped by the depressing times. 'Of course it is hard to do any painting at the moment', Brecht wrote back to Tombrock in Sweden, after he himself had arrived in Helsinki; but he implored him, in spite of everything to 'try it—work is a good tonic'.

24

Waiting for Passports

With each report of a Hitler victory my
importance as a writer diminishes.

Brecht wanted to make arrangements for going to America while
he was in Sweden. But the Nazi military advance came quicker
than a satisfactory answer to the visa question. A week after the
Wehrmacht entered Denmark and Norway Brecht, to be on the
safe side, took his family and Margarete Steffin out of Sweden
which, at the end, had become almost a second home to him.
Whereas the transfer from Svenborg to Lidingö had still been
almost like moving house, the further transfer to Finland in April
1940 was a hurried departure for a country where it was still
possible to find refuge free from Nazi control. They left the
furniture and library behind with Swedish friends, taking with
them only the cases of manuscripts. In Helsinki, too, the refugees
were able to count on help from progressive artists and others who
had been notified from Stockholm. The writers Hella Wuolijoki
and Elmer Diktonius, the 'Finnish Horace', assumed the main
responsibility, finding them lodgings and seeing that they were
favourably received in official circles. Finland at that time was in a
very difficult position: it was a very poor country with a serious
shortage of foodstuffs due to the fact that it was cut off from
imports; moreover it had not yet recovered from the consequences
of the civil war. As they had to wait for their American visas, the
Brechts rented a small apartment in the working-class district of
Tölö in order to save money and be able to do their own cooking.

Auf der Flucht vor meinen Landsleuten
Bin ich nach Finnland gelangt. Freunde
Die ich gestern nicht kannte, stellten ein paar Betten
In saubere Zimmer. Im Lautsprecher
Höre ich die Siegesmeldungen des Abschaums. Neugierig

267

Betrachte ich die Karte des Erdteils. Hoch oben
in Lappland
Nach dem Nördlichen Eismeer zu
Sehe ich noch eine kleine Tür.

(Fleeing from my countrymen I have now reached Finland. Friends who
yesterday were strangers have put some beds in clean rooms. Through
the loudspeaker I hear announcements of the victorious scum. Anxiously
I scan the local map. Far up in Lappland, towards the Arctic Ocean, I can
still see a small door.)

They hoped to get a ship to the United States in August, sailing
from Petsamo. In addition to his family Brecht had to look after his
two friends, Margarete Steffin and Ruth Berlau, for whom he had
accepted responsibility. The former was very ill and hardly able to
travel any longer; he constantly had to encourage her not to give
way to exhaustion and to remind her that she was 'needed': 'But I
need you, whatever happens. I say I, and could as well say we'. By
now Helene Weigel had accepted Margarete Steffin as a member of
the household. Fear that the children might become tubercular,
not jealousy, had been the main reason why hitherto she had
always tried to find lodgings elsewhere for Brecht's co-worker and
erotic muse. But when it transpired that Ruth Berlau was now to
join the household as well, Helene Weigel refused. Brecht had sent
a message to his Danish mistress, who had returned to Denmark
for rehearsals in the spring of 1940, that in future he would always
include her in his travel arrangements. In Helsinki he immediately
asked Hella Wuloijoki to do something for Ruth Berlau, to write a
few lines to her direct and get her out of occupied Denmark: 'Only
so that you will understand how responsible for Ruth I feel; once
the Nazi machinery gets into its stride, all the work she has done
with me cannot possibly remain a secret . . . . In my view it won't be
possible for her to return until the war is over'.

His call to catch up with him quickly was very soon followed by
the arrival of Ruth Berlau herself. Recalling his professions of love
and the gramophone record of the poems 'Bivouac' ('Biwak') and
'Ardens sed virens', which he had had specially made for her in
Stockholm, she went to Kausala, to the Marlebaek property
where, in the meantime, Hella Wuolijoki had installed her German
friends. When she found there was no room in the house, Ruth

Berlau immediately pitched a tent close to the property. This importunate behaviour, which at first did not disturb Brecht in the least, struck his hostess as scandalous. She took Helene Weigel's part and forbade Ruth Berlau the house. It gradually dawned on the latter that she was not included in the travel arrangements. Helene Weigel, naturally, had booked only five passages on the ship. There were violent altercations, the excluded mistress was in despair, she started drinking fruit brandy and told everyone she had no intention whatever of allowing herself 'to be sent home'. Ruth Berlau's rebellious, overwrought behaviour caused Brecht concern and he was forced to concede: 'I realize there are others who would prefer to travel separately'. He reaffirmed his intention to stand by his promises, advised her to calm down, adopt a practical and critical attitude and show a sense of humour, 'as you always do when I want you to help me'. On 4 September he again assured his mistress: 'You must not be uneasy, I am thinking of you and shall not go without you'.

Brecht did not make that sort of statement lightly. His relations with the three women, with whom he lived constantly for several years, were based on warm affection and mutual gratification. For him they were all partners in whom he could fulfil himself and with whom he remained on friendly terms even when he was making love to one or other of them. Helene Weigel was the mother of his children and the actress best able to convey his idea of theatre from the stage to the auditorium. Margarete Steffin was a 'leader' in times of darkness, whose courage and strength made him sentimental and tender. Finally Ruth Berlau presented a challenge to Brecht because of her passionate nature and goodness. She indulged her feelings and kindness to the point of selflessness. Her desire to be good constantly led her into difficulties from which there was no way out; she then took refuge in alcohol, which made her surprisingly malicious, so that her friends were eventually forced to concern themselves with her problems. In Ruth Berlau's case love, for Brecht, meant something 'perpetually capable of turning into solicitude and then back from solicitude into love again, and into many other things and always back again'.

At the beginning of October 1940 Hella Wuolijoki was compelled, for financial reasons, to sell her property. Finland's economic situation had become still more precarious and, in the meantime, the government had had to give the Nazis a right of passage into Norway. Brecht now found a small apartment in the harbour area of Helsinki in which, while the wireless was daily giving out fresh news of the Third Reich's irresistibly mounting power, he wrote *Refugees in Conversation,* where he described Finland as a nation whose people were silent in two languages. The scene of the 'whispered' conversations between the physicist Ziffel and the worker Kalle was the Helsinki station restaurant, where Brecht often joined Diktonius or Hermann Greid in a glass of beer. Nazi informers made their appearance with increasing frequency, so that for emigrants, waiting for travel documents, which had become man's 'most precious component', was now a race against time. The prospect of getting out of Finland without being subjected to questioning was growing less every day, while there was also the danger of being refused entry into the United States if, as was to be expected, it came into the war. When, in December, Brecht received an entry visa into Mexico, for which he had also applied, many of his friends urged him to make the voyage immediately. But he refused, because there were no papers for Margarete Steffin.

Although by now there was not the ghost of a chance of getting one of his plays performed, and although he was completely isolated in his work, Brecht kept himself going by writing for the theatre. If he could possibly help it, he did not intend to let things get on top of him or to give the Nazis the satisfaction of being able to cross his name off the list of their opponents. In March, in the midst of all the confusion over travel documents and chances to leave, he decided to write a 'gangster play' for the American stage, which would explain the events leading up to Hitler's seizure of power. The alienation necessary to the political argument was to be obtained through the gangster milieu and the grand manner. Instead of using the gangster plot to symbolize political events, therefore, he treated it as an independent story of a 'revelatory' nature. *The Resistible Rise of Arturo Ui (Der aufhaltsame Aufstieg des Arturo Ui)* was conceived as a gangster tale, not as a cryptographic play about Hitler's career. After writing it, which took him barely three weeks, Brecht noted: 'I am anxious to see if I have succeeded in giving pace to the epic style—it is wrong to imagine that it must of necessity be leisurely. In principle one can employ quick motion as well as slow motion in epic writing. Needless to say liveliness, open conflict, the clash of antagonists,

270

are also as possible in the epic as in the "dramatic" style'. Brecht then spent several further days polishing his iambics, a task to which he was held by Margarete Steffin, whose persistent criticism was always aimed at getting the correct and most accurate results. A new formal apparatus had to be devised for modern verse with irregular rhythms. Exercises of this sort, another example of which was the effort he made to keep his manuscript on a high aesthetic level, were Brecht's antidote to the collapse of all human values and the realization that for the time being all literary endeavours were futile. He worked on the realistic assumption that his ideas needed a certain amount of time to gain acceptance. He therefore aimed at endowing his works with long life.

In *Arturo Ui* Brecht continued the dismantling of great historical figures which he had started in his Caesar novel. What he wanted to do was to demolish the romantic notion of history held by the petit bourgeoisie, and destroy people's respect for killers. Like Chaplin, who at the time was making his film *The Great Dictator,* Brecht believed that a blood-stained character like Hitler could be portrayed satirically and made ludicrous: 'When those in power allow a little scoundrel to become a big scoundrel he should not acquire a special place, not merely as a scoundrel but in our view of history. And in general it is probably true to say that tragedy more often makes light of human suffering than comedy'.

In Finland Brecht also put the finishing touches to his parable play *The Good Woman of Setzuan,* which set out to show how pleasant it is to be kind and good and what a strain it is to be evil. The wicked world compels people to behave inhumanly because to be good does not pay and exposes one to danger. The metamorphoses of the good Shen Te into her wicked male cousin Shui Ta are shown to be necessary in a world in which sheer interest alone, 'callous payment in cash', determines the relations between individuals. Financial conditions prevent the natural development of love and productivity. The play used many of the devices of the Chinese theatre; the author laid great stress on bringing out the unambiguous demonstrational character of the scenes. He wanted the form of the play to convey an idea of the Utopia of unrestricted, pleasurable productivity.

On 12 May 1941 the long-awaited American travel documents finally arrived, with a visitor's visa for Margarete Steffin, which meant that she did not first have to submit to the compulsory

271

health inspection. To avoid the risk of being arrested in Petsamo they decided to take the trans-Siberian railway to Vladivostock. On the journey Margarete Steffin's health became worse every day. In Moscow, where they made a brief stop, her transfer to hospital became imperative. Brecht wanted to remain there but was urged to continue the journey because the June sailing from Vladivostock to the United States might be their last chance to get away. Margarete Steffin accepted this decision quietly and calmly, consoled by a parting-gift of a ring and a small elephant: 'I shall follow, only two things can stop me—illness and the war . . .. Thanks to the things you said to me, I am quite at peace'. Four days later, after they had passed Lake Baikal, Brecht received a telegram from the writers Apletin and Tadejev telling him that his little teacher had died.

> Im neunten Jahr der Flucht vor Hitler
> Erschöpft von den Reisen
> Der Kälte und dem Hunger des winterlichen Finnland
> Und dem Warten auf den Pass in einen andern Kontinent
> Starb unsere Genossin Steffin
> In der roten Stadt Moskau.

(In the ninth year of the flight from Hitler, exhausted by travelling, by the cold and the hunger of wintry Finland, and by waiting for a passport to another continent, our comrade Steffin died in the red city of Moscow.)

25

Herr Puntila and his Servant Matti

The attempts by someone who has fallen into a swamp to reach solid ground are not, of course, experiments. To want something new is out of date, what is new is to want something old.

'These clear nights are very beautiful. Just before 3 o'clock I got up, because of the flies, and went outside. The cocks were crowing but it had never been dark. And I do so love to urinate in the open'. The days when he swam in lakes and rivers as he wandered with his Augsburg friends along the Lech or drove into the Allgäu, never again seemed so close as they did in the summer of 1940 on the Marlebaek property in Kausala. The lakes and streams full of fish, the birch woods, the smell of berries and the clanging of milk cans filled him with a happiness, of which he could not feel ashamed but which, nonetheless, seemed wrong when he thought of the war. While the Battle of Britain was raging, and the Nazis were preparing their campaign against the Soviet Union, he was intoxicated by the summer nights in Finland and wrote a comedy about a rich farmer who is only human when he is drunk, 'because then he forgets his own interests'. The title character and the framework of the plot were taken from a farce by his hostess Hella Wuolijoki. Brecht's task, as he saw it, was to 'tear down' the psychologizing talk of this comedy of manners in order to 'make room for tales of Finnish national life or for opinions, to give dramatic expression to the contrast between "master" and "servant", and give back to the subject its poetry and comedy'. In contrast to *Refugees in Conversation,* which was written immediately after *Herr Puntila and his Servant Matti (Herr Puntila und sein Knecht Matti)* and in which the author divided his personal views and experiences between the bourgeois scholar and the worker, he here puts everything personal into the character of the rich farmer. In the 'Nocturno' scene, which was entirely new,

Brecht makes Puntila rhapsodize: 'I could never live in a town. Why? Because I want to walk straight out and urinate in the open, under the stars. Otherwise what do I get out of it? They tell me it's primitive to do it outside, but I call it primitive to do it into a piece of china'. The practice of literature turned out to be far removed 'from the centres where all the decisive events are taking place'. Brecht had to admit that '*Puntila* means almost nothing to me, the war everything; I can write almost anything about *Puntila* but nothing about the war'. Just how important Brecht felt this comedy to be and how greatly affected he was while writing it by the discrepancy between art and reality—a discrepancy he constantly noted down—can be seen from the fact that when he was in Zurich, on his return from America, he immediately produced it and also chose it for the opening performance of the Berliner Ensemble. The outward incentive to write *Puntila* was a competition for a 'Volksstück', or folk play, which Hella Wuolijoki wanted to enter with Brecht. When the latter told her of his Setzuan play, which he had just finished, and of the girl in it who led a double life as a good and as a wicked person, she remembered her comedy about the rich farmer who makes promises in his cups that he cannot keep when he is sober. This story of a drunkard with two sides to his nature was based on a true incident, the mad driving-escapade of her uncle Roope, which in the mid-nineteen-twenties had caused something of a sensation in Kausala. She had also used the subject for a film script, with the title *The Sawdust Princess*. What disturbed Brecht was not the play's construction, in the form of a farce, but simply the conventional dramatic technique with which the subject was presented. When he first published *Puntila* in 1950, in the tenth volume of the *Versuche,* Brecht commented: 'It is a folk play and was written in Finland in 1940; it is based on stories and the outline of a play by Hella Wuolijoki'. Both these originals, however, were complete dramatic works and had been preceded only by a short sketch in prose. There are no stories among Hella Wuolijoki's works. What Brecht was referring to were stories which his hostess used to tell him and which impressed him far more than her literary work; he often got Margarete Steffin to take them down. When she told stories she was 'an entrancing epic poet'; but in her plays he missed any observation based on reality, he could find no trace in them of her rich experience of life.

Hella Murrik, who was Esthonian by birth, had gone to Helsinki in 1904 to study philology, and while there had married the lawyer and social democrat politician Sulo Wuolijoki. Before starting to write plays she had been manageress of various timber firms as well as a diplomat and journalist. She spoke six languages. She had remarkable stories to tell of Finland's 'heroic' days during the civil war of 1918. Her sympathies were with the 'reds', her manner when telling stories was that of a woman of the people: 'everything was biblically simple and biblically complex', was how Brecht put it. But in her approach to art she belonged to a different world, to the class of society she wanted to fight. By supplementing Hella Wuolijoki's play with her stories Brecht hoped to make her artistically a socialist too. Although he incorporated many elements of the plot, almost all the characters and some actual phrases, the new play, which took him barely three weeks to write, was radically different from the original.

The central character of Hella Wuolijoki's *Sawdust Princess* is Eva, the daughter of a farmer named Puntila, who has in mind for his daughter's husband a man from the upper classes. To the father a socially acceptable son-in-law is worth a dowry of a saw-mill. At the Kurgela estate, which is financially dependent on him, Puntila drinks heavily with the local bigwigs and sets out to serenade his hostess Aunt Hanna. To prevent things getting out of hand the women hide the bottles. In protest at the forcible removal of the alcohol the humiliated farmer decides to go and get some illicit schnaps. The newly engaged chauffeur, Kalle, uses the time when he is away to court Eva. When Puntila, on his return, announces that all men are his brothers, tells of his engagement to five women and distributes currency notes, Kalle seizes the opportunity to try to come to an agreement with his employer on the subject of Eva. As a reward for helping his master to dispossess himself of his fiancées, who are now claiming their rights, Puntila agrees. To show his loved one that it is not the dowry he is after, Kalle tells her of the romantic bliss of a poor life and tries to abduct her. When his master, who is now sober again, wants to dismiss him, Kalle discloses his real identity as Dr. Vuorinen, so that nothing any longer stands in the way of a respectable marriage. Puntila, for his part, submits to the strict regimen of Aunt Hanna.

As this brief summary shows *The Sawdust Princess* is a comedy like a thousand others, devoid of genuine incongruities; all the conflicts are amicably resolved. One cannot help being struck by its similarity to Carl Zuckmayer's comedy *Der fröhliche Weinberg*, in which the wealthy owner of the vineyard, Gunderloch, wants to marry his daughter Klärchen to the university Student Knuzius, but in the end is glad for her to get the honest sailor Jochen. And there is even a fine strapping woman for Gunderloch. As Hans Peter Neureuter has pointed out, the play is a also a variation, in comedy form, of the battle of the sexes in Strindberg's *Miss Julie*. Brecht left intact the comedy scheme of his model, changing only the perspective of the story. In his play the class differences remain intact throughout the comedy. Kalle really is a chauffeur, a man very much to the taste of both Eva and Puntila—only he is not socially acceptable. Master and servant like each other, but they can have no personal relationship: 'Because in this life the corn does not thresh the flail, and because oil does not mix with water'. Puntila is no longer a man 'torn in two', who is overcome by remorse and ill-humour when he is sober, but a man with twin natures that throw into relief the division into human being and representative of his class imposed on him by social conditions. According to Brecht's first sketch, entitled 'The twin natures of Herr Puntila or Rain always falls down': 'Herr von Puntila has twin natures. When he is drunk he is a human being, but when he is sober he is a rich farmer. When he is sober he beats his chauffeur, but when he is drunk he engages a chauffeur who refuses to put up with that sort of treatment. When he is drunk he marries any woman who gets up early and deserves a good life, but when he is sober he does not want to part with his money, and asks indignantly if he is supposed to give an annuity to every dairy maid he sleeps with. When he is drunk he promises his daughter to the chauffeur, but when he is sober he gives her to the attaché to marry. Drunk once more he disowns her for obeying him. Drunk he blames his housekeeper for ill-treating the servants, sober he marries her. He has a servant who knows all this and proves to him that all the things he wants when he is drunk are impracticable in real life'. When he wrote the play Brecht kept to this sketch. The housekeeper, whom Puntilla finally marries and who was based on Aunt Hanna, was the only character he eventually dropped. He confined himself to a determined manageress and an Aunt Klinkmann who never appears.

The servant Kalle acts as the mouthpiece of plebeian intelligence, making sure that class antagonisms are not simply ignored. He adds the dimension of social categories to the rich farmer's thinking. As a human being Puntila is not affected by this, on the contrary his intoxication is supposed to have something about it of 'divine, Dionysian drunkenness'. Brecht, however, does not regard Kalle but the women of Kurgela as the true key figures representing an opposing social viewpoint. It is they who tell the stories which Hella Wuolijoki did not think capable of literary treatment. In her play there had been room only for 'upper class' anecdotes and witticisms, such as the attaché, provost, judge and advocate had at their command. But in her case they were introduced for their own sake, not for that of the 'Sprachgestus' or underlying attitude.

Out of the farce about a marriageable daughter whose father when drunk plays some mad pranks which he later regrets, come scenes about 'Tavast drunkenness'. Brecht's first version contains more stories than the later ones. Kalle, who is later given the name Matti, is also rather more talkative; he strives still harder for equality with Eva and Herr Puntila, being the latter's social conscience rather than his social critic and opponent. A 'Gesindemarkt', or fair where servants could be hired, held in the vicinity of Marlebaek, gave him the idea for the scene of this name which he added to the manuscript.

To work from Brecht used a new version of Hella Wuolijoki's Puntila comedy, which she had made after talking the play over with him and had dictated in German to Margarete Steffin. The Finnish authoress was considerably upset by the greater artificiality of the new play, by its narrative elements and by the fact that the points she made in it had been discarded. But Brecht succeeded in convincing her to some extent that his alterations made sense and in persuading her to start translating it into Finnish. By and large Hella Wuolijoki accepted Brecht's version and, although she did not keep exactly to the text, she retained the scenic structure almost unaltered. She added Herr Kurgela (in other words Klinkmann) because she was clearly unenthusiastic over Brecht's idea of making Puntila think from time to time of marrying Kurgela's widow in order to save his wood. In her version she also dispensed with the 'Nocturno' scene and the great story of Emma the smuggler.

The Finnish version, published by Hella Wuolijoki in 1946, was called *Squire Iso-Heikkilä and his Servant Kalle,* the name Puntila being omitted for personal reasons, because the manor belonging to Uncle Roope's stepfather was called Puntila and the landowner portrayed under this name was still alive. Apart from cuts and slight alterations the play remained essentially unchanged until 1948. In Zurich Brecht wrote the poem 'The Plum Song' ('Das Pflaumenlied') for Therese Giehse, who played the part of Emma the smuggler. Because Puntila engaged people's sympathies too strongly, and in order to give added force to the social criticism voiced in the play, Brecht added the character of Surkkala, a red, for the production by the Berliner Ensemble, in order to give Matti, who is merely his master's servant, the support of a genuinely proletarian character. The addition was made chiefly because it was thought that the political background, with the rich farmer, had become historic in the context of the new social realities of East Germany. The intention was to show something of the history of the class struggle. A further addition was the Puntila song, performed, while the scenery was being changed, by the actress who played the cook; it was meant as a comment 'from the kitchen' on what went on on the Puntila estate.

Along with *The Threepenny Opera, Herr Puntila and his Servant Matti* must today be Brecht's most frequently performed play. It is considered to be his funniest and seems to be 'indestructible'. While its social criticism is regarded as out of date, it is praised for its universal human qualities as exemplified by sex and drink. At last a play that is not epic, that parades no theory, but is simply a superb comedy of human types. The farce, which the play was originally designed to refute, seems to be visible once more through the back door. Is Puntila really dated? In his book *Letzten Endes* Fritz Kortner has answered this question with an emphatic 'no': 'To prove how valid it is, transfer the setting to Texas, for example, dress Puntila as a Texan and make Matti black. The play would then be condemned as a flagrant piece of literary engagement by the very people who now complain that it has no topical interest . . . Be that as it may, in some recent productions the Puntilas of the day have been transferred to *Der fröhliche Weinberg,* the social monsters acclaimed as jovial drunkards and the guilty sybarites not been pilloried for what they are: smarmy spongers, robber barons at the expense of the public good, drinking companions for whose drinking the public has to pay, descendants of those Junkers who said fatherland when they meant my estates, who allied themselves to big business and, in order to protect this unholy alliance, introduced compulsory military service to preserve and extend their estates'.

Kortner's arguments in favour of a Brecht text not being a libretto and against rendering it harmless by turning it into a farce are valid; he is also right to resist the all too transparent political complaints that Brecht is out of date. But to make the play topical in the way he suggests is to ignore completely the human traits undeniably inherent in the character of Puntila. Politically a play against Puntila, the Junker, no longer has much to say to us. The equation of landowner with capitalist is convincing only if we set the play in the Finland of 1940. As we see it today the landowner type portrayed by Brecht appears politically dangerous, but not representative, and on its way out. Of much greater interest are the autobiographical, Baal-like elements of the character, all the things, in fact, about the man Puntila that are 'worth preserving'. The tendency of the audience to identify itself with the more complete, more vital, character of Puntila, and to dismiss Matti as insipid, should be exploited. How far is it possible to go with Puntila, and how far is it not (any longer) possible to go with Matti?

There is nothing wrong with the basic construction of the comedy. It demonstrates 'what servitude is in relation to authority' (Hegel). Matti's servitude is his apprenticeship. With the sure instinct of a man who longs for authority, he senses that the unpredictability of his master and his attacks of humanity can harm him. Matti fears those moments when his master addresses him as a human being and in this way might quite irrationally bind him to him. By forgetting that he needs his servant, Herr Puntila prevents the latter from developing his 'servile awareness'. But this, as Hegel attempts to show in his *Phenomenology of Mind,* is the prerequisite for true independence. In Diderot's novel *Jacques le Fataliste* the servant, being a fatalist, remains faithful to his master; he is content merely to know of the freedom to get along without him. Brecht's Matti is an optimist. He wants not only authority but power as well. He wants to be his own master. One suspects that he is looking for a new place only with a master for whom he is more than a match. He is prepared to wait until the Surkkalas have brought about a revolution or, to bring it more into line with the social realities of our own day, to profit by the

279

economic reasoning that will rationalize Puntila's estate away.

Puntila owns an estate, a saw mill, a mill and ninety cows. He is a big landowner, an influential man in Kausala and is anxious to acquire more influence with the government in Helsinki. Hence his idea of marrying Eva to the attaché. The planned union is even worth a wood to him. And this wood could be saved if he were to marry the attaché's aunt, who has had her eye on him for a long time. But the old woman is disagreeable, a termagent and hideously ugly. The human being in Puntila rebels against all these manipulations and marriages of expediency. He much prefers to get engaged without ulterior motives and as often as he feels like it. When drunk his human qualities come out and he speaks almost like a communist. When sober he is repulsive, a man who has 'gone wrong'. To enjoy things is easy when one has money, that is obvious! It is all very well for Herr Puntila to praise the cows and become intoxicated with the sound of milk cans, the cowman sees it differently; the lumberman will only be able to curse the trees that do not belong to him, whereas Herr Puntila's heart is warmed by the sight of them. Yet this Puntila is no drunken drone, no social monster, he is a great national figure, a 'Tavast Bachus'. There is something biblical, something godlike about him. He is certainly not a 'money-grubber'; he is not a Sternheim character nor a George Grosz type. Puntila, and one must not try to hide the fact, is a reactionary numskull, a member of the Finnish *Heimwehr*. As a politician he can still afford to indulge in a certain drunken anarchy; nevertheless he is more sober than drunk. We must not be blind to the dangerous side of Puntila, but what makes him sympathetic and important to us is his ability to give free play to his imagination, his charm, his gift for enjoyment.

Puntila is an irrational person, like Herr Quitt in Peter Handke's play *Die Unvernünftigen sterben aus (Irrational People are Dying Out)*. He is going to die out too because he does nothing to safeguard his property, to save his estate in the new age. If he knew anything about earning power and profits, the most sensible thing he could do would be to bind Matti to himself and the estate by tying him to Eva. Matti is the only one who is in a position to manage the estate as an economically profitable concern, the only one who has any experience of machinery. If he were to give Matti a share in his possessions, his problems of economic survival would be over. But any cooperation between the vital giant and the ascetic functionary and technocrat is out of the question. Puntila gradually realizes that Matti is not the man he took him to be at first. Red Surkkala would be much better suited to him, a man 'who will do anything for his convictions'.

Matti is a rebel but he is no revolutionary. He is a Schweyk character, the prototype of the little man who makes his way in the world with a certain cunning, and always knows in good time when he must accommodate himself to changed conditions. The qualities in Matti that grate on one are, above all, his inability to enjoy himself and his rather stuffy morality. His attitude to Eva is petit-bourgeois pure and simple and is seen at its most unpleasant in his idea of what a good working-class wife should be.

In his *Working-Diary (Arbeitsjournal)* Brecht wrote of Puntila; 'It is a fat little calf of a play. More of the countryside in it than in any other of my plays, except perhaps *Baal*'. Puntila is even more reminiscent of *In the Jungle of the Cities* than of *Baal,* the comedy being like a cheerful paraphrase of the early play. The relationship between Puntila and Matti reminds one of the fight between Shlink and Garga. When Matti leaves Puntila he is giving up the fight, because he realizes that his own hour has come—he assumes power, though not at Puntila's side. The new age simply passes Puntila by. Matti will clear things up and put the estate in order, where things are going increasingly to rack and ruin.

When he was working out the scenes involving the women of Kurgela, who are the real heroes of the play and the bearers of the people's hopes, Brecht noted: 'For the lower classes we have only mawkishly sentimental models and ones prior to 1848. Sympathy leads to everything being seen in a good light, to the popular (or folklorist) affability of romanticism'. So Brecht sketched out a coarsely sensual, wonderfully comic, group of four women to whom Puntila, drunk, immediately becomes engaged. These engagements can also be seen as anticipating subsequent consent *(Einverständnis),* which is destined to be lasting and in which all who spring from the Finnish countryside, and are tied to it, unite. Puntila thus belongs to these women, whereas Matti emerges as the enemy of this picture of happiness. Matti simply represents the state, he can never know the anarchy of happiness.

26

Hollywood

Scarcely anywhere have I found life more
difficult than here in this show place of 'easy
going'

America had long since ceased to be the country of Brecht's
dreams. He had not left Europe until it was absolutely necessary.
But more and more countries had succumbed to the Nazi armed
forces. Even in the Pacific Ocean one had to count on running into
German naval squadrons. The refugees were less afraid of a
typhoon in that area than of German 'pirates', considering their
chances of survival better in the first case. On 21 July Brecht
arrived in San Pedro on board the *Annie Johnson,* sailing from
Manila, where it had put in for several days. Here, in the port of
Los Angeles, he was met by Marta Feuchtwanger and Alexander
Granach. A great many of his artist friends had already found
sanctuary in America. Wilhelm Dieterle, Oskar Homolka, Fritz
Kortner, Fritz Lang and Ferdinand Reyher had been prominent
among those who had helped him to obtain entry permits and
money for the voyage. Even a house had been rented for him in
advance, and Lion Feuchtwanger, who had spent the first months
of the war in a French internment camp and escaped arrest only at
the last moment, urged him to settle in Hollywood, in spite of all
his reservations about it, because by American standards it was not
expensive and it was still the place where work was easiest to find.

The house in Santa Monica, the residential district of
Hollywood, had little appeal for Brecht; it was much 'too pretty'
and also much too small, so that Ruth Berlau had to take a room in
the neighbourhood with a Dutch couple who were painters. To the
political refugee from Europe the idyllic landscape seemed
extraordinarily unrealistic; all of a sudden he was a gold-digger by
profession. Although the Mediterranean resort of Sanary

resembled the Californian landscape more closely than the Danish Sound, Feuchtwanger also remarked, 'one has to keep very clearly in mind the horrors of Europe to find living here agreeable'. Brecht felt worse than he had ever felt in his life. The discrepancy between the wretchedness of the individual and the wealth of the community, from which everyone wanted to profit as much as possible, made him lose his bearings to some extent; he felt like a being from another age. It was a hell that looked like paradise: 'And here of all places I am without Grete. It is as if someone had taken my guide away on the edge of the desert'. Nothing ever affected Brecht more than the death of Margarete Steffin. And now he had to add the name of Walter Benjamin to the casualty list, a friend and conversationalist, on whom he counted to advise and contradict him; he had taken his own life on the Franco–Spanish border while fleeing from the Gestapo. When Günther Anders brought him the news and gave him Benjamin's last work, Brecht remarked on its clarity of thought and reflected with horror on 'how few people there are who are prepared even to misunderstand a thing of this sort'.

Surrounded by the many emigrants, and all the artists waiting for jobs in the ante-rooms of film studios, Brecht felt more isolated than in the solitude of the Finnish forests. Hitherto political events had cast a shadow on his work as a writer, and it had been political conditions that he had had to consider in the countries which gave him refuge. But now, in America, there was no demand for him simply as a writer. Theatre here was a means of making money, and commercial considerations alone determined whether a story could be used. The most important reason for staying was the hope of somehow earning some money. To develop an idea in association with others was madness from a business point of view, because every idea was worth the dollars it earned. The army of writers engaged at any one time on a project exemplified the perverted and totally commercialized form of Brecht's collective method of working. The mode of living and the social life were nomadic. There were no culture, tradition, taste or absolute values. A city like Los Angeles seemed to have been built for the sole purpose of making money; a house was merely somewhere to sleep, people did not learn professions they went after jobs. Brecht had his first taste of our modern way of life, of throwing things away and eating standing up.

283

And so, in one of the first film scripts he sketched out in Hollywood, with Ferdinand Reyher, he turned his attention to a 'venerable' subject, the art of baking bread. Because he enjoyed eating fresh bread and butter at night, it irked him to find that the shops sold bread only ready sliced and hygienically packed: 'They have to be slices that can be eaten quickly, standing up or as one goes out of the door. These people are genuine nomads. They change occupations like boots, they build houses to last only twenty years and then don't live in them as long, so that home to them is not a locality'. Nevertheless Brecht was cautious of making over-hasty judgements about America. He was aware that one could not judge the character of the country simply from impressions and experiences gained in Hollywood. Reyher, however, was an American to whom he looked to prevent him drawing false conclusions from individual phenomena. Brecht regarded this writer, whom he had first met in Berlin in 1927, as his American 'cicerone'; he had a high regard for him as an expert on sport and as a partner at chess, who always had entertaining stories to tell. He had once recommended one of Reyher's plays, translated by Elisabeth Hauptmann, for performance in Germany. Reyher, who was a friend of Sinclair Lewis and Dorothy Thompson, had met Brecht again in Copenhagen in October 1938, when he was touring Europe, and had offered to help him to get to America should the need arise. He also promised to do his best to obtain a film contract for him in Hollywood. On his return to America Reyher adapted some scenes from *Terror and Misery of the Third Reich* for the American stage under the title *The Devil's Sunday*. He was unable to find a producer for *Galileo,* which Brecht sent him as soon as he had written it.

Brecht owed his residence permit to the consequences of a liberal policy which, like the policy of the Popular Front in France some years earlier, sapped the working classes of all will to revolt. President Roosevelt's great achievement at home consisted of radical economic and socio-political reforms that were bitterly opposed by the largely reactionary press and big business. But as a result of his New Deal programme, the Democrat Roosevelt gained the support of the trade unions and the sympathy of the liberal and left-wing intellectuals. In 1942 Brecht saw the New Deal era in retrospect as a gigantic drama, comparable to *Hamlet:* the American working-class movement showed itself to be incapable of pursuing a dialectical policy, and a questionable trade union boss like John Lewis entered the political arena as the winner, like Fortinbras.

But the emigrants had every reason to support the Roosevelt government. After petitioning the 'Committee for Refugee Writers of the League of American Writers' in favour of his German colleague, and mobilizing numerous American writers to intercede for Brecht, Reyher had managed to enlist the support of Dorothy Thompson; as a journalist she had actively supported the Republican Party for many years but then, as a result of numerous talks with Fritz Kortner and other emigrants, had decided to support the policies of Roosevelt, in whose re-election in 1940 she played a decisive part.

After some hesitation Roosevelt did what the emigrants longed for him to do, he backed America's entry into the war against fascism, a step that was only possible because the economy had been stabilized. Brecht was not an enthusiastic supporter of Roosevelt. In his view the most that could be said was that the latter's policies were the right ones under the circumstances. He had no illusions at all about the true nature of American democracy. The president was not elected, he was 'made': 'Many people feel this democracy to be such that it can vanish from one hour to the next. Few dare to envisage what the hideous brutality engendered by the economic struggle on this continent would then make of it'. In this land the ideas of those in power held almost unrestricted sway.

Living in a villa and in safety had he any right whatever to complain? But then it occurred to him that these pretty Hollywood villas seemed to be built of the same materials as the ruins on the other side of the Atlantic, 'as if one and the same vicious wind that demolished the buildings over there whirled all manner of dust and dirt into villas over here'. Removal to another, better situated and older house did little to modify Brecht's impression that he had been banished to discreditable surroundings. The American way of life struck him as 'ignoble', because the pressure to be constantly on the alert and 'sell' each movement, each thought, was degrading: 'And so one is forever buying or selling; one sells, one might say, one's urine to the urinal'.

Kortner regretted that circumstances led people to speak 'with their pay cheques between their teeth'. The behaviour of those emigrants who had found sanctuary in Hollywood, in particular, was conditioned by the pressure to conform. Everyone distrusted everyone else, everyone suspected his neighbour of having made more concessions than he need. Those who had money awakened suspicion, those who had none were thought tiresome and inept. In the eyes of writers who were less successful in America Thomas Mann was corrupt and a vassal of the Hearst press; Brecht was looked upon as unrealistic and an incorrigible communist. As time went on solidarity became rarer and rarer. Occasionally writers like Thomas Mann, Heinrich Mann, Ludwig Marcuse, Bruno Frank, Leonhard Frank, Alfred Döblin and Brecht were prepared to put their names to a manifesto or to a tribute in honour of one of their number, but there was no such thing as a joint political forum or joint activities. As Brecht wrote in horror to Karl Korsch, who was living in Boston on a small stipend from the Frankfurt Institute of Social Research: 'Animosities flourish here like oranges, and like them have no core. The Jews charge each other with anti-semitism, the Aryan Germans accuse each other of philo-Germanism'. Feuchtwanger also wrote to a friend of 'utterly revolting gossip' and a mass of squabbling.

Brecht tried to keep out of all the petty quarrels, group intrigues and niggling wars of nerves. As he had always done he strove to make contacts that cut across all groups and factions. At first he refrained from taking part in any sort of political activity; he wanted to remain as inconspicuous as possible and to avoid being subjected to any form of victimization, or redrazzia as he called it. He hardly ever went to the parties given by the film community, unlike his friend Hanns Eisler who, as many emigrants testify, used to hurry, loaded with alcohol, from one dinner to another. It was generally Eisler who persuaded Brecht to attend an occasional garden party or birthday party as part of his education. It was in this way that Brecht met the members of the Frankfurt Institute for Social Research, which had emigrated to America; already amply informed on its leading figures, Max Horkheimer and Friedrich Pollock, through the descriptions of Walter Benjamin, he now began whole-heartedly to despise them. Their subsequent rejection of Marxism was already an established fact in his mind. For Brecht the 'Frankfurtists' were Marxists devoid of politics, empty intellectuals whose thinking was limited to cultural criticism.—The scholars of the Institute did not relish discussions with the Marxist trained writer, because in their view his arguments were too flatly materialistic and too dogmatic. It was only with the physicist Hans Reichenbach and with Theodor W. Adorno, whose ideas on the sociological aspects of music interested him, that Brecht could hold worthwhile conversations. He agreed with the theses, developed jointly by Adorno and Eisler, concerning the function and dramatic purpose of music in films and on the stage, but it was only reluctantly that he could share their liking for twelve-tone music. It seemed to him too 'heady', too unnatural, and unsuited to his purpose. While he was astonished at the manifestly logical and mathematical nature of the musical material, the unnatural declamation of the words seemed to him at variance with this. When Adorno played Schoenberg's settings of George's poems, or his own compositions, and sang them in his rasping voice, Brecht was tempted to ask what made the musician 'neigh like a lot of dying war-horses'. But when Adorno played him Eisler's music to the documentary film *Rain* by Joris Ivens, Brecht became more thoughtful: these 'fourteen ways of describing rain' reminded him of Chinese wash drawings. He had to admit that the quintet was beautiful and he himself suggested to Eisler that they write some new folk-songs together, 'composed in the new manner'. Why shouldn't the people learn to sing in this way too? Here in America, where voices speaking in chorus were used in advertising, their own massed choirs and provacative songs seemed squalid and banal, 'one cries out in despair for *l'art pour l'art*'.

When Eisler decided to introduce his friend to his teacher Arnold Schoenberg, Brecht was forced to revise completely his views on the New Music. He was impressed by Eisler's respect and veneration for Schoenberg. What he himself owed as a craftsman to Karl Valentin, he pointed out to Ruth Berlau, had clearly been liberated in Eisler by Schoenberg. In July 1942 Brecht attended a lecture by Schoenberg on modern composition. The arguments, which he understood only imperfectly, gave him the impression of being crystal clear: 'A pity we weren't even sufficiently trained in music at least to understand what we don't understand'. Like Brecht in his field, the composer had the attitude of an engineer, who deplored 'handiwork' in music and the lack of any purely musical language in which to express music.

Hanns Eisler had succeeded in establishing himself in

Hollywood, and in 1940 had been appointed head of a film music project, under the auspices of the New School for Social Research and financed by the Rockefeller Foundation, which gave him the opportunity to compose experimental music for a period of two years. In addition he wrote a number of film scores. To Eisler a celebration was an excuse to celebrate on his own account; he enjoyed his food and ate heartily. In many respects he was more open-minded and less prejudiced than Brecht. For instance he enjoyed the company of upper middle-class writers. In his opinion Brecht's approach to art, and above all to music, was often too puritanically educational. Eisler was opposed to applying very radical arguments to aesthetic matters. On occasion he successfully questioned Brecht's implacable or unjust attitude to some of his colleagues. In the case of Thomas Mann, however, Brecht refused to budge. Once when Eisler told him how much he had enjoyed having supper with Thomas Mann and talking about Wagner, Brecht maintained a polite silence, though he regarded such aberrations on the part of his friend as treason. Brecht simply refused to acknowledge Mann's humanity and his opposition to fascism. He continued to see his old enemy as a 'reptile', basking in his wealth, whose every phrase, every political statement, was made solely with an eye to its effect on his paying public. Whenever he ran into the odious man in Santa Monica he felt as if three thousand years were looking down on him. Added to this was the suspicion, which someone had put into his head, that Thomas Mann had denounced him to the American authorities as a communist writer in thrall to Moscow. It was an utterly absurd supposition because Thomas Mann had helped many communists and later did not hesitate to form an aid committee when Hanns Eisler was under interrogation by the House Committee for Un-American Activities.

Thomas Mann's every initiative and every gesture received an adverse verdict from Brecht, whereas he came to think more and more highly of his elder brother Heinrich, whom he treated with the utmost sympathy. Heinrich Mann, like Brecht, expected the defeat of fascism to be brought about by the Soviet, rather than the Allied, armies. They both greeted the heroic resistance of the Russian people with enthusiasm. Heinrich Mann was 'radiant' and 'delighted' when Brecht commented on the first military defeat of the Nazis and spoke of the resistance of the civil population of

288

Rostov. The lack of success in America of writers like Heinrich Mann and Alfred Döblin, for whom Thomas Mann had obtained a film contract with Metro–Goldwin–Mayer on their arrival in 1940 but which had been terminated a year later, disgusted Brecht, especially as he had to witness the generosity with which lavish pay cheques were handed out to completely untalented writers. It hurt Brecht to see Döblin and Heinrich Mann surrounded by these compliant Hollywood writers, every one of whom drank. They were reduced to the level of supplicants, of parasitical hangers-on of a travelling circus. Brecht himself felt like 'Lenin in the Prater'.

Brecht and Helene Weigel were touchingly solicitous about Döblin's and Heinrich Mann's personal circumstances, and did what they could to help. When Brecht noted in his diary that Thomas Mann was allowing his brother to starve, it was certainly not true: a small sum was made over to him each month, and Heinrich Mann also regularly received a small amount of money from books of his published in the Soviet Union. Nevertheless Heinrich Mann must have felt he had been forsaken by his successful brother. In 1947 for instance, when Brecht left Santa Monica, he wrote to Maximilian Brantl: 'I have known only one charitable organization and that will cease to exist when Brecht and his wife leave for Europe'. Alfred Döblin felt the same and after the war, although he had frequently received praise and assistance from Thomas Mann, he publicly launched a totally unjustified campaign of hatred against the 'great writer', calling him a 'perfect example of upper middle-class degeneration'. The help, recognition and advancement which many needy writers in exile had begged, and received, from the popular, comfortably off Thomas Mann was put down after the event to patronizing generosity. The support given only deepened the existing gulf between the benefactor and the emigrants forced into the role of supplicants. At least Brecht made no secret of his antagonism to Thomas Mann, he was never two-faced. Döblin on the other hand, only a few months before launching his attack against the 'opportunist' and 'epigone', wrote a eulogy of the 'Joseph novel' in gratitude for the 'beautiful, thoughtful and carefully chosen words' which Thomas Mann had spoken with practised skill, but sincerely, on the occasion of his sixty-fifth birthday. On the same occasion, on the 14 December 1943, Alfred Döblin surprised his friends and colleagues with a tangled confession of guilt that embarrassed everyone who heard

289

it: because he had not turned sufficiently to God, he was partly to blame for the rise of the Nazis. Brecht, who together with Helene Weigel had arranged the celebration in a small theatre, was particularly incensed at this statement by his friend, it was so completely divorced from all political reality. He wrote a poem about the 'embarrassing incident' which severely wounded the irreligious feelings of most of those present. One of his 'gods' had let him down, while the artists he had invited, people like Hanns Eisler, the pianist, Eduard Steuermann, the actors Blandine Ebinger, Alexander Granach, Peter Lorre and Fritz Kortner, declared that they had been made fools of. When Eisler stood up in a fury, Brecht implored him with a 'Psst' not to say anything. It was a time to swallow one's anger, he did not want to be rude and discourteous to a writer he admired. Thomas Mann, naturally, reacted with well-bred reserve, but avoided adopting a positive attitude to the celebration on the grounds of his protestant and humanitarian background. He least of any wrote Döblin off as a writer at that time. Meanwhile his sympathy merely aggravated the latter's Thomas Mann complex. The birthday party for Döblin was one of the rare occasions when artists and writers of varying backgrounds who lived in Hollywood, made common cause. Even Franz Werfel, whom Brecht and Döblin had once insulted in Dresden, sat in the stalls paying his tribute.

More than a year passed before Brecht could really work in this Hollywood paradise. Never in his life had he been surrounded by so many potential 'collaborators' and people to discuss things with, but the feeling, which they all shared, that they were drowning men put a stop to all productive impetus. Collaboration on work that was not for present use was out of the question anyway. So Brecht passed his days listening to the radio, reading crime novels and playing chess. His favourite chess partner was the actor Oskar Homolka, with whom he would have liked to stage *Galileo* and who urged him to write a play about the founder of the Red Cross. In Henri Dunant Brecht saw a mixture of Timon of Athens and St. Antony and he wanted to fashion this material into the tragedy of a philanthropist who cannot resist the seductive charms of charity and is ruined.

But until the necessities of life were assured, and he had converted one of his many film projects into cash, the question of setting aside a quiet period for work, such as he needed to write a play, did not arise. He also had to shelve for the moment his idea of writing a play about a Joan of Arc of the year 1940, based on Lion Feuchtwanger's book *Unholdes Frankreich*. Thus his main occupation during these first months in Hollywood was considering and drafting stories for films. On the one hand Brecht tried to get a foothold in the business by working with script writers like Ferdinand Reyher, Robert Thoeren and Salka Viertel, an authoress who had written many of Garbo's films, while on the other he associated with actors like Fritz Kortner, Peter Lorre and Elisabeth Bergner, who had connections with American producers or studios. In addition he had hopes of gaining admission through the film directors William Dieterle, Paul Czinner, Fritz Lang, Jean Renoir and Berthold Viertel. With Kortner he worked out a plan for a film with the emigrant French actor Charles Boyer. Kortner's gift for story-telling fascinated Brecht and in his opinion Kortner's gifts as an actor were surpassed at that time only by those of Charlie Chaplin. But because he made difficulties, and insisted on the acceptance of his own highly individual ideas, most of his projects came to nothing. In his diary Brecht noted admiringly that Kortner 'set an example by his ability not to conform'.

As Elisabeth Bergner was looking for a part to play in New York, Brecht set about trying to make his Setzuan play, which she found 'as boring as it was splendid', palatable to her. A talk with her husband, Paul Czinner, then made it clear that what they really had in mind for Broadway was a classical thriller or a play by Shakespeare. Before they finally started work on Webster's *The Duchess of Malfi* Brecht suggested 'as an exotic titbit' a version of Thomas Heywood's *A Woman killed with Kindness,* 'produced in the Elizabethan style'.

The moment he became seriously involved in an idea, Brecht's interest in a film rapidly extended far beyond its commercial aspects. He saw a film's technical possibilities, in the aesthetic sphere, in direct relation to his epic view of dramatic art. He was interested in fusing the documentary and the feature film, the documentary corresponding to the commentary in his plays. He had already discussed plans on these lines in Paris with Carl Koch, Jean Renoir's assistant, and Bartosch, a director of trick films. In Hollywood he now got Herbert Kline to show him his new films of Spain and Czechoslovakia (1938) and England (1939). Most recently Kline, in collaboration with John Steinbeck, had made

The Forgotten Village, a film about Mexico for which Hanns Eisler had composed effective music. Brecht also grappled with Eisenstein's film technique. Both methods, the way in which they broke down stories into individual incidents, consisted of a series of 'pregnant moments'. Roland Barthes has made an anlysis of how in every social attitude ('Gestus') in Brecht 'the idea of the pregnant moment' is renewed. 'Every morning, to earn my bread and butter, I go to the market where lies are bought. Hopefully I take my place among the sellers'.

At the end of May 1942 a Hollywood project finally took concrete shape: Fritz Lang had the idea of making a film about Reinhard Heydrich, the Nazi leader murdered by patriots, and the resistance of the Czech people. Because of his political knowledge Brecht seemed to Lang to be the ideal collaborator. Together they wrote a story about 'Prague, the Gestapo and hostages', with the title *Silent City,* which Lang successfully offered to the producer Arnold Pressburger. Brecht was given a contract as script writer under which he was to receive five thousand dollars for the script and an additional three thousand dollars for further collaboration. John Wexley, an American writer who spoke German, was engaged by United Artists to prepare the American script. The nearer the day for shooting approached the clearer it became that Lang intended to produce a Hollywood film, not omitting 'little bits of suspense, drab touches of sentimentality and falsehoods'. Suddenly Lang forgot his promise to consider Brecht's suggestions about specific actors; even Helene Weigel was not allowed to play the small part of a vegetable-woman that had been reserved for her. In order to avoid misunderstanding, the director did not want any German faces for Czech parts. Brecht considered this to be ill-conceived naturalism, and saw Lang's refusal as a further concession to his financial backers. In the hope of still being able to convince Lang he wrote, in conjunction with Wexley, an additional 'ideal script', only to find that Wexley, who was a member of the Communist Party and by general consent a 'good fellow', did not want to lose his job either. Behind Brecht's back Wexley re-inserted into the script all the principle stupidities of the story which Brecht had spent ten weeks in carefully removing. The script was found to be too long and had to be hurriedly cut, this time by another writer who made no difficulties. Brecht wanted to call the film *Trust the People,* a title that did not stand the slightest chance of being accepted by the film company. Lang then proposed *Never Surrender,* but before the film was finished a book with this title was published. A competition in the studio eventually produced the title *Hangmen Also Die.*

The experiences he went through with his friends were a considerable strain on Brecht: 'The spectacle of mental deterioration makes me physically ill'. To crown everything he had to appeal to the arbitration court of the Hollywood Screen Writer's Guild over differences with Wexley, who for the sake of his reputation wanted to be named as sole author of the script, and insist on being credited as co-author of a film which corresponded only vaguely with his own ideas as an artist. If he wanted to get another film job later, it was important that his name should appear among the credits. Although Lang and Eisler endorsed his claim, the court sided with Wexley. After the sitting Brecht and Lang never saw each other again. Lang proved not to be the 'heretic' Brecht took him to be by sending him a good luck charm. But to wax indignant over personal immorality when they were living under such inhuman conditions was not really possible. In his diary, however, Brecht qualified this: 'On the other hand one cannot direct one's indignation—that most socially productive emotion—only against conditions, because by doing so one would completely impersonalize these conditions, never concern oneself with people again and thus never again treat people as indictable and possible to change.'

As we have already seen in the case of the *Pagliacci* film Brecht was not content merely to see his draft script used. Without the hope of achieving something decisive he could never have written a line. The 'hostage film', in fact, he considered so important that he thought of including the text in his *Versuche.* In the end, however, the several months he spent on it were virtually wasted. The only pleasant aspect of the whole affair was the financial one, because his work with Lang procured him 'breathing-space for three plays': *The Visions of Simone Machard (Die Gesichte der Simone Machard), The Duchess of Malfi* and *Schweyk.* Brecht never succeeded in climbing on to the great film bandwaggon. In the six years he lived in America he worked on more than fifty film projects. The hostage story was the only one to be sold. At the end of 1943 he received some money for a script from Peter Lorre, who had arranged for the production of the film but then failed to clinch it. Then in his last year in Hollywood he acted as a sort of 'script doctor' during the filming of Erich Maria Remarque's novel *The Arch of Triumph,* a bread-and-butter job that Charles Laughton put in his way. The film was directed by Lewis Milestone, whom Brecht later tried unsuccessfully to interest in a film version of Offenbach's opera *The Tales of Hoffman.* The largest sum of money he earned was in 1944 for his share of the sale of the film rights of Feuchtwanger's novel *Simone,* based on the play, *The Visions of Simone Machard,* which they wrote together. On the proceeds of this, according to Feuchtwanger, he was able to 'live in relative luxury' for about a year, and write the play *The Caucasian Chalk Circle (Der kaukasische Kreidekreis).*

27

New York, 57th Street

> And these are dark times in the other city, yet
> the step still keeps its spring and the forehead
> is unfurrowed.

Since the beginning of the Second World War the United States
had been the principal land of exile for German refugees; there
they at least felt immune from the need to flee yet again. In spite of
the rather stringently administered immigration regulations, and a
State Department policy that was if anything anti-foreign and not
free from anti-semitic tendencies, the biggest colony of German
emigrants had collected in the United States. Since 1940 it had
been possible once more for foreigners to find adequate work, the
cultural field being the only one badly served in this respect
because it was still suffering from the effects of the economic
depression of 1930. Half the theatres were still closed and
publishers were not exactly doing a roaring trade. This meant that
most writers and actors pinned their hopes on the film industry in
Hollywood. There the state of the market, already appalling, was
made still worse by the influx of exiled artists. The pressure to
conform became stronger. This apart, however, the contribution
made by the immigrants was seen as a valuable addition to
American scholarship and culture. In America, more than in any
other country that attracted refugees, integration of this foreign
element was not only made possible, it was welcomed. If the older
immigrants found it difficult to come to terms with the new way of
life, their children fitted into it easily, and their grandchildren
actually had difficulties with the German language.

In relation to the large number of refugees, the immigrant
organizations and clubs played only a small role. The American
public paid no attention whatever to their activities. Nor were
English versions of German masterpieces, such as Jessner's
production of Schiller's *Wilhelm Tell* in Los Angeles, well

received. Foreigners were forced to take note of American requirements and conventions and come to grips with them. Max Reinhardt, whose productions in Berlin, Vienna and Salzburg had once been so much admired by American travellers in Europe, now met with almost no response in America. Only a few artists managed the integration successfully, and many of those who did lost their true identity in the process. If one lived in America, and wanted recognition and success, one had to become an American. Otherwise one remained isolated and a foreigner. To be different aroused suspicion and was considered discourteous; to conform, generally speaking, was synonymous with talent and virtue. It was also advisable for refugees not to admit to having communist convictions. Since 1938 there had existed the notorious House Committee on Un-American Activities, which had a say in granting entry permits and, after Roosevelt's death, specialized in hunting down communists. During the months when a curfew was in force, and all Germans, Italians and Japanese living in the United States were declared enemy aliens, it was especially important not to make oneself conspicuous.

Brecht, though anxious to find an American public, remained an outsider and a foreigner. He had no intention of jettisoning his principles as a writer. The examples of his friends Kurt Weill and George Grosz showed him what sacrifices one had to make as an artist in order to become an American. But Brecht also remained aloof from the emigrant organizations. He hoped to find an adequate personal answer, a sensible compromise, on the lines of Hanns Eisler or Erwin Piscator: they accepted posts as teachers, of film music and theatrical art respectively, within the organization of the New School of Social Research, and trained young American artists according to their principles. It was the only means by which rudimentary beginnings could be developed and become effective changes. It was, in fact, Piscator's Dramatic Workshop, which he directed from 1939 until 1951 and to which a studio theatre was attached, that produced the actors Marlon Brando and Rod Steiger, as well as Julian Beck and Judith Malina, founders of The Living Theatre.

Despite his abortive experiences in 1935, despite the defeats suffered by Fritz Kortner and other famous directors and actors, Brecht was drawn to New York, to a truly big city whose theatres he was determined to conquer. Hollywood offered him a chance to make money, but in Hollywood, once he had delivered his merchandise, he had no further say in how it was used. In New York he hoped to play a greater part as a producer. Another thing that drew him to the centre, not merely of America but of the emigrant colony, was the prospect of political discussions with companions he had known in Berlin, Paris or Stockholm. In a city like New York it was much easier to remain unobserved, while engaging in political activities. But the main reason for his prolonged visits, lasting several months, to New York between 1943 and 1947 was Ruth Berlau. Had he succeeded in making a successful start on Broadway, he would probably even have given up his house and family in Santa Monica.

In Hollywood Ruth Berlau suffered from being totally dependent on Brecht; she was unable to take any further initiative on her own that might be of help to him. Latterly, it is true, she lived round the corner from him, in a wooden cottage where he spent his afternoons; but she was not welcome in Brecht's house when Helene Weigel had guests. So when she received an invitation to Washington, in the spring of 1942, to speak at a women's congress on democracy, she jumped at the opportunity. Brecht did not like letting his 'sister' go alone, but he gave her some addresses in New York and the advice to stress in her speech the fact 'that democracy is not something one has or has not got, but something one has to fight for constantly'. In the first letters she wrote to him, while still on her way, she already hinted that she had made up her mind to stay in New York and try to find work there. As she had done in Paris, when on the spur of the moment she decided to go to Spain, she yielded to a sudden impulse and made a decision which to Brecht was both incomprehensible and challenging: 'You really have in you something of Galy Gay, who went out to buy a fish—and conquered the Himalayas'. He shook his head over her arguments, justified though they were in part. When she reproached him with doing too little to stop Helene Weigel from treating her so badly, he answered resignedly: 'But what do you expect me to do if I am not on very good terms with Helli?' Brecht found Ruth's extortionary remarks, her constant 'talk of first we must settle everything between us', both depressing and horrible. He asked her to return as soon as possible. But even his assurance that 'no one here takes your place, in any way' failed to bring her back. There were new calls to return from

297

Brecht in August 1942 when he moved again, this time to a spacious two-storey house on 26th Street, where he had a large study with a second entrance through the garden, which one could reach unobserved by other people in the house. For the first time since he arrived he now felt 'half-way well' in America. He immediately sent Ruth Berlau a plan of the house and a key to the garden entrance. He sorely missed her. It was true that no one else had taken her place, and Brecht found solace only in playing chess with Eisler: 'If Eisler does not come in the afternoon, there is only Simenon'.

At the end of the year Ruth managed to get a job in the Office of War Information at the Danish short wave radio station. Now Brecht also saw the advantages of her move to New York. Tired, and out of temper from working on the Fritz Lang film, he now wanted to go to New York as soon as he could raise the money. In December Ruth rented an apartment in New York and in turn sent the key to Brecht. Although he was going to be busy in Santa Monica until February 1943, in thought he had long been walking down Broadway with Ruth. After this he was somewhat taken aback to discover that his mistress was clearly in no great hurry to see him. The truth was that she had started a relationship with a Danish sailor and, contrary to all her protestations, had simply no longer been using the 'chastity belt', a stone which Brecht had given her for the express purpose of warding off sexual temptation. But he soon got over his touch of chagrin and they were close once more, almost as close as in the early days.

New York had a stimulating effect on Brecht; he met a whole crowd of his friends from the Berlin days of 1930, people with whom he used to work and discuss things, and this promising beginning increased his desire to put on a play there. He had not seen Elisabeth Hauptmann since 1935, or Karl Korsch since 1936. He went to see the Cantonese Players in the Chinese quarter with Heinz Langerhans, whom he found 'as sympathetic as ever'. In Piscator's Dramatic Workshop Brecht lectured on the principles of the epic theatre. George Grosz told funny stories as he had always done, but as a draughtsman he had become very tame; he earned his living as a portrait painter. There were fierce political discussions with Fritz Sternberg; and with Hans Borchardt, author of *Die Bluttat von Germersheim* who had collaborated with Brecht on *St Joan of the Stockyards* and in 1933 had gone to Russia to teach, keen arguments about Soviet politics and socialism under Stalin. Finally Hermann Budzislavski talked about his experiences as Dorothy Thompson's secretary.

Encouraged by Ernst Bloch, Ferdinand Bruckner, Oskar Maria Graf, Berthold Viertel and F. C. Weiskopf, Wieland Herzfelde endeavoured to establish a new publishing-house for German literature in New York. The original idea was to call it *The Tribune*, but Brecht and Feuchtwanger intervened and it was eventually given the name *Aurora*. The first book appeared in 1945. Since 1942 the above named authors, with organizational and financial aid from the art historian Friedrich S. Alexan, had been sponsoring literary evenings and performances; Berthold Viertel had undertaken to rehearse some scenes from *Terror and Misery of the Third Reich* and now this 'Tribune for Free German Literature and Art' arranged a Brecht evening. During the preparations for this Alexan introduced Brecht to Paul Dessau, who was to be responsible for the music. When the woman who was to sing Dessau's setting of the 'Battle Hymn of the Black Boaters' ('Kampflied der Schwarzen Strohhüte') let them down at short notice, Brecht said 'Eisler sometimes sings his own songs'. This intervention marked the beginning of Brecht's collaboration with Paul Dessau, who later moved to Santa Monica where he married Elisabeth Hauptmann. After this evening at the studio theatre of the New School of Social Research, in which, in addition to Wieland Herzfelde, Elisabeth Bergner and Peter Lorre took part, Brecht did everything in his power to bring himself to people's notice again and realize his plans for theatrical production.

Finally Brecht and Paul Czinner agreed on an adaptation of *The Duchess of Malfi* for Elisabeth Bergner. The contract guaranteed Brecht five hundred dollars for the adaptation. Czinner also arranged for him to meet the English poet W. H. Auden, who was later called in in an advisory capacity. A further attempt to promote a stage production was made by Ernst J. Aufricht. He had already discussed plans for a sequel to *Schweyk* with Brecht and Piscator in Paris. Now the theatrical entrepreneur arranged a meeting with Kurt Weill, who conceded that there were chances in America for an adaptation of Hasek's novel. Weill also enquired about the Setzuan play, and later suggested making a partly operatic version, for which he would use his influence on

Broadway. Brecht suspected that all Weill was interested in was a good part for Lotte Lenya and asked Ruth Berlau to take up the matter, though he would prefer her to try once more to get Elisabeth Bergner for a production.

After three months, with considerable hopes but with no actual contract in his pocket, Brecht returned to the Californian coast in order to write his version of *Schweyk* in peace, as well as the play he had started during the winter with Feuchtwanger about the visions of a French girl who wants to rouse the people to resist the Nazis. He asked Ruth in the meantime to be practical, gay, inquisitive, eager to learn, and faithful. He held out the prospect of his imminent return. On his way to California he wrote her an urgent request to hide the white nightdresses, which she always had to wear for him, from the eyes of Ida Bachmann, the other occupant of the apartment: 'I always see you in them, and in this there is something both of good times past and of good times to come'. Brecht had to stay longer in Hollywood than he had planned, because he had no money left for the autumn and wanted to remedy this before he returned. A surprise visit from Ruth in Santa Monica, by night through the unlocked door, was no more feasible than a lightning visit to New York—'but of course it's impossible, we have no money'.

As time passed Ruth Berlau became nervous and impatient again, liberally upbraiding him with reproaches and suspicions: she thought another woman was involved and pictured her lover being indulged and spoilt beneath the fruit trees of California. When she had to give up her job and her Danish colleague, Ida Bachmann, insisted on prompt payment of the rent, she was threatened with the loss of her apartment. Brecht assured his plaintive mistress that there was nothing against her coming to California, except perhaps 'that we shall be better off in New York'. Once Ruth Berlau got an idea into her head, she never let it go. She felt she had been unfairly treated and blamed Brecht for everything; at the same time, however, she followed his daily instructions carefully and energetically. To Brecht her complaint that he did not love his distant 'sister' sufficiently was petit-bourgeois and unnecessary. When he was working, impatience, 'weakness' and lack of discipline on the part of those he was fond of and trusted bothered him. At this particular moment, when he was in financial straits, he found his family something of a burden.

How willingly he would have exchanged his villa in California for the balcony of the New York apartment on 57th Street, and how content he would have been to eat onion soup out of a tin: 'But you choose to humiliate me the whole time by accusing me of simply wanting to preserve a bourgeois idyll here and of being afraid that your presence might disturb my domestic happiness'.

Although it very soon became clear that Weill had expected something much less committed and more entertaining, Brecht did not give up the *Schweyk* plan. Hanns Eisler now agreed to compose the songs and in New York Ruth Berlau did all she could to find another producer. Brecht's first choice for the principal part would have been Peter Lorre, but there was also talk of a cast that would include an American film comedian of the stature of W. C. Fields. At all events, as soon as the play was written he sent it to Ruth Berlau, who passed it on to the American writer Alfred Kreymborg to translate. The latter's fee was covered by a cheque from Peter Lorre, who once again during these financially critical months of 1943 assumed the role of Brecht's Maecenas. Brecht himself did his utmost to deliver a good piece of work for this money; he looked upon sums of this sort as payments in advance rather than financial aid. Kreymborg's translation proved to be inadequate and inaccurate, he had been unable to find any American form of speech to correspond to the 'Schweyk idiom'; it was only with the help of Ruth Berlau, Stefan Brecht, Mordecai Gorelik and Hans Viertel that an actable American version of *Schweyk in the Second World War (Schweyk in Zweiten Weltkrieg)* was produced. When Piscator heard from Kreymborg that Brecht had written a *Schweyk* he felt hurt and disillusioned. He considered he had been by-passed and gave notice that he intended to intervene by claiming rights in the project and the subject-matter. He also had had in mind a Broadway version with the assistance of Kreymborg, and now he discovered that Brecht had 'enticed' his collaborator away from him. Brecht in fact wanted to direct the play in association with Piscator, on condition that he had the final word in the rehearsals. In order not to discourage Weill, negotiations were also entered into with an American director. The part of Kopecka, the landlady, had been expressly written for Lotte Lenya, and Brecht saw in this an additional means of making the project palatable to Weill. But the composer hesitated; he thought the war too delicate a subject and doubted whether it would be possible to make a box-office draw out of the play. Brecht for his part could not satisfy Weill's ideas of a theatrical draw, he was simply unwilling to compromise beyond a certain point. He was totally unfitted to be the librettist of a Broadway musical: 'There are political questions involved in this play. I must have a say in it'.

As it turned out no one was prepared to take the risk of staging this biting comedy, in which Brecht had incorporated as many effects and elements of show businesss as he could in order to combine its political message with an adequate sop to Broadway. In those days scarcely anyone was prepared to accept the subtle juxtaposition of clever entertainment and serious didactic purpose; the play was too dry and not sufficiently sentimental for the American theatre world, while the emigrants objected to comedy as an art form being used to portray the war and the Nazi leaders. One of the few enthusiastic admirers of the play was Charles Laughton, through whom Brecht hoped to get an opportunity to stage the play in the spring of 1944. Laughton at least roared with laughter over *Schweyk* when he read it and thoroughly appreciated 'all the jokes'.

Schweyk in the Second World War was not a melodrama and, as in the case of *Mother Courage,* this anti-hero from the people was not intended as a classic resistance fighter. He was simply the sly obverse of the eternal little man, determined to survive, from whom one can expect everything but heroism. Brecht was aware of the contradictions in the character: it was because of Schweyk that wars were possible, yet at the same time he embodied the hope that there would be an end to oppression: 'The fact that he was indestructible made him both an inexhaustible object of abuse and the breeding-ground of liberation'. The question 'how is it possible to grant the proletariat's claim to leadership and permit irresponsibility' was one the audience was expected to ask.

After again spending several weeks from morning till night in search of a chance that would take him to New York, he was able to tell Ruth Berlau definitely at the end of October that his financial situation was assured for the next few months. In spite of the need to economize—'We shall have to live simply, a little'—he was certain they would fight through and make good provided only that Ruth remained staunch and cheerful and his 'good creature'. As his son had still found the current version of *The Duchess of*

Malfi 'a little thin', he decided he would immediately take it up again in New York with Elizabeth Bergner. Whereas on the one hand he was anxious to put on a play with the famous actress, to whose strange charm he was not insensitive, his pleasure in the idea was considerably damped by the everlasting cautious provisos and representations of Paul Czinner. When the production finally became reality, in the autumn of 1946, he had long been hard at work with Laughton on his Hollywood plans for *Galileo,* which from every point of view interested him more. A last hope that he might still make his appearance on Broadway with a play materialized in March 1944, when the actress Luise Rainer procured him a contract to make a version of *The Caucasian Chalk Circle.*

This project also came to nothing: the producers had misgivings on the grounds that there was too little dramatic tension and too much political commentary. *The Caucasian Chalk Circle* was the last play Brecht wrote in his American exile; he did not want to increase further his gallery of stage characters until he was able to work in a theatre. The part of Grusche, the motherly servant who saves the child of the governor's wife and behaves as if she were the real mother, had been reserved for herself by Luise Rainer, whose husband was the playwright Clifford Odets. It was not least because of this that Brecht, who did not want to throw away all chance of a performance at the outset, made the character much too pure, too good and too chaste. 'While retaining the old-fashioned characteristics of her class', he noted in criticism when he was writing the play, 'Grusche should be less easily identifiable and thus exist objectively as, in a certain sense, a tragic figure'. Although she became an admirable fairy-tale Gretel who, in the end, gets her honest Hänsel as a reward, she ought to make one taste the 'saltiness of the earth' and look like Breughel's 'marvellous Gretel'.

While the author invested Grusche with far too little gumption and cunning, he bestowed a superabundance of these qualities on the corrupt, unheroic and pleasure-loving judge Azdak, a down-at-heel Galileo who commands the style of a Schweyk. The play, originally conceived as a parable about conditions in the old days of bloodshed and oppression, was no more than a golden legend interspersed with wise social judgements and commentaries delivered by a singer. In spite of all its concessions the play was still

303

too bold technically for those days and too political in its statement. It was already clear to Brecht, when he was writing the final scenes, that Luise Rainer would turn down the play; he soon found her 'most unpleasant' and considered plans to put it on without her. Feuchtwanger's criticism caused him to tone down some of the play's loftier moments and Grusche's 'nice' traits, as well as to re-write the prologue and epilogue.

Brecht really had Ruth Berlau in mind when he wrote the part of Grusche: she was expecting a child and the play was intended to give her courage and awaken her maternal instincts. The name given to this child by his parents had no power to protect him: called Michel, like Grusche's child in the play, he died when he was only a few days old. As always Brecht worried a great deal about Ruth, but she could not count on having him by her side during these difficult weeks. For the time being no one in Santa Monica was to know about the child. Shortly before the baby was born Peter Lorre gave Ruth Berlau her air fare from New York to Los Angeles and the key to his villa in Hollywood. On 3 September 1944 Brecht made the purely factual entry in his diary: 'Ruth to be operated on in Cedars of Lebanon'. The doctor looking after her in the Cedars of Lebanon hospital was not to know the relationship between the visitor, who presented himself so discreetly, and Ruth Berlau: 'I will try to have a word with the doctor. Can you ask him to tell me how you are getting on (for your friends in New York?)'

When Ruth Berlau subsequently discovered the matter-of-fact entry in Brecht's diary, she took it as proof of his cold and cowardly attitude towards her, forgetting that he almost never entered in it anything of a personal nature. All the same he apologized: 'I was feeling very down when I wrote it, so I made it dry'. Because she made things so difficult for everyone round her when she was desperate and took to drink, answering all efforts to help with fresh accusations, Brecht became angry and withdrew; but he sent his Lai-tu friendly admonishments and messages in verse telling her of his love and dismay. Working for her beloved poet she regained courage and strength. Before returning to New York she arranged a film library of all his mansucripts, and compiled several copies of a little *War Primer (Kriegsfibel)* from the four-line epigrams in verse he had composed to newspaper photographs.

Once again he could not understand her sudden departure, but now it disturbed him less than formerly becaue he no longer had any effective advice to offer against the periodic return of her phases of depression. From time to time he found it necessary to maintain a certain distance from Ruth, just because he still loved and needed her. What he found hardest to bear was the accusation that he was responsible for the situation she was in. Instead of following him into exile in America, so she told him at the end of 1945, she could have fought with the underground movement in Denmark and played a useful role in the political field. Even if performances of his anti-fascist plays no longer carried any weight with workers in Denmark and Sweden, was not the publication of the *Svendborg Poems,* for instance, or her work at the Office of War Information a political activity? Had he really prevented his 'sister' from fighting? He still continued to believe that her decision to play her part at the front in Spain, for example, had been a mistake: it was not a political act but a compromise carried out in a spirit of political romanticism. He interpreted her sort of desire to fight as an 'escape', which not only hurts those who stay behind but harms the person involved: 'Not every mistake can be rectified, not every unrectifiable mistake is fatal, but no mistake can be rectified by another mistake'.

28

Interrogation

> My activities, even those directed against
> Hitler, were always purely literary and they
> were dependent on no one. As a guest of the
> United States I have engaged in no activities,
> and that includes literary ones, affecting this
> country.

In New York Ruth Berlau often wondered why, when the war was over, Brecht decided to stay on in America instead of wanting immediately to play an active part in building 'another Germany', in whose existence he had so firmly believed. Was it not one's duty, now that the Nazi régime had been defeated, to hurry to the aid of the German people? Why did Brecht hesitate? Why did he consider 'putting the Communist Manifesto into verse', and working with Charles Laughton on *Galileo,* more important?

There was nothing at that time to which Brecht gave more thought than his return to Germany. He did not aspire to American citizenship, which by now his son Stefan already had. But in 1945 it was still impossible to foresee what attitude the victorious powers would adopt towards Germany. What, throughout all these years, he thought would probably happen, namely that the German working-classes would exploit zero hour for their own ends, did not happen. After reading the newspaper reports about Germany he noted, disillusioned: 'Ruins and no sign of life from the workers'.

In America Brecht could exert no political influence whatever, hard though he tried from time to time. He was not allowed to take any part in the propaganda campaign against the Nazis. He would have liked to speak over the radio to listeners in Germany, as Thomas Mann did. He offered his cooperation to an American colleague in the White House: 'It could be of importance if broadcasts to Germany, in which the people were enlightened on the world situation, were to be arranged at this time. . . . As you know I could really make myself useful in this field'. When his offer was rejected, the only opportunity left to him was to address the German soldiers over the Soviet radio:

> Tausend Jahre war da nur ein Gelächter
> Wenn die Werke von Menschenhand angetastet wurden.
> Aber jetzt wird es sich herumsprechen auf allen Kontinenten:
> Der Fuss, der die Felder der neuen Traktorenfahrer zertrat
> Ist verdorrt.
> Die Hand, die sich gegen die Werke der neuen Städtebauer
>   erhob
> Ist abgehauen.

(For a thousand years there was only laughter when the works of man's hand were violated. But now the news will spread through every continent: the foot that trampled the fields of the new tractor drivers is withered; the hand that was raised against the works of the new town builders has been cut off.)

When talking with German emigrants Brecht got very heated over the nationalism of his 'poet friend' Johannes R. Becher, and asked for a spittoon whenever the 'genius of an eternal Germany' was invoked. But Brecht, like Becher, declared that a 'national' front for peace and liberty against Hitler was necessary tactically and as a political measure for establishing social democracy in Germany after the war. He wanted to differentiate between Nazi Germany and Germany. This is why in 1943 he immediately welcomed the establishment of the National Committee for Free Germany in Moscow, and initiated a call for solidarity among German writers living in America. Thomas Mann, who at first was inclined to support this action, dissociated himself from it when he learned that the formation of this committee had been un-favourably received in the White House. He confined himself to a carefully phrased, non-committal, address of welcome. In New York Brecht joined a committee formed to start a 'Freies Deutschland' movement in America; this eventually came into existence as the Council for a Democratic Germany. When Thomas Mann refused the presidency, the Protestant theologian, Paul Tillich, was chosen to fill the post in order to attract as broadly based a following as possible. The manifestos and statements were correspondingly free of ideology and contained no declarations of socialism. The intention was not to sit in judgement on the German people but to act as counsel for the defence. 'The whole thing is stuff and nonsense', Brecht complained, 'but even so no one wants to be associated with it. The cowardice is prodigious.' He, of all people, was given the task of winning Thomas Mann over to the movement. The latter's reaction confirmed Brecht in his assertion that Thomas Mann does what the White House tells him to. It was clear that for the spokesman of bourgeois culture there was no such thing as 'another Germany' in the sense of an anti-fascist, communist one. Convinced of the need for unity among the exiled opponents of Hitler, Brecht did what he could to dispel the other's doubt that there was any difference between the followers of Hitler and the democratic forces in Germany. But Thomas Mann had made up his mind simply to deliver an address of welcome and leave it at that. In his public pronouncements he maintained that the German people had to assume a 'certain joint responsibility' for the crimes of the Nazis; but he also declared that the world democracies had to bear a heavy share of the responsibility, and scoffed at the 'imbecile panic of the bourgeois world in the face of communism'. Thomas Mann pinned his hopes on a 'cleansing' revolution in Germany for which the prerequisite, in his view, was an allied victory over Germany. He regarded assistance from 'German bodies' before Germany was defeated as mistaken and premature. His answer to Brecht was: 'In fact there is not merely the risk, but the certainty, that our alliance would be interpreted as nothing but a patriotic attempt to protect Germany from the consequences of its crimes. By excusing and defending Germany, and by demanding a strong German democracy, we should find ourselves, at this moment, flying dangerously in the face of the feelings of those nations who languished under the Nazi yoke and are close to ruin. It is too early to draw up German demands, and make an appeal to world sentiment for a power that still holds Europe in its grip and whose capacity for crime is still by no means crushed. . . . Let the military defeat of Germany be effected, leave time for the Germans to settle their account with the destroyers completely and mercilessly, to an extent that the world scarcely dares to hope for from our unrevolutionary people, and then will be the moment for us over here also to testify: Germany is free, Germany has truly cleansed itself, Germany must live'.

Even if Thomas Mann was not such a passionate advocate of the so-called Vansittart plan as Emil Ludwig, his confirmed disbelief in German democracy allied him very closely to this idea. Lord Vansittart had spoken of the unity of the German national character and was the spiritual father of a policy evolved at the time by the American Secretary of State Morgenthau; this was that after the war Germany should be kept under control politically by dismantling its industry and splitting the country into a number of small states, and that a comprehensive system of re-education should be introduced. Brecht saw this idea of 'punishing' Germany as the beginning of American power politics, aimed at preventing a democratic revolution. He called the idea of 'educating' an entire nation by force absurd: 'Nations can only educate themselves; and they will not establish rule by the people with their brains, but only with their hands'. Thomas Mann's anti-fascism was unpolitical; he regarded Nazism as something that sprang from the German character. He repeatedly stressed what he wrote in his *Entstehung des Doktor Faustus:* 'There are not two Germanys, a bad and a good, but only one whose best side was turned by diabolic cunning into evil'. Brecht's political attitude in 1943 was correct as far as his assessment of the American idea of democracy and its political interests in Europe was concerned but, compared to that of Thomas Mann, it was too optimistic as regards the political forces and possibilities of the 'other Germany'. The effects of fascism on people were much worse and much more profound than Brecht had always assumed from a distance, but this was something he could judge accurately only after he returned to Europe.

After Roosevelt's death, American policy changed. Truman's government veered in the direction of violent anti-communism. The victorious powers soon exhibited widely different interests with respect to Germany. America was no longer prepared to adopt Morgenthau's policy on Germany and deny it all economic recovery. Instead it produced the Marshall Plan, and decided in favour of profitable investment in the western zones. Brecht was forced to realize that Germany was a completely vanquished capitalist state. The Soviet Union, itself severely affected by Germany's war of conquest, insisted on reparations. In the zone of Germany allotted to it, it applied a sort of Morgenthau plan of its own. Both psychologically and economically the Soviet course of action was understandable: 'A capitalist state cannot be spared for the sake of its workers'. For the time being there was no prospect of socialism developing. So what could Brecht do but await developments, and explore the possibilities of returning to some worthwhile activity.

It was only very rarely in the second post-war year that he was able to settle down and concentrate on his work as a writer. His efforts to find a financial backer for *Galileo* cost him a great deal of time and made great demands on his persuasive powers. When Charles Laughton was not working on a film, he and Brecht discussed the new viewpoints necessitated by the dropping of the first atom bomb and the questions of scientists' responsibilities that arose from it. Laughton's ability, when working, to reconcile 'sense and sensuality' appealed to Brecht: 'He could expatiate on, and give physical reality to, the great physicist's contradictory personality without suppressing or obtruding his own thoughts on the subject'. After all their plans for a production with Orson Welles and Paul Czinner had come to grief over the problems of financing it, they eventually found a dedicated producer in the person of T. Edward Hambleton, the New York theatrical agent. The young film director Joseph Losey took over the production and the play received its first performance at the Coronet Theatre in Beverly Hills at the end of July 1947.

Meanwhile Brecht had resumed contact by letter with his friends and followers who had remained in Germany, and he now started to discuss with them various possibilities for his return. He had also applied for an exit visa, which had to be approved by the State Department; moreover, because he did not wish to return to a specific occupied zone in Germany, he wanted to be issued with American travel documents, as a stateless person. As his first stopping-place in Europe he had Switzerland in mind, where a number of his plays had been performed in recent years and where the publishing house of Reiss looked after his interests. At any rate he urged Caspar Neher to make up his mind to go there; Neher, whom he had tried unsuccessfully to lure to America to design the sets for *Galileo*, had already established initial contacts with the Zurich Schauspielhaus. With the political situation in war-ravaged, occupied Germany in mind, he set about trying to create the most favourable conditions he could for the realization of his plan to establish a theatre on his own lines, with a permanent company.

While Helene Weigel sent 'Care' parcels to relatives, as well as to Neher, Peter Suhrkamp, Otto Müllereisert and Herbert Ihering, Brecht studied and discussed ways and means to get the family back to Europe. One idea, precipitated by a Milan publisher's plan to bring out an edition of Brecht's works, was to settle temporarily in Upper Italy. But from the beginning all Brecht's deliberations were centred on Berlin. Through Herbert Ihering, who put in a word with the competent authorities there, came a proposition to place the Theatre am Schiffbauerdamm at Brecht's disposal 'for certain things'. Brecht's idea was to obtain several offers, in order to get the best terms he could. He spoke to Peter Suhrkamp of his conviction 'that we shall establish a theatre again'. At the beginning of 1947 he asked Piscator what he thought of the 'theatrical prospects in Berlin'. Although relations between the two men were very strained in America—a production of *Terror and Misery of the Third Reich* in New York in 1945 which, at Brecht's instigation, Berthold Viertel took over from Piscator, had once again showed how irreconcilable their theatrical standpoints were—Brecht felt it advisable not to sever the connection entirely. In regard to Berlin, while he had no intention of opening a theatre jointly with Piscator, he thought it might be a good idea to take up the fight against provincialism from two different angles: 'For one part of my work for the theatre I have to develop a quite specific theatrical style, which differs from yours. This is the only reservation, and it seems to me to have possibilities'.

At the end of March 1947 Brecht received an 'exit and re-entry permit' for Switzerland. Because of the impending production of *Galileo* he put off his departure until the autumn. Meanwhile the change in the political climate began to have a disastrous effect on cultural life as well. The great communist 'witch hunt' in America had started. Brecht found himself caught up in the maelstrom of the investigations. Hollywood was to be cleansed of its allegedly communist infiltrated writers and artists. Ever since he had been denounced by one of the German emigrants Brecht had been under observation by the F.B.I. When he was already engaged in winding up his home in Santa Monica he received a summons to appear before the House Committee for Un-American Activities in Washington. Nineteen writers, directors and actors, among

311

them Brecht and Chaplin, neither of whom was American, had been summoned to the so-called Hearings Regarding the Communist Infiltration of the Motion Picture Industry. The summons to Chaplin, who informed the committee by telegram that they could have interrogated him and his friend Hanns Eisler in Hollywood and saved the country money, was dropped; but Brecht, who was not sufficiently prominent to indulge in irony of that sort, had to comply because, as a foreigner, he had no legal right to refuse, and in any case he did did not want to risk losing his exit visa.

During the interrogation of the 'nineteen' both 'friendly' and 'unfriendly' witnesses were heard. Among the former, those prepared to testify in support of the charge, were Adolphe Menjou, Robert Montgomery, Gary Cooper, Robert Taylor and Walt Disney, who positively vied with one another in denouncing alleged communists. The 'unfriendly' witnesses, those who appealed to reason like the director of western films Edward Dmytryk or the script writer Dalton Trumbo, lost their jobs and were ostracized. Anyone who exercised his right to refuse to testify was charged with 'contempt of Congress' and sent to prison. The real purport of the investigations, in fact, was to intimidate all those actively engaged in the arts and sciences who were not prepared simply to stop thinking. Artists unwilling to conform did not lose their lives but merely their livelihoods. Looking back, Brecht wrote in 1950: 'I escaped conviction because, not being an American, I had to answer the questions; I was not protected by the Constitution. My American colleagues were protected by the Constitution, but the Constitution itself was not protected'.

All the interrogations always centred round the question of membership of the Communist Party. Brecht answered truthfully: 'I was not, and am not, a member of any Communist Party'. For the rest he circumvented any precisely formulated questions that might have got him into trouble with extreme cunning and incredibly quick-witted obtuseness. His most precise answer was 'I think I am sure'. Towards the close of the interrogation the chairman said to the examining judge: 'He is doing very well. He is doing much better than many other witnesses you have brought here'. In Brecht's case the questions about his activities in Hollywood were simply a pretext to clarify his relations with the brothers Hanns and Gerhart Eisler, who had already been interrogated in another context. Gerhart Eisler, who played the key role in the Council for a Democratic Germany and acted as liaison with Soviet bodies, was suspected at the time of being a 'red atomic spy', and had been accused before the committee by his sister, Ruth Fischer, of being a leading agent of the Soviet secret police and a dangerous terrorist. Gerhart Eisler had been detained against his will since 1941, when he was on his way to Mexico via the United States; and now Hanns Eisler was also prevented from leaving the country. The latter was expelled in 1948, but Gerhart only succeeded in giving the F.B.I. the slip in 1949, when he boarded a Polish ship illegally in New York harbour. During the interrogation Hanns Eisler allowed himself to be provoked into giving polemical and affirmative answers, and into calling Stalin 'one of the greatest men of our time'; Brecht, on the other hand, adopted the role of wag, attributed any possible revolutionary statements in his songs and plays to wrong translations, and whittled himself down to being the author of 'historical plays' against Hitler, which naturally could not have been written had he not made a study of the Marxist theory of history. Eisler proudly acknowledged all the charges made against him, thus demonstrating his contempt for the committee, whose chairman was the reactionary politician Karl E. Mundt; other members were the Congressman J. Parnell Thomas, who was later gaoled for fraud, and Richard M. Nixon, who became one of the most inglorious presidents in United States history.

On the afternoon of 30 October 1947, the day of his interrogation, Brecht drove back to New York with his companions Edward T. Hambleton and Joseph Losey, who were preparing the Broadway premire of Galileo. In the evening he laughed as he listened to parts of his interrogation on the radio at Hermann Budzislawksi's. The headlines he feared never materialized. When Brecht said good-bye to Charles Laughton the following morning, the latter was evidently very relieved that it now required no particular courage to act in *Galileo*—its author had not exhibited any courage either. In fact Brecht did not recant at his interrogation, as many disillusioned friends accused him of doing; he simply withdrew into his role of author who wanted to write and do what he thought right, and whose life's work was inconsistent with membership of the Communist Party.

313

Twenty-four hours after his interrogation he was in an aeroplane bound for Paris. He had concluded his statement, which he had not been allowed to read to the Committee in Washington, by submitting a critical balance-sheet of his artistic activities and outlining the task which was to determine the last ten years of his life: 'We may be the last generation of the human species on this earth. Ideas on how to use new productive facilities have not progressed very far since the days when the horse had to do what man was unable to do. Do you not think that in such a hazardous situation every new idea should be carefully and freely examined? Art can make such ideas clearer and, indeed, nobler'.

PART FOUR

Before us lie the toils of the plains

29

Zurich

He is very far to the left, as always, and in my
heart of hearts I have to admit he is
right.   CASPAR NEHER

Brecht did not want to return to Berlin unconditionally. When he
heard in Paris that Anna Seghers was coming there from Berlin to
visit her children, he put off his departure for Zurich in order to get
authentic information from her about conditions in Germany and,
in particular, about the situation in Berlin. His talk with her
convinced him that, if he wished to maintain contact with the
theatres in all the zones of Germany, he would have to have 'a
residence outside Germany'. Although the 'iron curtain' had not
yet fallen, it was already clear that there were going to be two
ideologically opposed German states. As far as opportunities for
work in Berlin were concerned, Brecht received the impression
that it would only be possible to accomplish anything there as a
member of a powerful group: 'One cannot exist there on one's
own, or almost on one's own'. Anna Seghers told him of spying and
intrigues. In order to keep her Mexican passport she did not live in
the Russian sector but in Zehlendorf, in Herbert Ihering's house.
She expressed a fully justified fear that if she did otherwise she
would lose her readers in the Western Zone. On the other hand it
was only in the Russian sector that writers returning from exile
were given the privileges 'without which work is impossible'.
   Zurich appealed to Brecht as a suitable neutral base from which
to observe developments in occupied Germany. The
Schauspielhaus am Pfauen was still run by Oskar Wälterlin, Kurt
Hirschfeld, Leopold Lindtberg, Leonard Steckel and Teo Otto
who, during the war, had given first performances of three of the
great plays Brecht wrote in exile, and would certainly put on other
plays of his, if possible under his artistic supervision. Brecht was
also attracted by the idea of collecting round him a company of

actors and sending them to tour Germany with individual plays. As a beginning he hoped in any case to be able to negotiate an engagement for Helene Weigel at the Schauspielhaus. Initially his wife had gone to Vienna with Barbara; in the meantime he moved heaven and earth to find a room for himself, where he could be independent of his family. After he had spent a few days in the Hotel Urban, the dramaturg Uz Oettinger let him have the use for several months of his studio in the Garten Strasse, a solution which Caspar Neher greeted a little enviously with the remark, 'it is a revelation how he is handed what he needs from every side'. The problem of finding adequate lodgings for the family was also soon solved. The young Mertens offered them a small attic apartment, overlooking the lake, in their parents' house above the railway embankment at Feldmeilen.

At the very moment when he was settling down in Zurich, though only for a short while as he expressly told Ruth Berlau, Brecht was also picturing to himself the advantages of spending some time in Italy. Still hoping to achieve his big break-through on Broadway with *Galileo,* and earn a lot of money, he planned to go to Italy with his mistress as soon as possible. Ruth Berlau had stayed on in New York in order to complete the photographic and film documentation for *Galileo* and, at the same time, maintain contact with Edward T. Hambleton and Joseph Losey, with whom Brecht had discussed plans for a film of *Galileo,* to be made in historic settings in Italy. But when the stage performance failed to get good press notices, and very soon had to be taken off, the American producer's courage failed him. In April 1948 Brecht still spoke optimistically about the *Galileo* film to Ferdinand Reyher: 'We could write the script in Italy and have a lot of fun doing it'.

It proved to be excessively difficult, however, to obtain travel documents from Switzerland to visit other countries in Europe; to say nothing of the lack of money. Brecht had to consider himself fortunate that the aliens office in Zurich twice extended his residence permit. After his depressing experiences in America, Brecht found living conditions generally in Switzerland extra-ordinarily pleasant, in spite of all his political reservations. He was in Europe again, nature seemed less artificial, the colours much fresher: 'The planning is not governed by mathematics as it is in the flower gardens and plantations of California. And at least the villas symbolize old sins'. In the 'Kropf', a magnificent Bavarian beer hall with painted ceilings, he could revive memories and generate feelings of home.

In order to improve his financial position Brecht tried, as usual, to obtain a film contract. When drafting a film script of Gogol's story *The Overcoat,* in the spring of 1947, he already counted on selling it in Switzerland. What in fact he hoped to do was to conclude an agreement with Lazar Wechsler, whose Zurich firm of Praesens had assisted financially in the making of *Kuhle Wampe.* But neither *The Overcoat,* nor the newly sketched story *The Great Clown Emaël,* for which he negotiated with film people in Bâle, came to anything. Brecht's activities during his stay in Switzerland were limited to minor undertakings: to a reading in the bookshop in the basement of the Zurich Volkshaus (community house), at which Max Frisch made some introductory remarks and Therese Giehse and Helene Weigel recited poems; to discussions with Arnold Niederer and Konrad Farner, who edited the socialist students' newspaper *Bewusstsein und Sein* and had published Brecht's Stockholm lecture *On the Experimental Theatre* in it; to controversies with young Zurich intellectuals in the Odeon café; and to numerous meetings with writers, publishers and theatre people passing through Zurich.

Although it proved impossible to create the right conditions for systematic theatrical work, two opportunities to produce a play did occur. Brecht regarded the stage designer Caspar Neher as his most important theatrical partner; but the latter, who was also in Zurich, having arrived from Hamburg, did not feel really happy about it as a place to work in. Brecht, while still in America, had let him know that throughout his exile he had found no one in any country 'capable of doing the scenery for my plays (or any other plays)'; and when Cas had complained that the old horrors were reappearing in Germany, and that the habitual fascism still continued, he received this edict: 'But as they continue, we shall continue. The old centre of contagion is being rebuilt there, and it is there that the other building will take place'.

Brecht's arrival in Zurich on 5 November 1947 was a memorable day for Neher; their future undertakings and the constructive work they envisaged were to start there: 'I felt pretty depressed the whole time, nothing seemed to come off and I was already in the doldrums again, abandoning myself to the old Zurich jog-trot. Then came the news. It was good to see one another after such a

321

long time. He had grown fatter, more masculine, more reserved, and his gentleness was more in evidence than formerly. His facade of hardness had gone completely. His native goodness came to light . . .. The long awaited day had arrived, and this was certainly important to both of us. Naturally all our plans will change now. Various matters of importance will have to be attended to'. Immediately after he arrived, for example, Brecht conceived the idea of putting on *Galileo* with Neher at the Schauspielhaus. Work on translating the American version he had made with Charles Laughton was started at once. But those in charge at the Schauspielhaus felt that the five years which had passed since the first performance were an obstacle. Friendly though they were, they remained extremely sceptical about Brecht's wish to produce plays. And they had no part for Helene Weigel. Was this caution, tactics, fear, or simply ignorance? 'We come to grief over mediocre things', Brecht sighed repeatedly, while Neher was still more critical of his Zurich colleagues' traditional attitude to the theatre: 'We have witnessed the destruction of Europe. It has passed over us and here in Switzerland they have the most antiquated theatre imaginable. No thinking is done'.

During his years of exile Brecht had not been exactly spoilt, he had had to work with small amateur companies and emigrant theatres. Even under the most difficult and least promising conditions he developed a productivity that ultimately benefited everyone concerned. Consequently he did not hesitate for an instant when Hans Curjel, formerly Otto Klemperer's dramaturg at the Kroll opera in Berlin, offered him the Stadttheater in Chur, of which he was now head, for a play. On 24 November 1947 Brecht and Neher went to see Curjel, who lived in Zurich, 'in order to go further into the question of some performances at his theatre and how to realize them'. In the course of that evening the following plays were discussed: *Antigone, Phaedra, Macbeth, Mother Courage* and *St. Joan of the Stockyards.* They decided on *Antigone,* which Brecht immediately started to adapt, using Hölderlin's translation as his basis. On 29 November, only five days later, he submitted the first scene; after this Curjel accepted every suggestion put to him. By mid-December the work was finished. Brecht had discovered Swabian cadences and some school Latin in Hölderlin's text, and this made him feel 'at home': 'There are also reminders of Hegel. Presumably it is being surrounded by the German language again that drives me to do it. As far as the dramatic side is concerned, "Fate" is eliminated automatically, as it were, as one goes along . . .. Gradually, as the adaptation of the scenes progresses, there emerges out of the ideological mist the intensely realistic popular legend'.

Brecht regarded the Chur performance as a sort of 'preview for Berlin', an exercise in practical theatre, arranged more or less for his own benefit. Helene Weigel, who had not appeared on the stage for years, was to play Antigone, with an eye to playing the name part in *Mother Courage,* which, in the meantime, Brecht had proposed for his first production in Berlin. The Chur production took place in the most unpropitious circumstances imaginable. There were several serious disagreements between Brecht, Neher and Curjel, although on each occasion they were resolved as the work progressed. The first rehearsals took place in the Zurich Volkshaus after which, on 16 January, they moved to Chur, where rehearsals were held sometimes in the theatre and sometimes in the Volkshaus. Work was made still more difficult by the fact that every few days the actors had to leave to give guest performances in Arosa or some other town. Later, however, Brecht stressed the great interest shown by the actors. He was particularly pleased with Hans Gaugler who played Creon, a part he only took over on 20 January, after a long search for a suitable actor. Whereas Brecht could improvise and, even if he did not make a virtue of every necessity, at least found a productive way out, Neher felt more like giving up. After the scenery rehearsal he made this note: 'Two or three times an evening the theatre is degraded into a cinema, and is in a condition one wouldn't find anywhere in Germany. Add to this the fact that depredations have caused a great deal of damage and it becomes clear that improvisation is better than a theatre gone to rack and ruin through bad management. What is needed here is an enthusiastic Jack of all trades; he could get more done than people with literary ambitions like Curjel, who is overwhelmed by the inadequacies. Although the company acts very passably, the theatre is only half full, and this makes a lot of difference when working to a small budget'.

In the light of *Antigone* Brecht took another look at his thesis that it would be useful if productions were handed down by means of models. Ruth Berlau arrived at exactly the right moment to take the necessary pictures. It was she who had laid the foundations of

Brecht's theory of models at the time of the production of *The Mother* with Danish working-class actors. Photographs of the Berlin production, with Helene Weigel as Vlassova, had served for Dagmar Andreasen's performance of the same part. Ruth Berlau followed the same principle when rehearsing *Senora Carrar's Rifles*. The idea was not to copy the model slavishly but to use it creatively, in other words to develop it further: 'The alterations, if made correctly, themselves have the character of models, the learner becomes the teacher, the model changes'.

The greatest importance was attached to this development, the idea being not to produce unique, inimitable achievements, but to create utilizable models. The *Antigone* model, which the Berlin publisher Weiss very quickly decided to publish, provided an initial foretaste of Brecht's future theatrical work. Included in its experimental nature was the demand to transform the individual act of creation into a collective creative process, and thus to establish a continuum of a 'dialectical kind'.

The experimental nature of the *Antigone* adaptation was not recognized until much later; the 1948 production remained virtually unnoticed and was discussed only among Brecht's friends in Zurich. It was given four times in all in Chur, and in the middle of March there was a single Sunday morning matinée at the Zurich Schauspielhaus. Brecht was very disappointed that Oskar Wälterlin and Kurt Hirschfeld did not have sufficient faith in the work to make more than one performance possible. Caspar Neher, who owing to other commitments had followed the Chur production only to the extent of the technical installations, found the Zurich performance 'remarkably good', and could now feel proud of the praise lavished on him from Chur after the first public rehearsal: 'Your staging of *Antigone* (including costumes, props and basic groupings) is exemplary and must be retained, all the more because it is susceptible to any number of variations. To my mind your treatment of the chorus also belongs to your lasting contributions. I am very happy that we were able to do this'.

While work on *Antigone* was still in progress, Kurt Hirschfeld reached agreement with Brecht to stage *Puntila* at the Schauspielhaus at the end of the season. First choice for the title role was Hans Albers, but he was not free at the time in question. Brecht was very taken with this actor's vulgar charm, which at the same time was 'not without violence'; in his view Albers had all the

324

qualities of a people's actor *(Volksschauspieler)*. This opinion, which was formed from films, was confirmed when he saw Albers give a guest performance in Molnar's *Liliom* at the Schauspielhaus. Brecht immediately thought of writing an Eulenspiegel play for him, and then proposed sending *The Threepenny Opera* on tour, with Albers as Mac the Knife, although this ran counter to his declared intention not to allow this work to be performed in Germany for the time being.

Brecht's search for the actor best suited to play Puntila finally ended with the choice of Leonard Steckel, whom as a director he did not find very convincing. After they had jointly decided on a conception, and a large number of sketches had been produced, it was suddenly found that Neher would not be available; he had undertaken to do the décor for opera productions in Italy and Salzburg. To avoid interrupting the work, Brecht turned to Teo Otto, whose settings for *Mother Courage* he had quite liked. When, subsequently, Neher unexpectedly had some time to spare he was asked to provide further drawings for *Puntila;* he was also roped in to work on a new play, *The Chariot of Ares (Der Wagen des Ares)*, a revue on the political situation after the Second World War, which had as its target the lofty vantage point 'from which the Swiss (intellectuals) viewed the misery and distress'. Officially *Puntila* was directed by Kurt Hirschfeld, because Brecht did not have a work permit and they wanted to avoid difficulties with the aliens office. Brecht regarded this production, too, as a preliminary exercise in which he could only try out basic arrangements for 'unchaining' the actors. Under the circumstances the 'time devoted to discussion' had to be reduced to three minutes every four weeks. And yet astonishing artistic results were achieved; in spite of inadequate lighting the 'landscape' of the comedy was very effectively realized. It was a long time since the public and the critics had been so unamimous about his work. Pleased with his success Brecht for once dropped his shyness and appeared on the stage, in 'working clothes' as the critic of the *Basler Nationalzeitung* remarked, a little shocked; but in view of the 'simple and unceremonial style' of the production this dress, unusual though it was at a first night during the June festival, was accepted as appropriate.

Theatre as an aesthetic undertaking in Brecht's sense was simply not practicable at the Schauspielhaus, where the company as a unit bore the imprint of its artistic 'mission' during the Nazi era. Conditions for producing plays could hardly have been worse. Routine and inefficiency were the hallmarks of the working-day. While the situation was better than on Broadway, it was obvious that here too nobody found thinking a pleasure. Brecht had the very highest opinion of the great theatrical potential of the Schauspielhaus, on which its reputation was to feed for a long time to come, but in those days, alongside a Therese Giehse or the young Regine Lutz, there was a growing influx of actors like Walter Richter and Will Quadflieg who brought with them the style of the Berlin Staatstheater under the Nazis. After a rehearsal of *Woyzeck* Brecht noted in disgust, 'Before ever I see the ruined theatres I get a sight of the ruined acting'. In his reminiscences of Brecht Max Frisch has described the former's rage after his first post-war visit to a German theatre. The vocabulary of the actors at the Deutsches Theater in Constance, their self-importance and arrogance, rendered him speechless until a remark by Wilfried Seyferth, who had travelled with him from Zurich, brought an explosion: 'The German theatre was in Berlin, and not in Constance, he asserted, only because Heinz Hilpert was in Constance. Seyferth could not understand what was the matter with Brecht. The vocabulary these survivors used, however untarnished their records, their behaviour on the stage, their blissful unawareness, their effrontery in simply carrying on as if nothing had been destroyed but their houses, their starry-eyed attitude to art, their premature conclusion of peace with their own country—all this was worse than he had feared'. As Brecht had suspected, and since this day in August 1948 had known, it would be impossible to resume where he had left off in 1933; a completely new start would have to be made.

Fritz Kortner arrived in Zurich from Germany and lashed out still more violently, and even Berthold Viertel, of whom Brecht had a high opinion as a thoughtful craftsman, said much the same thing: 'The style of presentation I saw in operation in Germany sidesteps drama . . .. One detects a cold emotionalism that sounds as if it were frozen solid, a false matter-of-factness that is a survival from the style of speech of Nazi days. This is bad enough. But what perhaps is even more open to question is the flippancy, the outward accomplishment, the choreographic element, that sets in motion a neat and tidy world, a smooth mechanism of illusion: a world with no perspectives, no half tones, conceived and executed like a painting; soaring, light as a bird, in ecstasies that are tinged with coquetry. It is acting that lacks reality, incisive motivation and characterization, power and weight of expression'.

Brecht wanted to go to Berlin as a claimant, not a suppliant. The more alternatives he had, the better his position would be; and he attached great importance to maintaining contact with all German speaking countries. Thus he unhesitatingly accepted the offer of the Austrian composer, Gottfried von Einem, to discuss the reorganization of the Salzburg Festival. At the same time Kurt Hirschfeld was trying, through Benno Frank the United States officer for cultural affairs, to obtain an entry visa to the American zone of Germany for Brecht, who also wanted to explore the possibilities of working with Erich Engel at the Munich Kammerspiele. The visa was first promised, and then refused because of an objection by the State Department in Washington. After a long wait the travel documents for Salzburg arrived from Berne in the autumn of 1948. In the meantime, however, no essentially new viewpoints had arisen there. Talks continued and, on Berthold Viertel's advice, Brecht asked that the Vienna Burgtheater be included in the Salzburg deliberations.

On 22 October 1948 Brecht, travelling by way of Prague, entered the eastern sector of Berlin. Suddenly he was a person of note. He had already been greeted by a delegation of cultural and party personnel, led by Ludwig Renn, when he crossed the Czech–German border. A big array of photographers and radio reporters gathered round him 'as they did in the U.S.A.' at his interrogation by the House Committee for Un-American Activities. At the city boundary of Berlin the home-comer was received by Alexander Abusch and escorted to the *Kulturbund* where Herbert Ihering, Johannes R. Becher and Slatan Dudov were waiting for him. Brecht at once agreed with Becher that he should 'say nothing' at the official reception given by the *Kulturbund*. On the occasion of a peace rally two days later, at which Arnold Zweig made a speech, Brecht noted: 'I do not speak myself, have decided to get my bearings and not take part'. He had received no definite offer of a theatre, this being merely the goal which he and some of his friends had in mind. Prominent among those who spoke up for Brecht were Wolfgang Langhoff, Herbert Ihering and the Soviet officer for cultural affairs Alexander

327

Dymshitz; although acknowledged by the 'Moscow lot' to be anti-fascist, Brecht was not considered by them to be a loyal champion of socialist realism. The wreckage of the Nazi theatre was also much more to the taste of Stanislawski's followers than the postulates of the epic theatre. The gulf that separated Brecht from Oscar Fritz Schuh and Heinz Hilpert also separated him from Ottofritz Gaillard, Maxim Vallentin and Gustav von Wagenheim. The first production Brecht saw at the Deutsches Theater was Julius Hay's *Haben,* a play he loathed: 'Miserable performance, hysterical, inhibited, completely unrealistic'. Brecht had a horror of emotionalism, false sentiment, fulsomeness or glossing things over. He could be convinced only by realistic attitudes, truth, and sobriety.

He had been invited to stage one of his plays at the Deutsches Theater. It was only shortly before the opening night of *Mother Courage and Her Children,* on 6 January 1949, that the first meeting took place at which a 'theatre project' was officially discussed with Brecht. No great enthusiasm was shown for his suggestions. Chief Burgomaster Ebert and the other party and government representatives gave the poet a taste 'of the stinking provincial atmosphere one breathes here'. Eventually it was agreed that Brecht should form his own company which, for the time being, would have the right to give guest performances at the Deutches Theater, then under the management of Wolfgang Langhoff. Helene Weigel assumed the task of organizing the whole thing and became head of the Berliner Ensemble. She had her office in the 'Möwe' cultural club. Meanwhile Brecht took a thorough look round and had numerous talks with workers and students. Gradually he became familiar with all the advantages and disadvantages of the cultural and education policy followed in the Russian occupied zone of Germany. The Aufbau publishing house was to bring out a volume *New Poems* of his, but it never got beyond the make-up stage because many of the poems were unwelcome, politically inopportune or too 'formalistic'. Brecht was thus well aware of what lay in store for him.

In order to remain as independent as possible, and be able to work effectively, he needed some means of protecting himself against unwarranted censorship. To support the aims of the party and the socialist state voluntarily, as an outsider, made better sense than to be manacled to opportunist party politics. Indicative of this was a quarrel with an official of the Freie Deutsche Jugend who asked Brecht to alter the line, 'And no leader (Führer) leads us out of this mess!', in his 'Songs of Reconstruction' ('Aufbaulied'), because, while no one was any longer interested in the subject of Hitler, what was needed was guidance in party matters. The poet, who was always ready to listen to constructive criticism or suggestions, had no suitable answer to this sort of thing: 'The verse is built on the theme, be your own leader—as is the whole song'. Brecht had made up his mind to play his part in building a socialist order of society. He rejected the western concept of democracy, and considered the imperialistic policy of America and the American way of life, even in its peaceful form, to be inhuman. He was confirmed in this view by Karl Korsch who, in 1947, felt compelled to modify his previous attitude to the Soviet Union 'in spite of the terrible savagery in the occupied zone and, still more, in Russia itself': 'World domination by the Yankees (sic) would not only be the worst fate I can imagine for this world, it would also be merely a reactionary Utopia. Even imperialism has to be learned and the Americans, unlike the British, would only spend ages fiddling around with the problem, and the rest of the world would have to suffer from other things besides American imperialism. Put differently, U.S. imperialism as hitherto practised in the Carribean, in Central and South America, and in the Phillipines, and probably about to be practised in new forms in Japan, will not even serve the interests of U.S. capitalism as a whole, but always only those of a relatively small specialist group of predatory colonial exploiters. In all these respects Russian imperialism is a better thing for the world today than Yankee imperialism; and there is really no third prospect'.

The problem of starting afresh in the Russian occupied zone of Germany lay in the initial conditions: a prescribed socialism, represented by fighters who had survived the concentration camps, and by those who had returned from exile, and led by a party which had to take its orders from Moscow. The population regarded the Russians, not as liberators, but as oppressors. No one remembered who had unleashed the barbarism. The idol of the Germans was the rich uncle from America. 'The great impulses come from the Russians', was Brecht's comment on the political situation in Berlin, 'but the Germans tend to be caught in the

329

vortex caused by opposition to the movement by the other occupying powers.'

To the extent that emigrant artists could make up their minds to return to Germany in the immediate post-war years, they were drawn in the main to the Russian occupied zone. In spite of all the restrictions, this was where the most stimulating cultural climate was to be found; here, too, artists were given work and granted rights. Brecht also profited by this special position accorded to artists and intellectuals, concerned though he was that the party authorities' motive was not exactly the creation of socialist awareness. They were much more concerned to demonstrate to the outside world how attractive their political system was. They wanted to parade as many eminent names as possible. The vital factor was not the socialist interpretation of art but readiness to ally oneself with the Socialist Unity Party. Germany was still not irrevocably divided. Brecht still believed in the power of progressive ideas and social awareness to penetrate all the zones. His view was that ideological war should be waged throughout Germany: 'Literature cannot withdraw behind the Elbe and simply help to build a model province defended by Russian arms (and Russian police)'. He himself, at any rate, wanted to carry the fight into the whole length and breadth of Germany.

As final official consent to the plan for the Berliner Ensemble had still not been given, Brecht returned with Ruth Berlau to Zurich, to his observation post beyond the German border. He took a room in the house 'Au bien être' in the Hottinger Strasse, set himself up as a casting-office in conjunction with Helene Weigel in Berlin, with whom he kept in touch by telephone and letter, and together with Ruth Berlau and Caspar Neher wrote the play *The Days of the Commune,* with which he wanted to open his theatre in the autumn. Repercussions from the production of *Mother Courage* at the Deutsches Theater, he was pleased to discover, had reached Zurich. The Berlin undertaking attracted genuine interest because the company at the Schauspielhaus showed increasing signs of disintegrating: 'The bonds between Giehse and Steckel grow weaker all the time, Knuth spends most of his time in Munich, Seyferth is leaving for good. No director. Principal actor Quadflieg . . .. I shall return as soon as I can'. Brecht found Zurich 'terribly boring' after Berlin.

Brecht was still a stateless person. He had no particular desire to get a German passport in Berlin. So he tried to get travel documents, valid for as long as possible, in Berne, for himself and his daughter Barbara, who was now to go and live with her parents in Berlin. But the Swiss authorities put great difficulties in their way. As Gottfried von Einem had been in touch with him again, commissioned him to write a festival play and worked out a long term strategy for Salzburg, it now occurred to him to ask for a passport instead of an advance payment on the play: 'If such a thing were possible, it should naturally be done entirely without publicity. Perhaps something on these lines would be best: Helle (Helene Weigel) is Austrian (Viennese) by birth and, like me, has been stateless since 1933; and there is now no German government. Could she get an Austrian passport again? And could I, as her husband, then get one too? The thing is, I don't know the legal procedure. But a passport would be of enormous importance to me. I cannot settle in one part of Germany and, as a result, be dead as far as the other part is concerned'.

On 20 April 1949, official permission having been granted in the meantime to go ahead with the Berlin theatre plan, Brecht applied for a passport to Dr. Felix Hurdes, minister in the Austrian federal government, and Josef Rehrl, governor of Salzburg; in these applications he expressed a longing for Austria and promised that everything he wrote in future would be at the disposal of Austria, adding that foremost in his mind were the Salzburg festival and the Burgtheater in Vienna. Brecht, who was never at a loss in such matters, actually started to write the festival play, which was intended to replace *Everyman*. For this purpose he made use of some dialogue and notes which he had appended to an old sketch for a play called *Der Pestkaufmann* and which he had jotted down, following a visit to Bâle at carnival time in March 1949, for a play *Der Tod von Basel*. At the end of May Brecht returned to Berlin, visiting Salzburg on the way. Quite apart from the passport question, the plans for the festival were of great concern to him because he hoped to be able to collaborate in such a way that directors like Fritz Kortner and Berthold Viertel and actors like Therese Giehse, Käthe Gold, Helene Weigel, Oskar Homolka and Peter Lorre could belong to both the Berliner Ensemble and the Salzburg Festival Company. The plans broke down, but not over the poet who wanted a passport and who, in fact, received it a year later. On 14 September 1950, when he was staging *Mother Courage and Her Children* at the Kammerspiele in Munich, Brecht was able to tell Gottfried von Einem that he was now an Austrian citizen. In December 1950 Brecht and Neher resumed work on the Salzburg festival play, which was to be called *The Salzburg Dance of Death (Der Salzburger Totentanz)*; it was hoped that the cast would include Fritz Kortner, Therese Giehse, Karl Paryla, Peter Lorre and Rudolf Forster. The storm of indignation that broke out when, following an indiscretion in the summer of 1951, it became known that Brecht had been granted Austrian citizenship, proved that his cooperation in the Salzburg Festival would never have been accepted in any form whatever. The resulting commotion forced Gottfried von Einem to resign from the governing body of the festival. On 18 October 1951 Brecht wrote to him: 'Cas has told me, what unfortunately I also see from the newspapers, that you have landed yourself in difficulties through helping me. Write me at once if you need any statements or letters from me. Shall I send you some pages of *The Salzburg Dance of Death,* which is already complete in my head? I don't understand how, as an artist, you can be blamed for helping another artist—I had no papers of any kind at the time! Cordially, your old Bertolt Brecht'.

30

Away with the old state, bring on the new!

*It is one of the great misfortunes of our history
that we are forced to build the new without
first tearing down the old.*

The Berliner Ensemble in East Berlin, which in its early years was
merely a company that gave guest performances in another
theatre, was not a generous gift from the party to a theatrical
personality it admired. Brecht and his friends had extracted the
consent and the money from the responsible authorities in a series
of tough negotiations. The playwright was not invited 'into the
kitchen'; it would be truer to say that he forced his way in,
convinced that he could work more successfully here under new
social conditions. A 'standard', a continuity of development, could
be achieved only with generous state support. Brecht's demand to
be allowed to create a progressive cultural centre in Berlin was met
in 1949 with shrugs; to do right by everyone and offend no one was
the order of the day. In the understandable endeavour to start by
gaining a large number of adherents, and to try out a policy of
taking things step by step, the socialist viewpoints were neglected
and the great opportunities of 'zero hour' lost. 'My remarks on the
deplorable artistic state of the theatre in the former capital of the
Reich', Brecht complained, 'were brushed aside as the more or less
offensive carpings of a place-seeking artist who overrated himself.'
Because of his weak position relative to the authorities, com-
plaisant allegiance to whom secured privileges for too many of his
less gifted colleagues, Brecht let no opportunity pass to persuade
artists of standing whom he admired to return to Berlin. He asked
Piscator to direct Grieg's play *The Defeat:* 'It would be a good
opportunity for you to have a look round and take stock'. He also
urged Kortner and Lorre to come to Berlin. It was vitally
important to occupy as many positions possible, he argued, in
order to prevent the wrong people from gaining influence: 'It is a

good moment, one should not put it off much longer, everything is still in a state of flux and the direction things take will be determined by the forces at hand'.

The creation of the Federal Republic and the election of Adenauer's government were the prelude to the final division of Germany, the Socialist Unity party reacting in October 1949 by setting up the German Democratic Republic. This made it more difficult for politically uncommitted emigrants to decide to accept Brecht's invitation to go to Berlin. In spite of the changed political situation, Brecht still held firmly to his intention to create a theatre that would serve as an example for the whole of Germany. He encouraged Peter Huchel, chief editor of *Sinn und Form,* the literary magazine run by Becher and Paul Wiegler, to adopt an equally open-minded attitude with his newspaper and aim at a pan-German reading public. It was a matter of establishing as many bases as possible, and manning them with competent people who would be responsible for distributing progressive ideas over a fairly wide area. By exchanging artists the Berliner Ensemble would maintain contacts with Zurich, Munich, Hamburg and Vienna. Ruth Berlau took over a production of *Mother Courage and Her Children* in Wuppertal and then went on to rehearse *The Mother* in Leipzig. Soon Brecht was the chief driving force in the German Democratic Republic, not merely in the theatre, but throughout the whole field of culture and education. In the nineteen-fifties the artistic conscience of 'the other Germany' was represented by Brecht and, in addition to him, Becher, Anna Seghers, Arnold Zweig, Ludwig Renn, Peter Huchel, Hanns Eisler, Paul Dessau, Ernst Bloch, Hans Meyer, Paul Rilla, Walter Felsenstein, Wolfgang Langhoff and Helene Weigel. At international congresses and meetings they campaigned for peace and international understanding. Brecht spoke out in criticism of all the political steps taken by the West German government; they made re-unification more and more difficult. He protested against re-armament, against West Germany's inclusion in the European Defence Community, and against the reintroduction of military service in both parts of Germany: 'When one day Germany is united—everyone knows it will come, no one knows when—it will not be through war'. It was not strange, but obvious, for Brecht to live in the part of Germany in which the fight for a new and better way of life had begun and was continuing.

If, in spite of this, Brecht had difficulties in East Germany, it was not because he advocated too little communism but because he demanded too much. His play *The Days of the Commune,* for example, dealt with a theme that was much too disruptive politically for the East Germans. Originally he had intended to open in Berlin with Nordahl Grieg's *The Defeat.* After a close study of this play, written under the impact of the defeat in Spain, he started to adapt it, and drafted a counterwork, a play in which he kept strictly to the truth, 'which, as we know, some people don't like'. Because a comedy was much less controversial, it then occurred to him that it might be better to open with *Herr Puntila and His Servant Matti.* In December 1949 his plan to stage *The Days of the Commune* had to be deferred once again, if only because the Volksbühne, which provided most of the audience, had few workers among its members. On the basis of the new social order, there was now a socialist state, but first it had to be made palatable to the masses by convincing them that it was a good thing. The main impetus behind Brecht's plays, the possibility of changing things, was now no longer valid: the object to be achieved had been achieved. Brecht was not prepared simply to accept this dialectical standstill. He, therefore, sought a compromise that would take into account the particular social realities of East Germany and at the same time activate awareness of the dialectics of contradiction. In the theatre this meant avoiding topical subjects, if they could not be treated in a radical way. Brecht's idea was to create social awareness in his predominantly petit- bourgeois audience by the roundabout process of educating them aesthetically. He felt he wanted to stimulate his audience to see things differently in future, with reference to a different social perspective. The *Commune* play was untimely because it portrayed an assumption of power by the lower classes in which the party did not play a leading role and which demanded the destruction of an order that at the moment was necessary.

The official opening of the Berliner Ensemble took place on 12 November 1949, with a performance of *Herr Puntila and His Servant Matti,* in the presence of the new government under Otto Grotewohl, the members of which, to Brecht's satisfaction, withheld neither laughter nor applause. The press also reacted favourably to this second joint production by Brecht and Erich Engel. The new style of performance was accepted. In the opinion

335

of Brecht and Engel, however, it was 'only epic theatre to the extent that this can be accepted (and offered) today'. It was a first step; 'but when will there be a true, radical epic theatre?'

Brecht not only behaved very loyally towards the East German government, he also tried, by means of constant discussions with politicians, to maintain contact with it in a way conducive to his own work and to be effective on its behalf in promoting socialist awareness. He had a high opinion of Wilhelm Pieck, the first President of the Republic, whose assumption of office he expressly welcomed and who, he hoped, would recite his poem 'To My Countrymen' ('An meine Landesleute'). The people Brecht liked best were old comrades who, like Jakob Walcher, had passed through the school of Rosa Luxembourg, Karl Liebknecht and Lenin, had seen the world, had learned to think for themselves and had fought against the fascists. He felt no personal ties to Walter Ulbricht. He paid this politician, who often made dilettante excursions into the world of literature, an oblique, ironic tribute with an old Chinese popular play, which Peter Palitzsch and C. M. Weber staged in the Berliner Ensemble in 1955, under the title *The Day of the Great Scholar WU (Der Tag des grossen Gelehrten WU)*. For Brecht a petit-bourgeois outlook, narrow-mindedness and worthiness were the worst qualities a person could have, even if that person were what was known as a good, honest socialist, a social democrat turned Socialist Unity party member like Chief Burgomaster Friedrich Ebert for instance. In his view the man was simply out of place in a city like Berlin: 'What is needed here is a socialist with the qualities of a gangster, a socialist anti-gangster'. Brecht was worried by the insufficiently bellicose climate, the stuffiness, the hypocrisy; but when it was a question of defending the socialist achievements of East Germany, and standing up for the Communist Party, Brecht could be counted on for his support. He found it easy to get on with Gerhart Eisler or Paul Wendel, but he was on far less good terms with most of the politicians in the cultural field, whom he accused of basing their standards on the bad taste 'forced' on the proletariat 'by the bourgeoisie'. They were always on the defensive, were afraid of engaging in arguments and taking risks, and issued instructions to artists. They were afraid of being criticized and contradicted, while they rewarded opportunism and subservience. The result was that literature became disastrously atrophied and controversial socialist theory

336

completely eliminated. 'It is not easy to get pre-eminent works from cowed people'—this warning of Brecht's fell on deaf ears.

At short notice he took *The Days of the Commune* out of the repertory and replaced it by Lenz's *Der Hofmeister (The Private Tutor)*, a play about the shocking conditions in Germany, in which a man castrates himself in order to remain socially acceptable. Brecht's adaptation, which emphasized the tragi-comic character of the original, was intended as a contribution to the great East German educational reform. The serious aspect of the play was the fact that a man was tyranized, the comic that he was prepared to submit to such humiliating treatment: 'Pupils and teachers of a new age, observe how gladly he accepts his bondage, and liberate yourselves from all such usage'. Germany, even the other, better Germany, now made Brecht feel a little uneasy; from time to time it gave him an 'eerie, sinister feeling', something that had seemed quite impossible to him in exile. Should he instil hope into the young people? Suddenly the question whether one could regard the young 'without apprehension', seemed to him more important. The sight of 'ruined people' was a greater shock to him than the sight of ruined cities. The young intellectuals he spoke to were already in search of a 'great aim', and ideals, again: 'It is as if you are looking around for someone who might be able to use you again. You hope that this time he won't misuse you? But why hope that anyone will want to use you?' When he talked with students in Berlin or with those attending Hans Meyer's lectures in Leipzig, when he talked with scholars and scientists or went to meetings at the Academy, Brecht's attitude of sceptical commitment was clear to all. His idea of socialist realism, which he advocated in his own way, rarely coincided with the official doctrine of art: 'I do not take the view that the theatre should develop along the lines of the positive hero'. He rejected facile generalizations, the regimentation of artists, and enforced prescriptions based on the theory of art. His reply to the demand for more optimism was: 'They can lick my arse slowly. Then art will be well and truly degraded'.

Generally speaking the claim of the first six productions staged by the Berliner Ensemble, in 1949—1951, to contribute towards building a new Germany and a national theatre, received official approval and appreciation. The qualities of these productions— *Mother Courage and Her Children, Herr Puntila and His Servant Matti*, Gorki's *Vasya Shelesnova, The Private Tutor, The Mother*,

337

and *Biberpelz und roter Hahn*—which Brecht and his fellow-workers documented in the book *Work in the Theatre (Theaterarbeit)*, were respected as attempts to give new artistic form to what was new socially. The theatrical means employed frequently aroused opposition and gave rise to misunderstandings, but the quarrels were aired in public and did not hamper the artistic work.

In 1951 the political climate in East Germany deteriorated. In part this reflected the increasing economic difficulties facing the republic, and in part it was traceable to the Soviet purges which in turn sparked off similar purges in the other socialist countries, where they were directed principally against comrades who had emigrated to the West and whose backs had not yet been broken. Jakob Walcher, for example, who together with Hermann Duncker and Albert Schreiner had advised Brecht in New York over putting the Communist Manifesto into verse, and was one of the poet's closest friends in East Berlin, lost all his appointments and was once again expelled from the party. But even a man like Alexander Abusch found himself relieved of all his political functions, and subsequently had to prove himself a loyal comrade by being especially accommodating. In East Germany however, unlike Czechoslovakia or Hungary, this species of Stalinism was not accompanied by the death penalty. The masses were now no longer provided with any socialist subject-matter whatsoever; they were simply injected with Soviet propaganda, and in so far as this was dressed up as art it had to be dispensed in familiar forms. All genuinely political art was condemned as formalistic. Even John Heartfield's photomontages were discouraged. Those affected found 'freedom' in the West no more attractive. The United States was preparing for the Korean war; West Germany decided to rearm. Anti-communism was the dominant factor in all political decisions. Faced by such conditions Brecht noted: 'Time will show if pessimism is to be rated negatively'.

He therefore supported all the more insistently, and with all the means available to him, the demand for more politics; above all he dedicated himself passionately to East Germany's efforts on behalf of peace. When he told audiences in West Germany or West Berlin of the hard fight the Socialist Unity party was having, praised the land distribution policy or reported enthusiastically on the communist youth meeting, he was at best listened to politely, while

338

in the press he was rebuked as a propagandist and lackey of the East German Government. His addresses to the West German *Bundestag,* or to writers and artists, raised smiles but no echo. His privileges were cast in his teeth and he was regarded as corrupt. When he said 'I do not think as I do because I am here, I am here because I think as I do', he was not believed. There were times when Brecht's activities suddenly made him feel so alone in East Germany that it was as if no one, apart from himself and Becher, was honestly behind the republic. 'They are yes-men', he told Käthe Rülicke regretfully. In 1951 he declared himself ready to put aesthetic problems on one side, if it would lead to political progress. When Paul Dessau wanted to withdraw the opera, *The Trial of Lucullus (Das Verhör des Lukullus),* in order to avoid exposing it to the formalism debate, which he saw advancing inexorably in his direction, Brecht merely retorted laconically: 'One must never fear criticism, one either meets it or turns it to account, that is all'. To him it was important to stage the opera at a time 'when the American threats are so hysterical'; and of the objections, which were then forthcoming on a massive scale, he listened only to those which he could turn to account: the execration of Lucullus, the military commander, at the close of the opera was turned to concrete account by excluding defensive wars from the condemnation of war. In its revised form *Das Verhör des Lucullus* was performed at the Staatsoper in the autumn of 1951.

'It is casual work that turns an artist into a professional, and sometimes into a tradesman as well.' A poet's talent had to stand the test of commissioned work. What was good enough for the firm of Steyr would surely be suitable for the world youth festival. An understanding of art was necessary for both purposes. All the same Brecht set store by not making more of a subject or a commission 'than there is in it'. The text of a cantata by Paul Dessau, entitled 'Herrnburg Report' ('Herrnburger Bericht'), concerned a border incident near Herrnburg when several thousand young people, returning to the Federal Republic from the communist youth rally in Berlin, 'had their names taken' by the West German police. Essentially the text was based on the story told by three girls who were present at the Herrnburg round-up.

In West Germany works by Brecht like the 'Herrnburg Report' were greeted with indignant and derisive laughter. Even left-wing writers, prepared to accept only the image of the opposition poet who had made a pact with the devil in order to have a theatre of his own, and endured East Germany, regarded the 'Herrnburg Report' as an embarrassing lapse. Unlike bad seditious songs, and the carefully rhymed little political verses of the proletarian magazine poets, there was in Brecht's effusions of this sort an underlying attitude which gave support to the political argument and, at the same time, mildly satirized the disreputable genre itself. Seen in this way the 'Herrnburg Report' has wit, satirical bite and the effortless ease of a nursery rhyme. It is not a work for a German men's choral society, nor is it a paean to beer or war, but a mixture of political reportage and a ballad interspersed with songs. The young people, of whom we hear, simply ignore the border between the two Germanys and present a picture of a peaceful 'other' Germany without oppression or police. 'Barriers and entrenchments, what purpose do they serve? Watch us as we dance across them and away.' — 'The moon he stepped from out the clouds and saw a laughing throng, and when he saw policemen there, he too laughed loud and long.' Brecht did not foam at the mouth when delivering a lecture, nor did he make heavy weather of writing verse to order, he argued light-heartedly, without exceeding the limits of the commission or the genre. 'Schumacher, Schumacher, your shoe is too small, Germany won't fit into that one at all. Adenauer, Adenauer, show your hand! For thirty shekels you'll sell out our land.' His patrons in East Berlin did not like this at all. On instructions from the party leaders the performance of the Cantata, which had been rehearsed by Egon Monk, was cancelled. Paul Dessau then arranged a private performance for Brecht, to which Wilhelm Pieck, Otto Grotewohl and other members of the government were invited. The attitude was now more conciliatory: the objections raised by junior officials had been exaggerated. Nevertheless, the displeasure could still be felt. Grotewohl let fall the expression 'lecture-room'. The formal construction had deprived the songs of their immediate impact. Creative political writing had to come from the heart, here one was aware of the 'chill', of the writer's pleasure in his own cleverness. 'With judgements of this sort one is up against the desire to see artistic expression simply as heightened expression without transformation into a new quality, the quality of art.'

The obligation to achieve higher and higher production, the raising of quotas without any quid pro quo, aroused indignation and opposition in the factories. The party could no longer cherish the illusion of being able to count on the spontaneous consent of the working-class. The Socialist Unity Party, therefore, increased its efforts to gain the people's confidence in this workers' and farmers' state. Artists were to contribute by providing an ideological feeder service. Art having been proclaimed to be realistic and linked to the people, writers were expected to announce 'the beautiful truth of our age', and to give literary expression to experiences which the politicians conceived in the form of wishes and ideas. 'The workers', Brecht wrote after that 17 June 1953 when the party was brought back to reality, 'were urged to increase production, the artists to make this palatable. A high standard of living was granted to the artists, and promised to the workers. The artists' production, like that of the workers, assumed the character of a means to an end; in itself it was not looked upon as either aggreeable or free.'

The classics, enlisted to help in solving the dilemma, were declared by the party schoolmasters to be the immediate precursors and prototypes of the socialist national culture that was about to be created anew. Everything fragile, contradictory, inharmonious was branded as formalistic and inimical to the working-class. Brecht and Eisler, having already had their fingers burned in the expressionism debate, decided to contribute something more useful to the argument over the classical heritage. In their attempt to offer new interpretations of the Faust subject, however, they ran into the most violent opposition. Encouraged by alert guardians of the heritage like Alexander Abusch and Wilhelm Girnus, Walter Ulbricht expressed the will of the Socialist Unity Party by not permitting 'one of the most important works of our great German poet Goethe to be formalistically defaced by caricaturing the great ideas of Goethe's *Faust,* a thing that has already been done in a number of works, even in the German Democratic republic, in the so-called *Faust* by Eisler, for example, and in the production of the *Urfaust'*.

The controversy which flared up in 1952/53 over the libretto of the opera *Johann Faustus,* planned by Hanns Eisler, centred mainly on the historical assessment of the title character: was Faust a hero, a man of learning who advocated heretical ideas and fought for the cause of progress—or was he a scholar who, faced with revolution and force, betrayed the cause of the people and

341

retracted the utopian claim of his scholarly activities, a 'renegade' as Ernst Fischer somewhat ambiguously called him? One can avail oneself of both possibilities, the positive and the negative view, in dealing with the Faust subject. For good reasons Hanns Eisler decided on the second interpretation. He intended to write a seditious opera and to treat his subject in as popular a way as possible. Like Brecht in *Galileo* he wanted to present the dilemma of a scholar who, at the decisive moment, takes the coward's course and shirks the social mission which his origins, training and mental capabilities have equipped him to carry out.

Brecht and Eisler wanted to stress the power of scientific ideas that are of benefit to mankind, and it is as the representative of such ideas that a Faust or a Galileo is to be seen; but at the same time they wanted to condemn the type of bourgeois intellectual who regards his activities as unpolitical and, in the name of some supposedly priceless scientific knowledge, imagines that he also can make a pact with the devil. Brecht took great interest in the genesis of Eisler's Johann Faustus, because at the time he was preparing his production of the *Urfaust*. Brecht saw Goethe's Faust entirely in terms of Galileo: 'What is historically new about this man is that he longs and strives to develop himself, to educate his faculties and to be the embodiment of everything of which nature and society seek to deprive him'. But the enlightened mind immediately turns out to be also a social delinquent.

The arguments over Faust, which dragged on for months, robbed Eisler of all desire to compose the opera. Deeply hurt and misunderstood he went to Vienna for several months where Brecht, who with Manfred Wekwerth staged *The Mother* there in October 1953, encouraged him to embark on new projects and convinced him that he should return. Eisler explained to the central committee of the Socialist Unity Party how necessary an atmosphere of confidence and friendly criticism was to him: 'After the Faustus attack I found I had lost all incentive to go on writing music. The result was that I got into a state of depression such as I have scarcely ever known. But I have no hope of finding the incentive to write music, which is so vitally important to me, anywhere except in the German Democratic Republic. . . . I can see my place as an artist only in that part of Germany where the foundations of socialism are being laid'. Brecht did all he could to hold this circle of friends and collaborators together, in order to be able to confront stupidity with as strong a force as possible and with artistically competent people. Many of his friends could could not endure the unpleasant cultural and political climate and found the gulf between their special privileges and the restraints to which the East German people were subjected too much to bear. Months now passed before the newspapers even mentioned performances given by the Berliner Ensemble, and there were often more people in the audience from the West than from the various districts of East Berlin. In March 1953 Brecht was forced to realize that the Ensemble's performances aroused almost no interest any more. Berthold Viertel could not make up his mind to undertake any further productions; Erich Engel, who was to make the film of *Mother Courage and Her Children,* had had his fill of the sterile wrangles with East German film officials and worked again for a time in West Germany; as long ago as 1950 Teo Otto had refused a call to teach a class in stage design at the Academy, and after what happened on 17 June 1953 Therese Giehse did not want to act again. Finally, Caspar Neher himself came only rarely and did not enter into any new agreement with the Ensemble. When he asked for the *Private Tutor* sketches in 1955, Brecht replied: 'The sketches, Cas, are the only point over which I might really fall out with you. You shouldn't touch them. They are what remains to us of our happy and successful work together'. The individual artists all had somewhat different reasons for the decisions they reached, but they forced Brecht to reconsider his concept of the theatre, to drop his plans to treat the whole of Germany as a single entity, and to give more work to young actors. Apart from this, he felt the time had come to look more closely into the question of portraying on the stage the contemporary situation in East Germany, with the aid of Erwin Strittmatter's play *Katzgraben.*

My Pupils and Friends

If I love, if I'm roused, I am worn out just the
same. But then, once the flame is doused, I'm
once more aflame.

If Brecht never realized his intention to leave Helene Weigel, at
which he hinted to friends from time to time, it was due more than
anything else to his wife's good sense and her unwavering respect
for agreements, once they had been made. Her gift for organization
made his work easier for him. Her 'masculine' side, if one wants to
put it that way, was the stabilizing element in their relationship.
She was capable of making her own decisions, and in her career she
had consummate achievements to her name. As an actress she was
independent of Brecht and it was only as an actress that she could
seduce him. It was in America that the marriage was subjected to
its greatest test, because in America the only role available to
Helene Weigel was that of housewife. She had no part in Brecht's
work as a writer, she could not even type; she did not play chess
either. Nor did she obey most of the other 'Ten Rules for Actors'
which Brecht sent to Käthe Reichel in 1951: she could not play the
lute and she never made notes about her work. A great many
outlines of Brecht's plays originated in conversations with Fritz
Kortner, Oskar Homolka and Elisabeth Bergner. With Charles
Laughton he spent almost two years on constant, absorbing
detailed work on the text of *Galileo,* which neither of them found
boring or unprofitable. Clearly what Helene Weigel had to say was
of significance only when she was on the stage. Between 1938 and
1948 Brecht did not dedicate a single line to his wife. Only on the
opening night of *Antigone* did he become aware of her again, and
from that moment her value to him grew with every day that
passed. Without Helene Weigel it is possible that there would have
been no Berliner Ensemble.

When Brecht first met his wife his attitude to women was still purely that of a consumer. Friendship with them only existed independently of romantic attachment. Later he loved Helene Weigel as the mother of his children. There was no longer any irrational element in their relationship. He could count on Helene Weigel; she had an inflexible will, and was kind and considerate. She was obstinate and tough. Brecht had complete faith in her qualities, but at the same time tried to extricate himself from them. He was excessively sensitive and vulnerable, characteristics which in his youth he masked with cynicism and frequently with great contempt for his fellow human beings. Later, as he began to feel more secure, he learned to let himself get involved with people, and towards his mistresses he was 'too weak to be wise'.

Helene Weigel, and in a different way Elisabeth Hauptmann, kept their independence in their relationships with Brecht, whereas Ruth Berlau lost hers. She loved him too much. The unconditional nature of her feelings, her devotion, her incorruptible sense of justice and, along with these, her inconsequence attracted him. She could not be 'sensible'. What finally destroyed her was her inability to discipline herself. She did not work for herself, but only for Brecht. Her gifts as a writer and actress went into her work with Brecht. But when she saw that she was strong only with Brecht at her side, she lost her self-confidence; she became unsure of herself and malicious. She needed Brecht but also blamed him for her misfortune. She reproached him more and more frequently for her lack of money and her lack of success without him. And with the years her plight became so desperate that she became transformed increasingly often into Shui-Ta, the wicked cousin who drank and nagged and scared all her friends away. What did she get in return for her goodness, what recognition did she get for the sacrifices she made? When she drank senselessly and went to pieces, Brecht opened her letters as if they were baskets of vipers: 'There is no pleasure in taking when the bill is forwarded afterwards. Giving is no pleasure when it is demanded of one'. But she was lured into provoking Brecht, into vitiating his ability to set aside personal difficulties, and the misfortunes of those round him, by working. In America Brecht could still understand her 'illness', seeing it as a consequence of her refusal to accept unjust conditions. Once, when he went to see her in the neuropathic hospital at New Island

City, she showed him the door when he refused to take all the other patients away with him. She was the 'good' person he could never be.

Ruth Berlau's mistake was to want to be too sure of Brecht's love, the slightest negligence on his part led her to question every promise he had made. Even though Brecht was not 'faithful' to her, he kept strictly to his agreements, and the promise he made to his mistress in Stockholm in 1940 he regarded thenceforth as binding. He kept on reiterating: 'I love you and will never leave you'. When it mattered he never failed to mention what she had done and to praise her 'pioneering work': 'You did this work virtually in the face of everyone, without fear of laughter or intrigue. The thousands of photographs you took of manuscripts and performances are witness to a diligence worthy of the Chinese and to an independence of spirit scarcely to be found'.

The last years of his life with Ruth Berlau put a strain on Brecht and were often more than disagreeable. The periods when she was sober and worked grew shorter and shorter. All Brecht's attempts to create a new situation, and persuade his mistress to abandon the convenient romantic attitude of 'it is all over', were of little use. After each cure or course of medical treatment in the private ward of the Charité hospital in East Berlin Brecht hoped that things would once more be on the old basis, that they would greet each other with offers not demands, with help not resistance: 'For the years have not been harmful but beneficial. You would know without asking that your beauty has not gone, and will not go, but has changed, and this is as it should be. Don't let me be your prisoner, Ruth, but your guest'.

The effect of the alcohol was that the marvellous picture Brecht had of his 'sister' Lai-tu gradually faded: 'Once you were only Shen-Te, then the cousin appeared from time to time, now only the cousin remains'. Ruth Berlau became an issue, a talking-point in East Berlin. Occasionally her rampages caused a stir and she found herself in trouble with the police. When she was drunk she developed astonishing strength; she screamed and became aggressive. One day in the theatre she hit Brecht in the presence of Helene Weigel and other colleagues; as a result she was forbidden the 'Schiff' (Theater am Schiffbauerdamm), an order she naturally ignored. And in 1954 when her lover was in Paris with the Berliner Ensemble, she simply followed him there uninvited.

346

He refused to see her, telling her in a note: 'And I am always afraid when I see you, because you can always turn out to be drunk. For me there is nothing more terrible than for a person to drink away his reason'. A year later, in Berlin, Brecht asked her to leave and make a new start in Copenhagen, and to return only as Shen-Te, never again as Shui-Ta. Only because she was a long way off there did he still feel close to her. He bought her a house near Copenhagen, provided for her and again loved her very dearly.

The fact that he was living with another woman did not, in Brecht's view, prejudice existing relationships. Marriage and adultery, for him, were concepts of a bourgeois morality. Unless his relationship with a woman was purely sexual, he fought against having to endure a loss. 'There is nothing better than friendship; anything more than that is good only if there is friendship.' To the actress Käthe Reichel, who like Ruth Berlau loved Brecht too much and for a long time was unable to regard her love as a 'source of productive activity', he dedicated a Keuner story in which he tried to explain what he understood by passing love and attachment: 'It is a widespread folly that love is higher than friendship and, what is more, is something entirely different. But love is worth only the friendship it contains and from which alone it can constantly re-establish itself. One is simply cheated by the ordinary sort of love if it does not extend to friendship'.

Käthe Reichel's first part with the Berliner Ensemble was the serving-girl in *The Mother*. It was the part Margarete Steffin had played in 1932. Käthe Reichel was also the child of working-class parents, she wrote stories and poems. One day during a rehearsal Brecht took her on one side and asked her, 'are you getting any fun out of this?', and she thought to herself, 'When you put me in a good mood . . . I should be happy to the end of my days.' Although at the end of 1950 he was feeling very tired and exhausted, the ageing poet instructed Fräulein Reichel in the art of love, and succeeded in giving her 'a lovelier mouth and more skilful legs'. When she sent him a bunch of yellow leaves, he wrote: 'The year is nearly over, love is just beginning'.

Brecht was not ashamed of his feelings, nor did he deliberately hide them, but he was reluctant to subordinate his work, which aimed at domesticating the world, to his weakness. He wanted at least to be 'steadfast' in his art. It was not he who had to interest people but his work. He advised his pupils to live in the third person, by which he meant 'to make a note of whatever they were engaged on at a given time, and to do it as though it were for a biography, written for the class for which they intended to fight'. The fact that this aspect of his work was so little understood made him nervous and impatient, as well as often unjust to many of those who worked with him. He was not diffident about his feelings, he was simply afraid that to spend too long over personal problems might rob him of the strength he needed for social tasks. He did not want anyone to cling to him. He was soon calling Käthe Reichel his 'dear clamp', from which he had to free himself, but he did not give her up. He wrote to her shortly before he died: 'We must do these necessary things for which we are trained, without regard for our inclinations and personal happiness. Much in our personal relationship has been difficult for me too, for much of it I am still paying, but the teacher in me and the artist in me are steadfast, I hope. So please do not let the thin thread which is so necessary snap from without. When the inside is in darkness, the outside becomes clear'.

When Ruth Berlau started to fail in her capacity as Brecht's constant companion and secretary, the young assistant director Käthe Rülicke took her place. She did everything for him, was more interested in his teachings than his feelings, and made herself indispensable through her work. Her adviser was Elisabeth Hauptmann, who in Berlin was now once more among the group of regular assistants, and supervised the book publications in an editorial capacity. Käthe Rülicke took reliable minutes of all the working sessions and of Brecht's conversations with workers and writers. She followed the advice contained in the little love song he wrote for her: 'Seven times I shall call you, six times stay away, but the seventh time promise to come when I say'. On occasion, when she showed signs of jealousy by expressing herself too critically on the subject of Käthe Reichel's acting, she was forbidden to attend rehearsals for a few days. She found this actress, who made so many demands on the director, 'simply asocial'. But Brecht liked to be seduced by an actress's work. There was no way of telling whether it was still work or already love. In 1928, during the rehearsals for *The Threepenny Opera,* the other members of the cast would willingly have lynched Carola Neher, for whom Brecht was for ever writing new lines; and during the rehearsals for *The Trial of Joan of Arc at Rouen in 1431 (Der Prozess der Jeanne d'Arc zu Rouen 1431)* her colleagues made bids for 'someone to wring that Reichel's neck'. Of course Brecht gave Käthe Reichel preferential treatment. Of course his intensive work with her was unfair to the others. But a play was in production.

When things got out of hand, and there were too many nervous crises and scenes, Helene Weigel stepped in to restore order. She always knew what to do; she threatened, she turned on her charm, and saw that her husband got the freedom of action he needed. Brecht's 'last' mistress was Isot Kilian. One day when the Polish director Konrad Swinarski, who was visiting the Berliner Ensemble as an observer, was seen flirting arm in arm with her, Helene Weigel asked him to go to her office, where she discreetly explained the situation. It distracted the playwright when other men behaved intimately with the women he loved. When Brecht first started to notice Isot Kilian she was still married to the philosopher Wolfgang Harich who, with a group of opposition Marxist intellectuals and artists, wanted to set up a sort of counter-government to the existing one, and in this connection also conspired with left-wing social democrats in West Berlin. Helene Weigel occasionally attended their meetings, while Brecht preferred to remain aloof; but at the beginning of 1954 he asked Harich to give up his wife in favour of him: 'Divorce her now and marry her again in about two years time.' As a result, Brecht enjoyed the attentions of 'sweet A.T.' for two years. It was Isot Kilian to whom he dictated his will, telling her to write it out and get it attested by a notary. Owing to a careless oversight this was never done. When Brecht died Helene Weigel suddenly became small-minded; now, when it was all over, she wanted her husband to herself. She successfully contested the will, in which he left the royalties from certain plays to Elisabeth Hauptmann and Ruth Berlau and in which, in addition to his family, he also remembered Käthe Reichel, Isot Kilian and Jakob Walcher; she contented herself with giving the legatees in question a share of her own inheritance. The gifts, needless to say, were a mere trifle compared to the fortune represented by the royalties from a single play. In Elisabeth Hauptmann's case Peter Suhrkamp, knowing how much work she had put into the plays, intervened and insisted on her being given a fairer share of the royalties. At the end the marriage law, to which throughout his life Brecht had attached no particular importance, acted in accordance with respectability and rewarded only the 'lawful' widow.

> Dauerten wir unendlich
> So wandelte sich alles
> Da wir aber endlich sind
> Bleibt vieles beim alten.

(If our span were infinite, everything would change, but as our span is finite, much remains the same.)

32

The truth unites

Ignoramuses! I cried, conscious-stricken.

When he invented the term 'epic theatre', Brecht had no intention of coining a phrase to describe a new poetic genre. There had always been an epic element in drama. What concerned him was the attitude of the audience to what was going on on the stage and, consequently, to reality. He thought of his public as 'interested persons', who did not think without a cause. He found old legends, untragic heroes, typical events, which made apparent the nature of the story as a process, better suited to his purpose than sensational subject-matter. Surprisingly he told the journalist and dramatic critic Ernst Schumacher, who had written a work on Brecht's early plays: 'I must admit I did not succeed in making it clear that the epic element of my theatre is a social category, not an aesthetic and formal one'. Brecht always took form as his starting-point, and it was this fact alone which, in his eyes, proved he had become a realist. He then used the dialectical method to demonstrate the appropriateness of his subject-matter. In order to ensure that his art made a topical appeal to the senses he had to make the subject-matter itself sufficiently detached, or 'alien', and maintain his own distance from present-day events. Following the unpleasant discussions on formalism he took the precaution of admitting that he had doubts about the 'epic theatre' and proposed 'dialectical theatre', a term more accurately descriptive of his method, in order to stress his intention to use the theatre to portray reality for the purpose of influencing reality: 'The Shakespearian theatre could take it for granted that its audience would never worry its head about the play, though it would about life'.

He was quite unable to understand the charge that his sort of drama presented something merely in order to elicit knowledge, but that it did not move the audience or incite it to act, because to him knowledge implied the desire to know and to act. At all events he now wanted increasingly to organize people into taking pleasure in changing reality. It was largely because of this that Brecht welcomed Erwin Strittmatter's comedy *Katzgraben*, which not only 'showed', but implicated the audience directly in , the process of transforming productively a village where the 'modern class struggle' was in full swing. At the same time Brecht wanted to make it clear that *Katzgraben* was not a 'tendency play' but a 'historical comedy'. After working for months with the author, who was able to tell him a lot about the everyday life and discussions of the farmers in the Lusatian villages, Brecht produced a version of the play for the Berliner Ensemble, and staged it himself. He was well aware that the result was a compromise, but it interested him to try his hand at a topical subject and political possibilities in a familiar theatrical technique. He had no other way of giving practical consideration to what was not yet possible.

At the back of his head he still clung to the idea of reverting to the form of his didactic plays. He still had in mind as a model his *Large Manual of Pedagogics (Grosse Pädagogik)*, in which only actors who were also students were recognized. Because it put into practice the principle that all should study for the benefit of all, it assumed for Brecht the character of a concrete Utopia. To prepare for it, during the transition period of the first revolution, a *Small Manual of Pedagogics (Kleine Pädagogik)* was to usher in the democratization of the theatre. The little didactic plays, written before 1933, were to anticipate elements at least of the *Large Manual of Pedagogics*. His intention was to continue the didactic form in a play about the first activist of the German Democratic Republic, the stove-fitter Hans Garbe who, in the course of several sessions, told his life story to Brecht and Käthe Rülicke. In 1951 Brecht saw this Garbe material, which in the meantime Käthe Rülicke had put in order, as a fragment 'in large rough blocks' in the manner of *The Fall of the Egoist Johann Fatzer*. At the centre of this play, later called *Büsching* after one of the characters in *Johann Fatzer*, there was to be an enquiry into the question of what changes for the worker when he ceases to be the object of history and becomes its subject, 'with the proviso that this is not a purely personal affair because, after all, it concerns the class'. In Vienna, in 1953, Brecht and Hanns Eisler discussed a plan to write the play about Garbe in the style of *The Measure Adopted* or *The Mother*, and in it also to introduce the theme of the 17 June. But conditions in East Germany were far from auspicious for political theatre in the sense of a modified form of the didactic play. When in 1956, a few days before Brecht died, Manfred Wekwerth asked him which of his plays he though represented the theatre of the future, Brecht answered: '*The Measure Adopted*'. It is an answer that reminds one of an interview with the Protestant pastor, Karl Kleinschmidt, in which Brecht referred to certain possibilities that he might remain troublesome even after he was dead.

In her 'Reflections on the poet Bertolt Brecht and his relation to politics', Hannah Arendt takes the view that the political opinions of eminent artists should not be taken too seriously, provided that their work does not suffer from them. Thus Ezra Pound, who, as she says, probably had periods of insanity and was not much of a man of the world either, could permit himself certain follies which the healthy and extremely shrewd Brecht could not afford in the same way. As far as Pound is concerned Brecht would certainly have agreed with Hannah Arendt, although he rejected the popular classification into poets and politicians. A human being was by nature inconsistent and contradictory and he had a right to his mistakes. Brecht had defended Karl Kraus against too short-sightedly framed moral demands, and subsequently adopted the same attitude towards Pound, who had given wildly enthusiastic support to Italian fascism. He conceded 'feudal dignity' to the American poet, who had been arrested in Italy in 1945 and then been declared insane and imprisoned in his own country; he grouped him with Kipling, D'Annuncio and Stefan George among the élitist poets, who were not to be found in the market-places themselves but 'rather in the temples—on the periphery of the market-places'. At any rate they were not Tuis.

It was only natural that Brecht should have a higher opinion of an Ezra Pound than of some committed poet of the left who was only capable of putting his views into rhyme and poured out his heart's blood in doing so. Conversely however, and Hannah Arendt was not alone in wishing to do this, should not Brecht's literary output be defended against his political opinions? For Hannah Arendt Brecht was a 'sinner' because, as a writer who had to be taken seriously politically, he had damaged his work, intentionally as it were, by espousing the East German cause and its Stalinist practices. Above all, by praising Stalin, he had trifled away his poetic 'gift'. But Stalin was far from being a 'poetic mishap' on Brecht's part. In *Me-ti*, or *The Book of Changes*, he criticized and paid tribute to the Soviet dictator as Ni-en, a name that in itself signifies 'no'. Brecht was not passing a moral but a historical verdict. In common with Isaac Deutscher he considered Stalin to be a great revolutionary despot and placed him in the company of Cromwell, Robespierre and Napoleon, because like them he had translated into practice the idea of a fundamentally new social organization, 'order on a grand scale'. He emphatically rejected any comparison with Hitler, obvious though it was in many respects.

When Stalin died, in March 1953, Brecht wrote an obituary notice that was indicative of his attitude and was published in a special issue, compiled by Peter Huchel, of the magazine *Sinn und Form*: 'The hearts of all who are oppressed throughout the five continents, of all who have already found their freedom, of all who are fighting for world peace, must have missed a beat when they heard the news, Stalin is dead. He was the embodiment of their hopes. But the spiritual and material weapons he made are there, and so also is the teaching to make new ones'. Whereas other poets, on hearing the news of Stalin's death, declared that their hearts had stopped beating for a moment, Brecht simply gave a factual description of the feelings of people for whom Stalin represented the embodiment of their hopes. Apart from this, Stalin's name occurs exactly twice in Brecht's works: in *The Cultivation of Millet* (*Die Erziehung der Hirse*), however, the poet does not praise Stalin but lets 'Stalin, the great leader of the harvest', praise Millet; and in the cantata, 'Herrnburg Report,' Stalin and Mao Tse-tung convey a greeting to the young people with the 'new ideas'. It is not the political leaders who are exalted, but it is they who have to declare their admiration to the masses.

Stalin's death brought the first indications of a liberalizing process in the socialist countries. In East Germany there were arguments within the party as to what the general line should be. Two politicians in particular, Rudolf Herrnstadt and Wilhelm Zaisser, spoke in favour of a more realistic assessment of the material needs of the workers. Before any agreement could be reached, the dissatisfied masses took up the cudgels on their own behalf. Local factory meetings and demonstrations were the prelude to a spontaneous uprising of workers on 17 June 1953, an action that was immediately boosted for propaganda purposes in the west, where people wanted to see it as a purely anti-Communist demonstration. The East German government was completely at a loss and could think of no other solution than to demonstrate its strength by calling out Russian tanks.

On the evening of 16 June, Brecht arrived in Berlin from Buckow in order to take part in a discussion, arranged a long time previously, on problems arising out of the current work programme of the Berliner Ensemble; owing to the unrest in the streets, however, it turned into a discussion on the political situation in East Germany. Brecht found it understandable that the population was indignant. In his opinion the party officials had completely forgotten how to speak to the people and handle them. They had withdrawn into their ideological cages, where they insisted that what should not be done could not be done. They could no longer understand the language of those with whom they had once shared 'the intolerable life in the abyss': 'Now, they are the rulers and speak a new idiom, the jargon of their class, which is spoken with the threatening voice of the schoolmaster, and fills the shops—but not with onions'. The 'jargon of their class' consisted of ideological phrases, bad socialist propaganda and promises that could not be kept. In 1953 there was no famine in East Germany, but there were serious bottlenecks in supplies and the shops often lacked the most important basic foodstuffs. In those days a veritable migration could be observed from the depths of Saxony to the flesh-pots of West Berlin: 'If a calf is neglected, it turns to every coaxing hand, even to the hand of its butcher'.

The public's anger finally vented itself in emotional scenes. But unleashed German masses were what Brecht feared: comparing them to Jacob's sons who went into Egypt to buy corn, he considered them capable of selling themselves 'for a small cask of wine, for a small sack of flour' and becoming mercenaries. As he walked through the streets he saw no sign of revolutionary forces being organized. The *Don Juan* rehearsal arranged for the morning of 17 June was replaced by worker's meetings in the Berliner Ensemble's Reinhardt Strasse rehearsal building. Brecht asked his colleagues to attend these, obtain a detailed picture of the situation, keep their ears open for the arguments put forward by the insurgents, and hold themselves in readiness for militant propaganda programmes on the radio. But those in authority at the broadcasting station adopted a hesitant, wait-and-see attitude and rejected the Ensemble's offer as too political for the moment.

That same morning Brecht dictated letters in similar terms to Walter Ulbricht, First Secretary of the Socialist Unity Party, Otto Grotewohl, Minister-President of the German Democratic Republic, and Semjonov, the Soviet High Commissioner. To Ulbricht he wrote: 'History will respect the revolutionary impatience of Germany's Socialist Unity Party. The great discussion with the masses on the tempo of socialist construction will lead to the socialist achievements being sorted out and safeguarded. I feel the need at this moment to express to you my loyal allegiance to the Socialist Unity Party'. Meanwhile Russian tanks had appeared in the streets of Berlin, and American tanks stood in readiness at the sector boundaries. The danger of a Third World War, which Brecht had so often invoked in his political declarations, was never greater than on that day. The uprising was bloodily suppressed. Fortunately the tanks of the Western powers did not intervene. On 21 June the party newspaper *Neues Deutschland* published the last sentence of Brecht's letter to Ulbricht which, though written as a request for talks with the workers to clarify the situation, could have been interpreted in the west as merely a statement approving the government's measures. Brecht was annoyed by this somewhat inept 'censorship' of his letter, because he wanted the public to regard him as an author with a mind of his own. He had no wish to be confused with a writer like KuBa (Kurt Barthel), for whom everything the government did was automatically right.

As he had no chance of getting a correction published, he insisted on his right to explain his view briefly in a new article: 'On the morning of 17 June, when it had become clear that the workers' demonstrations were being misused for warlike purposes, I expressed my loyal allegiance to the Socialist Unity Party. I now hope that the provocateurs will be isolated and their communications network destroyed; but I hope that the workers, who demonstrated because of justifiable dissatisfaction, will not be put on a level with the provocateurs, so that the much needed talks on the mistakes made by all sides may not be obstructed at the outset'. Brecht pleaded for the workers' demands to be examined in the light of their political aims, and for them to be given a genuinely socialist perspective. When his friend and publisher, Peter

356

Suhrkamp, asked him to explain his attitude, he again pointed to the serious mistakes made by the Socialist Unity Party, which had led to the revolt by the workers, while he also confirmed that on 17 June there had been grounds to fear a repetition of the National Socialist 'revolution', because 'all manner of young riff-raff', and brutal types from the Nazi days, had joined the workers, 'whole columns of whom had been channelled through the Brandenburger Tor, across the Potsdamer Platz and onto the Warschauer Brücke'.

The events of 17 June were a bitter disillusion to Brecht, he felt totally 'alienated'. How little claim East Germany had to be called a socialist state had been revealed all too clearly. The legacy of the Third Reich had not yet been overcome, so many of the old habits and practices still remained. The party had simply fallen in love with a concept of the working-classes that had no basis in reality. Chaotic, feeble and mismanaged though it was, the revolt nonetheless woke the party up: 'There was cause for it to be alarmed, but no need for it to despair . . . The great opportunity to win over the workers came very inopportunely. Because of this I did not see the 17 June in a merely negative light'. At last, Brecht hoped, they would decide to adopt a thoroughgoing socialist policy. The course things had taken, the clarity with which one had seen how easily the proletariat could throw itself into the arms 'of the re-emergent fascism of the fascist era', strengthened him in his conviction that he could persuade the party not only to advocate, but to apply, historical materialistic dialectics, and so engage in open debate with bourgeois and revisionist attitudes. He thought it much better not to wipe out the still existent class differences between the workers and the petite-bourgeoisie. As he saw it the workers would have to bring the petite-bougeois ranks under their leadership. 'We have our own West right here!' he wrote to Paul Wandel, commenting on his poem 'The Truth Unites ('Die Wahrheit einigt'):

Freunde, ich wünschte, ihr wüsset die Wahrheit
                                                und sagtet sie!
Nicht wie fliehende müde Cäsaren: Morgen kommt Mehl!
So wie Lenin: Morgen abend
Sind wir verloren, wenn nicht . . .

(Friends, what I want is that you should know the truth and speak it. Not like tired, shifty Caesars: tomorrow there'll be food. But like Lenin: tomorrow evening all will be lost, unless. . .)

The party, said Brecht, should not react defensively but offensively, they should encourage every initiative to promote the attractions of socialism. The events of 17 June at last led to a wide-ranging discussion of failures and omissions. Brecht violently attacked the government's unsuccessful cultural policy, and raised the subject of the disastrous roles played by the State Commission for Art and the Office of Literature, which were finally abolished. In place of these instruments of state control a Ministry of Culture was created, of which Johannes R. Becher became minister at the beginning of 1954. Brecht attended meetings, 'on the subject of the Augean stables', at both the Academy of Arts and the Cultural Association. In an article in *Neues Deutschland*, on 12 August 1953, he declared that covering things up and glossing things over were the greatest enemies of beauty and political reason: 'The fight against formalism must not be seen merely as a political task, it must also be inspired with political meaning. It is part of the proletarian fight for genuine social solutions; consequently false artistic solutions have to be fought as false social solutions—not as aesthetic mistakes . . . The question of quality is politically decisive for genuine socialist art'. As open discussions were avoided in the German Democratic Republic—often with a reference to the way in which enemies of the working-class could make wrong use of this criticism—Brecht answered the praise in the West German press for his courageous words by publishing the poem 'Not meant like that' ('Nicht so gemeint'), in which he protested against applause from beyond the border: 'Even the lowest brows that harbour peace are more welcome to the arts than the art lover who is also a lover of the art of war'. In the fight against war and fascism Brecht felt at one with the East German government and the Socialist Unity Party. He preferred the authoritarian communist form of government for Germany, if only to prevent Nazis, aided by a 'free democratic constitutional structure', from being able once again to capture key posts in society.

358

33

Turandot or *The Congress of Whitewashers*

> In *Turandot* formulating, unproductive
> thinking is caught at a moment when the
> (capitalist) method of production no longer
> permits the facilities for production to go on
> developing; it shows itself to be impractical
> and therefore ridiculous. And it will still
> continue for a time, until the intellectuals no
> longer confront the rest of the population, but
> the whole population is intellectualized.

Apart from adaptations and projects like the drama *Einstein,* Brecht's last play was the comedy *Turandot or The Congress of Whitewashers (Turandot oder Der Kongress der Weisswäscher),* written in Buckow in July and August 1953. Subsequently the so-called first version, which Brecht gave to his collaborators and certain actors for their opinions, was subjected to slight alterations and changes in the order of the scenes. The version considered to be the last bears the date 10.8.1954. The play was written for the Berliner Ensemble and Käthe Reichel was Brecht's choice for the title role. The first rehearsals took place in the spring of 1954 but were soon broken off. The director was to be Benno Besson, to whom Brecht sent a telegram in January 1956, after the opening night of *The Good Woman of Setzuan* in Rostock: 'I look forward to the Tuis'. But *Turandot* was not given until 1969 when Besson directed it at the Zurich Schauspielhaus.

'I already had the idea of writing a *Turandot* play in the thirties', Brecht noted. At that time he wanted to make a version of *Turandot* based on themes from the old fairy-tale and on Gozzi's play, which Schiller, using Werthes' prose translation, had put into iambics; Carola Neher was to have played the title role. This plan had been inspired by Wachtangov's famous production of *Turandot.* During his exile Brecht did some preliminary work on a novel about the Tuis, and repeatedly thought of combining the Turandot material with his Tui project. In *Galileo* he wanted to depict 'the approaching dawn of reason'; the Tui play was to depict its twilight, the twilight, that is, of 'that sort of reason which, towards the end of the sixteenth century, had ushered in the capitalist age'. Although *Turandot or The Congress of Whitewashers* was written immediately after the events of 17 June, it did not owe its existence to them. What is certain, however, is that in the course of his work on the play Brecht introduced allusions to specific attitudes and utterances of certain 'whitewashers' in his own ranks. Thus he varied the poem 'The Solution' ('Die Lösung') by making the highwayman Gogher Gogh say to the Emperor in *Turandot* what Ku Ba said to Walter Ulbricht: 'What do you mean, the people must be able to choose their own régime? Can the régime choose its own people? It cannot. Would you have chosen precisely these people, for example, if you had your choice?' There were other allusions to the debates on popular appeal and realism. Brecht's Tui congress, too, was an allusion to the 'Congress for the Defence of Freedom of Culture' that was meeting in West Berlin.

The story, which is about China, is analogous to the events under the Weimar Republic that led to Hitler's seizure of power. The Emperor is in a serious dilemma because news has started to trickle through everywhere that, in order to restore his financial position, he has organized a cotton shortage. He has hoarded the rich cotton harvest in his storehouses, in other words taken it off the market, in order to keep up the price. The people murmur and demand to know what has become of the cotton. Kai-Ho, who has trained the 'friends of armed revolt' ideologically and militarily, sets to work to enlighten the people. He wants to make China 'a land fit to live in' at last. Public opinion in China is still formed by the Tuis, the Tellect-Ual-Ins. They operate the squalid business of thought; they live by dealing in opinions. To be anyone in the country, one has to be a Tui. There are Tui schools and a Tui university, where they teach the art of being a Tui and of producing suitable opinions. Kai-Ho himself comes from the Tui caste, but as he does not misuse his intellect the Tuis have expelled him from their ranks on the grounds that he mixes 'with the scum'. If the Federation of Clothesmakers and the Federation of the Clothesless could reach agreement the Emperor's reign would be finished. But the Tui members of these two mass associations hate

360

each other more than they hate the enemy. They quarrel about the right course to take, but mainly about the role of force; both claim allegiance to Marx and batter each other's heads in with his books. The feeble Emperor is not the only one who profits by their quarrel, the man who profits most is the former highwayman Gogher Gogh, who only became a highwayman in order to become a Tui. But he fails to gain admittance to any of the numerous Tui schools, and so goes into politics. In the hour of need this Gogh, with his bodyguard, is chosen as helper in preference to the Tuis, because at the critical moment the latter proves to be incapable of guaranteeing the Emperor's rule. The Tui council, the Congress of Whitewashers, convened by the Emperor to clear him of the suspicion of having stockpiled cotton, breaks down. Princess Turandot is to be given in marriage to the man who succeeds in diverting suspicion from the Emperor. No one has been successful, all the suitors have been beheaded. Gogher Gogh now approaches Turandot, who at first is enthusiastic. The wedding is fixed. Gogh seizes power and sets fire to part of the royal stocks of cotton with the intention of fastening responsibility on the Clothesmakers, the Clothesless and the Tuis; at the same time he sells the remaining cotton at a good price. Gogh persecutes the Tuis and destroys their works of art, but does not make much headway as a ruler: Kai-Ho and his followers have entered the capital, determined to remove the corrupt Emperor and dictator and establish a people's government.

There is not much of the Turandot material left in this story. The tale of Princess Turandot comes from the oriental collection, *Arabian Nights' Entertainments,* where it is called *The Story of Prince Calaf and the Princess of China.* Calaf is a prince of royal blood whose family has suffered great hardship, having been deprived of its kingdom and its power. Calaf goes to China and to its capital Peking, where he hears of Turandot, the beautiful daughter of the Emperor Altun Khan, who is a violent misanthrope but whose beauty entices the princes of all the neighbouring countries. Turandot is a thorn in her father's flesh because, apart from this headstrong daughter, he has no heir. She is so proud and so vain that she rejects all her suitors: 'I hate men and have no wish to marry', she declares. She will take as husband only the man who has answered every question put to him by Turandot in the presence of all those in the capital versed in the

361

law. All who cannot answer will be beheaded. Finally the princess puts her questions to Calaf, who is the first to be able to answer them. Turandot is aghast and says to her slave: 'His correct answers have turned me utterly against him'. The prince is willing to renounce his right provided that Turandot in turn answers the questions he puts to her. She is to guess his name. She cannot do so, and asks for a reprieve until the following day. She sends a girl, one of her slaves, to the prince charged with the task of discovering his name. This slave, herself a princess living in Peking as the King's prisoner, falls in love with the prince and tries to persuade him to run away with her. The next day Turandot knows the prince's name. The slave has told her in order to prevent the prince from marrying Turandot. Calaf, utterly disconsolate, sinks to the floor. The victorious Turandot, however, announces that she has decided to marry the prince. The slave stabs herself to death. 'Everyone present, it is said, trembled at this deed.' No lucky star watches over this marriage, and the dark clouds lift only slowly, but in the end the old possessions are restored in the happiest way though, needless to say, not without bloody warfare. There are several hundred thousand victims to be mourned but, says the story-teller of the prince whose misfortunes are now at an end, 'bloody though the battle was, it was at least decisive'.

This story of Calaf and the Princess of China is a great fairy-tale, cruel and realistic. How often the original richness and realism of old subjects are lost in later adaptations. Gozzi's fairy-tale play still retains much of the cruelty of the original, but there are already conciliatory touches here and there, as well as *commedia dell'arte* figures, introduced to give the fairy-tale a veneer of popular appeal. The determinant factor was what interested Wachtangov in his 1922 production of Gozzi's *Turandot*: 'in our fairy-tale we want to show the peripeties in man's fight for the victory of good over evil, for our future'. Wachtangov decided in favour of Gozzi rather than Schiller: the latter was not sufficiently rooted in the people, sufficiently 'cruel', for him. In *Turandot* Schiller struck him as being simply a stylist.

In construction and plot Schiller followed Gozzi's play, cutting out only one burlesque scene. In Gozzi's play the role of the slave is already watered down, the girl becoming a lovelorn schemer who, when she is about to take her own life, is generously forgiven by the prince and Turandot. Schiller went further than this, made all the characters noble and dispelled all the cruelty. Whereas in Gozzi Turandot stills acts merely at the dictates of her whim, without any further psychological motivation, Schiller's Turandot is a noble woman with a craving for freedom.

Brecht completely reversed the character of Turandot. She is not, as she is in the old fairy-tale, a misanthrope who takes a husband only after endless vacillation and then only because she has reduced him to submission. She is much more like a man-mad tart, lascivious, and perverted into the bargain. She insists on Tuis. And a Tui is in her bad graces the moment he fails intellectually or, in concrete terms, fails as a whitewasher. Good lying is what she wants, bad lying costs the man his head. This Turandot becomes more lascivious still when men find 'clever' answers and pretty ways of saying things. In Brecht the riddles Turandot sets her suitors become the task set by the Emperor to the Tuis: to whitewash him by clever talk of being suspected of manipulating the economy. Princess Turandot rewards the best whitewashers with a nod. The Divan, the gathering of those in the capital who are versed in the law, has become the Council of Tuis, which is at the centre of Brecht's play. Following a suggestion by his friend Hanns Eisler, Brecht also intended to make this Council of Tuis the point of departure and centre of his Tui novel, which had been planned independently of a possible adaptation of Turandot.

The Tui novel was one of Brecht's great prose projects. He intended this novel about the intellectuals to follow immediately after completion of the *Threepenny Novel*. Walter Benjamin mentions this work in his Svendborg diary of September 1934: 'on the one hand there are drafts of prose writings to be worked out, the smaller being the UI—a satire on Hitler in the style of the Renaissance historiographers—and the large one the Tui novel. The Tui novel is to be an encyclopaedic review of the assininities of the Tellectual-Ins (the intellectuals); part, at least, of it will be set in China, it seems. A small working-model of this book is finished'. Brecht's intention was to describe the role of the intellectuals in the capitalist state, how dependent it was and how distorted. He wanted to show, in the Tui novel, how the supposed democracy of the Weimar Republic led to fascism. He chose a Chinese setting for this. He saw the Weimar Republic, with its broad concept of freedom, as the 'Golden Age of the Tuis'. To Brecht Tuis were intellectuals who know the truth but, for reasons

363

of personal advantage, do not speak it, who see their social function as mere purveyors of marketable opinions. In *Me-ti* he says of the Tuis, who are also known as brain workers: 'The brain workers see to it that their brains feed them. In our day their brains feed them better when they hatch out something that injures a lot of people. This is why Me-ti says of them: their diligence causes me concern'.

Certain specific writers' attitudes, their vanities, their tactics, their artful little moves, provided Brecht with his basic material. But he still lacked the great plot he needed. A further complication arose when he discovered that the phenomenon of Tuism did not vanish with the introduction of a socialist order of society. In *Me-ti* he says: 'Even Su, the workers' and farmers' state, succumbed to the influence of the Tuis a decade and a half after its formation'. The spokesmen for Stalinism and Trotskyism proved to be model disciples of the Tui cause when they abused each other for being Tuis, and 'in the worst sense of the word'. While *Me-ti* was intended to be in the nature of a didactic story about the genesis and consolidation of the Soviet Union, based on the teachings of the socialist classics, the Tui Novel was conceived as a *roman à clef* about the Weimar Republic. But the two projects occurred to Brecht in a haphazard way—because of outside circumstances such as developments in the Soviet Union and because of difficulties caused by discrepancies in the position of the intellectual in the capitalist state—so that he was no longer able to keep them strictly apart. Side by side with the planned Tui Novel individual Tui stories came into being, and parts of these bear a strong resemblance to the Me-ti texts. Brecht once referred to them as 'Chinese moralities, stories of morals and manners from the Tui age'.

The various aspects of the subject proved too big and too ramified for him to be able to start work on the novel in earnest. In 1938 Brecht intended to set it alongside his Caesar novel, as a satiric companion piece, in the same way that he wanted his whole diverse output to be treated as 'an assemblage of self-contained works': 'To *The Transactions of Mr. Julius Caesar (Die Geschäfte des Herrn Julius Cäsar)* must be added the Tui Novel. To the drama the didactic plays'. In 1939 he wrote to Korsch: 'The Tuis are truly inexhaustible'. But Brecht also had to remind himself constantly that the Tuism of the emigrants was far less mischievous than the degeneracy of thought in fascist Germany:

'The Golden Age of the Tuis is the liberal Republic, but Tuism reaches its peak in the Third Reich. Idealism, having reached its lowest ebb, celebrates its most gigantic triumphs. Philosophically—and hence adequately—expressed: at the moment when consciousness is most deeply enslaved to the social entity, it presumes to try to dictate to it in the most imperious way. The "idea" is nothing more than a reflex, and this reflex assumes a particularly dictatorial and terroristic form when confronted with the reality'.

Hollywood proved to be one big mine of Tui material. Here too, at first, it was the attitudes of individual Tuis that Brecht recorded with bitter sarcasm, the attitudes of bourgeois thinking intellectuals from Thomas Mann and Leonhard Frank to Erich Maria Remarque who, as he saw it, politicized from an idealistic standpoint but were cautious and craven when it really came to putting across a political point of view. There were times when he did not exempt even his best friends from the suspicion that they might be Tuis. And it was also clear to him that, as a candidate for a film contract in Hollywood, he himself was in a Tui situation. The reality exceeded anything satire could attempt. In 1942 he noted resignedly: 'This country is smashing my Tui novel to pieces. Here there is no question of exposing the sale of opinions. It goes around naked. The great comic situation, which they think they are controlling and by which they are controlled, the quixotry of the consciousness which imagines it is determining the social entity—this presumably exists only in Europe'. A chance that he might still hit upon a suitable plot for this novel then presented itself in the varied activities and attitudes of the members of the Frankfurt Institute for Social Research, which had moved to America and almost all of whose members lived in Hollywood: Max Horkheimer, Friedrich Pollock, Theodor W. Adorno, Leo Löwenthal, Herbert Marcuse and Günther Anders. The wealthy Horkheimer and the economist Pollock, in particular, provoked Brecht to indulge his taste for sarcastic criticism: 'At a garden party given by Rolf Nürnberg met the twin clowns Horkheimer and Pollock, the two Tuis from the Frankfurt Sociological Institute. Horkheimer is a millionaire, Pollock merely comes from a good family, so it is only Horkheimer who can buy himself a professorship wherever he happens to be, as a cover for the revolutionary activities of the institute'.

The institute had been founded by the liberal Jewish merchant Hermann Weil, who had emigrated from Germany to the Argentine in 1890, where he amassed a considerable fortune from wheat. His son and heir Felix Weil had studied in Frankfurt and written a thesis on the practical problems of establishing socialism. At a Marxist study-week, organized by Weil, which took place in Thuringia in 1922 and was attended by Karl Korsch, Georg Lukács and Friedrich Pollock, the idea was born of a self-financing institute for social reform, independent of the rigid university system, at which subjects like the history of the labour movement and the origins of anti-semitism could be studied. Weil enabled many Marxist scholars to carry out projects at that time, while left-wing artists like Grosz and Piscator could also always count on his support. The institute's most important undertaking was the 'Journal for Social Research', the final issues of which were published in English in New York. Brecht accused the institute of concealing the real causes of fascism, to avoid destroying its own material foundations. The institute's representatives, he claimed, had feared they might be victims of a 'redrazzia' in America, and so had used their money to maintain a dozen intellectuals on the other side of the Atlantic, among them Benjamin, Korsch and Langerhans, on condition that they sent all their work to the institute, but with no guarantee that the institute's journal would ever publish it. The main concern of these Tuis, according to Brecht, had been to save the institute's fortune, and it was this that they had regarded as 'their primary revolutionary duty throughout all these years'.

Coming from lunch with Horkheimer, one day in May 1942, Hanns Eisler, who had also benefited from Weil's patronage, suggested to Brecht that he build his Tui Novel round the story of the Sociological Institute: 'A rich old man (the wheat speculator Weil) dies, haunted by the misery in the world. In his will he leaves a large sum of money to establish an institute to investigate the source of the misery. This, of course, is he himself. The institute's investigation takes place at a time when the Emperor himself wants to name a cause of the evil, because the people's anger is growing. The institute participates in the Council'.

The chief object of interest for Brecht was Theodor W. Adorno, whom he considered to be the institute's most experienced theoretician, a man whose fluency of speech and attractive turn of phrase appealed to him as a good basis for a stage character: 'Adorno is incapable of pulling a long face, and this stands him in good stead as a theoretician'. Brecht despised scholars like Adorno, as 'disinterested admirers of the idea of materialism', whose insistence that the theory must be absolute caused them largely to ignore the practice. He dedicated to the institute his Tui story *The Theory of Knowledge or The River Mis-ef (Die Erkenntnistheorie oder Der Fluss Mis-ef)*, which was based on a conversation with Adorno. His arguments with the institute's representatives covered not only the political questions of the day and the position of the Soviet Union, but the problems of the authentic interpretation of Marx, the members of the institute regarding themselves as the lawful trustees of the Marxist heritage. Their views on the Jewish question were also the subject of controversy. Brecht adhered to the Marxist standpoint of defining the Jew in social terms, 'formed by persecution and resistance, in his economic specialization and dependence on ready money (the need to buy himself out or in)', and demurred at explaining anti-semitism as a psychological implication of an authoritarian disposition that tended to fascism. Brecht regarded the New York Jewish financiers as much more likely to be potential fascists than the great mass of people who, stupefied by anti-semitic prejudices, gave support to the fascist system.

Now *Turandot or The Congress of Whitewashers,* this satire on the liberal democratic state and its intellectuals, is certainly not a portrait of members of the Frankfurt Institute; Eisler's suggestion is followed only in the nucleus of the plot and the council of Tuis, while Brecht used his talks with members of the Institute to define the attitudes of individual characters. In the little scene in which Munka Du, the cleverest and vainest of the Tuis, the idol of the philosophic seminar at the Tui University, has himself made up, while he practices his phrases as a singer practices his arias, before making his appearance at the congress, there are satirical reminiscences of Adorno's entrances, and of Thomas Mann too, who used to practise his celebrated impromptu speeches in front of the mirror and was especially fond of showing off with his recitations in front of women. A weakness of the play is that the various Tui attitudes are inadequately differentiated. Circumstances compel the Tuis to walk the streets or become revolutionaries. This is the alternative to which the author of the play has reduced the intellectual in the liberal democratic state. As a result *Turandot* is only the satiric counterpart to *Galileo;* Brecht never wrote *The Life of Einstein (Das Leben des Einstein)*, which was to be the companion play for our age.

Side by side with the satire on the intellectuals is a farcical parable on the rise of fascism, the central character of which is Gogher Gogh, a blend of Mac the Knife and Arturo Ui. From the simple highwayman who, at the beginning, 'has all the ladies of Peking at his feet because of his manliness', Gogh gradually progresses to the ruthless gang leader who wields political power. Just as Hindenburg nominated Hitler to be Chancellor, the Emperor in Turandot clears the way for Gogher Gogh, who then sets fire to the cotton storehouses and inaugurates the persecution of the communists (Federation of Clothesmakers), the social democrats (Federation of the Clothesless) and the intellectuals (Tuis). But fascism stands no chance, Kai-Ho has entered the city in time. The saviour never appears himself, we only hear of him. His presence is felt in the transformation, or learning process, of the peasant Sen, who goes to Peking in order to become a Tui student, but after seeing how depraved this intellectual caste is thinks better of it and decides to learn the A B C of Kai-Ho.

His play *Turandot,* Brecht said, lay right outside the stream of German literature and, as solitary people often do, gave the impression of being 'insubstantial': 'Were I entirely a writer of comedies, which I almost am, but only almost, a work like this would at least be surrounded by relatives, and the clan could hold its own'. Malicious satire and gruesome political fairy-tale stand side by side. The play must be acted at great speed. Slapstick entrances, like that of the Emperor's mother who always comes on merely to hand poison to her son, follow grotesque satiric showpieces, like the pupil in the Tui school who, during his speech-making exercise, has the prize snatched away each time his wording approaches the truth. The comedy has to be accepted in all its banal superficiality, the schematic contradictions have to be made realistic by heightening the situations to the point where they are no longer plausible. One can only regret that Brecht never adapted the old Turandot material. He might have extracted a great realistic plot from the cruel fairy-tale.

34

A great time, wasted

Who else has said harsh things so gently! Who
else could be so stubborn and so gentle at the
same time! Who else has said gentle things so
harshly!   JOHANNES R. BECHER

In the spring of 1954, when the Volksbühne was once more housed
in its own theatre, now rebuilt, on the Luxemburg Platz, the
Berliner Ensemble was able to move into the Theater am
Schiffbauerdamm. For the first time Brecht now had complete
freedom of movement, as well as the space and financial conditions
needed for long-term projects and extensive theatrical experiments. The Ensemble opened with an adaptation of Molière's *Don
Juan,* directed by Benno Besson. The production of *The Caucasian
Chalk Circle,* into which more than eight months work had gone,
provided an opportunity fully to test the ideal conditions now at
the Ensemble's disposal. To Brecht the relaxed atmosphere, with
no deadlines to worry about, meant a great deal. It was a luxury to
be able to practise his art in this way, a foretaste of better times to
come. But although Brecht allowed adequate time for rehearsals,
he worked indefatigably. He was delighted that he now had an
apartment close to the theatre, and no longer had to travel several
miles a day from Weissensee to the centre of town. His day was
strictly planned; in these last years of his life he lived 'with his
watch in his hand'.

At the Deutsches Theater there had been constant quarrels
between him and Wolfgang Langhoff over the number of stage
rehearsals and the opening dates; both frequently lost their
tempers, each being convinced that the other was intriguing
behind his back. In any case Brecht rather enjoyed shouting in the
theatre from time to time, and on these occasions indulged in abuse
that was out of all proportion; he reacted with particular violence
against mistakes and negligence on the part of the technical staff.

Like Fritz Kortner he would immediately make a political issue out of slovenliness and call those concerned Nazis. Needless to say his outbursts were planned stage entrances, because as far as he could he kept to the rule of avoiding unplanned rows: 'Peace and quiet is as much a part of directing as anything else'. He did, however, cherish a deep and growing mistrust of all those round him who had spent the Nazi era in Germany: these people, who formerly never risked a thing, should learn to keep quiet, and trust the anti-fascists in the government, before criticizing conditions in the German Democratic Republic. One day it suddenly struck him that less than ten years previously his pupils in the Berliner Ensemble would have handed him over to the Gestapo:

> Da war eine Zeit
> Da war alles hier anders.
> Die Metzgerfrau weiss es.
> Der Postbote hat einen zu aufrechten Gang.
> Und was war der Elektriker?

(Time was when things were different here. The butcher's wife knows about it. The postman holds himself too erect. And the electrician, what was he?)

When, following *The Caucasian Chalk Circle,* Brecht staged Johannes R. Becher's play *Winterschlacht,* it was not an opportunist act of homage to the Minister of Culture, but the outcome of political considerations: in his view the important thing about the play was the way in which the account with the Nazi era was settled ideologically. Hitherto East German writers had neglected this subject; moreover it was one which the party preferred to pass over in silence. Generally Brecht, like others, found Becher's emotional appeal insufferable. Compared to the Minister, who in his personal appearance and behaviour conformed more nearly to the popular idea of a poet, Brecht seemed like an ordinary workman. When they appeared on a political platform together, Brecht was the bolder; he did not hesitate to indulge in virulent polemics. Although the initiative for such East-West discussions usually came from Brecht, he then sheltered behind Becher, let him call the tune and contented himself with playing second fidddle. In their attitudes to poetry and drama the two men were miles apart, but politically their confidence in each other was absolute.

Brecht not only gained increased standing in East Germany after 1954, thanks to Becher's support, his position also became more secure, largely because of the Berliner Ensemble's success abroad. Even in the Soviet Union they gradually began to appreciate him, and at the end of 1954 he was awarded the International Stalin Peace Prize. Admittedly he received this prize for occasional works like 'Song of Peace' ('Friedenslied'), and for his political activities, rather than in recognition of *Mother Courage,* just as Picassso was honoured for his dove and not for *Guernica.*

By now the recipient of many official honours Brecht, national prizewinner, Stalin prizewinner and Vice-President of the Academy, intended to remain controversial in spite of this. *The Caucasian Chalk Circle* production was perhaps the finest theatrical achievement of his life, a fact the Berlin critics fully realized only after its success in Paris in 1955. But he had no intention of resting on his laurels. Was not *The Caucasian Chalk Circle* an aesthetic transfiguration of the old dialectical theatre? The play, with prologue and epilogue, took as its starting point a social situation in which class distinctions were no longer known. The conflicts were shown in retrospect, as dangers that had been successfully overcome. In 1944, when the play was written, this had the force of a bold anticipation of a happier human state of affairs. In 1954, however, inhuman conditions represented by the stage equivalent of historical woodcuts failed to carry conviction in face of the contemporary socialist reality. So Brecht was probably by no means loath to accept Becher's unsuccessful play, because the antagonisms with which it dealt had immediate relevance for the social realities of the German Democratic Republic.

Brecht's continuing inability to find any satisfactory 'poetic detachment' from the social facts of the German Democratic Republic was due, not to him, but to the reality, on which he did not want to turn his back. In comparison with the number of works he wrote in exile, his literary output during his years in the German Democratic Republic was relatively small: one play, some adaptations, songs for children and young people, and the magnificent *Buckow Elegies (Buckower Elegien).* But Brecht was never unproductive. His work in the theatre, his sociopolitical activities, were part of his production as a poet. His work was more than ever 'in a state of flux', and because of this he had come a little closer to his Utopian demand to put an end to the distinction between art and life.

The 'toils of the plains' gave Brecht a great deal of trouble. He was glad to be wanted but unhappy about wasted time. Since he was now confronted from morning to night with problems relating to his theatre and cultural policy, and was engaged in a daily battle with visitors and deadlines, he felt a great need for peace and quiet. Thus, from 1953 onwards, he retired as often as he could to Buckow in the Märkische Schweiz, to the garden house of a property containing one other building and big old trees, situated on the edge of an 'ill-favoured petit bourgeois little place'. Here, too, there were always swarms of visitors, but in the mornings he allowed himself time and quiet, and even had sufficient leisure occasionally to read Horace again. In Buckow he wrote his most reflective and formally most polished poems, his 'work of mourning' as he called it. In them he took stock of his life, alluded to the wretched plight of his country, and made a plea for productive impatience.

> Ich sitze am Strassenrand
> Der Fahrer wechselt das Rad.
> Ich bin nicht gern, wo ich herkomme.
> Ich bin night gern, wo ich hinfahre.
> Warum sehe ich den Radwechsel
> Mit Ungeduld?

(I am sitting by the roadside, the driver is changing the wheel. I do not like it where I have come from. I do not like it where I am going. Why do I watch the wheel-change impatiently?)

In old age Brecht did not look back longingly to his childhood in Augsburg. That period of his life was finished and done with. At the most it was an occasional, tender, elegiac memory. He did not deny his bourgeois origins, but he tried to discard them and learn a different social attitude. The future interested him only as a perspective, not as a final outcome. The present was important, working for history. Brecht watched the 'wheel-change' from the past to the future in East Germany impatiently, because it progressed so listlessly and was so lacking in perspectives. The

372

new state was not being built for history, and hence for mankind, but for statistics. Inadequate use was being made of the opportunity to undertake sweeping changes: 'What are cities then, if built without the wisdom of the people?'

Contrary to what Brecht hoped, dialectics continued to languish in East Germany. The Socialist Unity Party failed to learn the lesson he expected it to learn from the events of 17 June 1953. It improved only statistics. Many critics of its policy were relieved of office, and provocateurs were not the only ones to be put on trial. To Brecht, the overthrow of Stalinism meant to have scope for dialectics again: 'Without a knowledge of dialectics, transitions like that from Stalin as a motivating force to Stalin as a brake cannot be understood . . . . Stalinism can be liquidated only if the party mobilizes the wisdom of the masses on a gigantic scale'. In Brecht's view the only dialectician since Lenin among the political leaders of the socialist countries was Mao Tse-Tung. During the last years of his life he regarded Mao's essay *On Contradiction* as one of the most important of books.

The subject of the essay is the continued existence of opposing structures even after the capitalistic society has been abolished. In it Mao draws special attention to the unversally operative law of contradictions, and resolves them into dynamic activity; in fact he is more interested in the eternal play of contradictions than in the definitive form of communism: 'the contradiction between the new and the old is to be found in every phenomenon, and provokes an unceasing and complex struggle. In the outcome of this struggle the new grows and rises to the dominant position, while the old declines and begins to die out. As soon as the new gains supremacy over the old, the essential features of an old situation are transformed into those of a new one'.

Ever since he became engrossed in Marxist theory, Brecht had taken a great interest in the art and philosophy of the far east. He had an especially high regard for the theory of behaviour advanced by the old Chinese dialectician Mo Di or Me-ti, for whom art and science were still one and the same thing. In 1948 an ode by Mao Tse-Tung elicited this observation from Brecht: 'My calculation that there would be a renaissance of the arts, triggered off by the upheaval in the far east, seems to be paying off sooner than one would have thought'. Only since the victory of the Chinese communists and the establishment of the People's Republic in 1949 had he been certain that the face of the world was going to change completely. Since that time he had followed with great interest the reports and accounts given by East German writers who travelled to China in the nineteen-fifties. In the summer of 1952, when he was feeling depressed over the fusty petit bourgeois atmosphere in East Germany, and the re-miltarization in West Germany, he discussed with friends the possibility of going into exile in China. No doubt it was more of a mental game than a plan he seriously thought of putting into effect. His frequent references to the 'wisdom of the people' during the last years of his life reflected a political idea gleaned from the writings of Mao Tse-Tung, rather than any actual experience made in the German Democratic Republic: 'The wisdom of the people must have the last word in everything, and yet it is mingled with superstition. We have to start somewhere, we may never stop anywhere'.

Brecht lived to the end in the country where he was best able to realize his artistic projects, and where his suggestions had most chance of being accepted. His death in 1956 came as a surprise and, for East Germany, meant the loss of a writer who, more than any other, had helped by his interventions and suggested changes to mould its cultural policy. So long as Brecht was there no artist, scholar or scientist of real significance in East Germany thought of giving up his post. Then, as time passed, it became very obvious that his advice and protecting hand were no longer available. His work, however, was declared to be an incontestable part of the classical heritage: it was rendered harmless and canonized.

During his life Brecht had done all he could to avoid being canonized. He was anxious never to be praised by those in power. Before flying to Moscow in May 1955 to receive the Stalin Prize he wrote to the Academy of Arts, in the person of Erich Engel: 'Should I die, I do not wish to lie in state anywhere or to be exposed to public view. I want no speeches at my graveside. I should like to be buried in the cemetery near the house where I live, in the Chaussee Strasse'. The site of the grave, diagonally across from that of Hegel, had been chosen by Brecht himself. His prophecy that his choice would set a fashion, and that one day the Dorotheen-Friedhof would become a meeting-place like the 'Möwe' artists' club, came true: Johannes R. Becher chose a grave in the immediate vicinity of Brecht's, and later they were joined by

Arnolt Bronnen, Hanns Eisler, Erich Engel, John Heartfield, Helene Weigel, Elisabeth Hauptmann and Ruth Berlau.

Brecht died on 14 August 1956. At the beginning of May he had entered the Charité hospital to be treated for the after-effects of virus influenza. After his discharge he still felt so weak that he let Peter Suhrkamp persuade him to go with him for treatment, to a private clinic in Munich, for the rest of August and the first two weeks of September. Helene Weigel supported this plan, and in addition asked Therese Giehse to advise Brecht to consult a further specialist: 'I hope you won't give me away, because he would probably be more likely to listen to your advice than to my chatter, which he has had ringing in his ears for so many years'. Being too exhausted to work, Brecht could not ignore the fact that he was ill, although he gave scarcely a sign of it to those round him. On 9 August he arrived in Berlin from Buckow. On the following day he attended two rehearsals, necessitated by changes in the cast, for the forthcoming London appearance of the Berliner Ensemble; but he had to leave the theatre early because he suddenly felt weak. He intended to leave for Munich on the evening of 14 August, but at midday the doctors found he was suffering from a severe heart attack, which must have occurred at least three days previously. From six o'clock in the evening he was unconscious; shortly before midnight he died. He was buried very quietly, at nine o'clock in the morning, on 17 August.

> Hier, in diesem Zink
> Liegt ein toter Mensch
> Oder seine Beine und sein Kopf
> Oder noch Weniger von ihm
> Oder nichts, denn er war
> Ein Hetzer.

(Here, in this piece of zinc, lies a dead man, or his legs and head, or still less of him, or nothing at all, because he was an agitator.)

The *Burial of the Agitator in a Zinc Coffin (Begräbnis des Hetzers im Zinksarg)*, of a comrade who had called for solidarity with the oppressed, and on people to think, had been ordered by men who feared the return of a troublesome fighter. The agitator Brecht had also given instructions that he be buried in a zinc coffin—as a protection against worms; a final demonstration of the vitality of his favourite idea of the wisdom of the people, mixed with superstition. The coffin was escorted to the grave by his family, those most closely associated with him in his work, and his friends Hanns and Gerhart Eisler, Paul Dessau, Jakob Walcher, Fritz Cremer, J. R. Becher, Erich Engel and Paul Wandel. When Peter Suhrkamp reached the cemetery at a few minutes past 9.0 it was all over. Suhrkamp wrote to Caspar Neher, who could not go to Berlin: 'The 'Prize Song' ('Preislied') and 'Farewell Canon' ('Abschiedskanon') can only be sung among intimates. In Brecht's case this meant only a few men. The house in the Chaussee Strasse is now a house filled with melancholy women'. At the grave in the nearby cemetery a constant coming and going was to be seen for days: 'Everything changes. You can make a new start with your last breath. But what is done is done'.

REFERENCES AND NOTES

In the following pages the sources are given of all quotations from Brecht and other authors, in the order in which they occur in this book, with the exception of those contained in Brecht's *Gesammelte Werke* (vols. I–VIII, Frankfurt 1967), *Texte für Filme* (Frankfurt 1969), *Arbeitsjournal* (two volumes, Frankfurt 1973), and *Tagebücher 1920–1922 | Autobiographische Aufzeichnungen 1920–1954* (Frankfurt 1975).

CHAPTER 1

Max Frisch, *Erinnerungen an Brecht;* in *Kursbuch 7,* Frankfurt 1966.— *Dreizehn Bühnentechniker erzählen;* in *Sinn und Form,* second Brecht number, Berlin 1957.—Letter from Brecht to Herbert Ihering, October 1922; in *Sinn und Form,* vol. 1, Berlin 1958.—Robert Minder, *Brecht und die wiedergefundene Grossmutter;* in *Dichter in der Gesellschaft,* Frankfurt 1966. In his story, *Die unwürdige Greisin,* Brecht gives his grandmother's age as seventy-two. He wrote the poem, 'Aufgewachsen in dem zitronenfarbenen Lichte der Frühe' for her eightieth birthday on 17 September 1919; it was reprinted in Werner Frisch and K. W. Obermeier, *Brecht in Augsburg. Erinnerungen, Dokumente, Texte, Fotos,* Berlin and Weimar, 1975.—Brecht's famous answer, 'You will laugh— the Bible', was printed in the magazine *Die Dame,* Berlin, 1 December 1928, in the supplement *Die losen Blätter.*—Erich Maiberger, *Bert Brechts Augsburger Jahre;* reprinted from *Hundert Jahre Realgymnasium Augsburg,* 1964.—Wilhelm Brüstle, *Wie ich Bert Brecht entdeckte;* in *Die Neue Zeitung,* 27 November 1948.—The article *Turmwacht* appeared in the *Augsburger Neueste Nachrichten* 8 August 1914, and was reprinted in Frisch and Obermeier, op. cit.—Otto Müllereisert, *Augsburger Anekdoten um Bert Brecht;* in *Erinnerungen an Brecht,* Leipzig 1964.— Letter from Brecht to Caspar Neher, 10 November 1914; printed in Frisch and Obermeier, op. cit.

CHAPTER 2

Thomas Mann, *Lübeck als geistige Lebensform;* in *Altes und Neues,* Berlin and Weimar 1965.—Erich Maiberger, *Bert Brechts Augsburger Jahre;* reprinted from *Hundert Jahre Realgymnasium Augsburg,* 1964.—Hanns Otto Münsterer, *Bert Brecht. Erinnerungen aus den Jahren 1917–1922,*

Berlin 1966.—Meinhard Adler, *Untersuchungen zum Studium Bert Brechts;* in *Neue Deutsche Hefte* 111, Jahrgang 13, Heft 3.—Letter from Brecht to Heiner Hagg, 23 November 1917; printed in Frisch and Obermeier, *Brecht in Augsburg,* Berlin and Weimar 1975.—*Zeitgenossen geben zu Protokoll,* statement by Pauline Sch., secretary at the Haindl paper-mill; in *Kultur und Leben,* week-end supplement to the *Augsburger Allgemeine,* 10 February 1968.—Letters from Brecht to Hanns Johst, 1919 (undated), 1920 (beginning).—'Lied der Kavaliere der Station D', quoted by Münsterer op. cit., and *BBA,* Mappe 800, Blatt 11.—Letters from Brecht to Caspar Neher: 8 June, beginning of September, October, 23 November 1917; beginning of February, middle of March, 8 April, 10 April, end of April, 11 May, June, beginning of July, 22 July, 26 August 1918.

CHAPTER 3

Hanns Otto Münsterer, *Bert Brecht. Erinnerungen aus den Jahren 1917–1922,* Berlin 1966.—Rosa Luxemburg, *Gesammelte Schriften,* Berlin 1951, vol. 2, p. 597.—Lion Feuchtwanger, *Bertolt Brecht;* in *Erinnerungen an Brecht,* Leipzig 1964.—Marieluise Fleisser, *Frühe Begegnung;* in *Akzente,* vol. 3, Munich 1966.—Letter from Brecht to Paula Banholzer, beginning of December 1921; printed in Kurt Fassmann, *Brecht. Bildbiographie,* Munich 1963.—Letter to Caspar Neher, end of April 1918.—*Volkswille* appeared from 1 September 1919 to 13 January 1921 and was the forerunner of the *Bayrische Arbeiterzeitung.* In addition to the criticisms reprinted in the *Gesammelte Werke,* the criticism of performances of Max Halbe's *Jugend* and Björnson's *Über unsere Kraft,* which appeared on 13 October 1919, was probably also by Brecht. Reprinted in Frisch and Obermeier, *Brecht in Augsburg,* Berlin and Weimar 1975, pp. 188–191.—Letters from Brecht to Dora Mannheim, see Doris Hasenfratz, *Aus dem Alltag eines Genies, Die Zeit,* 19 August 1966.

CHAPTER 4

The motto is from the *Arbeitsjournal,* 11 September 1938.—Hanns Johst, *Der Einsame. Ein Menschenuntergang,* Munich 1917.—Brecht, *Baal. Der böse Baal der asoziale. Texte, Varianten und Materialien.* Critical edition with commentary by Dieter Schmidt, Frankfurt 1966.—See also Dieter Schmidt, *Baal und der junge Brecht,* Stuttgart 1966.—Letters from Brecht to Caspar Neher, middle of March 1918 and beginning of September 1917.—Friedrich Engels, *Ludwig Feuerbach und der Ausgang der klassischen deutschen Philosophie;* Marx/Engels, *Werke,* vol. 21, Berlin 1962.—Karl Marx, *Ökonomisch-philosophische Manuskripte;* in Marx/Engels, *Werke,* supplementary volume, part one, Berlin 1968.—

Herbert Marcuse, *Triebstruktur und Gesellschaft*, Frankfurt 1965.—The Wedekind quotation from the *Lulu* tragedy is from an early version of the play and is taken from *Notizbuch 15* in the Wedekind archives of the Stadtbibliothek in Munich. See also Klaus Völker, *Wedekind*, Velber 1965, p. 37.

CHAPTER 5

Arnolt Bronnen, *Tage mit Bertolt Brecht*, Munich 1960 (also contains Brecht's letters to Arnolt Bronnen).—Letter from Brecht to Paula Banholzer, end of 1921; printed in Fassmann, *Brecht. Bildbiographie*, Munich 1963.—On 24 December 1921 Brecht signed a contract with the Erich Reiss Verlag for the '*Buch und Bühnenvertrieb*' of his works; it had been negotiated by Klabund. The contract contained the passage, 'If the publisher refuses to publish a play, although a leading theatre has acquired it for performance, the author may transfer the copyright and selling-rights to another publisher, provided that the latter assumes responsibility for printing it,' and it was this that enabled Brecht to conclude a contract for *Baal* with Kiepenheuer in 1922.—*Arnolt Bronnen gibt zu Protokoll*, Hamburg 1954.—Brecht, *Im Dickicht der Städte. Erstfassung und Materialien*. Edited with a commentary by Gisela E. Bahr, Frankfurt 1968.—Undated letter from Brecht to Caspar Neher, 1922.—Marieluise Fleisser, *Frühe Begegnung;* in *Akzente*, vol. 3, Munich 1966.—Herbert Ihering, *Der Dramatiker Bert Brecht, Berliner Börsen-Courier*, 5 October 1922.—Hanns Otto Münsterer, *Bert Brecht*, Berlin 1966.—Letter from Brecht to Herbert Ihering, middle of October 1922; Published in *Sinn und Form*, vol. 1, Berlin 1958.—Texts of the *Hannibal* fragment, *BBA 520/37 and 520/17*.—Bernhard Reich, *Erinnerungen an Brecht;* in *Studien*, supplement to *Theater der Zeit*, vol. 14, Berlin 1966.

CHAPTER 6

Brecht, *Leben Eduards des Zweiten von England. Vorlage, Texte und Materialien*. Edited by Reinhold Grimm, Frankfurt 1968.—Bernhard Reich, *Erinnerungen an Brecht;* in *Studien*, supplement to *Theater der Zeit*, vol. 14, Berlin 1966.—Herbert Ihering, *Die zwanziger Jahre*, Berlin 1948.—Karl Valentin's suggestion for the soldiers' make-up in *Eduard* is quoted from Walter Benjamin, *Versuche über Brecht*, Frankfurt 1966. See also Asja Lacis, *Revolutionär im Beruf*, edited by Hildegard Brenner, Munich 1971.

CHAPTER 7

The motto is from Brecht's article in the programme of the Heidelberg production of 1928.—Letter from Brecht to Caspar Neher, 31 May 1918.—Quotations from the working-notes for *Im Dickicht;* in Brecht,

Im Dickicht der Städte. Erstfassung und Materialien, edited by Gisela E. Bahr, Frankfurt 1968.—Karl Marx, *Ökonomisch-philosophische Manuskripte.* Using *Die Phänomenologie des Geistes* as a basis, Marx embarks on a criticism of Hegel's dialectics and philosophy in general; in Marx/Engels, *Werke,* supplementary volume, part one, Berlin 1968, p. 574. In the *Ökonomisch-philosophische Manuscripte* Marx also writes on the problem of work alienation, p. 514 f.—Johannes Vilhelm Jensen, *Das Rad.* 5th–9th. edition, Berlin 1921.—Herbert Marcuse, *Neue Quellen zur Grundlegung des historischen Materialismus;* in *Philosophie und Revolution,* vol. 1, Berlin 1967.

CHAPTER 8

Brecht's four-line poem 'Über die Städte' was written in 1927. In the original version, entitled 'Die Städte' and published in *Simplizissimus,* the third line read, 'We were within them. And enjoyed them'.—Walter Benjamin, *Versuche über Brecht,* p. 68.—Marieluise Fleisser, *Zu Brecht.* Written in 1966 as a suggestion for announcing a film she had written about Brecht for the Westdeutscher Rundfunk. Printed in *Materialien zum Leben und Schreiben der Marieluise Fleisser,* edited by Günther Rühle, Frankfurt 1973.—Bernard Guillemin, *Was arbeiten Sie? Gespräch mit Bert Brecht;* in *Die Literarische Welt,* Berlin 30 July 1926.—The report of Brecht's motor car accident appeared in *Uhu,* vol. 2, year 6, November 1929.—*Bert Brechts Erwiderung auf H. Schlien* appeared in *Die neue Zeit,* vol. 5/6, Dresden 1927.—*Arnolt Bronnen gibt zu Protokoll,* Hamburg 1954. For the adventure of the 'three gods' in Dresden see also Hans Mayer, *Gelegenheitsdichtung des jungen Brecht,* in *Anmerkungen zu Brecht,* Frankfurt 1965.—Thomas Mann, *German Letter No. 3,* September 1923, in *The Dial,* New York, vol. 75 No. 4, p. 375; *German Letter* No. 5, October 1925, in *The Dial,* New York, vol. 77 No. 5, p. 417 ff.—Thomas Mann, *Die neuen Kinder;* in *Uhu,* vol. 11, Berlin, year 2, August 1926.—Klaus Mann, *Die neuen Eltern,* ibid.—Thomas Mann, *Die Unbekannten;* in *Gesammelte Werke,* XI, p. 751 and p. 754.—Thomas Mann, *Worte an die Jugend;* in *Gesammelte Werke,* X.—The questionnaire, *Worüber lachen Sie?,* appeared in the *Film-Kurier,* Berlin, 11 June 1927.—Gershom Scholem, *Walter Benjamin—die Geschichte einer Freundschaft,* Frankfurt 1965.—Karl Marx, *Thesen über Feuerbach;* in Marx/Engels, *Werke,* vol. 3, Berlin 1962.—Walter Benjamin, *Versuche über Brecht,* Frankfurt 1966, pp. 67 f. and p. 65.

CHAPTER 9

The motto is from the draft of a letter to a dramatic critic; in *Gesammelte Werke,* VIII, p. 104.—Bernhard Reich, *Erinnerungen an Brecht;* in *Studien,* supplement to *Theater der Zeit,* vol. 14, Berlin 1966.—The first performance of Bernhard Reich's production of *La Dame aux Camélias* was on 10 March 1925. Herbert Ihering's notice appeared in the *Berliner Börsen-Courier* of 11 March; Alfred Kerr wrote in the *Berliner Tageblatt* and Monty Jacobs in the *Vossische Zeitung.*—Fritz Sternberg, *Der Dichter und die Ratio. Erinnerungen an Bertolt Brecht,* Göttingen 1963.— Marieluise Fleisser, *Frühe Begegnung;* in *Akzente,* vol. 3, Munich 1966.—Elisabeth Hauptmann, *Notizen über Brechts Arbeit 1926;* in *Erinnerungen an Brecht,* Leipzig 1964.—The recorded discussion on *Trommeln in der Nacht* (Brecht, Piscator, Sternberg) is printed in Brecht, *Schriften zum Theater,* vol. 2, Frankfurt 1963.—Erwin Piscator, *Politisches Theater heute;* in *Aufsätze, Reden, Gespräche,* Berlin 1968.

CHAPTER 10

The motto is Brecht's reaction after reading Boris Souvarine's 'depressing' book on Stalin; *Arbeitsjournal,* 19 July 1943.—Karl Marx, *Das Kapital;* in Marx/Engels, *Werke,* vol. 23, Berlin 1962, p. 445 f.

CHAPTER 11

The motto is Brecht's reply to a questionnaire sent out by the Eigenbrödler Verlag concerning the future of Germany, 1928; in Brecht, *Schriften zur Politik und Gesellschaft,* Frankfurt 1968, added by the editor Werner Hecht, p. 43.—Ernst Josef Aufricht, *Erzähle, damit du dein Recht erweist,* Berlin 1966.—Lotte Lenya, *Das waren Zeiten!;* in *Brechts Dreigroschenbuch,* edited by Siegfried Unseld, Frankfurt 1960.— Marieluise Fleisser, *Der Tiefseefisch;* in *Gesammelte Werke,* vol. 1, Frankfurt 1972.—Marieluise Fleisser, *Der Rauch;* in *Abenteuer aus dem Englischen Garten,* Frankfurt 1969.—Henning Rischbieter speaks of the 'dubious myth' of the *Dreigroschenoper* in his *Brecht-Monographie,* vol. 1, Velber 1966, p. 84.—Harry Kahn's notice of the *Dreigroschenoper* appeared under the heading '*Traum und Erwachen*' in *Die Weltbühne,* 20 November 1928, with an additional statement by the editors.—Kurt Tucholsky wrote of the protests against Brecht performances in *Die Weltbühne* 3 April 1930.—Kerr's charge of plagiarism in the *Berliner Tageblatt* brought answers from Brecht in the *Film-Kurier,* year 11 no. 106, 4 May 1929, and in the *Berliner Börsen-Courier,* 6 May 1929. That in the *Börsen-Courier* was reprinted by the review *Die schöne Literatur* in its July number, 1929, with the comment: ' "Fundamental laxity" means, in German, a sinister determination to get rich at other people's expense. This corresponds exactly with the views of that portion of the nation which derives amusement from Bert Brecht'.—Kurt Tucholsky gave his views on the plagiarism controversy in *Die Weltbühne,* 28 May 1929.— Karl Kraus, *Kerrs Enthüllung;* in *Widerschein der Fackel,* Munich 1966.—Walter Benjamin, *Karl Kraus;* in *Schriften,* vol. 2, Frankfurt

1955.—Brecht on *Pioniere in Ingolstadt* by Marieluise Fleisser; in *Das Stichwort*, the Theater am Schiffbauerdamm newspaper, April 1929.— Marieluise Fleisser, *Avantgarde*, Munich 1963.—Up until now *Happy End* has been published only as a stage manuscript (Bloch Erben, Berlin n.d.). The phrase, 'What is a picklock compared to an investment, what is breaking into a bank compared to founding a bank.', originally written for *Happy End*, was incorporated by Brecht in the first book edition of the *Dreigroschenoper* and also in the *Dreigroschenroman*.—Sigmund Freud, *Das Unbehagen in der Kultur; in Gesammelte Werke*, vol. 14, London 1948.—Elisabeth Hauptmann in a letter to the author dated 14 February 1969: 'For him the "Ku-Damm", from the Gedächtniskirche to the Halenseer bridge and on into the amusement parks, was a sort of Mahagonny; in this glittering, sparkling excrement Salvation Army squads moved about, one saw men disabled in war, etc.'—Theodor W. Adorno, *Mahagonny; in Moments musicaux*, Frankfurt 1964.—Herbert Rosenberg wrote of promoting 'the power to form communities' through the communal performance of musical works in his essay *Neue Musik und neue Zeit; quoted by Ernst Schumacher in *Die dramatischen Versuche Brechts 1918—1933*, Berlin 1955.

CHAPTER 12

Motto from Walter Benjamin, *Aus dem Brecht-Kommentar; in Versuche über Brecht*, Frankfurt 1966.—Fritz Sternberg, *Der Dichter und die Ratio. Erinnerungen an Bertolt Brecht*, Göttingen 1963.—Bertolt Brecht, *Der Jasager und Der Neinsager. Vorlagen, Fassungen und Materialien*, edited by Peter Szondi, Frankfurt 1966. This volume also contains *Die Oper als Predigt* by Walter Dirks.— Bertolt Brecht, *Die Massnahme*, critical edition, with a guide to performance, by Reiner Steinweg, Frankfurt 1972. This volume also contains Alfred Kurella's critical essay *Ein Versuch mit nicht ganz tauglichen Mitteln*.—Fritz Sternberg (op. cit.), and before him Martin Esslin (*Brecht—Das Paradox des politischen Dichters*, Frankfurt 1962), see Brecht's turn to Marxism as a search for an ideological anchor. In the opinion of Gerhard Szczesny (*Das Leben des Galilei und der Fall Bertolt Brecht*, Frankfurt/Berlin 1966) the 'anchorless' Brecht threw himself into the arms of communism which, like all authoritarian systems, had an attraction for immature and frustrated people: 'subjectively Brecht sacrificed the entire development of his human and artistic individuality to a system that relieved him of individual responsibility.'—For Otto Wels's speech and the policy of the Social Democrat Party (SPD) see Theo Pirker, *Die SPD nach Hitler*, Munich 1965.— The author obtained the verse about Friedrich Ebert in the *Kriegsfibel* from Ruth Berlau, who arranged the material for the book-edition and supplied the copy. See *BBA 2101/81*.

CHAPTER 13

Karl Marx, *Das Kapital;* in Marx/Engels, *Werke,* vol. 23, Berlin 1962. See in particular p. 476 and p. 620. Cf. the analysis of the plot in Käthe Rülicke-Weiler, *Die Dramaturgie Brechts,* Berlin 1966, p. 137–146.— Upton Sinclair, *Der Sumpf,* Berlin 1923.—W. I. Lenin, *Der englische Pazifismus und die englische Abneigung gegen die Theorie* (also refers to Upton Sinclair); in Werke vol. 21, p. 261.—Elisabeth Hauptmann, *Bessie soundso. Eine Geschichte von der Heilsarmee;* in *Uhu,* year 4 vol. 7, Berlin 1928.—Bertolt Brecht, *Der Brotladen, Bühnenfassung und Texte aus dem Fragment,* Frankfurt 1969.—Bertolt Brecht, *Die heilige Johanna der Schlachthöfe. Bühnenfassung, Fragmente, Varianten,* critical edition by Gisela E. Bahr, Frankfurt 1971.—Herbert Ihering's introduction to the broadcast of *Die heilige Johanna der Schlachthöfe* appeared in *Charivari,* Berlin, 13 May 1932. Quoted by Ernst Schumacher in *Die dramatischen Versuche Bertolt Brechts 1918-1933,* Berlin 1955, p. 486.—Gustaf Gründgens, *Briefe, Aufsätze, Reden,* Munich 1970.

CHAPTER 14

The Lenin quotation used as a motto is taken from *Ein Schritt vorwärts, zwei Schritte zurück;* in *Werke,* vol. 7, Berlin 1960, p. 419 f.—Ernst Bloch, *Ein Leninist der Schaubühne;* in *Erbschaft dieser Zeit,* Frankfurt 1962.—Andor Gabor attacked Brecht's epic theatre in an article, *Zwei Bühnenereignisse,* in *Die Linkskurve,* year 4 vol. 11/12, Berlin 1932.— Serge Tretyakov, *Die Arbeit des Schriftstellers. Aufsätze, Reportagen, Porträts,* edited by Heiner Boehncke, Reinbek bei Hamburg 1972.—On Tretyakov see also Fritz Mierau, *Tatsache und Tendenz. Der Schriftsteller Sergej Tretyakov;* in *Weimarer Beiträge,* vols. 3 and 4, Berlin and Weimar 1972.—Walter Benjamin, *Der Autor als Produzent;* in *Versuche über Brecht,* Frankfurt 1966.—George Lukács, *Reportage oder Gestaltung?* Critical observations occasioned by Ottwalt's novels; in *Die Linkskurve,* year 4, Nos. 7 and 8, Berlin 1932.—Gottfried Benn, *Die neue Literarische Saison;* in *Gesammelte Werke,* vol. 1, Wiesbaden 1959.—*Kuhle Wampe oder Wem gehört die Welt?* Filmprotokoll und Materialien, edited by Wolfgang Gersch and Werner Hech, Leipzig 1971.—Klaus Pfützner, *Die Gruppe Junger Schauspieler in Berlin (1928–1933);* in *Schriften zur Theaterwissenschaft,* vol. 4, Berlin 1966.—Walter Benjamin, *Ein Familiendrama auf dem epischen Theater;* in *Versuche über Brecht,* Frankfurt 1966.—W. I. Lenin, *Was tun?;* in *Werke,* vol. 5, Berlin 1959, p. 394 ff.—Karl Korsch, *Die materialistische Geschichtsauffassung. Eine Auseinandersetzung mit Karl Kautsky,* Leipzig 1929.—The correspondence between the Polizeidirektion in Munich and the Polizeipräsidium in Berlin is printed in Werner Mittenzwei, *Brecht. Von der Massnahme zu Leben des Galilei* Berlin 1962, p. 365 ff.

CHAPTER 15

Hans-Christoph Wächter, *Theater im Exil,* Munich 1973.—Hans-Albert Walter, *Asylpraxis und Lebensbedingungen in Europa. Deutsche Exilliteratur 1933–1950,* vol. 2, Darmstadt und Neuwied 1972.—Karl Kraus, *Die Fackel,* No. 888, October 1933, Vienna.—Karl Kraus, *Warum die Fackel nicht erscheint;* in *Die Fackel,* No. 890–905, end of July 1934, Vienna.—Undated letter from Brecht to Helene Weigel, autumn 1934 from London.—Walter Benjamin to Gershom Scholem, 15 September 1934; in Benjamin, *Briefe,* vol. 2, Frankfurt 1966.—Hans Richter, *Die Kläbers;* in *Köpfe und Hinterköpfe,* Zurich 1967.—Undated letter from Brecht in Lugano to Helene Weigel in Vienna, spring 1933.— Letter from Brecht to Kurt Kläber; in Marianne Kesting, *Bertolt Brecht in Selbstzeugnissen und Bilddokumenten,* Hamburg 1959.—Postcard from Brecht to Helene Weigel, Paris, 10 June 1933.—Brecht, *Die Ware Liebe;* in *Materialien zu Brechts Der Gute Mensch von Sezuan,* Frankfurt 1968.—Karin Machaelis, *Der kleine Kobold,* Vienna 1948.—Hanns Henny Jahnn, *Vom armen B.B.;* in *Sinn und Form,* second Brecht number, Berlin 1957. Brecht also wrote briefly about Jahnn in 1954, in a *Festschrift* for Jahnn's sixtieth birthday issued by the Freie Akademie in Hamburg; 'Dear Hans Henny Jahnn, perhaps you were never told, but I once conducted rehearsals for your fine play *Pastor Ephraim Magnus.* It was in Berlin, in the early nineteen-twenties, and my artistic activities lasted only a few days. To this day I can still hear that tremendous dying lament; it is one of the grandest monologues in German literature. I can no longer find the book—disgraceful! Well, we met in exile in Denmark, and we even meet here in Germany. And I am glad that you existed, and I am glad that you exist.'—Harald Engberg, *Brecht auf Fünen,* Wuppertal 1974.—Brecht, *Das Zehnte Sonett* ('Am liebsten aber nenne ich dich Muck'), *BBA 152/67.*—The poem, later published by Brecht in his *Studien* with the title 'Über die Gedichte des Dante auf die Beatrice', is the twelfth love-sonnet he wrote for Margarete Steffin.—Hermann Kesten, *Wiedergefundene Briefe;* in *Süddeutsche Zeitung,* No. 115, 19/20 May 1973, Munich.—Jean Renoir, *Mein Leben und meine Filme,* Munich 1975.—*Deutsche Literatur im Exil. Briefe europäischer Autoren 1933–1949,* edited by Hermann Kesten, Frankfurt 1973.—Letters from Brecht to Benjamin, April 1936 and 22 December 1933; in *Zur Aktualität Walter Benjamins,* edited by Siegfried Unseld, Frankfurt 1972.—Letter from Brecht to J. R. Becher; in *Brecht. Reihe Schriftsteller der Gegenwart,* with contributions by Hans Bunge, Werner Hecht and Käthe Rülicke-

Weiler, Berlin 1963.—Kurt Tucholsky, *Ausgewählte Briefe 1913–1935*, edited by Mary Gerold-Tucholsky and Fritz J. Raddatz, Reinbek 1962, p. 230.—Maximilian Scheer, *So war es in Paris*, Berlin 1964.

CHAPTER 16

The motto is from the poem 'Über die Bezeichnung Emigranten'.— Letter from Brecht to Karl Korsch, January 1934, *BBA* 2181/40–42.— Letter from Karl Korsch to Brecht, 17 March 1934; in *Jahrbuch Arbeiterbewegung*, vol. 2, *Marxistische Revolutionstheorien*, Frankfurt 1974, p. 123.—Michael Buckmiller and Jörg Kammler, *Revolution und Konterrevolution. Eine Diskussion mit Heinz Langerhans;* in *Jahrbuch Arbeiterbewegung*, vol. 1, *Über Karl Korsch*, Frankfurt 1973.—On 29 August 1935 Karl Korsch wrote to Paul Mattick from Skovbostrand: 'This really very pointless occurrence, sad though it was, had a great many unpleasant and painful consequences for me through the stupid intrigues of female democrats with nothing to do and malicious socialist, communist and labour—or independent labour—people; these were crowned by the unexpected refusal to extend my residence permit, so that in the middle of July, immediately after the arrival of your last letter, I had to leave that ultrareformist Eldorado within a week.' Korsch included with this letter the copy of an explanation of Comrade Dora Fabian's suicide; her death was followed by that of Comrade Mathilde Wurm. In *Jahrbusch Arbeiterbewegung*, 2, op. cit. p. 151 ff.—In his book, *Brecht auf Fünen*, Harald Engberg quotes a number of Danish interviews given by Brecht and also deals fully with the reception of Brecht's plays in Denmark.—Walter Benjamin, *Gespräche mit Brecht;* in *Versuche uber Brecht*, Frankfurt, 1966, pp. 125/126.—Letter from Walter Benjamin to Margarete Steffin, end of October 1935; in Benjamin, *Briefe*, vol. 2.

CHAPTER 17

The motto is taken from Brecht's notes on Gide's book on the Soviet Union, made in 1936; they have been collected by Werner Hecht under the title *Die ungleichen Einkommen, Gesammelte Werke*, VIII, p. 664.— Hermann Haarmann, Lothar Schirmer, Dagmar Walach, *Das Engels— Projekt. Ein antifaschistisches Theater deutscher Emigranten in der UdSSR (1936–1941)*, Worms 1975. This book contains the letters quoted from Brecht to Piscator and from Wilhelm Pieck to Piscator.—Undated letter from Brecht to Helene Weigel, from Moscow, spring 1935.

CHAPTER 18

Hans-Christoph Wächter, *Theater im Exil*, Munich 1973.—Berthold Viertel, *Bert Brecht;* in *Die neue Weltbühne*, 3 February 1938.—Fritz Kortner, *Aller Tage Abend*, Munich 1959.—Hans Bunge, *Fragen Sie mehr über Brecht. Hanns Eisler im Gespräch,* Munich 1970.—Ruth Berlau's book of short stories, *Ethvert Dyr Kan Det,* was published in Copenhagen in 1940 under the pseudonym Maria Sten.—Undated letter from Brecht to Ruth Berlau, written from Stockholm in 1940 before he left for Finland. Quoted by Hans Bunge in his speech at Ruth Berlau's graveside. Manuscript.

CHAPTER 19

The motto is from Brecht's notes on the American production of *Die Mutter* in New York, 1935; in *Materialien zu Bertolt Brechts Die Mutter. Zusammengestellt von Werner Hecht,* Frankfurt 1969, p. 101.—Letter from Brecht to Paul Peters, end of August 1935, ibid. p. 91.—Undated letters from Brecht to Helene Weigel, New York, beginning of November 1935.—Sydney Hook, *A Recollection of Bertolt Brecht;* in *The New Leader,* 10 October 1960.—Mordecai Gorelik, *New Theatres for Old,* New York 1957.—The Correspondence of 1935 between Brecht and the New York Theatre Union (edited by James K. Lyon) is printed in the *Brecht-Jahrbuch* 1975, Frankfurt 1975.—Letter from Brecht to Erwin Piscator in Moscow, 8 December 1935; in Eberhard Brüning, *Das amerikanische Drama der Dreissiger Jahre,* Berlin 1966, p. 61.—correspondence between Brecht and V. J. Jerome; in *Progressive Labor,* December 1965.—Harald Engberg, *Brecht auf Fünen,* Wuppertal 1974.—Bertolt Brecht, *Über mein Theater* (Skovbostrand 1934); in *Brecht im Gespräch.* Diskussions, Dialogues, Interviews, edited by Werner Hecht, Frankfurt 1975. The piece appeared, with a foreword by Luth Otto who took part in the conversation, in the Danish newspaper *Ekstrabladet,* 30 March 1934, under the heading *Funny tragedy, doleful comedy.*—Undated letter from Brecht to Karl Korsch, end of 1936 or beginning of 1937; quoted in Wolfdietrich Rasch, *Bertolt Brechts Marxistischer Lehrer, Merkur,* year 8 vol. 10, October 1963.

CHAPTER 20

Werner Mittenzwei speaks of the history of the play's origins in an appendix to his book, *Brecht—Von der Massnahme zu Leben des Galilei,* where he gives examples of dialogue from earlier versions of the play (p. 384–387), Berlin 1962.—The version *Die Spitzköpfe und die Rundköpfe* is printed in Brecht, *Versuche,* parts 5–8, Berlin 1963.

CHAPTER 21

The motto comes from the essay *Kunst oder Politik?,* February 1938, *Gesammelte Werke,* VIII, p. 252.—Letter from Walter Benjamin to Alfred Cohn 18 July 1935; in Benjamin, *Briefe 2,* Frankfurt 1966, p.

670.—Letter from Heinrich Mann to Feuchtwanger, spring 1936; in Hans-Albert Walter, *Deutsche Exilliteratur 1933–1950,* vol. 7, Exilpresse I, Darmstadt and Neuwied 1974, p. 302.—Letter from Walter Benjamin to Fritz Lieb, 9 July 1937; in Benjamin, *Briefe 2,* Frankfurt 1966, p. 732.—For the additions made for the Swedish production of *Carrar,* see *BBA* 167/24–28, written 22 May 1939. Cf. Werner Mittenzwei, *Brecht— Von der Massnahme zu Leben des Galilei,* Berlin 1962, p. 226 f.—Hugh Thomas, *Der spanische Bürgerkrieg,* Frankfurt and Berlin 1964.—Letter from Brecht to Erwin Piscator, 21 April 1937; cf. Wolfgang Gersch, *Film bei Brecht,* Munich 1976, p. 186 f.—Letter from Brecht to M. Gorelik, 19 March 1937.—Letter from Brecht to Jean Renoir, 17 March 1937.— Brecht, 'Als er sie abholen kam', poem written in 1937 for Ruth Berlau.— Letter from Brecht to Korsch after the Paris production of *Carrar;* in Wolfdietrich Rasch, *Bertolt Brechts Marxistischer Lehrer, Merkur.* Year 8 vol. 10, October 1963.—Undated letter from 'Steff und Bidi' to Helene Weigel, end of 1937.

CHAPTER 22

The motto is taken from the notes to the essay on *Volkstümlichkeit und Realismus, Gesammelte Werke,* VIII, p. 331 f.—For Lukács's meeting with Brecht in Moscow in 1941 see *Georg Lukács im Gespräch mit Iring Fetscher,* Ms Hessischer Rundfunk, 9 January 1968.—Brecht's remark about Kafka is referred to by Gershom Scholem, as a note made by Benjamin in June 1931, in *Walter Benjamin—die Geschichte einer Freundschaft,* Frankfurt 1975.—Georg Lukács, *Mitten im Aufstieg verliess er uns;* in *Neues Deutschland,* 21 August 1956.—Georg Lukács, *Skizze einer Geschichte der neueren deutschen Literatur,* Neuwied 1963.— Georg Lukács, *Es geht um den Realismus;* in *Das Wort,* vol. 6, Moscow 1938.—Georg Lukács, *Ästhetik I,* 2 half-volumes, Neuwied 1963.— Ernst Schumacher, *Brechts Galilei: Form und Einfühlung;* in *Sinn und Form* vol. 4, Berlin 1960.—Georg Lukács, *In memoriam Hanns Eisler;* in *Die Zeit,* no. 36, Hamburg 1965.—Georg Lukács, *Der russische Realismus in der Weltliteratur,* Neuwied 1964.—Georg Lukács, *Erzählen oder Beschreiben?;* in *Internationale Literatur,* vol. 11, Moscow 1936.—Georg Lukács, *Marx und das Problem des ideologischen Verfalls;* in *Internationale Literatur,* vol. 7, Moscow 1938.—Ernst Bloch, *Der Expressionismus, jetzt erblickt;* in *Erbschaft dieser Zeit,* Frankfurt 1962.—Ernst Bloch, *Diskussionen über Expressionismus;* in *Das Wort,* vol. 6, Moscow 1938.— Ernst Bloch and Hanns Eisler, *Die Kunst zu erben;* in *Die neue Weltbühne,* vol. 1, 1938.—Hanns Eisler, *Antwort an Georg Lukács;* in *Die neue Weltbühne,* vol. 50, 1938.—Georg Lukács, *Grösse und Verfall des Expressionismus;* in *Internationale Literatur,* vol. 1, Moscow 1934.

CHAPTER 23

The motto is from *Galileo*.—Ernst Niekisch, in particular, welcomed the writer's attempt, in the Caesar Novel, to establish a new concept of the world in the historical novel: 'The Transactions of Mr. Julius Caesar constitute a dagger that strikes to the ground a social type which can never be revived. Brutus had tradition behind him but the tendencies of his age against him, so he did not escape his Philippi. Brecht is a Brutus who has the needs of his age and the pressure of historical development behind him. He is a tyrannicide who, unlike Brutus of old, does not indulge the rancour of men who are done for but carries out the orders of things to come.'; Ernst Niekisch, *Heldendämmerung;* in *Sinn und Form,* special Bertolt Brecht issue, Berlin 1949. In contrast to Niekisch, the Italian Germanist Franco Buono gives the *Threepenny Novel* precedence as an example of a 'true and great historical novel', because of 'the remarkable inquiry conducted by this novel into the classical capitalist society'; Franco Buono, *Zur Prosa Brechts,* Frankfurt 1973, p. 106. Finally Hans Dahlke calls the attempt to destroy the Casear myth 'chasing a phantom', and ascribes the novel's failure to, among other things, Brecht's attempt to reduce Caesar to the level of an average businessman: 'In the historical Caesar there must also have been the sort of objective qualities, such as his ruthless energy in the struggle for power, that promotes the emergence of fame.'; Hans Dahlke, *Cäsar bei Brecht. Eine vergleichende Betrachtung,* Berlin and Weimar 1968.—In a note dated 5 March 1939 Brecht joins issue with representatives of realistic American literature, like Hemingway and James Mallahan Cain, calling them members of the 'great emotion racket'.—Ernst Schumacher, *Drama und Geschichte. Bertolt Brechts Leben des Galilei und andere Stücke,* Berlin 1965.—Letter from Brecht to Henry Peter Matthis, 11 April 1939; in Manfred Gebhardt, *Fahndung nach John Kent, Das Magazin,* vol. 2, Berlin 1966.—Harald Engberg, *Brecht auf Fünen,* Wuppertal 1974.—Brecht's commentary on *Was kostet das Eisen?, BBA* 209/45.—Brecht, *Über einen Courage–Film* 1950; in *Brecht im Gespräch.* Diskussions, Dialogues, Interviews, edited by Werner Hecht, Frankfurt 1957.—*Über Dialektik,* talk between Brecht and Hermann Greid in Lidingö, 1939, ibid, pp. 53–56.—Letters from Brecht to Hans Tombrock; in *Bilder und Graphiken zu Werken von Bertolt Brecht,* catalogue IV, Neue.Münchner Galerie, Munich 1964.

CHAPTER 24

The motto is from a note in the *Arbeitsjournal,* 20 April 1941.—Undated letter from Brecht to Hella Wuolijoki, Helsinki 1940.—Letters from Brecht to Ruth Berlau, 4 and 15 September 1940, written in

Marlebaek.—Manfred Gebhardt, *Zwischen Wartesaal und Weissem Gut;* in *Das Magazin,* vol. 1, Berlin 1965.—A chronicle of Brecht's stay in Finland has been compiled by Hans-Peter Neureuter; in *Mitteilungen aus der Deutschen Bibliothek,* No. 7, Helsinki 1973, pp. 11–35.

CHAPTER 25

The motto is from a note in the *Arbeitsjournal,* 16 October 1940.— Manfred Peter Hein reports on *Leben und Werk der Hella Wuolijoki* in *Mitteilungen aus der Deutschen Bibliothek,* No. 9, Helsinki 1975.—This same work also contains a full account of the genesis of the comedy *Herr Puntila und sein Knecht Matti* by Hans-Peter Neureuter, who is also preparing a critical edition of the various editions, as well as a volume of material for the play.—First draft of the plot of *Puntila, BBA* 178/16.— Fritz Kortner, *Letzen Endes,* Munich 1971, p. 90 ff.—Georg Friedrich Wilhelm Hegel, *Phänomenologie des Geistes,* Frankfurt 1970, p. 150 ff.— Brecht on the Women of Kurgela, *BBA* 566/09.

CHAPTER 26

The motto is from a note in the *Arbeitsjournal,* 1 August 1941.—Letter from Lion Feuchtwanger to a woman friend and assistant left in Berlin, 19 July 1941; in *Literatur und Kunst* des 20 Jahrhunderts, catalogue 18 of the antiquarian bookseller Herbert Blank, Stuttgart 1975.—James K. Lyon, *Bertolt Brecht's American Cicerone;* in *Brecht heute. Jahrbuch der Internationalen Brecht-Gesellschaft,* Frankfurt 1972.—Letter from Brecht to Karl Korsch, end of September 1941.—Hans Bunge, *Fragen Sie mehr über Brecht. Hanns Eisler im Gespräch,* Munich 1970.—In a letter to Ruth Berlau, written in summer 1942, Brecht wrote: 'Valentin was for me roughly what Schoenberg was for Eisler'.—Letter from Heinrich Mann to Maximilian Brantl, 2 September 1947: in Klaus Schröter, *Heinrich Mann in Selbstzeugnissen und Bilddokumenten,* Reinbek 1967, p. 155.—Letter from Alfred Döblin to Hermann Kesten, 30 July 1946; in Döblin, *Briefe,* Olten and Freiburg 1970, p. 353.— Letter from Alfred Döblin to Thomas Mann, 20 August 1943, ibid. p. 293.—Roland Barthes, *Diderot, Brecht, Eisenstein;* in *Filmkritik* No. 215, November 1974.—The *Hangmen Also Die* story is fully documented in *Filmkritik* No. 223, July 1975.—Letter from Lion Feuchtwanger, 27 March 1945, also in the above-mentioned catalogue of the Stuttgart antiquarian bookseller Herbert Blank.

CHAPTER 27

Letters from Brecht to Ruth Berlau, all undated, May and end of July 1942.—Paul Dessau, *Begegnungen mit Brecht;* in *Notizen zu Notizen,*

Leipzig 1974, p. 40.—Letter from Brecht to Ruth Berlau, 26 May 1943; in Stargardt's auction catalogue No. 16, Marburg 1963.—Letters from Brecht to Ruth Berlau, 27 August, 9 August and 7 September 1943.— *Materialien zu Bertolt Brechts Schweyk im Zweiten Weltkrieg*, edited by Herbert Knust, Frankfurt 1974.—Letters from Brecht to Ruth Berlau, 12 October and 20 October 1943, undated beginning of June and undated September 1944, 20 December 1945.

CHAPTER 28

The motto is taken from the statement Brecht prepared for his interrogation in Washington, *Gesammelte Werke* VIII, p. 861.—Brecht's question about broadcasting against the Nazis is quoted by Hans Bunge in the *Bertolt Brecht* volume in the series *Schriftsteller der Gegenwart,* Berlin 1963, p. 121.—Letter from Brecht to Ruth Berlau, 15 August 1943.—Thomas Mann asnwered Brecht's letter of 1 December 1943 on 10 December 1943; in Thomas Mann, *Briefe 1937–1947,* Berlin and Weimar 1965, p. 363 ff.—Thomas Mann, *Die Entstehung des Doktor Faustus. Roman eines Romans;* in *Zeit und Werk,* Berlin and Weimar 1965.—*Materialien zu Brechts Leben des Galilei*. Edited by Werner Hecht, Frankfurt 1963.—Undated letter from Brecht to Caspar Neher, autumn 1946; in *Kultur und Leben,* supplement to the *Augsburger Zeitung,* Augsburg, 14 February 1970.—Undated letters from Brecht to Erwin Piscator, February and March 1947.—Brecht's interrogation before the committee of enquiry into un-American activities is contained in the volume *Brecht im Gespräch. Diskussion, Dialogues, Interviews,* edited by Werner Hecht, Frankfurt 1975.—Excerpts from Hanns Eisler's interrogation are contained in the article *The Artist on Trial,* with commentary by Eric Bentley, in the magazine *Encore,* vol. 11 No. 5, London 1964.—

CHAPTER 29

The motto comes from an entry in Caspar Neher's diary, 6 November 1947, Neher estate, Nationalbibliothek, Vienna.—Letters from Brecht to Ruth Berlau, 4 and 5 November 1947.—Neher's diary, 18 November 1947.—Letters from Brecht to Ferdinand Reyher, April 1948; in James K. Lyon, *Bertolt Brecht's American Cicerone, Jahrbuch 2,* Internationale Brecht-Gesellschaft, Frankfurt 1972, p. 202.—Undated letters from Brecht to Caspar Neher, autumn and December 1946; in *Kultur und Leben,* supplement to the *Augsburger Zeitung,* Augsburg 14 February 1970.—Neher's diary, 5 November 1947, 1 December and 24 November 1947.—Brecht speaks of the *Antigone* production as 'a sort of preview for Berlin' in a letter to his son Stefan in America; in Bertolt Brecht, *Die Antigone des Sophokles. Materialien zur Antigone.* Edited by Werner

Hecht, Frankfurt 1965, p. 113.—Neher's diary, 12 December 1948.—
Brecht/Neher, *Antigonemodell 1948,* edited by Ruth Berlau, Berlin
1949.—Letter from Brecht to Caspar Neher, 7 February 1948; in *Bertolt
Brecht—Caspar Neher,* exhibition catalogue of the Hessisches
Landesmuseum, Darmstadt, 1963.—*Der Wagen des Ares* quotation,
BBA 814/23.—Notice of the first performance of *Herr Puntila und sein
Knecht Matti* in the *Abendblatt* of the *National Zeitung,* Bâle, 8 June
1948.—Max Frisch, *Erinnerungen an Brecht;* in *Kursbuch* No. 7,
Frankfurt 1966, p. 68.—Berthold Viertel, *Wiedersehen mit dem Berliner
Theater;* in *Schriften zum Theater,* Munich 1970, p. 265.—Undated
letter from Brecht to Helene Weigel, end of February or beginning of
March 1949; in *Helene Weigel zu ehren,* Frankfurt 1970.—All Brecht's
letters on the subject of his Austrian passport quoted in Siegfried
Melchinger, *Bertolt Brechts Salzburger Totentanz;* in *Stuttgarter
Zeitung,* 5 January 1963.

CHAPTER 30

Brecht, after the meeting with the Chief Burgomaster of Berlin, *BBA*
523/19.—Letter from Brecht to Erwin Piscator, 5 March 1949.—Letter
from Brecht to Helene Weigel, 21 April 1949.—Letter from Brecht to
Helene Weigel, 21 April 1949; in *Helene Weigel zu ehren,* Frankfurt
1970.—Brecht's remark about Ebert's competence to fill the role of Chief
Burgomaster of Berlin was supplied by Wolfgang Harich in a manuscript
originally intended as additional material for *Geschichten von Herrn B,*
published by the Insel Verlag, 1967.—Brecht on 'positive heroes': *Brecht
im Gespräch,* edited by Werner Hecht, p. 132.—Brecht on 'optimism':
ibid., p. 143.—Note by Käthe Rülicke, 12 March 1951, *BBA* 1264.—
Brecht, 'Herrnburger Bericht'; in *Neues Deutschland,* 22 July 1951.—
Walter Ulbricht, *Zur Geschichte der Arbeiterbewegung,* vol. 4 p. 604.—
Ernst Fischer, *Doktor Faustus und der deutsche Bauernkrieg;* in *Sinn und
Form,* vol. 6, Berlin 1952.—Letter from Hanns Eisler to the central
committee of the Socialist Unity Party, 30 October 1953; quoted from
Louise Eisler-Fischer, *Faust in der DDR. Dokumente betreffend Hanns
Eisler, Bertolt Brecht, Ernst Fischer;* in *Neues Forum,* Vienna, October
1969.—Undated letter from Brecht to Caspar Neher, August or
September 1955, *BBA* 654/103—104.

CHAPTER 31

The motto is the second verse of the poem, 'An Ruth', written in 1950;
printed in *Gesammelte Werke* IV under the title 'Geh ich zeitig in die
Leere'.—The *Zehn Vorschriften für Schauspieler,* sent by Brecht to Käthe
Reichel in November 1951, are printed in *Gesammelte Werke* VII (pp.
742–744) under the heading *Über den Schauspielerberuf.*—Letters from

Brecht to Ruth Berlau, 19 July 1954, 14 March 1950, 1 December 1951, June 1955, end of June 1954.—Undated letter from Brecht to Käthe Reichel, end of 1954 or beginning of 1955.—Brecht, *Herr Keuner sagte (über Liebe und Freundschaft), BBA* 2050/10.—The love songs, 'Als ich nachher von dir ging', 'Lied einer Liebenden' and 'Die Liebste gab mir einen Zweig', were written for Käthe Reichel.—Letter from Brecht to Käthe Reichel, August 1956.—Brecht wrote the poem, 'Sieben Rosen hat der Strauch', for Käthe Rülicke.—Notes by Käthe Rülicke, 22 November 1952, *BBA* 1264.—Brecht's question regarding Isot Kilian was supplied by Wolfgang Harich in the manuscript mentioned above.

CHAPTER 32

The motto is from the poem 'Böser Morgen'.—Ernst Schumacher, *Er wird bleiben;* in *Erinnerungen an Brecht,* Leipzig, p. 339.—Käthe Rülicke, *Hans Garbe erzählt,* Berlin 1952.—Manfred Wekwerth, *Die Letzten Gespräche;* in *Schriften. Arbeit mit Brecht,* Berlin 1975, p. 78.—Hannah Arendt, *Quod licet Jovi . . . Der Dichter Bertolt Brecht und die Politik;* in *Merkur,* year 23 vols. 6 and 7, Munich 1969.—Isaac Deutscher, *Stalin. Eine politische Biographie,* Stuttgart 1962.—The poems *Die neue Mundart (BBA* 153/8) and *Lebensmittel zum Zweck (BBA* 153/14) also belong to the *Buckower Elegien.*—Brecht's letters about 17 June 1953 to Walter Ulbricht, Peter Suhrkamp and Erwin Leiser are in Erwin Leiser, *Brecht, Grass und der 17 Juni 1953;* in *Die Weltwoche,* Zurich, 11 February 1966.—Letter from Brecht to Paul Wandel, middle of August 1953.—Undated letter from Brecht to Ruth Berlau, September 1953.

CHAPTER 33

The motto is from a note in Brecht's *Arbeitsjournal,* 13 September 1953.—*Tausendundeintag,* Vol. 1, Leipzig 1967.—Wachtangov's remark about *Turandot* is in *Meyerhold, Tairov, Wachtangov; Theateroktober,* Leipzig 1967, p. 361.—Walter Benjamin, *Gespräche mit Brecht;* in *Versuche über Brecht,* Frankfurt 1966.—Letter from Brecht to Karl Korsch, February 1939.—Karl Marx, *Zur Judenfrage;* in Marx/Engels, *Werke,* Vol. 1, Berlin 1961, p. 347 ff.

CHAPTER 34

The motto is from Becher's obituary on Brecht; in *Bemühungen 2. Gesammelte Werke,* Vol. 14 p. 587. Undated letters from Brecht to Ruth Berlau, August 1953 and December 1950.—Mao Tse-Tung, *Über den Widerspruch;* in *Ausgewälte Schriften,* Frankfurt 1964, p. 58.—Letter from Brecht to the Academy of Arts, containing instructions for his burial, 15 May 1955; in *Neues Deutschland,* Berlin, 17 August 1956.—

Therese Giehse, *Ich hab nichts zum Sagen. Gespräche mit Monika Sperr,* Reinbek 1976, p. 79.—Letter from Peter Suhrkamp to Caspar Neher, 21 August 1956.

Name Index

400

Tucholsky, Kurt 132, 133, 192

Ulbricht, Walter 151, 205, 336, 341, 356, 360
Ullstein, (publisher) 102, 108

Valentin, Karl 36, 40, 42, 61, 62, 72, 95, 121, 166, 287
Valetti, Rosa 127
Vallentin, Maxim 203, 235, 328
Vanderbilt, Cornelius 110, 153
Vansittart, Robert Gilbert 309
Veidt, Conrad 209
Verdi, Giuseppe 93, 107
Verlaine, Paul 10, 45, 78, 79, 133
Viertel, Berthold 55, 158, 210, 291, 299, 311, 326, 327, 343
Viertel, Hans 301
Viertel, Salka 291
Villon, François 10, 19, 45, 46, 126, 132, 134, 135
Vishnevsky, Vsevolod 205
Voltenen, Mogens 184

Wachtangow, Yevgeny B. 359, 362
Wagner (actress) 38
Wagner, Richard 288
Walbrook, Anton see Wohlbrück, Adolf
Walcher, Jakob 336, 338, 349, 376
Walden, Herwath 133
Wallace, Edgar 94
Walpole, Sir Robert 126
Wälterlin, Oskar 319, 324
Wandel, Paul 336, 357, 376
Walgenheim, Gustav von 203, 328
Warschauer, Frank 52
Weber, C. M. 336
Weber, Carl Maria von 8

Webster, John 291, 299
Wechsler, Lazar 321
Wedekind, Frank 10, 17, 18, 19, 20, 36, 46, 49, 111, 166
Wegener, Paul 51, 57
Weigel, Helene 35, 67, 68, 108, 129, 130, 163, 168, 169, 173, 174, 177, 178, 179, 182, 184, 203, 204, 221, 222, 223, 238, 259, 262, 264, 289, 290, 292, 297, 311, 320, 321, 322, 323, 324, 328, 330, 331, 334, 344, 345, 346, 349, 375
Weil, Felix 366
Weil, Hermann 366
Weill, Kurt 126, 127, 128, 138, 139, 141, 145, 179, 180, 181, 182, 198, 224, 225, 296, 299, 300, 301, 302
Weinert, Erich 203
Weisenborn, Günther 163, 164
Weiskopf, F. C. 174, 299
Weiss (Publisher) 324
Wekwerth, Manfred 342, 353
Welles, Orson 310
Wels, Otto 149
Weltzer, Johannes 198
Werfel, Franz 92, 93, 94, 187, 290
Werthes, F. A. C. 359
West, Mae 212
Wexley, John 292, 293
Whetstone, George 227
Whitman, Walt 78
Wiegler, Paul 334
Wifstrand, Naima 264
Wilde, Oscar 34
Wilder, Thornton 198
Willstätter, Richard 17
Wilson, Woodrow 22
Wittfogel, K. A. 196
Wohlbrück, Adolf 209
Wolf, Friedrich 203, 205

405

Title Index

Poems

412